Firewall Fundamentals

Wes Noonan
Ido Dubrawsky

Cisco Press

800 East 96th Street
Indianapolis, Indiana 46240 USA

Firewall Fundamentals

Wes Noonan
Ido Dubrawsky

Copyright © 2006 Cisco Systems, Inc.

Published by:
Cisco Press
800 East 96th Street
Indianapolis, IN 46240 USA

Printed in the United States of America   2 3 4 5 6 7 8 9 0

Second Printing   February 2007

Library of Congress Cataloging-in-Publication Number: 2004114308

ISBN: 1-58705-221-0

Trademark Acknowledgments

All terms mentioned in this book that are known to be trademarks or service marks have been appropriately capitalized. Cisco Press or Cisco Systems, Inc. cannot attest to the accuracy of this information. Use of a term in this book should not be regarded as affecting the validity of any trademark or service mark.

Warning and Disclaimer

This book is designed to provide information about firewalls. Every effort has been made to make this book as complete and as accurate as possible, but no warranty or fitness is implied.

The information is provided on an "as is" basis. The authors, Cisco Press, and Cisco Systems, Inc. shall have neither liability nor responsibility to any person or entity with respect to any loss or damages arising from the information contained in this book or from the use of the discs or programs that may accompany it.

The opinions expressed in this book belong to the author and are not necessarily those of Cisco Systems, Inc.

Corporate and Government Sales

Cisco Press offers excellent discounts on this book when ordered in quantity for bulk purchases or special sales. For more information, please contact: **U.S. Corporate and Government Sales**   1-800-382-3419   corpsales@pearsontechgroup.com

For sales outside of the U.S. please contact: **International Sales**   1-317-581-3793   international@pearsontechgroup.com

Feedback Information

At Cisco Press, our goal is to create in-depth technical books of the highest quality and value. Each book is crafted with care and precision, undergoing rigorous development that involves the unique expertise of members from the professional technical community.

Readers' feedback is a natural continuation of this process. If you have any comments regarding how we could improve the quality of this book, or otherwise alter it to better suit your needs, you can contact us through email at feedback@ciscopress.com. Please make sure to include the book title and ISBN in your message.

We greatly appreciate your assistance.

Editor-in-Chief	Paul Boger
Cisco Representative	Anthony Wolfenden
Cisco Press Program Manager	Jeff Brady
Executive Editor	Brett Bartow
Production Manager	Patrick Kanouse
Development Editor	Andrew Cupp
Project Editor	Interactive Composition Corporation
Copy Editor	Interactive Composition Corporation
Technical Editors	Randy Ivener, Eric Seagren
Editorial Assistant	Raina Han
Book and Cover Designer	Louisa Adair
Composition	Interactive Composition Corporation
Indexer	Tim Wright

CISCO SYSTEMS

Corporate Headquarters
Cisco Systems, Inc.
170 West Tasman Drive
San Jose, CA 95134-1706
USA
www.cisco.com
Tel: 408 526-4000
     800 553-NETS (6387)
Fax: 408 526-4100

European Headquarters
Cisco Systems International BV
Haarlerbergpark
Haarlerbergweg 13-19
1101 CH Amsterdam
The Netherlands
www-europe.cisco.com
Tel: 31 0 20 357 1000
Fax: 31 0 20 357 1100

Americas Headquarters
Cisco Systems, Inc.
170 West Tasman Drive
San Jose, CA 95134-1706
USA
www.cisco.com
Tel: 408 526-7660
Fax: 408 527-0883

Asia Pacific Headquarters
Cisco Systems, Inc.
Capital Tower
168 Robinson Road
#22-01 to #29-01
Singapore 068912
www.cisco.com
Tel: +65 6317 7777
Fax: +65 6317 7799

Cisco Systems has more than 200 offices in the following countries and regions. Addresses, phone numbers, and fax numbers are listed on the
Cisco.com Web site at www.cisco.com/go/offices.

Argentina • Australia • Austria • Belgium • Brazil • Bulgaria • Canada • Chile • China PRC • Colombia • Costa Rica • Croatia • Czech Republic
Denmark • Dubai, UAE • Finland • France • Germany • Greece • Hong Kong SAR • Hungary • India • Indonesia • Ireland • Israel • Italy
Japan • Korea • Luxembourg • Malaysia • Mexico • The Netherlands • New Zealand • Norway • Peru • Philippines • Poland • Portugal
Puerto Rico • Romania • Russia • Saudi Arabia • Scotland • Singapore • Slovakia • Slovenia • South Africa • Spain • Sweden
Switzerland • Taiwan • Thailand • Turkey • Ukraine • United Kingdom • United States • Venezuela • Vietnam • Zimbabwe

About the Authors

Wes Noonan, CISA, is a staff quality engineer at NetIQ working on their security solutions product line. Wes has more than 12 years of industry experience, specializing in Windows-based networks and network infrastructure security design and implementation. Wes is the author of *Hardening Network Infrastructure* (ISBN 0072255021), is a contributing/co-author of *CISSP Training Guide* (ISBN 078972801X) and *Hardening Network Security* (ISBN 0072257032), and is a technical editor for *Hacking Exposed: Cisco Networks* (ISBN 0072259175). Wes also maintains a Windows network security "Ask the Experts" section for Techtarget.com (http://searchwindowssecurity.techtarget.com/ateAnswers/0,289620,sid45_tax298206,00.html). Wes lives in the Houston, Texas, metropolitan area with his wife and two bulldogs.

Ido Dubrawsky, CISSP, is the strategic security advisor for the Communications Sector at Microsoft. Prior to working at Microsoft, Ido was the owner and president of Silicon Security, Inc. (http://www.siliconsec.com), a mid-Atlantic network security consulting company, as well as the acting national practice lead for the security consulting practice at AT&T/Callisma. Before joining AT&T/Callisma, Ido worked for more than four years at Cisco Systems, Inc., as both a network security engineer as well as a network security architect on the SAFE project.

About the Technical Reviewers

Randy Ivener, CCIE No. 10722, is a security specialist with the Cisco Systems product security incident response team. He is a CISSP and ASQ CSQE. Randy has spent many years as a network security consultant helping companies understand and secure their networks. Before becoming immersed in information security, he spent time in software development and as a training instructor. Randy graduated from the U.S. Naval Academy and holds a master's degree in business administration.

Eric S. Seagren, CISA, CISSP-ISSAP, SCNP, CCNA, MCP+I, MCSE, and CNE, has nine years of experience in the computer industry, with the past seven years spent in the financial services industry working for a Fortune 100 company. Eric started his computer career working on Novell servers and performing general network troubleshooting for a small Houston-based company. While working in the financial services industry, his duties have included server administration, disaster recovery responsibilities, business continuity coordinator, Y2K remediation, and network vulnerability assessment responsibilities. He has spent the past few years as an IT architect and risk analyst, designing and evaluating secure, scalable, and redundant networks. Eric lives in Missouri City, Texas.

Dedications

For SSgt. Anthony L. Goodwin, USMC. KIA 05/08/05. *Semper Fidelis, my friend—you will not be forgotten.*

Acknowledgments

From Wes:

I'd like to thank my wife for once again sacrificing the time it took me to work on another book. I couldn't do this without you.

I could not have done this had Brian Ford not been willing to take a chance on bringing me in on this project. Likewise, I appreciate the chance to work with Ido Dubrawsky and look forward to future partnerships. I want to thank both Brian and Ido for the opportunity and privilege of working with them both. To Brett Bartow and Andrew Cupp, I know we drove you crazy from time to time, but thanks for being patient and sticking with us and providing the guidance and encouragement we needed to finish this project.

Thank you to my colleagues both at Collective Technologies and NetIQ for giving me the opportunity to mature and grow as an engineer and a person. To Jeff Pollard for giving me the time I needed to finish this project, everyone should be so lucky as to work for a boss like you. I'd also like to thank Geri Williams for providing technical expertise on the late nights of writing. I'd be remiss if I didn't thank the technical and copy editors for helping to ensure not only the technical accuracy of what I wrote, but for making me sound far more intelligent than I am by making it appear that I have a much better grasp of English and the written word than I do!

Finally, thank you to my family and friends for all of their support and encouragement. Roll 20s and *Semper Fidelis.*

From Ido:

I would like to thank, first and foremost, my wife, whom I dearly love and treasure and without whom I would not be where I am today. Second, I wish to give my thanks to my wonderful children, who are truly the light of my life. I took time away from my family to write this book, and there were moments where I wished to be there more for them but could not be. I love all of you with all of my heart. May G-d bless you all and keep you. May G-d shine his countenance upon you all and be gracious to you. May G-d lift his countenance to you all and bring you peace.

I wish to also thank Wes Noonan for agreeing to work on this project as a great co-author and to thank Brett Bartow for being as patient an editor as he has been. My schedule notwithstanding, this has been a trial for both of them, too. Thanks also to Brian Ford for bringing me in on this project and for listening to me when I was frustrated with it.

To my good friend Ben Bazian who has been a source of humor and good counsel when I needed it I wish to give a very big thank you. A big thanks also goes to Nigel Willson for being a great national director for the Security Consulting Practice over at AT&T. I also want to thank Ricardo Farraj-Ruiz, Charles Outlaw, and Karl Weaver over at CRS in the Library of Congress for being great people to work with. And last but certainly not least, thanks to David Barak and Peter Griffin over at AT&T/Callisma. David has amazed me with his vast knowledge of service provider routing, and Peter has immense knowledge in the optical world and in that strange world that is Callisma management.

This Book Is Safari Enabled

The Safari® Enabled icon on the cover of your favorite technology book means the book is available through Safari Bookshelf. When you buy this book, you get free access to the online edition for 45 days.

Safari Bookshelf is an electronic reference library that lets you easily search thousands of technical books, find code samples, download chapters, and access technical information whenever and wherever you need it.

To gain 45-day Safari Enabled access to this book:

- Go to http://www.ciscopress.com/safarienabled
- Complete the brief registration form.
- Enter the coupon code UZGR-WUPF-DQ5Z-ITFF-DXJT

If you have difficulty registering on Safari Bookshelf or accessing the online edition, please e-mail customer-service@safaribooksonline.com.

Contents at a Glance

Contents

Icons Used in This Book

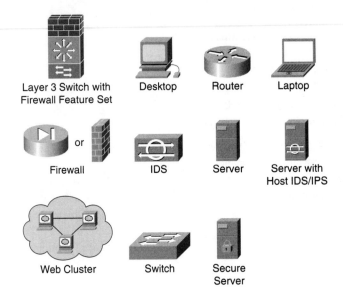

Layer 3 Switch with
Firewall Feature Set

Desktop

Router

Laptop

Firewall

IDS

Server

Server with
Host IDS/IPS

Web Cluster

Switch

Secure
Server

Command Syntax Conventions

The conventions used to present command syntax in this book are the same conventions used in the IOS Command Reference. The Command Reference describes these conventions as follows:

- **Boldface** indicates commands and keywords that are entered literally as shown. In actual configuration examples and output (not general command syntax), boldface indicates commands that are manually input by the user (such as a **show** command).

- *Italics* indicate arguments for which you supply actual values.

- Vertical bars | separate alternative, mutually exclusive elements.

- Square brackets [ ] indicate optional elements.

- Braces { } indicate a required choice.

- Braces within brackets [{ }] indicate a required choice within an optional element.

Introduction

Firewalls are a staple component of a secure network in today's Internet. This book provides network administrators who are more focused on the core network services and end users an opportunity to learn about modern firewall capabilities. This book is not an exhaustive reference on all possible firewalls nor is it a complete text on the firewalls that are mentioned in this book. Instead, this book provides a solid foundation of fundamental knowledge upon which readers can build their knowledge and skills in firewall administration and implementation (and security in general).

Motivation

The intent for this book is to provide information about the basic workings of firewalls, with a predominant slant toward the smaller appliance firewall, such as the Linksys and Cisco PIX 501E, as well as the personal firewall such as the Windows Firewall. Although vendors' firewall products vary greatly, fundamental underlying principles do not vary because of the nature of the technology. The hope is that this book provides readers with an understanding of these fundamental principles.

Goals and Objectives

The goal of this book is to provide a ready reference for the reader on firewall technology, especially where it pertains to the personal and desktop firewall. Readers will come away with enough knowledge that they will then be able to approach some of the references provided at the end of this book to learn more and expand their knowledge of this important class of devices in network security.

Target Audience

The target audience for this book is novice network administrators, home users, and corporate employees who are telecommuting but want to use a firewall to protect their network. This book does not aim to be a thorough reference on firewalls and all of their capabilities. Instead, the focus is predominantly on smaller firewalls such as the Cisco PIX 501E, Linksys, and personal firewalls such as Windows Firewall and Trend Micro's Firewall. The reader of this book is expected to have some knowledge of the basics of networking and of computer operating systems.

How This Book Is Organized

This book provides a building-block approach to the material. The initial focus is on the basics of firewalls and a review of TCP/IP. Although the book is intended to be read cover to cover, it can also provide point references for various products and concepts. Chapters 1 through 3 provide the necessary background to firewalls and TCP/IP concepts as they relate to firewalls. The core content lies in Part II and Part III, where the focus shifts to how various firewall products are implemented and how to manage firewalls.

A quick overview of the contents for the various chapters follows:

- **Chapter 1, "Introduction to Firewalls"**—This chapter introduces what a firewall is and discusses what a firewall can be reasonably expected to do. The focus is on what a firewall is, what security threats exist, what the firewall security policy is, and how you can use the firewall to protect against threats.

- **Chapter 2, "Firewall Basics"**—This chapter covers the basics of various firewall technologies. The focus is on explaining software firewalls, integrated firewalls, and appliance firewalls. These are further broken down into the various modes of operation such as personal, network, NAT, proxy, circuit, and transparent firewalls as well as how they work.

- **Chapter 3, "TCP/IP for Firewalls"**—This chapter is a primer on TCP/IP and how TCP/IP functions from the perspective of firewall administration. The various protocols, applications, and services in the TCP/IP world are reviewed, with a particular focus on IP, TCP, UDP, and ICMP (for an understanding of how a firewall can be configured to control them).

- **Chapter 4, "Personal and Desktop Firewalls"**—This chapter covers personal firewalls that can be found or installed on laptop and desktop systems. The two example systems provided in this chapter are Windows Firewall (found in Windows XP Service Pack 2 and Windows 2003 Server systems) and Trend Micro's Firewall (which is part of the Internet Security Suite).

- **Chapter 5, "Broadband Routers and Firewalls"**—This chapter looks at what a broadband router/firewall is, how it works, and how and where it should be implemented. The focus of the chapter is on the Linksys broadband routers, and a discussion of the basic features and functionality necessary to perform the initial configuration is provided.

- **Chapter 6, "Cisco PIX Firewall and ASA Security Appliance"**—This chapter looks at the Cisco lower-end firewalls: the PIX 501E and the PIX 506E. These devices are marketed to the end-user/small-office and remote-office markets. A quick overview of some of the PIX capabilities as well as how to configure the system initially is provided.

- **Chapter 7, "Linux-Based Firewalls"**—This chapter covers the evolution of Linux-based firewalls, from ipfwadm to ipchains to the latest incarnation, NetFilter. In addition, an overview of configuring Linux-based firewalls is provided.

- **Chapter 8, "Application Proxy Firewalls"**—This chapter looks at what an application proxy is, how it works, and how and where it should be implemented. The focus of the chapter is on the Microsoft ISA Server 2004 firewall, and a discussion of the basic features and functionality necessary to perform a basic configuration is provided.

- **Chapter 9, "Where Firewalls Fit in a Network"**—This chapter focuses on architecting and designing firewall deployments. The chapter discusses different types of firewall design architectures, including dual firewall and different types of DMZ implementations. This chapter also explores the different types of firewalls and where each type of firewall best fits in the network.

- **Chapter 10, "Firewall Security Policies"**—All firewalls function by virtue of how the firewall security policies are configured. This chapter covers the different types of firewall security policies and rulesets that exist with a focus on ingress and egress filters as well as how to provide for secure management access.

- **Chapter 11, "Managing Firewalls"**—The management of firewalls is a crucial issue. As firewalls become more and more complicated, the configuration of them and the management of them becomes harder and harder for the average user and for the novice administrator. This chapter covers some of the management tools used to manage personal and small firewalls.

- **Chapter 12, "What Is My Firewall Telling Me?"**—Some of the most valuable information a firewall can provide is from its log files. This chapter looks at the types of logging supported by most firewalls and the kind of information that can be gleaned from that information. This chapter explains how to read the information provided by the logs and how that information can be used for forensics analysis. This chapter also identifies the top 10 things to look for in log files.

- **Chapter 13, "Troubleshooting Firewalls"**—Regardless of how well you implement, sooner or later you are going to need to troubleshoot something regarding your firewall. This chapter examines how to build a troubleshooting checklist that you can use to troubleshoot traffic flow through the firewall (as well as through the firewall itself).

- **Chapter 14, "Going Beyond Basic Firewall Features"**—This chapter explores many of the advanced features that firewalls can provide, while at the same time illustrating the limitations of firewalls in providing these advanced features.

- **Appendix A, "Firewall and Security Tools"**—This appendix lists firewall and security tools and briefly discusses usage and situations in which each tool is appropriate.

- **Appendix B, "Firewall and Security Resources"**—This appendix lists online and traditionally published resources for additional learning. These resources provide a solid next step of more detailed and technical information to build on the fundamentals you have gained from this book.

Part I: Introduction to Firewalls

## CHAPTER 1

Introduction to Firewalls

Depending on whom you talk to, a firewall is either the cornerstone of their organization's security infrastructure, or it is a device that has woefully failed to live up to expectations. How can one device have such a contrast in perceptions? The biggest reason for this is a misunderstanding of what a firewall is and is not, and what a firewall can and cannot do.

This chapter looks at what a firewall is and how a firewall works to illustrate what are the reasonable expectations for a firewall. This chapter also examines the threats that exist and motivations of attackers to explore how firewalls can—and most important, cannot—protect against those threats.

What Is a Firewall?

When most people think of a firewall, they think of a device that resides on the network and controls the traffic that passes between network segments, such as the firewall in Figure 1-1 (a network-based firewall). However, firewalls can also be implemented on systems themselves, such as with Microsoft Internet Connection Firewall (ICF), in which case they are known as host-based firewalls. Fundamentally, both types of firewalls have the same objective: to provide a method of enforcing an access control policy. Indeed, at the simplest definition, firewalls are nothing more than access control policy enforcement points.

Figure 1-1 *A Network Firewall Enforcing Access Controls*

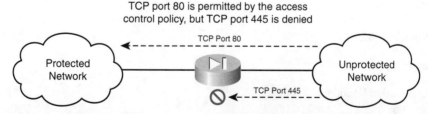

Firewalls enable you to define an access control requirement and ensure that only traffic or data that meets that requirement can traverse the firewall (in the case of a network-based firewall) or access the protected system (in the case of a host-based firewall). Figure 1-1 illustrates how you can use a network-based firewall to allow only traffic that is permitted to access protected resources.

What Can Firewalls Do?

Chapter 2, "Firewall Basics," and all of Part II, "How Firewalls Work," examine the details of how different types of firewalls work; before delving into more detail, however, you need to understand from a broad design perspective what firewalls can and cannot do. All firewalls (or at least all firewalls that you should be considering implementing) share some common traits and functionality that help define what a firewall can do.

Fundamentally, firewalls need to be able to perform the following tasks:

- Manage and control network traffic

- Authenticate access

- Act as an intermediary

- Protect resources

- Record and report on events

Firewalls Manage and Control Network Traffic

The first and most fundamental functionality that all firewalls must perform is to manage and control the network traffic that is allowed to access the protected network or host. Firewalls typically do so by inspecting the packets and monitoring the connections that are being made, and then filtering connections based on the packet-inspection results and connections that are observed.

Packet Inspection

Packet inspection is the process of intercepting and processing the data in a packet to determine whether it should be permitted or denied in accordance with the defined access policy. Packet inspection can look at any or all of the following elements in making a filtering determination:

- Source IP address

- Source port

- Destination IP address

- Destination port

- IP protocol

- Packet header information (that is, sequence numbers, checksums, data flags, payload information, and so on)

An important thing to keep in mind about packet inspection is that, to make a filtering decision, the firewall must inspect every single packet in every direction and on all interfaces, and access control rules must exist for every packet that will be inspected. This requirement can present a problem when it comes time to define an access control rule to address the return traffic from a permitted request.

Connections and State

For two TCP/IP hosts to communicate with one another, they must establish some sort of connection with each other. Connections serve two purposes. First, the hosts can use the connection to identify themselves to each other. This identification ensures that systems do not inadvertently deliver data to hosts that are not involved in the connection. Firewalls can use this connection information to determine what connections between hosts are allowed by the access control policy and thus determine whether data should be permitted or denied.

Second, connections are used to define the manner in which two hosts will communicate with each other. For Transmission Control Protocol (TCP), this type of connection is known as a connection-oriented session. For User Datagram Protocol (UDP) and Internet Control Message Protocol (ICMP), this type of connection is known as a connectionless session. Although connectionless session would seem to be contradictory in this context (how can a connection be connectionless?), connectionless session simply means that the hosts do not undertake any special mechanisms to ensure reliable data delivery, unlike TCP, which does undertake special mechanisms (specifically sequencing) to ensure that data is reliably delivered. Connections allow the hosts to know what the rules of etiquette for communications are. For example, when Host A makes a request for data from Host B using a protocol such as TCP, Host B responds with the data that was requested, not with a new connection request or with data other than what was requested.

This defined structure of a connection can be used to determine the state of the communications between two hosts. The easiest way to think of state is to think of a conversation between two people. If Bob asks John a question, the proper response is for John to answer the question. Thus, at the point that Bob has asked his question, the state of the conversation is that it is waiting for a response from John.

Network communication follows a similar format for tracking the state of a conversation. When Host A attempts to communicate with Host B, Host A initiates a connection request. Host B then responds to the connection request, and in doing so defines how the two hosts will keep track of what data needs to be sent and when it should be sent. So if Host A initiates a request, it can be assumed that the state of the conversation at that time is waiting for a response from Host B. Figure 1-2 illustrates this process in detail:

1. HostA initiates a connection to HostB.

2. HostB responds to the connection request from HostA.

3. HostA finalizes the connection with HostB, allowing for the passing of data.

4. HostA begins transmitting the required data to HostB.

5. HostB responds as required, either with the requested data, or to periodically acknowledge the receipt of data from HostA.

Figure 1-2 *Connections Between Hosts*

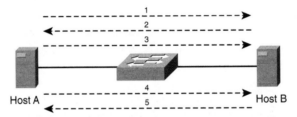

Firewalls can monitor this connection state information to determine whether to permit or deny traffic. For example, when the firewall sees the first connection request from HostA (Step 1), it knows that the next data it should see is the acknowledgment of the connection request from HostB (Step 2). This is typically done by maintaining a state table that tracks what the state of all the conversations traversing the firewall are in. By monitoring the state of the conversation, the firewall can determine whether data being passed is expected by the host in question, and if it is, it is permitted accordingly. If the data being passed does not match the state of the conversation (as defined by the state table), or if the data is not in the state table, it is dropped. This process is known as stateful inspection.

Stateful Packet Inspection

When firewalls combine stateful inspection with packet inspection, it is known as stateful packet inspection. This is the inspection of packets not only based on packet structure and the data contained in the packet, but also based on what state the conversation between hosts is in. This inspection allows firewalls to filter not only based on what the contents of the packet are, but also based on the connection or state in which the connection is currently in (and thus provides a much more flexible, maintainable, and scalable filtering solution).

A benefit of stateful packet inspection over the packet inspection discussed previously is that after a connection has been identified and permitted (after being inspected accordingly), it is generally not necessary to define a rule to permit the return communications because the firewall knows by state what an accepted response should be. This buys you the security of being able to perform inspection of the commands and data contained within the packet to determine whether a connection will be permitted, and then automatically have the firewall track the state of the conversation and dynamically permit traffic that is in accordance with the state of the conversation. This process is done without needing to explicitly define a rule to permit the responses and subsequent communications. Most firewalls today function in this manner.

> **NOTE**   For more information about TCP/IP packet structure and TCP/IP-based communications, see Chapter 3, "TCP/IP for Firewalls."

Firewalls Authenticate Access

A common mistake that people make when evaluating firewalls is to consider packet inspection of the source IP address and port as being the same as authentication. Sure, packet inspection allows you to restrict what source hosts are able to communicate with your protected resources, but that does not ensure that the source host should be allowed to communicate with your protected resources. After all, it is a relatively trivial task to spoof an IP address, making one host appear to be an entirely different host and thus defeating inspection based on source address and port.

To eliminate this risk, firewalls also need to provide a means of authenticating access. TCP/IP was built on the premise of open communications. If two hosts know each others' IP addresses and are connected to each other, they are allowed to communicate. Although this was a noble design at the time, in today's world you may not want just anyone to be able to communicate with systems behind your firewall.

Firewalls can perform authentication using a number of mechanisms. First, the firewall can require the input of a username and password (often known as extended authentication or xauth). Using xauth, the user who attempts to initiate a connection is prompted for a username and password prior to the firewall allowing a connection to be established. Typically, after the connection has been authenticated and authorized by the security policy, the user is no longer prompted for authentication for that connection.

Another mechanism for authentication of connections is through the use of certificates and public keys. A benefit of certificates over xauth is that the authentication process can typically occur with no user intervention, provided the hosts have been properly configured with certificates and the firewall and hosts are using a properly configured public key infrastructure. A benefit of this approach is that it scales much better for large implementations.

Finally, authentication can be handled through the use of pre-shared keys (PSKs). PSKs are less complex to implement than certificates, while at the same time allowing for the authentication process to occur without user intervention. With PSKs, the host is provided a predetermined key that is used for the authentication process. A drawback of this system is that the PSK rarely changes and many organizations use the same key value for multiple remote hosts, thus undermining the security of the authentication process. If possible, certificate-based authentication or xauth should be used over (or in addition to) PSKs.

By implementing authentication, the firewall has an additional method of ensuring that the connection should be permitted. Even when the packet would be permitted based on inspection and the state of the connection, if the host cannot authenticate successfully with the firewall, the packet will be dropped.

Firewalls Act as an Intermediary

When people are concerned that a direct meeting would be too risky for them, they commonly use intermediaries to act on their behalf, and thus protect them from the risk of direct interaction. In the same vein, a firewall can be configured to act as an intermediary in the communications process between two hosts. This intermediary process is commonly referred to as acting as a proxy.

A proxy functions by effectively mimicking the host it is trying to protect. All communications destined for the protected host occurs with the proxy, which to the remote host appears to be the protected host. Indeed, the remote host has no way of knowing that it is not actually talking directly to the protected resource. The proxy receives packets destined for the protected host, strips out the relevant data, and builds a brand new packet that is then forwarded to the protected host. The protected host responds to the proxy, which simply reverses the process and forwards the response to the originating host. In doing so, the proxy (in this case, a firewall) acts as an intermediary to insulate the protected host from threats by ensuring that an external host can never directly communicate with the protected host.

In many cases, this function as a proxy is complemented by using a firewall that is capable of inspecting the actual application data to ensure that it is legitimate and nonmalicious data. When functioning in this manner, the firewall is known as working as an application proxy, because it is proxying the actual application functionality. This allows the firewall to inspect the actual application data itself (for example, allowing it to differentiate between legitimate HTTP traffic and malicious HTTP traffic) before presenting the data to the protected resource. For more detailed information about application proxies, see Chapter 2.

Firewalls Protect Resources

The single most important responsibility of a firewall is to protect resources from threat. This protection is achieved through the use of access control rules, stateful packet inspection, application proxies, or a combination of all to prevent the protected host from being accessed in a malicious manner or being made susceptible to malicious traffic. Firewalls are not an infallible method of protecting a resource however, and you should never rely exclusively on the firewall to protect a host. If an unpatched host (that is, a host that is lacking security updates that would protect it from being exploited) is connected to the Internet, a firewall may not be able to prevent that host from being exploited, especially if the exploit uses traffic that the firewall has been configured to permit. For example, if a packet-inspecting firewall permits HTTP traffic to an unpatched web server, a malicious user could leverage an HTTP-based exploit to compromise the web server because the web server is not patched against this new exploit. The unpatched web server renders the firewall useless as a protection device in this case. This is because the firewall cannot differentiate between malicious and nonmalicious HTTP requests, especially if the firewall does not function as an application proxy, and thus will happily pass the malicious HTTP data to the protected host. For this reason, protected resources should always be kept patched and up-to-date, in addition to being protected by a firewall.

Firewalls Record and Report on Events

The simple reality is that regardless of what you do to protect resources with a firewall, you cannot stop every malicious act or all malicious data. From simple misconfigurations of the firewall to new threats and exploits the firewall cannot protect against yet, you have to be prepared to deal with a security event that the firewall was not able to prevent. As a result, all firewalls should have a method of recording all communications (in particular access policy violations) that occur to enable the administrator to review the recorded data in an attempt to ascertain what transpired.

You can record firewall events in a number of ways, but most firewalls use two methods, either syslog or a proprietary logging format. By using either method of logging, the firewall logs can be interrogated to determine what may have transpired during a security event. In addition to the forensic analysis benefits of recording events, this data can also frequently be used when troubleshooting a firewall to help determine what may be the cause of the problem that is occurring.

Some events are important enough that merely logging them is not a good enough policy. In addition to logging the event, the firewall also needs to have a mechanism of alarming when a policy has been violated. Firewalls should support a number of types of alarms:

- **Console notification**—This is the simple process of presenting a notification to the console. The drawback of this alarm method is that it requires someone to be actively monitoring the console to know an alarm has been generated.

- **SNMP notification**—Simple Network Management Protocol (SNMP) can be used to generate traps that are sent to a network management system (NMS) that is monitoring the firewall.

- **Paging notification**—When an event occurs, the firewall can be configured to send a page to an administrator. This page can be numeric or alphanumeric, depending on the type of pager carried by the administrator.

- **E-mail notification**—Similar to paging notification, but the firewall simply sends an e-mail to the appropriate e-mail address.

By having a method of recording and reporting events, your firewall can provide an incredibly detailed level of insight as to what is currently occurring, or what may have previously occurred in the event that a forensic analysis must be performed.

What Are the Threats?

One of my favorite quotes is from Sun Tzu's *The Art of War*:

> If you know the enemy and know yourself, you need not fear the result of a hundred battles. If you know yourself but not the enemy, for every victory gained you will also suffer a defeat. If you know neither the enemy nor yourself, you will succumb in every battle.

To this end, it is not good enough to merely know what a firewall does or how a firewall works. You need to understand the threats that exist, to ensure that you can effectively protect your environment from the threats.

Threats that most IT organizations need to deal with include the following:

- Targeted versus untargeted attacks

- Viruses, worms, and trojans

- Malicious content and malware

- Denial-of-service (DoS) attacks

- Zombies

- Compromise of personal information and spyware

- Social engineering

- New attack vectors

- Insecure/poorly designed applications

Targeted Versus Untargeted Attacks

On the surface, the difference between a targeted and untargeted attack may seem pretty unimportant. As the saying goes, an attack is an attack, regardless of source. While in the midst of an attack, whether the attack is targeted or not may fall down the list of priorities. However, it is important to define the difference because it could impact the ultimate level of response required to address the attack.

Untargeted attacks are attacks that are not directly motivated by the resources being attacked. In other words, the attacker is not necessarily being motivated to attack *your* resources, as much as the attacker is probably trying to gain access to *any* server that might be susceptible, and your server just so happened to fall in their sights. This is a common attack method for defacement-style attacks. In many cases, the attacker has not chosen to target your website because you own it, as much as they are trying to find websites running on certain versions of web server software, and you just so happened to be running that web server software. As a result, untargeted attacks typically do not have as much effort and motivation behind them and can be easier to defend against than a targeted attack is. In many cases, merely dropping the malicious traffic is enough to effectively defend against an untargeted attack and cause the attacker to move on to easier hunting grounds.

Targeted attacks, on the other hand, present an additional twist to the attack. For whatever reason, the attacker is interested in the resources and data you have, and has made a conscious and concerted effort to try to gain access to those resources. This makes a targeted attack of more concern than an untargeted attack, because in general it means that the attacker is going to continue to attempt to gain access to those resources, despite your efforts to protect them. Therefore, you must be even more vigilant in attempting to stop and ultimately catch the attacker so that the legal authorities can take the appropriate action. Indeed, if you suspect that your environment is under a targeted attack, it is a good idea to get the authorities involved sooner than later, because often attackers will not stop until they have been locked up by the appropriate legal authorities.

Viruses, Worms, and Trojans

It seems like as long as there have been computer systems, there has been someone willing to make malicious software to attack them. Although the terms *virus*, *worm*, and *trojan* are often used interchangeably to refer to malicious software, each term has its own distinct qualities and attributes that you need to understand.

Viruses are pieces of malicious code that typically are attached to legitimate software. For example, an attacker might make a game for use on a computer that includes the virus code as part of the game code. As the game is passed from computer to computer, typically through user intervention such as e-mail or sharing discs, the virus is able to spread, infecting computers that run the game software. Viruses have differing degrees of severity, ranging from merely annoying messages and content, to destructive code designed to erase or otherwise cause the loss of data or system functionality. The key attribute to a virus is that it cannot execute and spread by itself; it requires user intervention to allow it to function and infect other systems.

Worms are similar to viruses (sometimes even considered a subclass, or evolution of the traditional virus), with one major difference. Worms are self-replicating and can spread and infect systems with no help from a human user after they have been initially unleashed. In many cases, worms take advantage of system exploits in their propagation process, utilizing the exploit to allow the worm to infect a new system. Another common method of propagation is to utilize the e-mail client on an infected host to e-mail the worm to additional targets. This nature of a worm allows it to be much more devastating than a traditional virus because an infected host can effectively spread the infection to hundreds of thousands of systems at once, allowing the spread of the worm to grow exponentially after the initial host has been compromised. This propagation can be so disruptive as to actually cause an inadvertent denial of service against resources in some cases. For example, Code Red spread by attempting to connect to a large number of remote hosts, which in turn caused the routers connected to the networks that those remote hosts resided on to issue a corresponding amount of Address Resolution Protocol (ARP) requests in an attempt to connect to the remote hosts. Because of the sheer quantity of requests and the nature of how ARP functions (ARP is covered in more detail in Chapter 3), many routers were unable to handle the sheer volume of traffic and therefore stopped being able to forward legitimate data.

Trojans take the idea of malicious viruses and worms to a new level. Rather than functioning as a virus or worm, the objective of a trojan is to appear as a piece of useful software that has a hidden function, typically to gain access to the resources on the infected system. For example, many trojans will install back-door software (such as BackOrifice) on the infected system, allowing the designer of the trojan to be able to connect to and access the infected system.

Viruses, worms, and trojans can be difficult to defend against using firewalls alone, and generally require either the integration of virus-scanning software on the firewall itself or the use of third-party products in conjunction with a firewall.

Malicious Content and Malware

Malicious content is simply data that was written with a nefarious purpose in mind. In most cases, malicious content requires the user to undertake some action that allows the protected system to be exposed to the content. This action may be accessing a website or simply viewing an e-mail that contains the content. The users, by virtue of the fact that they undertook the risky action, inadvertently allow their systems to become compromised by the malicious content. Often, the malicious content is active scripting functionality that allows arbitrary code to be executed by the client web browser or e-mail client, thus allowing the malicious content to perform functions ranging from accessing/destroying client data to installing viruses, worms, trojans, back doors, or just about any malware (malicious software) the attacker desires.

Malware (malicious software) simply builds on the basic premise of malicious content and includes any software that has a nefarious purpose in mind. Malicious software includes software such as viruses, worms, and trojans, although those three types of malware warrant their own distinct discussions because of the specialized nature and impact of each.

Unlike most threats this book covers, malicious content and malware generally requires the user on the protected network or resource to purposely or inadvertently perform some action to allow the content to be executed. As a result, protecting against malicious content and malware frequently requires the firewall to be able to monitor and control traffic that may originate from a protected network or host, typically through the use of egress filters on the firewall itself and content-filtering software used in conjunction with the firewall.

Denial of Service

A DoS attack entails a threat that simply prevents legitimate traffic from being able to access the protected resource. A common DoS is one that causes the services or server itself to crash, thus rendering the service being provided inaccessible. This attack is commonly done by exploiting buffer overflows in software and protocols or by sending data to the host that the host does not know how to respond to, thus causing the host to crash.

A variant of the DoS that has gained traction and is much more difficult to protect against is the distributed DoS (DDoS). With a DDoS, the end purpose is the same, but the method of attack differs. DDoS attacks typically utilize thousands of hosts to attack a target, thus increasing the amount of traffic exponentially. The objective of the DDoS is to overload the target with so many bogus requests that the target cannot respond to legitimate requests. Consequently, the difference between a DoS and a DDoS is generally the number of hosts engaging in the attack and the fact that the attackers are distributed across these systems as opposed to attacks coming from a single attacker. In fact, many DDoS attacks are nothing more than a DoS that is being executed on a much larger scale.

One well-known method of performing a DDoS is what is known as a SYN flood. A SYN flood in and of itself is not necessarily a DDoS. A SYN flood functions by presenting a target host with thousands of connection requests that are not allowed to complete successfully. The target must wait a determined amount of time for the connection to be successfully completed, thus utilizing network traffic buffers to store the partially created connections. When these buffers fill up with these partially created connections, the target can no longer accept new connection requests, and therefore begins dropping new traffic. What makes it particularly potent as a DDoS attack, however, is when thousands of hosts undertake the SYN flood, thus exponentially increasing the amount of traffic the targeted host must deal with. If one host attempts a SYN flood, it might not be able to generate enough connection requests to cause the DoS, but when 1000 (or more) other hosts join in, suddenly the targeted host can be quickly become inundated. Another method of performing a DDoS is to simply saturate the target with so much data, legitimate or otherwise, that the amount of traffic exceeds the capacity of the network bandwidth. This type of DDoS is particularly difficult to protect against because by the time DDoS traffic is on the network, it is already too late to stop it. The only effective way to protect against this type of DDoS is to rely on an upstream partner with more bandwidth than you have to filter the malicious traffic prior to it traversing your network segments. More mundane forms of DoS, particularly a DoS that attempts a SYN flood, can be protected against by implementing the appropriate rules on the firewall.

Zombies

Zombies are systems that have been infected with software (typically trojans or back doors) that puts them under the control of the attacker. The zombies can then be used at some point in the future to launch an attack, frequently a DoS attack against the ultimate target of the attacker.

The most effective way to protect against zombies is to prevent a system from being used as a zombie in the first place. You can do so by implementing egress filtering (filtering of traffic from a protected network) at the firewall as well as content filtering to ensure that even if a system is somehow turned into a zombie, it cannot be used to execute the final attack. In this sense, it is the responsibility of the firewall administrator to not only ensure that the firewall protects the organization's resources, but also to ensure that the firewall protects others from the organization's internal systems.

Compromise of Personal Information and Spyware

Personal information, in particular financial information, is the holy grail of many attackers. With that information, an attacker can either use or sell the data to someone who will use it to engage in all sorts of financial-based frauds. Literally millions of dollars of fraudulent purchases are made every year using personal information that was obtained illegally.

Financial information is only one component in the compromise of personal information. Another risk is the compromise of private medical data. This information, if made public, could result in people being illegally discriminated against. For example, an insurance company that has full and unfettered access to a patient's medical data might not be willing to insure the subject.

The compromise of personal information has led to a slew of legislation, the most well known being the Health Insurance Portability and Accountability Act of 1996 (HIPAA), which requires companies and organizations to take steps to ensure that personal information is not exposed to unauthorized access. From a corporate perspective, this means that the systems that collect this kind of data need to be insulated and protected to ensure that only authorized access to the data is permitted. The penalties for failing to protect personal information range from legal penalties to the loss of business and trust from the users of your systems.

A variation of the compromise of personal information is the compromise of proprietary or confidential information of a company or organization. This compromise could include the loss of source code or trade secrets as well as more mundane items such as company strategies and future business initiatives, allowing your competitors to gain an unfair advantage in business operations and competition.

In all of the previous methods, firewalls can be used to segment and isolate the critical systems, allowing greater control over who and what types of access to the protected resources will be allowed.

The compromise of information is not restricted solely to the realm of business. Individuals also risk the loss of their personal information through the use of malicious software such as spyware. Spyware functions in many ways like a trojan and allows the designer of the spyware to track everything from what websites an individual frequents to the purchases (and potentially the credit cards used) that the user makes. Spyware is much more difficult to control using network firewalls because in most cases the spyware is distributed throughout the environment. Many personal firewalls have included spyware-detection and -removal functionality as a component of their firewall suite, however, and therefore these can be an effective solution to the problem of how to protect personal information on a local computer.

Social Engineering

Whereas brute-force hacking a system gets all the sex appeal, social engineering is the surgical strike to the carpet-bombing mentality of a traditional hack. Social engineering attempts to compromise what is often the weakest link in an organization's security, the wetware (or people).

A social-engineering attack typically involves attackers attempting to pretend to be someone they are not, sometimes a user in need of help, sometimes an administrator attempting to help a user in need, and then trying to get the information they need from their target. For example, someone might contact users asking whether they are having any computer problems (most all users have *some* problem). The attacker might then seem to be trying to help the users troubleshoot the problem by asking them their password so they can attempt to log in as the user and see whether they experience the same problem. If a user provides that password, the attacker can then attempt to use it to gain access to other resources. Let's assume that your virtual private network (VPN) requires user authentication. With this information, a remote attacker might then be able to successfully log on to your VPN concentrator, and thus gain access to the internal network.

Because of the nature of a social-engineering attack, all the firewalls in the world will not do anything to prevent the attack from being successful. Rather, the best defense against social engineering is a well-trained user community and staff (you would be amazed at how many IT administrators will turn passwords over to a "service provider" trying to help troubleshoot a problem) that knows what is and is not acceptable information that should be shared either over the phone or in person.

New Attack Vectors

A current buzz is the threat of the zero-day event or exploit. The zero-day event is a security vulnerability that is exploited on the same day it is discovered—before vendors can respond with the appropriate patch or solution. Although the zero-day event has not happened yet, the time between when vulnerabilities are discovered and exploited has continued to get shorter and shorter.

The decreasing time from vulnerability to exploitation presents a problem because most technologies today take a rather reactionary response to attacks. As new vulnerabilities are discovered and published, vendors often must figure out the solution and attempt to deliver it before the attack is attempted. During this time period, after a vulnerability has been discovered but before a solution is available, systems are completely vulnerable and susceptible to attack and exploit. As an administrator, the only effective way to deal with new attack vectors is to ensure that you have an aggressive patch management solution in place, and that you apply patches and access control rule updates in a timely fashion, thus reducing that period of vulnerability.

Insecure/Poorly Designed Applications

The ugly truth that few software vendors want to admit is that a sizeable number of successful attacks result from insecure and poorly designed applications. In some cases, the application was designed well at the time, but the times changed and the application did not. In other cases, the application is just badly designed and implemented.

Regardless of the reason, insecure and poorly designed applications are one of the most difficult threats to address. Unfortunately, we are all at the mercy of the software vendors to patch their systems; if they have not or will not undertake this, the best we can do is attempt to work around the insecurity or design flaw, or use a different vendor's products.

Application proxies can be an effective solution to this problem, because the application proxy can typically be configured to recognize malicious traffic that attempts to exploit the application insecurity, and thus protect the system running the insecure application. Another potential solution is to use the firewall to prevent connections to the vulnerable system that are not necessary for the system to perform its job. For example, if the protected system is running a web server that is insecure, but the web server does not need to be accessed from an external source, you can configure the firewall to prevent access to the web server, while allowing access to any other applications the protected system is running.

What Are the Motives?

There is no shortage of motives behind the threats that attackers come up with. Perhaps the most dangerous motive is the conscious decision to break the law, typically in an effort to gain some financial or monetary gain. Often, criminals develop attacks and exploits with the sole purpose of gaining illegal access to systems, typically for the purpose of monetary gain. This gain could come from obtaining personal information and committing fraud with that information, gaining access to data and blackmailing the victim into paying for that data, or stealing trade secrets from a competitor's system or undermining the financial stability of the company.

A less-driven, but still dangerous motive is the simple desire to cause mischief and wreak havoc on an environment. Mischief covers everything from bored teenagers looking to do something they consider exciting and interesting, to the disgruntled ex-employee who is just looking to cause trouble for his former employer. One of the most difficult aspects of attackers motivated by mischief is that often the attacks they engage in have logical reason, especially if the attacker falls into the category of the bored person just looking for something interesting to do. Many times, their attempts at what they consider mundane and harmless activities can inadvertently cause significant problems or outages. Many virus writers fall into this category, not realizing just how much damage their innocuous virus can cause if someone is able to modify it slightly.

Another angle for motivation is simple ego. Attackers are convinced that they are smarter than you, the defender, and an easy way to prove it is to compromise the system. They can then run off to their chat rooms and brag about how they were able to get the best of the company they targeted.

However, the most troublesome motive comes from attackers with multiple motives. In this case, the attacker is frequently so driven by boredom, ego, and criminal behavior that nothing short of legal intervention can stop the attacker. Indeed, a number of attacks that may have started as untargeted attacks against an environment have escalated with bad consequences when attackers realized that what they did has been patched. Their ego cannot handle that they were stopped, and they become willing to undertake more risky—and more costly—activities to prove that they are superior.

Motives are not solely the realm of the attacker, however. As administrators, we have to know what our motivation is in protecting our resources. Ensure not only that you are protecting your resources, but that you are doing so in the proper manner. Although it is human nature when presented with an attack to want to lash out and strike back at attackers to teach them a lesson, that is not our place or our role. In fact, in the case of zombies, the system that you decide to strike back against often becomes an unwitting victim not only of the original hacker's attack on their system, but of your attack in an effort to teach the hacker not to mess with your systems. As cliché as it sounds, there are good guys and bad guys, and as administrators we need to make sure that our motives and undertakings remain on the side of the good guys.

Security Policies

As mentioned previously, firewalls are nothing more than access control policy enforcement points. Consequently, a firewall is only as effective as the firewall security policy (as opposed to the enterprise security policy) that dictates how the firewall will be used. Firewall security policies are discussed in great detail in Chapter 10, "Firewall Security Policies," but we can look at the fundamentals of what kinds of firewall security policies exist and how to build an effective security policy now.

The first step to a good security policy is to perform a risk analysis to determine what the threats to the protected system are. After doing this, you can develop a strategy and policy for protecting the system from those threats with your firewalls. A key thing to understand when you develop this strategy is that you may not be able to protect against or prevent everything. The reasons for this range from technological limitations (technically the recommendation cannot be done) to practical limitations (it would not be practical to undertake the recommendation) to financial limitations (you do not have the money in the budget to undertake the recommendation). As a result, you need to approach the subject from the perspective of seeking to minimize the risk associated with the threat. In some cases, that means you can reduce the risk to zero (for example, if you use a firewall to prevent all access to a system). In other cases, you can only reduce the risk to a level that is acceptable by management. For example, management may not decide that they can afford to spend the money required to implement the security solution recommended. In this instance, it is absolutely critical to convey in an honest and accurate manner what the level of risk will be. The reason for this is that after an incident occurs, it becomes real convenient for people to suddenly "forget" that they agreed to that level of risk in the first place. This is the time that it comes in handy to be able to produce a signed document that proves everyone agreed that the level of risk that was settled on was appropriate.

Examples of Security Policies

You have two primary security policies to use as a baseline in designing your security policy. The first is the closed security policy, also known as the minimalist security policy. The other is an open security policy, also known as generally a bad idea.

The closed security policy is based on the premise that by default all access is denied, and only access that is explicitly required will be permitted. The benefit of this approach is that the security policy will be designed only to allow access that has been explicitly granted. This security policy is frequently implemented when dealing with granting access from an untrusted source to a protected system (sometimes referred to as ingress filtering). The drawback of this system is the same as its strength, however. Because the default action is to deny traffic, it can be a time-consuming process to identify, configure, and maintain the list of exceptions that must be permitted.

At the other end of the spectrum is the open security policy. It takes the exact opposite approach, by default granting all access and denying only the traffic that is explicitly configured to be denied. This type of security policy is frequently implemented for granting access from a trusted network to external systems (sometimes referred to as egress filtering). The benefit of this system is that it generally takes little to no configuration to allow systems to traverse the firewall and access resources. As a result, *many* firewalls by default apply this methodology to traffic that is sourced from the internal network to external networks such as the Internet. Although convenient, it is incredibly insecure because the firewall will allow legitimate and malicious traffic out with equal ease. Consequently, it is not recommended that you implement a firewall that is configured in this manner. Although more convenient, the risk is simply too great for most environments.

Firewalls and Trust

After the decision has been made to allow some traffic through the firewall, the administrator has effectively made the decision (intentional or not) to trust the traffic that will be permitted. This decision is part of defining an acceptable level of risk. A firewall typically does not exist to stop all traffic. If it did, you would be better served just to disconnect the system from the network entirely. Instead, the firewall exists to allow some traffic while stopping other traffic.

In these situations, you have to realize and accept that by permitting certain traffic, you are trusting that the traffic is safe and acceptable. However, this does not mean that by deciding to permit traffic you are effectively removing any security a firewall can provide. Simply put, just because you trust certain types of traffic does not mean you have to trust the traffic in its entirety and in every way.

In the continued pursuit of mitigating and minimizing risk, you can configure the firewall to authenticate connections that will access the trusted resource, adding an additional level of security and risk management to the access that is being granted. Doing so ensures that before access to the protected resource will be granted, the requesting system must be authenticated as a legitimate user of the resource.

Another option is to use the firewall as an application proxy, serving as an intermediary for providing access to the protected resource. As discussed previously in this chapter, this can help mitigate and minimize risk by ensuring that all access to the protected resource must go through the proxy, allowing the proxy to ensure that the data being transmitted is not malicious or harmful.

The biggest thing to remember about firewalls and trust is that no matter how much you trust the access being granted, it has to go through the firewall before gaining access to the protected resource as opposed to just bypassing or not using a firewall at all.

Determining If You Need a Firewall

It is convenient (and accurate) to say that you always need a firewall if you are connecting to the Internet. Firewalls should not be relegated exclusively to the realm of providing access to and protection from Internet-based resources. Instead, you should consider implementing a firewall any time a resource needs to be protected, regardless of where the protected resource is located, or where the requesting traffic will be coming from. Firewalls can, and in many cases should, be used to control access to important servers or different subnets within the corporate network. For example, if two branch offices should never need access to each other's resources, you should consider a firewall to enforce that policy and ensure that such access is never granted.

To help determine where you can implement a firewall, define what the cost of the data you are trying to protect is. This cost includes a number of variables. One variable to consider is the cost of restoring or repairing the data. An additional variable is the cost of lost work and downtime as a result of the data being inaccessible to employees. Yet another variable is the cost in lost revenue or income that might come as a result of the loss of data.

A common way of quantifying this kind of cost is known as determining the single loss expectancy (SLE) and annual loss expectancy (ALE). SLE is the expected monetary loss every time an incident occurs. The ALE is the expected monetary loss over the course of a year. The ALE is calculated by multiplying the annual rate of occurrence (ARO) by the SLE. The ARO is the probability that something will occur during a given year. The easiest way to understand how to calculate and determine this information is to go through a fictional scenario.

Suppose that your external web server is compromised and that web server is used to process incoming requests that 100 data processors work on. The first thing to do is to define the SLE, and doing that requires that you define the variables mentioned previously. First, you need to define the cost of restoring or repairing the data. This cost can range from the time it takes someone to reboot a server and apply a patch or to restore the server from a tape backup. For this scenario, assume that the cost to recover from this compromise is $500. Next, the loss of the web server and subsequent inability of the workers to do anything productive needs to be factored into the equation. Assuming the employees are paid $12 an hour (average salary of a data-entry clerk in the Houston, Texas, area) and the server is down for a half a day being rebuilt, the cost to the company in just lost time for the users of the web server is $4800. Finally, the cost of loss of revenue or income needs to be factored into the equation. There are a number of ways to determine this, which the accounting department should be able to help in defining. For example, if the application in question generates a certain amount of money per transaction, and the average number of transactions per day is known, you can easily determine the number of lost transactions, and thus revenue, for a given period of time. For example, suppose that the loss of revenue is $1000. This gives you a grand total of $6300, which is the SLE of the given scenario.

On the surface, considering that an enterprise-class firewall with failover can be had for less than $6000 (Cisco PIX 515E unrestricted license with failover), it would seem to make perfect sense that if a firewall could have prevented the incident, that there should be no question about whether a firewall should have been purchased and implemented. However, it is not quite that simple. With the benefit of hindsight, you can easily see that the firewall was worth the cost. Rarely do we have the benefit of hindsight when it is time to determine what to spend money on, which is where the ALE comes into play.

Defining the ALE is a little bit trickier than defining the SLE because it almost always requires you to make some educated guesses as to what the ARO is. For example, it is impossible to say with certainty that an event will occur a certain number of times a year or even a certain number of times over the course of many years. The ARO is more of a method of making an educated calculation based on historic data and information to determine what the expected probability of an occurrence is. For example, suppose that in reviewing insurance data the probability of a serious fire is once every 25 years. This does not guarantee that a fire will happen in any given year, or even at all during that time, but it does allow you to put a value to the probability that a fire will occur, in this case 1/25 or 0.04 percent in any given year. When the ARO is multiplied by the SLE, you can get the ALE.

Reviewing the scenario, suppose that the ARO is defined as 1 or greater. In that case, you can easily justify spending $6000 on a firewall that could prevent the loss ($6300), because it will pay for itself by preventing a single incident. What if the ARO is less than 1 (which it frequently is)? At that point, it can be tougher to make the case that a firewall should be implemented, because the cost of the firewall may not be less than the ALE. In this case, however, keep in mind that the ALE is the expected loss, not the actual loss, and although the cost of the solution may be less than the ALE, it may still be financially viable and a worthwhile endeavor. Conversely, if the probability that an event will occur is so low, the cost of the solution may never be justified. Of course, as the saying goes in technology, it is always difficult to get money for security before an event occurs. . .but after an event does occur, the pocketbooks open right up to prevent a recurrence.

Another variable is the cost of starting over. This variable is particularly important for smaller companies, because the majority of smaller companies that experience a week of downtime as a result of a security incident are rarely able to recover from that outage, and subsequently go out of business.

The cost of legal repercussions as a result of the data loss or compromise is another real cost that you must consider. The simple reality is that we live in a litigious society, and if a company is negligent in adequately protecting their data, especially if they maintain consumer data, there will be no shortage of lawyers seeking monetary compensation for the security incident. I would not want to be on the jury of a company being sued that admitted that they decided not to use a firewall, or do anything else to protect their resources, and were subsequently hacked.

Whereas the corporate user has many justifications for protecting their resources, home users tend not to share such concerns. Some home users might think, "What do I have that I need to protect?" and not come up with anything important. This is a deceptive line of thinking, however. The home user might be unaware of data that needs protection. We have all seen the news regarding identity theft and the loss of financial information; and if home users have used their computer to make online transactions or store their financial data, protecting that data can go a long way toward preventing them from becoming a victim of these types of crimes and events. Even going beyond protecting financial data, however, many home users maintain data such as personal or family information that they probably would not want to be made publicly available. Also, although home users might legitimately not have any data of any consequence that they believe they need to protect, if they leave their system unprotected it can relatively easily be used by someone else to engage in malicious activity, particularly by using the system as a zombie, and use a home user's computer to attack other systems on the Internet. Therefore, home users really have an obligation to implement a firewall (in addition to making sure that they run current antivirus and antispyware/malware software and keep their systems patched and up-to-date) not only to protect themselves, but to protect others from their systems being used as part of an attack.

Summary

Firewalls, regardless of how complex in design and implementation, have a simple responsibility to act as security policy enforcement points. Firewalls can do this by inspecting the data that is received and tracking the connections that are made to determine what data should be permitted and what data should be denied. In addition, firewalls can act as an intermediary and proxy requests to the protected host while at the same time providing a means of authenticating access to better ensure that only approved access is granted. Finally, firewalls can report and alert on events related to all of these processes to allow you, the administrator, to know what is going on with your firewall and the systems it is protecting.

Any number of motivations drive people to develop threats to our systems. By examining the threats and the appropriate responses, you can develop a security policy that minimizes the risk presented by a threat through the proper implementation and configuration of a firewall. Although a firewall cannot prevent all attacks, it is one of the best methods of protecting resources; and when in doubt, there is a good chance that a firewall can help make your resources even more secure than if there were no firewall at all.

## CHAPTER 2

Firewall Basics

This chapter covers the basics of firewalls. Firewalls can be distinguished in a variety of ways: from the size of the network they are designed to operate in to the way they provide protection. This chapter examines the basic taxonomy of firewalls and uses the convention of classifying firewalls based on "size"—personal or desktop firewalls, small office/home office (SOHO) firewalls, and enterprise-level firewalls. In addition, this chapter discusses the various ways firewalls defend the networks they are placed in, from simple packet filters to stateful packet filters to application proxies.

This chapter provides a high-level overview of the various firewall products discussed throughout the book.

Firewall Taxonomy

Firewalls come in various sizes and flavors. The most typical idea of a firewall is a dedicated system or appliance that sits in the network and segments an "internal" network from the "external" Internet. Most home or SOHO networks use an appliance-based device for broadband connectivity that includes a built-in firewall. In general, firewalls can be categorized under one of two general types:

- Desktop or personal firewalls

- Network firewalls

The primary difference between these two types of firewalls simply boils down to the number of hosts that the firewall protects. Within the network firewall type, there are primary classifications of devices, including the following:

- Packet-filtering firewalls (stateful and nonstateful)

- Circuit-level gateways

- Application-level gateways

The preceding list describes general classes of firewalls but, as discussed later, many network firewalls represent hybrids of the preceding classifications. Many firewalls have characteristics that place them in more than one classification.

Figure 2-1 shows a breakdown of the various firewall types currently available. This figure does not provide complete details of the various capabilities within each firewall type but rather shows the general taxonomy of the different firewalls available in the two primary types: personal/ desktop firewalls and network firewalls.

Figure 2-1 *Firewall Taxonomy*

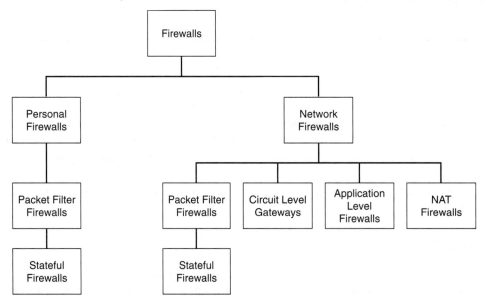

Given these various firewall types available, users may have a hard time identifying exactly what they need. In many cases, costs represent a driving factor in the purchase of a firewall, but knowing which types of firewalls are available and what capabilities they provide helps users make a more informed final decision.

Personal Firewalls

Personal firewalls are designed to protect a single host from unauthorized access. Over the years, this has evolved so that modern personal firewalls now integrate additional capabilities such as antivirus software monitoring and in some cases behavior analysis and intrusion detection to protect the device. Some of the more popular commercial personal firewalls include BlackICE as well as Cisco Security Agent. In the SOHO market Trend Micro's PC-cillin, ZoneAlarm, and the Symantec personal firewall are some of the more popular offerings. Microsoft's Internet Connection Firewall is also among the top personal firewalls installed because of the install base of machines running Windows XP with Service Pack 2.

Whereas personal firewalls make immense sense in the SOHO and home user market because they provide the end user protection as well as control of the policy, in the enterprise the issues are more complex. Perhaps the biggest concern for enterprise users with regard to personal firewalls is the ability to provide a centralized policy control mechanism for the firewall. The need to centralize policy control is critical to the use of personal firewalls in an enterprise environment to minimize the administrative burden. What is administrative burden? As the number of firewalls deployed in an organization increases, the network administrator must be concerned with the proper configuration and monitoring of each one of these firewalls. Therefore, it is extremely important that as the number of firewalls increases, the ability to administer them does not become overly burdensome. By centralizing policy control and monitoring, many vendors have eased the effort of properly configuring the firewall policy and of monitoring the events.

Network Firewalls

Network firewalls are designed to protect whole networks from attack. Network firewalls come in two primary forms: a dedicated appliance or a firewall software suite installed on top of a host operating system. Examples of appliance-based network firewalls include the Cisco PIX, the Cisco ASA, Juniper's NetScreen firewalls, Nokia firewalls, and Symantec's Enterprise Firewall. The more popular software-based firewalls include Check Point's Firewall-1 NG or NGX Firewalls, Microsoft ISA Server, Linux-based IPTables, and BSD's pf packet filter. The Sun Solaris operating system has, in the past, been bundled with Sun's enterprise firewall, SunScreen. With the release of Solaris 10, Sun has begun bundling the open source IP Filter (IPF) firewall as an alternative to SunScreen.

Many network firewalls provide enterprise users the maximum flexibility and protection in a firewall system. These firewalls have over the past few years incorporated many new features such as in-line intrusion detection and prevention as well as virtual private network (VPN) termination capabilities both for LAN-to-LAN VPNs as well as remote-access-user VPNs. Another feature that has been introduced into network firewalls is a deep packet-inspection capability. The firewall can identify traffic requirements not just by looking at Layer 3 and Layer 4 information but by delving all the way into the application data so that the firewall can make decisions as to how to best handle the traffic flow. This evolution in firewall design and capabilities has led to the development of a new firewall product, the integrated firewall, which is covered in more detail in the next section.

Firewall Products

You can find a wide variety of firewall products on the market today, comprising three basic physical firewalls: software based, appliance based, and integrated. Software-based firewalls, as discussed previously, typically run on top of a commercial operating system, such as Sun Solaris or Microsoft Windows. Appliance-based firewalls are purposefully designed devices in which the filter and inspection software is tightly integrated into a custom-built or hardened operating system. These firewalls include the Cisco PIX products as well as Juniper's NetScreen firewalls and the Symantec Enterprise Firewall. Finally, there is the integrated firewall, which is somewhat of a synthesis of other products with the traditional firewall. Whereas in the past multiple security devices such as firewalls, VPNs, and intrusion detection systems were all based on different devices, recent movement in the industry tends toward integrating all three devices into one platform. This synthesis has the benefit of reducing the number of hardware devices that require administration and thus lowering the administrative overhead necessary to deploy and manage these devices. Examples of integrated firewalls include the Cisco ASA and the TippingPoint X505 devices. The following sections discuss each of these firewall products in further detail.

Software Firewalls

Software firewalls are installed on top of an all-purpose generic operating system. Software firewalls include the Sun SunScreen firewall, IPF, the Microsoft ISA Server, Check Point NG, Gauntlet, Linux's IPTables and FreeBSD, and OpenBSD's pf packet filter. Typically, the vendor's firewall software suite includes patches as well as configuration changes that must be applied to harden the underlying operating system from attack or to include a kernel module or driver for the firewall to operate properly. The primary advantage of such firewalls is that you can task them to be multipurpose in nature. For example, a firewall can also be a Domain Name System (DNS) server itself or it can be the spam filter. Software firewalls lend themselves to multipurpose roles much more easily than dedicated appliance firewalls.

A significant disadvantage to these firewalls is the need to consider the potential vulnerabilities of the underlying operating system. Consider, for example, the SunScreen firewall and the Microsoft ISA firewall. Both are installed on top of a base operating system of Solaris or Windows 2000/ 2003, respectively. As new vulnerabilities are discovered in various aspects of the operating system, the administrator must consider whether to install the vendor patches or whether to forego the patches because of potential adverse effects on the firewall. What are the potential effects of patches? The firewall may not function properly after the installation of a patch. In many cases, the vendor (either the operating system manufacturer or the firewall software vendor) tests patches for compatibility with the firewall software and releases a bulletin recommending the installation or cautioning against the installation of the patches.

Additionally, in an enterprise environment, a software firewall may sometimes cross the "political" line between the systems group and the network group. The question of "who owns the box?" needs to be resolved. The systems group may claim that because the system has a generic operating system installed that the system belongs to them; similarly, the network group may claim that because the system role is that of a firewall it is under their administration. Issues such as this *can* crop up in larger environments.

The primary benefit of software firewalls is the ability to use commodity hardware for the device such that if the device should fail, then replacement of hardware is relatively straightforward. A significant drawback to software firewalls is that the firewall software vendor and the operating system vendor may simply point fingers at one another and blame the other whenever a problem arises that causes the firewall software or the operating system to fail. This issue normally does not apply when the firewall vendor and the operating system vendor are the same, as with Linux-based firewalls, Microsoft ISA Server, or OpenBSD's IPF running on OpenBSD.

Other drawbacks to software firewalls include the requirement to lock down the underlying operating system, maintaining patches of the underlying operating system, and potentially poorer performance because the operating system has not been tuned for a high-performance environment. Finally, software firewalls tend to underperform compared to appliance-based firewalls, because software firewalls typically do not run on an operating system that has been explicitly tuned for peak performance as a firewall.

In smaller environments, these issues typically do not come into consideration because the systems and network group may not be distinctly separate. Also, software firewalls can be useful low-cost devices for the technically savvy home user. However, for the more typical home user, the low-end appliance-based firewalls (such as Linksys, D-Link, and NETGEAR) provide greater benefit because of the ease of setup and the low maintenance they require.

Appliance Firewalls

Appliance firewalls are firewalls that are integrated tightly with custom-built hardware (or in some cases commodity hardware) and provide firewall services to a network. Appliance firewalls include the Cisco PIX, NetScreen firewalls, SonicWall appliances, WatchGuard Fireboxes, and Nokia firewalls all the way down to the Linksys, D-Link, and NETGEAR products for home users. The underlying operating system need not be a custom operating system. It can be a highly customized version of a commodity operating system as in WatchGuard's use of Linux or Nokia's use of FreeBSD as their base operating systems.

In many cases, appliance firewalls offer better performance relative to software firewalls because of the nature of the customized underlying operating system and the use of specialized processors and application-specific integrated circuits (ASICs) for data processing and handling input and output (I/O) requests. Additionally, these firewalls may have the benefit of fewer moving parts by eliminating the hard disk (or disks as the case may be) of the software firewalls. As firewalls have matured and become more complex, the gap between the appliance firewall and the software firewall has dramatically closed. Many of the features that have typically been the province of appliance firewalls have been filtering down into software firewalls.

Perhaps the main benefit of the appliance firewall may be technical support. As mentioned previously, with a software firewall at least three (and possibly more) vendors may be involved in the firewall: the hardware vendor, the operating system vendor, and the firewall software vendor. As is the case with many different parties involved in a given device, each will typically point the finger at the others whenever something goes wrong. With the appliance firewall, there is only one vendor for the entire device. If a failure occurs, that vendor is called on to make things right.

Other benefits typical of appliance firewalls are overall better performance, tighter security of the firewall operating system, and lower overall cost than commercial software firewalls.

The drawbacks of a single vendor for handling issues with the firewall is if the vendor chooses to discontinue a specific firewall model in favor of a more recent model, the possibility that the vendor will no longer be in business in the future (either due to bankruptcy or acquisition by a competitor), and the possibility that if a bug is found in the firewall software (or the underlying operating system) the vendor may determine when or whether to release a patch.

Additional drawbacks to appliance-based firewalls are that they may lack advanced features and functionality that software-based firewalls provide. It can also be more difficult to provide additional security functions, such as spam control, when compared to software-based firewalls. This drawback results from the fact that it is generally a trivial task to add additional applications to a software-based firewall; you simply install the new application. Appliance-based firewalls frequently require the implementation of additional hardware to provide similar functionality, increasing the complexity of the potential solution.

Integrated Firewalls

Integrated firewalls are multipurpose devices that combine the traditional firewall with other features such as remote-access VPN, LAN-to-LAN VPN, intrusion detection or prevention, spam filtering, and antivirus filtering. These devices are designed to provide an "all-in-one" approach to network-edge security by collapsing the responsibilities of several devices into one device. The benefit of integrated firewalls is that they simplify the network design by reducing the number of devices on the network as well as provide a single system for administration, thereby reducing the administrative burden on the network staff. Another benefit is the potentially lower cost of the device versus multiple devices from multiple vendors.

The major drawback is that the failure of such a device can lead to multiple exposures. Additionally, the complexity of such a device may make it difficult to troubleshoot connectivity problems because of the interaction of different capabilities in the device and how they affect the underlying fundamental operation of a firewall. Although an integrated firewall may be lower in total cost of ownership (TCO), the upfront cost may be significantly more. If a single integrated firewall is more costly than the component devices that provide similar functionality and only provides a marginal cost-benefit, it may be difficult to justify the purchase of an integrated firewall.

Firewall Technologies

This section focuses on the technologies used in various firewalls and how they work. The firewall taxonomy in Figure 2-1 shows the general types of firewalls. This section focuses more on the underlying technologies that devices that fall into those types utilize. In some cases, one technology discussed here can fall into multiple types in the taxonomy tree. The focus is on a wide range of firewall technologies, including the following:

- Personal firewalls

- Packet filters

- Network Address Translation (NAT) firewalls

- Circuit-level firewalls

- Proxy firewalls

- Stateful firewalls

- Transparent firewalls

- Virtual firewalls

Now, you might be thinking, "Wait, I thought there were three firewall products: software based, appliance based, and integrated." The firewall technologies discussed in this section may be used by any of the three basic physical firewalls. Indeed, these technologies simply allow us to define a firewall in a more granular fashion. So, for example, an appliance firewall can be further quantified as a stateful firewall. Each of these technologies is examined and discussed to provide you with an understanding of the differences between these technologies, and by extension the firewall devices that utilize these technologies. Each section focuses predominantly on the operation of the firewall in its function as a network security device. Discussion of the redundancy capabilities, performance, and management of specific firewalls is not covered. This section provides a brief introduction to some specific firewalls that subsequent chapters cover in greater detail.

Personal Firewalls

Personal firewalls are designed to protect a single host. They can be viewed as a hardened shell around the host system, whether it is a server, desktop, or laptop. Typically, personal firewalls assume that outbound traffic from the system is to be permitted and inbound traffic requires inspection. By default, personal firewalls include various profiles that accommodate the typical traffic a system might see. For example, ZoneAlarm has low, medium, and high settings that allow almost all traffic, selected traffic, or nearly no traffic, respectively, through to the protected system. In a similar vein, IPTables—which you can set up as a personal firewall as well as in a network firewall role—during the setup of the Linux system, enables the installer to choose the level of protection for the system and the customization for ports that do not fall into a specific profile.

One important consideration with personal firewalls is centralized management. Some vendors have identified that a significant barrier to deployment of personal firewall on every end system is the need for centralized management so that policies can be developed and applied remotely to end systems and have developed such capabilities within their products. Large enterprises are hesitant to adopt this personal firewall technology for their systems because of the difficulty of maintaining a consistent firewall policy across the enterprise.

Packet Filters

Packet filters are network devices that filter traffic based on simple packet characteristics. These devices are typically stateless in that they do not keep a table of the connection state of the various traffic flows through them. To allow traffic in both directions, they must be configured to permit return traffic. Simple packet filters include Cisco IOS access lists as well as Linux's ipfwadm facility to name a few. Although these filters provide protection against a wide variety of threats, they are not dynamic enough to be considered true firewalls. Their primary focus is to limit traffic inbound while providing for outbound and established traffic to flow unimpeded. Example 2-1 shows a simple access list for filtering traffic. This list is based on the network example in Figure 2-2. The access list is applied to the inbound side of the filtering device that connects the LAN to the Internet.

Example 2-1 *Simple Access List*

```
access-list 101 permit icmp any 192.168.185.0 0.0.0.255 echo-reply
access-list 101 permit icmp any 192.168.185.0 0.0.0.255 ttl-exceeded
access-list 101 permit tcp any 192.168.185.0 0.0.0.255 established
access-list 101 permit udp any host 192.168.185.100 eq 53
access-list 101 permit udp any eq 123 192.168.185.0 0.0.0.255
```

Figure 2-2 *Simple Access List Sample Network*

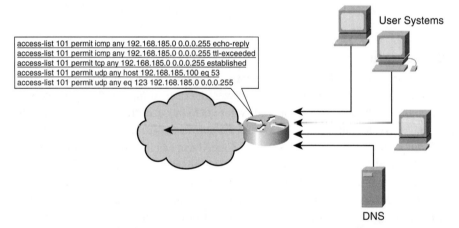

Note that inbound return traffic for DNS (53/UDP) and NTP (123/UDP) are explicitly stated toward the end of the filter list, as are Internet Control Message Protocol (ICMP) echo-reply and Time-To-Live (TTL)-exceeded responses. Without these statements, these packets would be blocked even though they are in response to traffic that originated in the protected LAN. Finally, note the following rule:

```
access-list 101 permit tcp any 192.168.185.0 0.0.0.255 established
```

This rule is required to allow return traffic from any outside system back to the 192.168.185.0/
24 subnet as long as the return traffic has the TCP ACK flag set. Packet filters typically do not
have any stateful capabilities to inspect outbound traffic and dynamically generate rules
permitting the return traffic to an outbound flow. Figure 2-3 shows a simple packet-filtering
firewall.

Figure 2-3   *Packet-Filtering Firewall*

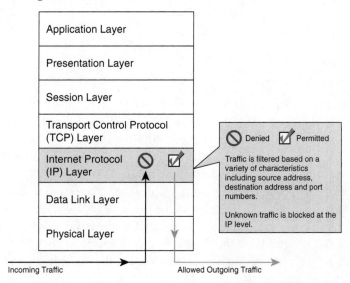

NAT Firewalls

A distinct firewall that existed for a short period is the Network Address Translation (NAT)
firewall. In today's firewall market, NAT is a part of almost every firewall product available.
From the lowliest SOHO firewall such as the Linksys BEFSX41 to the high-end enterprise
PIX 535, NAT is now a function of a firewall. NAT firewalls automatically provide protection
to systems behind the firewall because they only allow connections that originate from the
inside of the firewall. The basic purpose of NAT is to multiplex traffic from an internal network
and present it to a wider network (that is, the Internet) as though it were coming from a single
IP address or a small range on IP addresses. The NAT firewall creates a table in memory that
contains information about connections that the firewall has seen. This table maps the addresses
of internal systems to an external address. The ability to place an entire network behind a single
IP address is based on the mapping of port numbers on the NAT firewall. For example, consider
the systems shown in Figure 2-4.

Figure 2-4 *NAT Firewall*

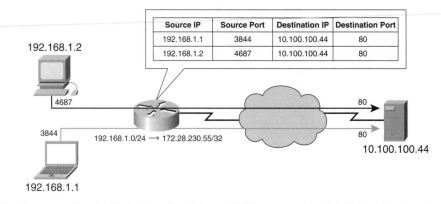

The hosts on the "inside" of the NAT firewall (192.168.1.1 and 192.168.1.2) are both trying to access the web server 10.100.100.44. Host 192.168.1.1 opens up TCP port 3844 and connects to the web server 10.100.100.44 at TCP port 80. Host 192.168.1.2 opens TCP port 4687 and connects to the web server 10.100.100.44 at TCP port 80. The NAT firewall is configured to translate the entire 192.168.1.0/24 network to the single IP address 172.28.230.55. When the firewall sees the outbound connections, it rewrites the IP layer information in the traffic and replaces 192.168.1.1 and 192.168.1.2 with the single IP address 172.28.230.55. Internally, the NAT firewall maintains a table that keeps track of the traffic flows and translates both 192.168.1.1 and 192.168.1.2 to the IP address 172.28.230.55. It does this by means of network sockets that uniquely identify a given connection. For the example shown in Figure 2-4, there are two unique sockets: 192.168.1.1:3844 and 192.168.1.2:4687. When this traffic is seen by the firewall, the NAT process replaces the 192.168.1 network addresses with the 172.28.230.55 address. Table 2-1 shows this process.

Table 2-1 *Network Address Translation*

Source IP	Source Port	NAT IP	NAT Port	Destination IP	Destination Port
192.168.1.1	3844	172.28.230.55	3844	10.100.100.44	80
192.168.1.2	4687	172.28.230.55	4687	10.100.100.44	80
192.168.1.1	4687	172.28.230.55	63440	10.100.100.44	80

The last entry in the table shows what a NAT firewall does when a specific source port is already taken by a previous connection. In this case, the client 192.168.1.1 is attempting to make a second connection to the web server 10.100.100.44. The client opens a connection on TCP port 4687; however, TCP port 4687 on the NAT firewall is already being used by the connection for the client 192.168.1.2. In this case, the NAT firewall changes not only the source IP address but also the source port and keeps that mapping in its translation table.

Circuit-Level Firewalls

Circuit-level firewalls work at the session layer of the OSI model and monitor "handshaking" between packets to decide whether the traffic is legitimate. Traffic to a remote computer is modified to make it appear as though it originated from the circuit-level firewall. This modification makes a circuit-level firewall particularly useful in hiding information about a protected network but has the drawback that it does not filter individual packets in a given connection. Figure 2-5 shows an example of a circuit-level firewall.

Figure 2-5   *Circuit-Level Firewall*

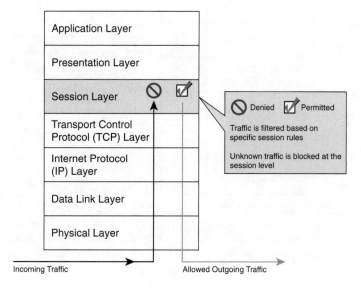

Proxy Firewalls

A proxy firewall acts as an intermediary between two end systems in a similar fashion as a circuit-level gateway. However, in the case of a proxy firewall, the interaction is controlled at the application layer, as shown in Figure 2-6. Proxy firewalls operate at the application layer of the connection by forcing both sides of the conversation to conduct the communication through the proxy. It does this by creating and running a process on the firewall that mirrors a service as though it were running on an end system. To support various services, the proxy firewall must have a specific service running for each protocol: a Simple Mail Transport Protocol (SMTP) proxy for e-mail, a File Transfer Protocol (FTP) proxy for file transfers, and a Hypertext Transfer Protocol (HTTP) proxy for web services.

Whenever a client wants to connect to a service on the Internet, the packets making up the connection request are processed by the specific proxy service for that protocol before being forwarded to the target system. Packets returning from the server on the Internet are similarly processed by the same proxy service before being forwarded to the internal system. In many proxy firewalls, a generic proxy service can be used by services that do not have a service specifically tailored to their needs. However, not all services can use this generic proxy. If there are no proxy capabilities for a specific service running on the firewall, no connection to outside servers running that service is possible, or the firewall utilizes other technologies such as circuit-level filtering to filter the connection.

Figure 2-6 *Proxy Firewall*

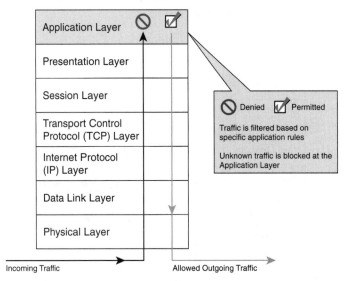

Because of their inspection capabilities, proxy firewalls can look much more deeply into the packets of a connection and apply additional rules to determine whether a packet should be forwarded to an internal host. The disadvantages of a proxy firewall can be in their complex configuration as well as their speed. Because the firewalls look deep into the application, they can introduce delay into network connections. Finally, if there is no specific proxy service for a particular network application and it cannot be made to work with a generic proxy service and the firewall cannot perform other methods of filtering, you cannot put that behind the firewall. Most modern firewalls include basic proxy server architecture in their operation by providing some form of proxy capabilities. For example, PIX OS 6 and earlier had the **fixup** command, and IPF provided an FTP proxy service to handle active FTP connections.

Stateful Firewalls

Modern stateful firewalls combine aspects and capabilities of NAT firewalls, circuit-level firewalls, and proxy firewalls into one system. These firewalls filter traffic initially based on packet characteristics like the packet-filtering firewall but also include session checks to make sure that the specific session is allowed. Unlike proxy or circuit-level firewalls, stateful firewalls are typically designed to be more transparent (like their packet-filtering and NAT cousins). However, they include proxy-filtering aspects by inspecting the application layer data as well through the use of specific services. This feature is best exemplified through PIX application-inspection capabilities (through the use of the **fixup** command in PIX OS 6 and the **inspect** command in PIX OS 7), which allow the PIX to support such protocols as FTP, SMTP, H.323, and many others. Figure 2-7 depicts stateful firewalling.

Figure 2-7   *Stateful Firewall*

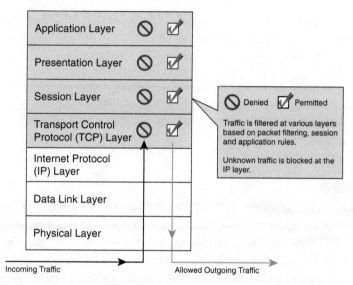

Stateful firewalls are more complex than their constituent component firewalls; however, nearly all modern firewalls on the market today are stateful firewalls and represent the baseline for security in today's networks.

Transparent Firewalls

Transparent firewalls (also known as bridging firewalls) are not a completely new firewall but rather a subset of stateful firewalls. Whereas nearly all firewalls operate at the IP layer and above, transparent firewalls sit at Layer 2, the data link layer, and monitor Layer 3+ traffic. Additionally, the transparent firewall can apply packet-filtering rules like any other stateful firewall and still appear invisible to the end user. In essence, the transparent firewall acts as a filtering bridge between two network segments. It represents an excellent way of applying a security policy in the *middle* of a network segment without having to apply a NAT filter. The benefits of a transparent, bridging firewall fall into three general categories:

- Zero configuration

- Performance

- Stealth

The bridging firewall requires no changes to the underlying network, which is possible simply because the transparent bridging firewall is plugged in-line with the network it is protecting. Because it operates at the data link layer, no IP address changes are required. The firewall can be placed so as to segment a network subnet between low-security and higher-security systems or to protect a single host if necessary.

Because bridging firewalls tend to be simpler than their Layer 3 cousins, they have a lower processing overhead. That lower overhead enables them to provide better performance as well as deeper packet inspection.

Finally, their stealth nature stems directly from the fact that they are Layer 2 devices. The network interfaces of bridging firewalls have no IP addresses (other than the management interface) assigned to them and therefore are invisible to an attacker. The firewall cannot be attacked because, basically, it cannot be reached.

Virtual Firewalls

Virtual firewalls are multiple logical firewalls running on a single physical device. This arrangement allows for multiple networks to be protected by a unique firewall running a unique security policy all in one physical appliance. A service provider can provide firewall services for multiple customers, securing and separating their traffic while managing the entire system on one device. Service providers do so by defining separate security domains for each customer with each domain controlled by a separate logical virtual firewall.

Typically, this capability is available only in higher-end firewalls such as the Cisco PIX 525 and 535 as well as the newer ASA line of devices (because of the memory requirements that each virtual firewall needs to operate properly as well as the necessary CPU capabilities).

Open and Closed Source Firewalls

You can find a wide variety of firewalls available on the market today. Some are open source, such as Linux's IPTables, OpenBSD's pf, and the Solaris IPF firewalls. Others are closed source, such as the Cisco PIX and ASA firewall operating systems, Juniper's ScreenOS, and Check Point's firewall software. Some even use an underlying open source operating system and firewall code with closed source modifications. The differences between these firewalls are most typically noticeable in the additional capabilities of the commercial firewalls.

Most commercial firewalls today provide for tight integration of VPN capabilities for remote users as well as deep packet inspection within the firewall itself. Open source firewalls tend to focus on the filtering capabilities in the firewall process rather than the integration of the firewall with other applications (and typically leave such capabilities as VPN and intrusion detection to other software systems). This focus can lead to integration issues between other applications and the firewall itself but does not represent an insurmountable obstacle.

New companies have emerged that have taken open source firewall code and have cleaned up the management and improved the firewall such that the product produced rivals many of the closed source commercial firewalls. The business model of these companies is to offer a trimmed-down version of the product for free and charge for the more complete version or charge for the support, which many business customers will want in addition to the actual firewall. A good example of this model is the Shorewall firewall.

Summary

Firewalls provide a wide variety of capabilities to administrators. From simple packet filtering to deep packet inspection, modern firewalls enable administrators to significantly improve the security of their network. Many of the previously "high-end" capabilities such as stateful packet inspection have been slowly making their way into the lower-end firewalls, such as the Linksys BEFSX41 and the PIX 501. Additionally, these higher-end capabilities have been making their way into the open source firewall codes, a fact that allows all administrators to secure their systems at very low cost.

## CHAPTER 3

TCP/IP for Firewalls

Much like humans may speak English, German, or Russian, computers may "speak" any number of languages: IPX/SPX, AppleTalk, and TCP/IP being just a few of them. Because of the portability and scalability of TCP/IP, TCP/IP has been settled on as the de facto standard method for providing communication services between hosts on a network and in particular across the Internet. Much like a human language, TCP/IP has a defined structure and set of rules that control how hosts communicate. Therefore, those who learn the structure and rules of TCP/IP, learn and become proficient in the language so to speak, will be able to truly understand how systems are communicating with each other.

This proficiency in TCP/IP is a critical skill for the firewall administrator because firewalls exist largely to protect systems from being accessed using TCP/IP. By understanding the intricacies of TCP/IP, a firewall administrator is much better equipped to effectively protect and defend systems from malicious access that uses TCP/IP as the communications protocol. Indeed, many security exploits and vulnerabilities that exist are based on taking advantage of misconfigurations and poor implementation of the TCP/IP protocols, applications, and services themselves.

Protocols, Services, and Applications

As mentioned, TCP/IP provides a mechanism to allow systems to communicate with each other across a network. If we refer back to our language analogy, most spoken languages have certain rules that define how the communications occurs. By adhering to these rules, one is then able to understand and comprehend what is being communicated. TCP/IP follows a similar process to define how the communications will occur through the use of protocols, services, and applications.

You cannot just start throwing words together in any order that you feel like and expect people to understand what you are saying. You have to follow certain rules that are understood by all parties involved for them to understand what you are saying. Network communications is no different. Although spoken languages have rules such as sentence structure and noun and verb usage to define how the communications occurs, network communication has protocols. The easiest way to think of a protocol is that it is merely a set of rules that defines how something occurs. So, much like how using a verb denotes an expression of existence, action, or occurrence, a network protocol defines how the method of communication will occur, such as how TCP defines a mechanism for connection-oriented communications. Protocols may be an open protocol (such as TCP, UDP, or IP), which means that the protocol is not "owned" by anyone in particular and can be used by anyone that wants to use the protocol or they can be closed protocols (such as Cisco Discovery Protocol [CDP]), which means that the protocol can only be used by licensed or authorized entities. In general, open protocols are used to facilitate most vendor-neutral communications processes; closed protocols are used by vendors to provide vendor-specific communications processes.

Whereas protocols define how something occurs, services typically define what is being done. The objective of a service is to produce some function or data of value and substance. This function or data can then be used by the systems to facilitate communications. In many cases, the function or data provided by a service is used by protocols, such as how services like addressing services such as Domain Name System (DNS) might be used by IP to facilitate communication between hosts.

Applications are nothing more than processes running on a host that take advantage of the network services and protocols to provide data to the end user. Applications are frequently known as end-user services because they exist to service end-user requests.

The concept of protocols, services, and applications can be a difficult one to grasp. After all, how do they interact with each other? Which is responsible for what? Network communications is a complex concept to master for many reasons, not the least of which is that the concept is so large. I refer to this as the elephant problem.

If you try to sit down and cook and eat an elephant all at once, you quickly realize that it is an insurmountable task. After all, there is a lot of elephant to chow down on. To be successful, one must take that elephant and break it down into smaller, easier-to-digest steak-sized pieces. In doing so, what was once an insurmountable task just became something easy to accomplish by virtue of the fact that you have taken a big thing and turned it into smaller, easier-to-manage pieces. To do this same thing with understanding network communications, it is important to break the total task of communications between hosts into smaller, easier-to-understand and define layers. The benefits of a layered approach to network communications are as follows:

- The complex process of network communications can be segmented into easier-to-understand components.

- It provides a standard interface to allow for multivendor integration. Each layer merely needs to have a standard interface to the layer above and below, without concern for the details of what is done at other layers.

- In conjunction with a standard interface, a layered approach allows the details of how something is done at a particular layer to be defined and changed without impacting the overall communications process at other layers.

There are two predominant models for network communications, the Open Systems Interconnection (OSI) model and the Department of Defense (DoD) model.

The OSI Model

The OSI model is a layered model that has been standardized for defining network communications. The OSI model breaks the complex process of network communications into seven distinct layers, each with it own distinct responsibilities. As shown in Figure 3-1, the seven layers of the OSI model are as follows:

- **The application layer (Layer 7)**—Primarily responsible for interfacing with the end user

- **The presentation layer (Layer 6)**—Primarily responsible for translating the data from something the user understands into something the network understands and vice versa

- **The session layer (Layer 5)**—Primarily responsible for dialog and session control functions between systems

- **The transport layer (Layer 4)**—Primarily responsible for the formatting and handling of the transport of data between systems

- **The network layer (Layer 3)**—Primarily responsible for logical addressing

- **The data link layer (Layer 2)**—Primarily responsible for physical addressing

- **The physical layer (Layer 1)**—Primarily responsible for the physical transport of the data on the network

Figure 3-1 *Layers of the OSI Model*

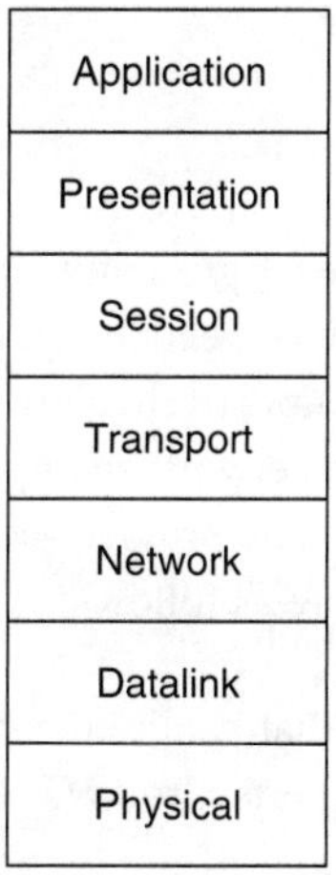

Application
Presentation
Session
Transport
Network
Datalink
Physical

Rather than focusing on detailing explicitly how communications occur, either in total or in each layer, the OSI model merely defines what needs to occur, and what each host attempting to communicate should be able to expect in the communications process. After this concept of what needs to occur has been defined, protocols, applications, or services can then be designed and implemented to handle the details of how the process occurs.

The Application Layer

The application layer provides the user access to network resources via network-aware applications. The application layer handles identifying and establishing that network resources are available and displays the data that is presented from the network in a format that is understandable to the end user.

Not all applications are defined at the application layer, only network-aware applications. For example, Microsoft Word is not a network-aware application and therefore is not really defined at the application layer. Web browsers, on the other hand, are network aware and therefore are defined at the application layer. Some common application layer protocols, services, and applications are as follows:

- **Messaging gateways**—Post Office Protocol (POP3), Simple Mail Transfer Protocol (SMTP), and x.400 e-mail gateways are used to deliver messaging data between systems.

- **Newsgroup, instant messaging and Internet Relay Chat (IRC) protocol applications**—Applications such as Forte Agent or Microsoft Messenger are used to communicate between systems using protocols such as Network News Transport Protocol (NNTP).

- **WWW applications**—Applications such as Firefox, Microsoft Internet Explorer, Apache Web Server, and Internet Information Services provide web-based access to and from resources.

The Presentation Layer

The presentation layer is responsible for presenting data to/from the application and session layers in a format that is understood by the respective layer. Therefore, the presentation layer is frequently referred to as the "translator" of the network. The presentation layer also handles encryption (not to be confused with network encryption such as IPsec or application encryption such as Pretty Good Privacy [PGP]) and protocol-conversion functionality. Some common protocols at the presentation layer are as follows:

- **Graphics formats**—Formats that handle the display and presentation of graphical data such as Joint Photographic Experts Group (JPEG), Graphics Interface Format (GIF), and Bitmap (BMP)

- **Sound and movie formats**—Formats such as Windows Media File (WMF), Digital Video Express (DiVX), and Moving Pictures Experts Group Layer-3 Audio (MP3) provide a means to translate and present sound and audio files across the network.

- **Network redirectors**—Handles protocol conversion for data from the application to the corresponding network format through the use of protocols such as Server Message Block (SMB) and Netware Core Protocol (NCP).

The Session Layer

The session layer is responsible for the establishment, maintenance, and teardown of communications channels that allow systems to differentiate network data that is received. The reason for this is that a network host may be communicating with multiple remote systems using multiple applications. Sessions allow the host to identify the data that belongs to a specific application or host, ensuring that data is not inadvertently delivered to the wrong application or remote host. Some examples of session layer protocols are as follows:

- **Remote procedure calls**—A client/server redirection mechanism for requesting data from and executing procedures on a remote system (the server) from a requesting system (the client).

- **NetBIOS**—An application programming interface (API) typically used on Microsoft systems to provide for remote network access to resources and data.

- **Structured Query Language (SQL)**—SQL provides the mechanisms and methods for connecting to, querying and retrieving remote data, typically from a database.

The Transport Layer

The transport layer is primarily responsible for the formatting and handling of the transport of data in a transparent manner. The transport layer provides an application independent method of delivering data across the network while doing so in such a manner as to ensure that the data can be properly put back together on the receiving end. This process is known as *segmentation and reassembly*, and in fact the data that is received from the higher layers are known as segments. Some examples of transport layer protocols are TCP and UDP, both of which are defined in greater detail later in this chapter.

The Network Layer

The network layer is responsible for the logical addressing and routing of data, known as packets at this point, across the network. This allows two hosts to communicate with each other regardless of physical location or direct connectivity by using logical addresses that have a global significance. Two common protocols that reside at the network layer are these:

- **Internet Protocol (IP)**—IP uses a hierarchal addressing scheme to identify hosts regardless of physical location. Because IP is hierarchal in nature, using subnets to define hosts that are local to each other, it scales to be able to provide a global addressing scheme and has become the de facto method of logical addressing across the Internet as well as within most organizations.

- **Internetwork Packet Exchange (IPX)**—IPX is used primarily on legacy Novell networks. IPX provides for logical addressing through the use of network and host addresses.

The Data Link Layer

The data link layer is responsible for the physical addressing of data, known as frames, across the network. Whereas logical addresses have a global significance and can be used to identify hosts regardless of physical proximity, physical addresses are used to differentiate between hosts that are able to receive the same electrical signal on the wire.

In addition to physical addressing, the data link layer also ensures the error free delivery of data through the use of a cyclic redundancy check (CRC) to ensure that the data that is received is the same data that was transmitted. Some common protocols that exist at the data link layer are as follows:

- **Institute of Electrical and Electronics Engineers (IEEE)802.2**—This protocol defines the interface between the network layer and the underlying network architecture. IEEE 802.2 is sometimes referred to as the logical link control (LLC) sublayer of the data link layer.

- **IEEE 802.3**—This protocol defines how the frames are transmitted and received on the physical media and defines the physical addressing that will be used to identify hosts. IEEE 802.3 is sometimes referred to as the MAC sublayer of the data link layers because it controls how the data will be transmitted on the media.

The Physical Layer

The physical layer is primarily responsible for the physical transmission of the data, generating the electric signals or pulses of light that contain the bits of data to be transmitted. The physical layer handles things such as the modulation of the data and how the hosts will access the media itself. Some examples of physical layer protocols are as follows:

- **10BASE-T**—10BASE-T is a form of Ethernet communications across twisted pair cables at 10 Mbps.

- **100BASE-TX**—100BASE-TX is similar to 10BASE-T but defines the communications of Ethernet at 100 Mbps, typically using Category 5 or greater twisted-pair cabling.

The Encapsulation Process

Although it is important to understand what processes and functions occur at each layer, the OSI model has no real value without understanding the process of encapsulation. Encapsulation is the process of taking the data received from a higher layer, adding the appropriate data and information for the current layer, and then passing the modified data down to the next layer. This process is repeated as the data passes down the OSI model and is eventually transmitted across the network. For the receiving host to be able to process the data it receives properly, it reverses this process, removing the data specific to each layer and passing the remaining data up to the next layer.

Figure 3-2 illustrates the encapsulation process of the OSI model. As the data from the application on the source host is defined it begins the process of being transmitted across the network. At the application, presentation and session layer, the data is manipulated and formatted in a manner that will be transmitted across the network. At the transport layer, the upper-layer data is encapsulated with the appropriate transport header information, (for example, the TCP header), creating a protocol data unit (PDU) known as a segment. The segment is then passed down to the network layer, where it is encapsulated with the network layer header information, such as the IP header, creating a PDU known as a packet. The packet is passed down to the data link layer, where data link header and footer information (the frame check sequence [FCS]) encapsulates the packet to create a PDU known as a frame. The frame is then passed down to the physical layer, where it is turned into the 1s and 0s that will be electronically transmitted across the network media.

Figure 3-2 *Encapsulation Process and OSI*

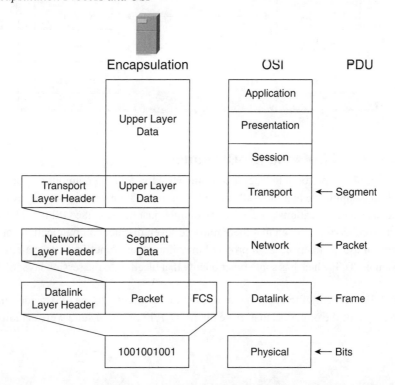

The encapsulation process allows each layer on one host to logically communicate directly with the corresponding layer on the other host, while at the same time providing the means for each host to know what to do next with the data (passing it up or down the communications stack to the next layer as appropriate). So, for all intents and purposes, the transport layer of the transmitting host is directly communicating with the transport layer of the receiving host, because the decapsulation process has removed all the lower-layer data by the time the transport layer sees it. From the perspective of the transport layer on the destination host, it merely has a segment of data that needs to be processed accordingly. Figure 3-3 depicts this process.

Figure 3-3 *Logical Communication Between Layers*

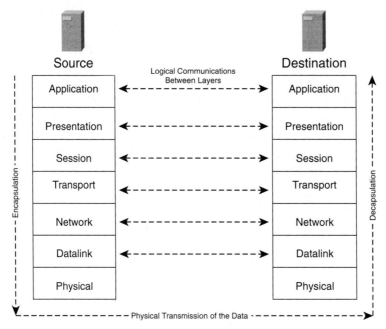

The Department of Defense (DoD) Model

Although OSI is a protocol independent framework for defining communications, and thus is portable and applicable to almost all network communications, it does not always map directly to a particular communications process. For example, just because the OSI model defines seven distinct layers does not mean that there must be seven distinct communications processes or protocols in use. In many cases, a protocol may implement functions that span multiple layers (for example, TCP which has some functionality that bleeds into the session layer of the OSI model).

The TCP/IP protocol suite in particular does not map directly to the OSI model, in no small part because most of the protocols that make up the TCP/IP protocol suite were actually based upon a four-layer model known as the DoD model. Figure 3-4 shows a comparison of the different layers in both the DoD and OSI models.

Figure 3-4   *Comparison of the DoD and OSI Models*

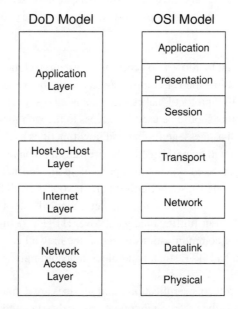

The four layers of the DoD Model are as follows:

■ **Application layer (Layer 4)**—The application layer is where higher-layer protocols, services, and applications such as HTTP, DNS, SMTP, and FTP function and reside. The application layer roughly overlays the application, presentation, and session layers of the OSI model.

■ **Host-to-host or transport layer (Layer 3)**—The host-to-host layer is where protocols such as TCP and UDP reside. It handles flow control, connection and session establishment, maintenance, and teardown. The host-to-host layer roughly overlays the transport layer of the OSI model.

■ **The Internet layer (Layer 2)**—The Internet layer is where protocols such as IP reside and handles the logical addressing and routing of data across the network. The Internet layer roughly overlays the network layer of the OSI model.

■ **The network access layer (Layer 1)**—The network access layer handles the physical addressing and delivery of data across the network and is where protocols such as 802.2, 802.3, and Ethernet reside. The network access layer roughly overlays the datalink and physical layer of the OSI model.

How Firewalls Use Protocols, Applications, and Services

Now that you understand what protocols, applications, and services are, how do firewalls use them? Because the primary objective of a firewall is to protect a host or network from access, and protocols, applications, and services define how hosts are accessed from the network, firewalls can use the information from protocols, applications, and services to make filtering decisions and grant or deny access.

For example, if you want to allow web access to a system, technically what you are doing is defining that you will allow the HTTP protocol to access the web server application running on the system. The HTTP protocol makes recommendations for things such as the default communications port that should be used for access to the web server application (TCP port 80) and defines things such as message format and how functions such as retrieving web pages as opposed to binary data will be performed. The firewall can then be configured to allow only TCP port 80 to access the protected system, thus preventing any traffic that does not use TCP port 80 from accessing the protected system. Furthermore, if your firewall has enough intelligence, it can use the information from the protocol itself to determine whether the access attempt should be permitted. For example, transmitting binary data over HTTP is defined by certain protocols; if you do not want this kind of communications to occur, the firewall can be configured to look for and identify binary data in an HTTP stream and block it accordingly.

Simply put, because protocols, applications, and services are defined, firewalls can use any of the information contained in the protocols, applications, and services to make filtering decisions about whether to permit or deny the corresponding network traffic.

Internet Protocol (IP)

In many ways, IP *is* the network. IP is a connectionless protocol that provides for the delivery of data to logically addressed hosts anywhere on the network. It is important to understand that IP is an unreliable delivery mechanism by design, leaving the responsibility of reliable delivery to higher- or lower-layer protocols such as TCP or IEEE 802.2 and 802.3. As far as IP is concerned, the data that is transmitted may be delivered, lost, sent out of order, duplicated, delayed, or otherwise mangled; it could not care less what the ultimate result is.

When we say that IP is connectionless, we mean that each packet that is transmitted is done so independent of every other packet. Consequently, packets that are transmitted may take different paths through the network and be lost or delayed, whereas other packets are successfully transmitted.

Although this concept of best-effort delivery may sound terribly unreliable, keep in mind that other protocols are designed that handle reliability, thus precluding the need for IP to handle such things. In addition, data is generally delivered successfully and true unreliability of data delivery is typically the result of an underlying network or communications failure of which IP would not be able to fix anyway (remember, each layer operates independent of each other, and a failure at the physical layer can only be fixed at the physical layer, not the network layer).

> **NOTE**   IP is defined by the following RFCs:
>
> ■ RFC 0791
>
> ■ RFC 2474
>
> ■ RFC 3168
>
> ■ RFC 3260

IP Packet Structure

An IP packet (sometimes referred to as a datagram) has a distinct and defined structure. In simple form, an IP packet is the IP packet data (which is nothing more than the segment that was passed down from the session layer) and the IP packet header, as shown in Figure 3-5.

Figure 3-5   *Simple IP Packet Structure*

IP Packet
(28 to 65535 bytes in length)

IP Packet Header (20 or more bytes in length)	IP Packet Data (variable length ranging from 1 to 65515 bytes in most cases)

The IP packet header is typically 20 bytes in length (unless IP options are used, in which case the length may be variable up to a maximum length of 60 bytes) and contains the information that allows systems to determine how to process the corresponding IP packet data. The IP packet data is a variable length, ranging from 1 to 65515 bytes in length in most cases. Obviously, if the header is larger than 20 bytes, the IP packet data maximum size will be reduced in size accordingly. This provides for a minimum IP packet size of 21 bytes (20-byte header, 1-byte data) and a maximum IP packet size of 65535 bytes (20-byte header, 65515-byte data).

The IP Packet Header

The IP packet header is what tells an IP-based host what to do with the packet that was received. Think of it as an instruction manual that contains the "how to process this packet" information. Therefore, an attacker wanting to generate malicious traffic will frequently modify the IP packet header in such a way as to instruct the receiving host to do something harmful with the packet, or to instruct the host to do something it is not capable of doing in hopes that it causes the host to generate an error condition that may allow the attacker to gain access to the system. Because of this, it is not good enough to understand that there is an IP header. As a firewall administrator, we need to understand what the contents of the IP header are and what the values represent so that we can identify and block potentially malicious traffic.

The IP packet header consists of 32-bit blocks of data known as words. These words are further broken down into numerous fields of various length and function. As mentioned previously, the typical IP packet header length is 20 bytes, which means that a typical IP packet header consists of 5 words. If any IP options have been configured, the packet header will contain the options values, and then the necessary padding to ensure that the header ends on a 32-bit boundary.

Figure 3-6 depicts the structure of an IP packet header.

Figure 3-6   *IP Packet Header Structure*

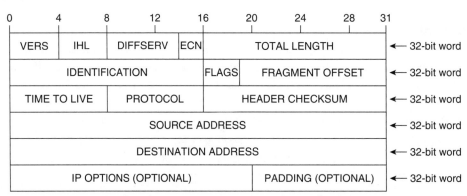

The fields of the IP packet header and their meanings are as follows:

- **Version (VERS, 4 bits)**—This represents the format of the packet header. In most cases, the value is 4, which represents IP version 4; or 6, which represents IPv6. If the value is 0, the packet should be destroyed; and in most cases, any value other than 4 or 6 is going to be considered invalid.

- **Internet Header Length (IHL, 4 bits)**—This field represents the length of the header in 32-bit words, typically with a value of 5. If IP options are included in the header, the value will be between 6 and 15. Any values less than 5 are invalid.

- **Differentiated Services field (DS field, 6 bits)**—This field was originally known as the Type of Service field, but RFC 2474 replaced this functionality with what is known as the DS field. The DS field is used to provide scalable service discrimination and guarantee quality of service (QoS) for the datagram transmission. The DS code point (DSCP) is the value that is encoded in the DS field to define the QoS and per-hop behavior (PHB) for a given datagram.

  In general, the DS field should have a DSCP value of all 0s unless QoS or a PHB class has been implemented for the data and in fact the default DSCP value and PHB class for Internet communications is 000000.

NOTE   For more information about PHB codes and usage, refer to RFC 2597, RFC 3260, RFC 3246, RFC 3140, RFC 3247, and RFC 3248.

- **Explicit Congestion Notification (ECN, 2 bits)**—This field is used to provide a congestion indication for incipient congestion through the use of ECN code points. If both bits are set to a value of 1, it indicates that congestion has been experienced.

- **Total Length (16 bits)**—This field is the full length of the datagram, including the IP packet header and the data itself. Because the Total Length field consists of 16 bits, it is impossible to have a packet size greater than 65535 bits, because the maximum value that can be provided by a 16-bit field is 2^16, or 65536.

- **Identification (16 bits)**—This field contains a value assigned by the sender and is used by the receiver to aid in assembling the fragments of a datagram.

- **Flags (3 bits)**—This field is used to specify whether the datagram can be fragmented. Bit 0 is reserved and must be 0. If bit 1 is a 0, the datagram may be fragmented. If the value is 1, the datagram may not be fragmented. If bit 2 is a 0, this packet represents the last fragment of the datagram. If bit 2 is a 1, there are more fragments of the datagram.

- **Fragment Offset (13 bits)**—This field indicates where in the datagram the packet belongs. The fragment offset is measured in units of 8 octets, and the first fragment has an offset of 0. The Fragment Offset field should only contain data if the packet is a fragment.

- **Time to Live (8 bits)**—The Time to Live field specifies how long the packet may remain on a network before the datagram must be destroyed. This provides a means for removing packets from the network that were unable to be delivered in the time specified. A time-to-live value of 0 indicates that the datagram must be destroyed.

- **Protocol (8 bits)**—The Protocol field indicates what protocol was used at the next layer to generate the data portion of the packet. For example, TCP has a protocol value of 6 (0x06 in hex) and UDP has a value of 17 (0x11 in hex). For a full list of protocols, refer to http://www.iana.org/assignments/protocol-numbers.

- **Header Checksum (16 bits)**—This field is a checksum on the header only to ensure that the header is complete and verified accurate at each point that processes the header (for example, at each router or by the destination host itself).

- **Source Address (32 bits)**—This is the source IP address of the transmitting system.

- **Destination Address (32 bits)**—This is the destination IP address of the receiving system.

- **Options (variable)**—The Options field contains optional pieces of information that can be used by hosts to assist in the processing of the packet. Because this field is not required, not all vendors successfully or properly know how to handle and process values in the Options field (even though they are supposed to), which makes manipulation of the Options field to contain "invalid" data a common attack method. In general, the Options field is not commonly used.

- **Padding (variable)**—This field is nothing more than bits with a value of 0 to pad the bits of the Options field to ensure that the header ends with a 32-bit boundary.

Figure 3-7 shows a screen shot of a packet sniffer to show the IP packet header contents in a decoded fashion.

Figure 3-7 *Sample IP Packet Header Contents*

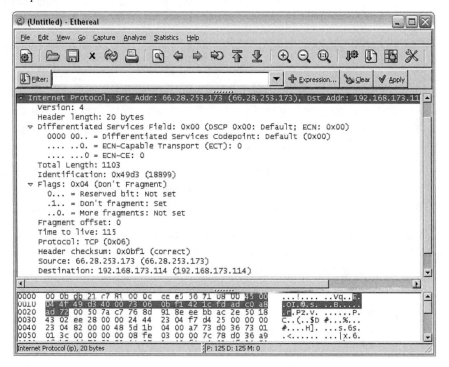

Bad IP Packets

In most cases, the IP packets that are received on a network can be successfully processed and acted upon accordingly. As is true with all network communications, however, it is possible for an IP packet to either be accidentally or intentionally designed in such a way as to be a bad packet. When we say "bad packet," we mean a packet that for whatever reason cannot be processed properly. In some cases, this may be the result of unreliable delivery of the data (for example, if a portion of the datagram is lost [remember, IP is an unreliable delivery mechanism, so a datagram could be fragmented and a fragment lost or something similar]).

In other cases, the packet may be intentionally crafted in such a way as to be an invalid or bad packet. This is normally done with the hope that when the destination receives the bad packet, it cannot properly deal with the packet, potentially leaving the host vulnerable to another attack.

Some examples of bad IP packets are packets that do not contain higher-layer contents such as TCP, UDP, or Internet Control Message Protocol (ICMP) contents. Another example is receiving packets that claim to be fragments, when no other packets correspond with the fragments to allow the destination to properly reassemble the datagram. In fact, sending IP fragments is a relatively common method of attacking a host with the objective typically being to cause the host to inadvertently process the fragment data, frequently an exploit of some sort. A common utility that leverages this is the tool "fragrouter," which can be used to circumvent firewalls and IDSs.

In general, the IP packet header should be interrogated to ensure that any fields that contain values contain accurate values. Any manipulation of this data could potentially cause a poorly designed host (see Windows systems for an example) to react in a negative fashion to the receipt of the data.

Transmission Control Protocol (TCP)

TCP is a connection-oriented transport mechanism that resides at Layer 4 of the OSI model. TCP implements the concept of sessions between hosts to serve as virtual circuits upon which higher-layer data and communications are delivered. In doing so, TCP addresses the inherent unreliability of lower-layer protocols such as IP, providing a means of ensuring that data is accurately and reliably transmitted between hosts.

The foundation of TCP is the creation of a session between hosts. This is performed through the use of a process known as the TCP three-way handshake. When a host decides it needs to transmit data to another host using TCP, it contacts that host with information regarding the initial sequence number that it will use for the session. This data is transmitted to the destination host in a segment known as a synchronize (SYN) segment. This is the first part of the handshake. The destination receives the SYN segment and responds with an acknowledge (ACK) segment to acknowledge the receipt of the SYN segment. In addition, it notifies the original source of its initial sequence number using it is own SYN segment. Although these are two distinct processes (the ACK and the SYN), they are typically combined into a single segment for efficiency of communication. Therefore, this segment is commonly referred to as a SYN/ACK segment and is the second part of the handshake. The originator then responds to the destination with its own ACK segment acknowledging the receipt of the SYN/ACK. This is the final step of the three-way handshake, and at this point the two hosts have established a virtual circuit between each other upon which all data will be transmitted. Figure 3-8 depicts the three-way handshake between hosts.

Figure 3-8 *Example of TCP Three-Way Handshake*

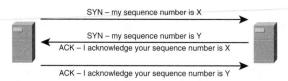

Reliability will be handled by each host periodically checking in with the other to confirm the successful receipt of data using a process known as sliding windows. If any data is lost, the hosts can retransmit the data upon discovery of the data loss, thereby ensuring the reliable and successful delivery and receipt of all transmitted data.

Because of the reliability of TCP, any application or protocol that requires data transmission to be verified typically implements TCP as a transport mechanism. This includes protocols such HTTP, FTP, SMTP, and most network file-sharing applications such as Microsoft Windows Server and Workstation services. As discussed when we examine the TCP segment header, TCP uses port numbers to identify the higher-layer application or protocol that the data came from and is destined to. These port numbers are assigned and maintained by Internet Assigned Numbers Authority (IANA), which provides a full list of registered port numbers at http://www.iana.org/assignments/port-numbers.

> **NOTE**   The following RFCs define TCP:
>
> - RFC 0793
> - RFC 3168

TCP Segment Structure

The TCP segment is structured similarly to an IP packet in that it contains two general components: a TCP header that contains processing information about the segment, and a data section that contains the data that was presented from/to higher-layer protocols and applications. The TCP header, much like the IP header, is typically 20 bytes in length. The data can be of variable length. Unlike IP, determining the maximum TCP segment length takes a bit of math. As a general rule, the maximum TCP segment length is calculated as being 40 bytes less than the maximum transmission unit (MTU) of the transmitting interface. This 40-byte subtraction represents both the TCP and IP header, so the remaining data would be the actual data contents of the segment. So, for example, using Ethernet with an MTU of 1500, the TCP maximum segment size would be 1460 (or 1460 bytes of data) with a 20-byte TCP header (1480 bytes total) and a 20-byte IP header (1500 bytes total).

TCP Segment Header

Like IP, the TCP segment header typically consists of five 32-bit words, with the potential for optional words containing additional options and the relevant padding to make 32 bits of data. Figure 3-9 depicts the TCP segment header.

Figure 3-9 *TCP Segment Header Structure*

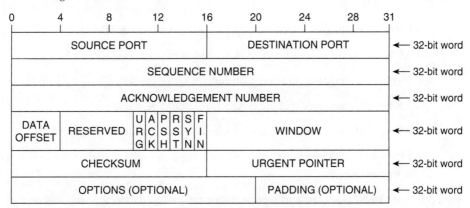

The fields of the TCP segment header and their meanings are as follows:

- **Source Port (16 bits)**—This field represents the source protocol or application. This allows the source to know which application the data belongs to so that responses can be delivered to the appropriate source application. In most cases, the source port is a random high-level port number (>1024) generated by the application.

- **Destination Port (16 bits)**—This field represents the destination protocol or application on the target host. This allows the destination to properly route the data to the appropriate higher-layer application or protocol. In most cases, the destination port is a defined (and in some cases well known) port number that is associated with the protocol or application in question.

- **Sequence Number (32 bits)**—This field contains the information necessary for the hosts to know what data has been transmitted. If the SYN control bit is enabled, this value is the initial sequence number (ISN) and the first data octet is the ISN+1.

- **Acknowledgement Number (32 bits)**—This field contains the value of the next sequence number the sender is expecting to receive. This field relies on the ACK control bit to be set and is always sent after a session has been established

- **Data Offset (4 bits)**—This field indicates where the actual data begins by specifying how many 32-bit words exist in the TCP header. It is also referred to as the Header Length (HLEN) field.

- **Reserved (4 bits)**—This field is reserved for future use and must have a value of 0.

- **Explicit Congestion Notification (ECN, 2 bits)**—This field is used, like in IP, for ECN information. The first bit is used to set the Congestion Window Reduced (CWR) flag; the second bit sets the ECN-echo (ECE) flag.

- **Control bits (6 bits from left to right)**—The control bits tell the hosts what they should be doing with the session. There are 6 bits that can be either on (1) or off (0) and from left to right they are as follows:

  - **URG**—This indicates that the Urgent Pointer field is significant.

  - **ACK**—This indicates that the Acknowledgment field is significant.

  - **PSH**—This indicates that the push function is requested.

  - **RST**—This indicates that the connection should be reset.

  - **SYN**—This indicates that the sequence numbers should be synchronized.

  - **FIN**—This indicates that there is no more data from the sender and the session can be terminated.

- **Window (16 bits)**—This field represents the number of data octets that will be transmitted before an ACK is expected.

- **Checksum (16 bits)**—This field verifies that the data received is the proper size as what was transmitted.

- **Urgent Pointer (16 bits)**—This field is only processed in segments where the URG control bit is set and communicates the value of the urgent pointer as a positive offset from the sequence number of the current segment.

- **Options (variable)**—The Options field contains any number of variable option values that must be understood by all TCP hosts, but in practice are rarely used.

- **Padding (variable)**—This field provides the necessary padding to the Options field to ensure that the data length is 32 bits.

Bad TCP

Because of how TCP functions, it is susceptible to a number of "bad" implementations and functions, starting with the manner in which sessions are established. When TCP hosts begin to initial a session, the destination host receives a SYN, responds with a SYN/ACK, and then waits for an ACK response. Malicious TCP traffic can take advantage of this process using what is known as a SYN flood. In a SYN flood, the host is inundated with session requests but no final ACK. Therefore, the host slowly fills its receive buffers with incomplete session requests waiting for the final ACK. When the buffers are full, the host can no longer accept new session requests and begins dropping the new session requests, effectively causing a denial of service.

Another example of bad TCP involves the use of non-random-sequence numbers. This allows a malicious host to determine what the expected sequence number is and insert itself into the conversations. Because the destination host uses the sequence number to put the data back together, it can be tricked into believing that the malicious data is the correct data.

If random-source and destination ports are implemented irresponsibly, they can also cause problems with TCP traffic, especially with firewalls. Most firewalls use TCP source and destination ports as part of the decision-making process for their rulesets. In particular, if an application uses random-destination ports, it can make it near impossible to protect the host behind a firewall because you cannot guess what port may be in use and therefore must potentially open multiple/all TCP ports to allow communications. With a stateful firewall, random-source ports are not as big a deal; in some circumstances, however (especially when implementing egress filters), they can make it all but impossible to allow hosts to securely respond to requests, such as when the communication is initiated on one port and then uses a different and/or random port. A good example of this is the X Display Management Control Protocol (XDMCP), which establishes the initial communications session on one port and then dynamically switches to a different port for the transmission of data.

User Datagram Protocol (UDP)

UDP is the polar opposite of TCP. Whereas TCP is connection oriented, reliable, and relatively complex, UDP is a connectionless, unreliable, and a relatively simple protocol. The initial response might be to ask, "Why use an unreliable protocol?" To understand this, you need to have the proper perspective of what we mean by unreliable.

Unreliable does not mean that it will not work or that the data will not get delivered. Indeed, when using unreliable protocols such as UDP, it is generally a safe bet that the data will be successfully delivered. Why? Because most networks today are designed to eliminate things such as latency and packet loss, thus ensuring that data gets delivered regardless of what protocol is used. Consequently, UDP was developed in large part to provide a simple, low-overhead method of delivering data across the network. Yes, UDP messages can be lost, duplicated, or sent out of order, but in most cases on most networks, they will not be.

The reason that UDP is low overhead is because two UDP hosts do not establish a session prior to transmitting data, and they do not periodically check to verify that the data was received as is done with TCP. This makes UDP an excellent choice for the transmission of small bursts of data or the transmission of data that handles reliability at the application layer. Some common applications that make use of this are things such as DNS, TFTP, and SNMP. Like TCP, UDP uses port numbers to identify the higher-layer application or protocol from which the data came and for which it is destined. These port numbers are assigned and maintained by IANA, which provides a full list of registered port numbers at http://www.iana.org/assignments/port-numbers.

> **NOTE** RFC 0768 defines UDP.

UDP Message Structure

Because of the simplicity of the design of UDP, the UDP segment structure is much simpler than the TCP segment structure. The UDP message contains two components: the UDP header and the UDP data. The UDP header is merely 8 bytes in length, again providing less overhead and thus more space for data than TCP (with its 20-byte header).

UDP Datagram Header

As shown in Figure 3-10, the UDP header is pretty simple and straightforward, containing the minimum required amount of information to allow for the delivery of data.

Figure 3-10 *UDP Header Structure*

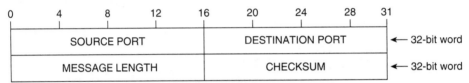

The UDP header contains two 32-bit words with the following fields and meanings:

- **Source Port (16 bits)**—This field represents the source protocol or application. This allows the source to know which application the data belongs to so that responses can be delivered to the appropriate source application. In most cases, the source port is a random high-level port number (>1024) generated by the application.

- **Destination Port (16 bits)**—This field represents the destination protocol or application on the target host. This allows the destination to properly route the data to the appropriate higher-layer application or protocol. In most cases, the destination port is a defined (and in some cases well known) port number that is associated with the protocol or application in question.

- **Length (16 bits)**—This field represents the length of the datagram in bytes, including the header and the data, and therefore has a minimum value of 8 (the length of the header).

- **Checksum (16 bits)**—This field is optional and if used represents a simple method to allow the destination to know that the full datagram was received. If not used, the value is 0.

Bad UDP

UDP is such a simple protocol that there is not a whole lot that can be done with the protocol itself to account for "bad" UDP traffic. UDP is particularly effective as a source of "bad" traffic because it is connectionless. Therefore, it is a great candidate for spoofing. Malicious users can generate traffic as a different host, and because UDP is connectionless and responses are not expected, they do not really care that the targeted host is sending the responses to the wrong host.

UDP is also a great candidate for flooding a network, in particular by flooding the network with malformed data or with UDP packets that contain no data whatsoever. One of the more effective methods of doing this is to flood the broadcast address of a network with UDP traffic, forcing all hosts to have to deal with and potentially respond to the traffic, thus creating an exponential amount of traffic from a single malicious datagram. These processes are referred to as denial-of-service (DoS) attacks.

Internet Control Message Protocol (ICMP)

TCP and UDP exist primarily to deliver upper-layer data across a network. Whether connection oriented or connectionless, fundamentally the process of delivering the data is the same: identify the source and destination application ports, format the data accordingly, and deliver the data to IP. This process works well when the network is functioning without error and when systems are operating correctly and know how to deliver data through routers and subnets to any destination, anywhere. The problem is that the network does not always work, routes fail, and data may not be able to be delivered (or it may need to be directed elsewhere to be successfully delivered). To facilitate this process, the ICMP protocol was developed.

In many ways, ICMP functions like the traffic cop and policeman of the network. Because IP (and UDP) lack any mechanism for identifying that failures may occur on the network, they need an external protocol that can provide information about routing failures and to report about delivery errors, congestion delays, and other conditions on the network. Indeed, like the traffic cop notifying motorists about congestion delays or blocked intersections (routers) on the street, ICMP provides a means to control the flow of traffic in an effort to ensure that the data can be reliably delivered.

An important distinction to understand about ICMP is that it is an error-reporting mechanism, not an error-correcting mechanism. That means that although ICMP can notify hosts of error conditions, ICMP natively has no means or method of actually doing anything about the error condition. Instead, ICMP relies on other protocols such as routing protocols or reliable protocols such as TCP to account for and address the particular error condition.

The most well-known use of ICMP is through the use of the ping application. Ping is a network troubleshooting application that makes use of ICMP echo request and echo reply (detailed in the next section) messages to determine whether a host is responding to network traffic. This allows the user to determine the reachability and status of the target host in a pretty simple manner. If a target host responds, it is reachable and available. If it does not, depending on the echo reply message, either the target host, target network, or network somewhere between the source and destination is unreachable and unavailable. We talk more about ping in Chapter 13, "Troubleshooting Firewalls," and Appendix A, "Firewall and Security Tools."

> **NOTE** RFC 0792 and RFC 0950 define ICMP.

ICMP Message Structure

ICMP controls the data being transmitted over the network through the use of numerous message types. Each ICMP message type contains specific formatting related to its function, but most implement a header and data field of varying lengths. All ICMP messages begin with the same 32 bits of data. First, 8 bits of data known as the TYPE field define the ICMP type. Next, 8 bits of data known as the CODE field provide additional information specific to the message type. Then, 16 bits of data known as the CHECKSUM ensure that the data that is delivered is the same amount of data that was transmitted.

Some of the more common message types are as follows:

- **Echo reply (Type 0)**—In concert with echo request (type 8), echo reply makes up one half of the messages that are used by the ping utility for testing destination reachability and status. As the name implies, this message is the reply to an echo request message.

- **Destination unreachable (Type 3)**—Destination unreachable messages are sent by intermediate routers to inform a host that it cannot forward or deliver the data. There are 13 codes associated with destination unreachable messages, each representing a specific failure condition. Common codes include the following:

    — **Network unreachable (Code 0)**—This typically indicates a failure of a router.

    — **Host unreachable (Code 1)**—This typically indicates that the destination network was reachable, but the host was unable to be contacted, and thus indicates a failure with the destination host itself.

    — **Protocol unreachable (Code 2)**—This typically indicates that the network protocol (for example, TCP or UDP) cannot be reached.

    — **Port unreachable (Code 3)**—Similar to protocol unreachable, this typically indicates that the given port (for example, the TCP or UDP port of the application in question) cannot be reached.

- **Source quench (Type 4)**—Source quench messages are used to rate limit traffic during periods of congestion. Routers typically reserve an amount of memory to store data in temporarily before it is delivered. If for some reason the router cannot efficiently deliver the data, it could run out of memory to store new data. Rather than drop the data packets (at which point if using a connection-oriented protocol such as TCP the data will need to be retransmitted), it will attempt to issue a source quench message. This message tells the source router to slow down the rate at which it is delivering the data in hope that whatever condition is causing the router to buffer data is fixed, at which point the normal flow of data can be reinstated and no data is lost or needs to be retransmitted.

- **Redirect (Type 5)**—Redirect messages are used to notify hosts to update their routing table to reflect a change in the routing environment. These are typically issued by routers that recognize that a host is using a nonoptimum routing configuration. A common instance of this is when a host's default gateway is on the same network as another gateway that it must use (such as a firewall). In that case, the router issues a redirect to inform the host to send the data to the other gateway directly, because that would be more efficient than going through the default gateway than the other gateway.

- **Echo request (Type 8)**—Echo request messages make up the other half of the messages used by the ping utility. As the name implies, an echo request message requests that the target host respond with an echo reply message.

- **Time exceeded (Type 11)**—Time exceeded messages are used to indicate that a circular or excessively long route has been detected and are a means of notifying the source host that the data was unable to be routed to the given destination.

NOTE For a list of all ICMP message types, refer to http://www.iana.org/assignments/icmp-parameters.

Bad ICMP

ICMP is one of the most abused protocols out there by the nature of what it exists to do. After all, if you want to attack a network or host, what better method to do so than to use the protocol that is designed to control network traffic in general? Consequently, a common example of "bad" ICMP is to allow any ICMP traffic from untrusted sources onto your trusted networks.

For example, if you allow ICMP redirects, you leave your Internet hosts susceptible to having their traffic inadvertently routed to the wrong location. This could result in a DoS in the best case (because the traffic never makes it to the hosts that are requesting data) or could result in a data compromise (in the event that the data can be redirected to a host that the attacker controls).

To address this, it is generally a good idea to block ICMP traffic, in particular between trusted and untrusted networks. The downside of this, of course, is that by blocking ICMP you also lose any of the benefits of ICMP, such as the ability to use ping to test the reachability of remote hosts. To mitigate this most firewalls allow you to define certain types of ICMP messages to permit or deny, thus allowing you to allow some ICMP traffic (such as time exceeded, destination unreachable, and echo replies) while blocking other ICMP traffic (such as redirects).

ICMP messages themselves are also susceptible to manipulation (as occurs frequently with the insertion of bogus or extremely large amounts of data in an ICMP message in hopes that the target host cannot properly process the message, which may leave it in a vulnerable state). Perhaps the most well known of this kind of manipulation is known as the "ping of death," which transmitted a message that exceeded the 65,535-byte limit of the IP protocol, which would cause many target hosts to crash, resulting in a DoS.

Addressing in IP Networks

Without an address, you can put a stamp on an envelope, put it in the mail, and it is not going to go anywhere. IP traffic on the network is no different. Without an address, it is impossible for hosts on a network to determine where the data should be delivered. To deal with this, two forms of addressing are used on IP networks:

- Physical/hardware addresses

- Logical/IP addresses

Physical Addresses

Physical addresses are used to identify the specific host that data is being transmitted to. The important thing about physical addresses is that they have a local significance only. What this means is that the physical address can only be used to communicate between hosts that share a common subnet or network segment. This is a legacy that goes back to the early days of networking where all hosts on a network received the electric signal that contained the data (such as how Ethernet functions). To ensure that only the host that the data belongs to processes the data, physical addresses were used to distinguish between hosts.

The most common form of physical address, and the physical address that is used for TCP/IP communications, is the MAC address. The MAC address is a vendor-assigned value that is supposed to be globally unique and that identifies the actual network card. MAC addresses are 6 bytes in length and typically consist of a 3-byte vendor identifier (known as the organizationally unique identifier or OUI) followed by a 3-byte unique identifier that is assigned by the vendor.

The use of physical addresses allows for network communications between two hosts on the same subnet regardless of logical address and is a key element to how routing works. For example, when two hosts on different networks want to communicate with each other, they use their logical addresses to identify each other from a global perspective. When they transmit the data to each other, each host physically addresses the frames to the hardware address of their corresponding router interface. This allows the routers to receive and process the frames directly, while still being able to use the logical addresses to determine the original source and final destination of the data. Figure 3-11 illustrates how this process works.

Figure 3-11 *Physical Addressing of Data Between Hosts*

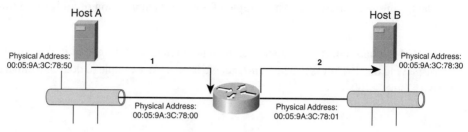

The process in Figure 3-11 is as follows:

1.   Host A logically addresses the data for Host B but physically addresses it to 00:05:9A:3C:78:00, the router interface physical address.

2.   The router receives the data, because it is physically addressed to it, but realizes that logically it must be delivered to Host B. Therefore, it rebuilds the frame, using the physical address of the interface on the same network as Host B (00:05:9A:3C:78:01) and physically addresses it to 00:05:9A:3C:78:30.

Logical Addresses

Logical addresses are the counterpart to physical addresses and allow for the identification of hosts and the delivery of data to hosts regardless of physical location or proximity to each other. Consequently, logical addresses must have a true global significance, and must be unique within all interconnected network segments. TCP/IP uses IP addresses as the logical addressing method. The following sections look at IP addresses in more detail.

IP Addressing

An IP address is a 32-bit universal identifier that provides a means of uniquely identifying from a global perspective. What we mean by global perspective is that the address is unique on all interconnected networks, such as all internal networks in an organization, or in a truly global sense on all networks across the Internet.

The 32-bit IP address is separated into four 8-bit octets, allowing each octet to have a value ranging from 0 to 255. Furthermore, the IP address is logically separated into two distinct components: the network ID and the host ID. The network ID is used to identify the subnet upon which the host resides. The host ID is used to identify the host itself within the given subnet.

IP addresses can be displayed in three typical formats:

■ **Binary notation**—Binary notation is the format that systems on the network use to process the address. An example of binary notation is 11000000.10101000.00000001.01100100.

- **Hexadecimal notation**—Hexadecimal notation is the format typically used when identifying IPv6 addresses. An example of hexadecimal notation of an IPv4 address is C0.A8.01.64

- **Dotted-decimal notation**—Dotted-decimal notation is the format that is typically used for displaying the IP address in a human-readable format. An example of dotted-decimal notation is 192.168.1.100.

IP Address Classes

Not all networks are the same size. Some are smaller than others; some are larger than others. To provide a hierarchy and structure to the assignment of IP addresses, they were broken down into distinct classes, with each class natively supporting a different number of networks and hosts.

For the public IP address space, which is managed by the IANA, three classes of addresses were defined:

- **Class A addresses**—Class A addresses provide for 128 (2^7) total networks, with each network containing 16,777,216 (2^{24}) hosts. This is achieved by designating the first octet as the network ID and the remaining 3 octets as the host ID. Class A addresses can be identified by the first bit of the first octet, which must be a 0, providing for a range of first octet values from 1 to 126 because the values of 0 and 127 are unusable (because 0 is all 0s and 127 is reserved for use as a loopback address).

- **Class B addresses**—Class B addresses provide for a greater number of network IDs at the cost of the total number of hosts per network. For the Class B address space, the first 2 octets are designated as network ID, and the last 2 octets are designated as the host ID. Class B addresses can be identified by the fact that the first 2 bits of the first octet must be a 10. This allows for the total number of network IDs to be 16,384 (or 2^{14} because the first 2 bits are defined) and the total number of hosts per network to be 65,536 (2^{16}). This provides a first octet range of values from 128 to 191.

- **Class C addresses**—Class C addresses provide for an extremely large number of networks, with a small number of hosts per network. For the Class C address space, the first 3 octets are designated as network ID, and the last octet is designated as host ID. Class C addresses can be identified by the fact that the first 3 bits of the first octet must be 110, which provides for a first octet range of values from 192 to 223. This provides for 2,097,152 total networks (2^{21}) with each network containing 256 host IDs (2^8).

In addition to the public address space, there are two additional address spaces, one for use in multicasting and the other for future use and testing:

- **Class D addresses**—Class D addresses are identified by the first 4 bits of the first octet having a value of 1110, which allows for a range of values in the first octet of 224 to 239. Unlike the public address space, which is designed to allow an IP address to be assigned to and represent the host on the network, the Class D addresses are used to assign multicast addresses (addresses that may be assigned to multiple hosts allowing them to receive the same data without the data needing to be transmitted uniquely to each host). In addition, Class D addresses have no network or host portion of the address, leaving the remaining 28 bits of the address to be the multicast address.

- **Class E addresses**—Class E addresses are identified by the first 4 bits of the first octet having a value of 1111, which allows a range of values in the first octet of 240 to 255. This address space should not be used in any circumstance. The address of 255.255.255.255 is used to indicate an "all subnets" broadcast.

Figure 3-12 shows the different address classes.

Figure 3-12 *Address Classes*

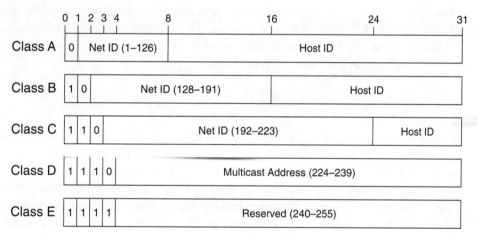

Classless Interdomain Routing (CIDR)

Although the classful address space is a great idea, the truth is that not everyone needs networks with the number of hosts that each class of address provides. For example, if you have more than 255 hosts that you need to connect to a network, using the classful address space you have to bump up to a full Class B, providing for 65,534 hosts on the network. Obviously, that is far more hosts than is necessary. To address this deficiency, CIDR was implemented.

One of the benefits of classful addresses is that they provide a hierarchy to the network through the use of the network ID. This translates into an efficient routing environment because it is easy for a router to determine what networks can be grouped together and treated as a single routing entry. CIDR adheres to this philosophy while allowing for administrators to create additional networks regardless of address class by using a strict interpretation of the subnet mask as the means of identifying a network. The subnet mask is used to determine the network prefix, which defines where the network ID portion of a given IP address ends. For example, a default Class B address (let's say 172.16.0.0) uses a network prefix of /16, or 16 bits. However, using CIDR, the administrator can elect to assign 20 bits of the IP address to the network, resulting in a network prefix of /20. This allows an administrator that has been assigned a single Class B address space to effectively turn that single network (172.16.0.0) into 16 individual networks (the result of 2^4, or the 4 additional bits that were borrowed from the host ID portion of the address and given to the network portion of the address). Similarly, because 4 bits have been taken from the host ID of the address, this leaves a total 12 bits for host ID assignment. This results in each of the 16 networks that were created having the potential for a maximum of 4096 hosts per network (2^{12}).

> **NOTE**   As you have read through this chapter, you may have noticed the use of (2^x) when referring to the number of hosts per network. This is the technically accurate representation of hosts per network. However, most networks reserve a host ID to identify the subnet itself (a host ID that consists of all 0s) as well as the broadcast ID for the subnet (a host ID that consists of all 1s). Consequently, the number of usable hosts per subnet is typically represented as (2^x)– 2 to account for the loss of those two host IDs.

Subnets

Throughout this section, I have mentioned subnets repeatedly, but what is a subnet and why are they important to firewalls? A subnet is nothing more than a group of IP addresses that are on the same network ID. By extension, a subnet is the collection of hosts that are on the same network segment. Subnets allow us to dissect the network into small, easier-to-manage chunks. The reason for this is simple: The fewer the number of hosts on a given subnet, the less extraneous the traffic and the smoother the flow of traffic will go because there are not as many hosts in contention with each other.

For communications to occur between subnets, a router needs to be involved. Routers keep track of the list of the subnets in existence through the use of a routing table. This allows a router to receive traffic and determine how to forward the traffic so that it can eventually be delivered to the destination network (and thus the destination host).

Subnets are important to firewalls because in many cases a firewall performs a similar function as a router. In fact, in most firewall implementations the firewall is implemented in such a manner as to explicitly reside between two subnets and thus restrict and control the traffic passing between subnets.

IPv6

Although the IPv4 address space provides for what would seem to be a virtually unlimited number of IP addresses, the reality is that with the growth of the Internet the number of IP addresses that are available for assignment has continued to decline. This served as the catalyst to motivate the designers of the Internet and IP to develop a new addressing system to address the lack of available IP addresses as well as a number of other issues that are covered here. They came up with IPv6.

Whereas IPv4 is based on a 32-bit address space, IPv6 is based on a 128-bit address space. This increased the total number of addresses from 4,294,967,296 (232) addresses to 340,282,366,920,938,463,463,374,607,431,768,211,456 (2^{128}) addresses. This will allow for an address space that is so large that it will not be depleted for the foreseeable future.

IPv6 also addressed a number of other deficiencies with IPv4, particularly around the areas of performance, security, control, and reliability. Whereas IPv4 needs to rely on numerous other protocols to handle many of these tasks, IPv6 includes new options and extensions that allow for performance, control, and reliability information and configuration to be handled natively by IPv6. This makes for a much more efficient communications system. Finally, IPv6 allows for a flexible header format, allowing for the implementer of the protocol to determine which optional header components they will or will not implement.

IPv6 is completely incompatible with IPv4, and with the widespread implementation of Network Address Translation (NAT) this has caused adoption of IPv6 to be dramatically slowed.

Network Address Translation (NAT)

NAT was developed to address a couple of concerns. First, the number of public IP addresses available on the Internet was becoming depleted. Second, because of the interconnectivity of networks, it was possible for an administrator to assign a set of IP addresses to a network that someone else might be using. This is a common situation when two companies and their respective networks are combined. NAT addresses these two concerns by providing a mechanism by which any number of IP addresses can be translated to a different range of IP addresses, or in some cases a single or smaller range of IP addresses.

To address the limitation of available IP addresses NAT can be used to translate hundreds or even thousands of IP addresses to just a couple of IP addresses or even a single IP address, thereby allowing a company to provide Internet access to their hosts without needing to allocate thousands of IP addresses on the Internet to do so. To address the issue of invalid networks, or in many cases duplicate networks, NAT can be used to allow each network to appear as a completely different network. Figure 3-13 illustrates the process of NAT and Internet connectivity.

Figure 3-13 *Example of NAT and Internet Access*

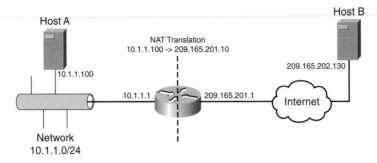

In this example, when Host A attempts to access the Internet, the firewall translates the request from having a source address of 10.1.1.100 to having a source address of 209.165.201.10 and transmits the data across the Internet. The firewall then stores this translation in its translation table so that it knows how to deal with the return traffic. When host B receives the data, it thinks it is communicating with 209.165.201.10 and addresses the return traffic accordingly. When the firewall receives the return traffic, it refers back to its translation table and determines that the traffic should be delivered to 10.1.1.100. The firewall repackages the packet, this time changing the destination IP address to be 10.1.1.100 and transmits it accordingly. In doing so, hosts A and B can communicate with each other, for all intents and purposes completely unaware that NAT is occurring.

Because NAT effectively hides the actual IP addresses that are in use, many networks have elected to use it in conjunction with private IP addresses. Private IP addresses are defined in RFC 1918 and are a predefined set of IP addresses that cannot be used on the Internet and therefore are referred to as being nonroutable. Because NAT prevents Internet-connected hosts from being able to ascertain what IP address is being used behind a NAT router, organizations have elected to implement the private IP addresses so that they can pretty much do whatever they want with them without concern with how they may interact with the Internet or other networks. The RFC 1918 IP addresses are as follows:

- 10.0.0.0/8

- 176.16.0.0/12

- 192.168.0.0/16

NOTE   RFC 3022 and RFC 2663 define NAT.

NAT Implementations

There are four primary NAT implementations. They all accomplish the same function, the translating of traffic from one IP address to another, but they go about the translation process in different manners. They are as follows:

■ **Static NAT**—Static NAT is sometimes referred to as traditional NAT, and refers to the mapping of one IP address to another IP address. Consequently, static NAT implementations require the same number of IP addresses as need to be translated. For this reason, static NAT is not an effective method of saving the number of IP addresses required for access to a network or the Internet.

■ **Dynamic NAT**—Dynamic NAT functions in a similar fashion to static NAT, but instead of each IP address having a one-to-one translation, a dynamic pool of IP address can be used for the translation. Doing so enables you to reduce the number of IP addresses in use because the pool of addresses can be smaller than the total number of IP addresses that must be translated.

■ **Port Address Translation**—Whereas static and dynamic NAT perform a translation from IP address to another, Port Address Translation (PAT) allows for the translation of a number of IP addresses to a single IP address. This is done by translating requests by TCP or UDP port. The translating router or firewall builds a NAT table, but instead of assigning an IP address for the outbound communications, it assigns a port number. When the response comes back to that port number, the translating router or firewall reverses the process.

■ **Bidirectional NAT**—In most cases, NAT is used to translate data in a single direction, typically from an internal or protected network to an external or unprotected network. Bidirectional NAT provides for the use of NAT regardless of the direction of the traffic flow.

NAT and IPsec: The Issues and the Solutions

Although NAT works in most cases, not all traffic can be successfully translated (in particular, when the original data cannot be manipulated, such as the case with IPsec). The reason for this is that the NAT process actually changes the data packet while it is being translated. Because of the nature of IPsec, when the data packet is rebuilt using NAT, the receiving router detects that the data has been changed (the source IP address is no longer the correct source IP address) and discards the packet. To address this, a process known as NAT traversal (NAT-T) has been developed.

NAT-T encapsulates the complete IPsec packet into either a TCP or UDP packet, which is then translated accordingly. By doing this, the traffic can be translated as required without the original IPsec data being changed. Figure 3-14 illustrates the encapsulation process and subsequent NAT.

Figure 3-14 *NAT-T Encapsulation*

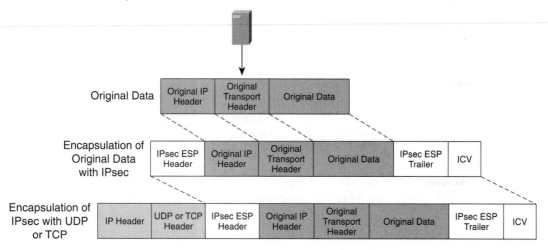

> **NOTE** RFC 3947 and RFC 3948 define NAT-T.

Broadcast and Multicast

Most of this discussion of IP traffic has revolved around the process of unicast traffic, which is traffic that is addressed for a single host. However, IP traffic can also be broadcast or multicast traffic, providing for some flexibility in how traffic is delivered.

Broadcast traffic is traffic that is destined to all hosts on a given subnet or to all hosts on all subnets. Broadcasts take advantage of the fact that the electrical signal is actually received by all hosts unless otherwise prevented. If a host needs to send the same data to multiple hosts, instead of needing to repeat the data in a unicast fashion to all destinations, it can just broadcast the data one time, allowing all the hosts to receive the data. For this reason, broadcast traffic is often referred to as "one-to-all" traffic. The drawback of broadcasts is that hosts that do not necessarily need to process the data will still receive the data because it is broadcast to every host on a network.

Multicasts attempt to bridge the gap between a unicast and a broadcast by functioning much like a broadcast, but limiting the destination hosts to only those which specifically register to receive the multicast. This allows a host to send the data a single time, but only the hosts that have specifically registered to receive that particular traffic will process it. Consequently, this is known as "one-to-many" or "one-to-some" traffic. Multicast traffic is typically used for applications that stream data, such as audio or video. It is also frequently used by routers to locate and pass routing protocol information between each other.

IP Services

When we talk about IP services, we refer to the applications, protocols, and services that not only use IP themselves, but also provide data to be used by other IP protocols. These IP services typically allow for IP communications between hosts by performing functions such as physical address resolution, automatic address assignment, name resolution, and time synchronization.

Address Resolution Protocol (ARP) is an IP service that was developed to map physical addresses to logical addresses. This resolution is required because hosts need to be able to physically address the data frames at Layer 2 to the appropriate destination. In most cases, the hosts only know each other by IP address. Consequently, ARP functions by broadcasting on the local subnet for the host that has the IP address that needs to be resolved. Because it is a broadcast, all hosts will process the packet, but only the host that actually has that IP address will respond with its MAC address, thereby allowing the original source to properly address the packet both logically by IP address and physically by MAC address.

DHCP exists to provide unconfigured hosts on a network with the appropriate IP addressing information necessary to enable them to communicate on the network. Because a host that is a DHCP client does not have an IP address to use, DHCP uses broadcasts between the DHCP client and the DHCP server. When a DHCP client is turned on, it issues a broadcast known as a DHCP Discover packet. The objective of this broadcast is to discover whether there is a DHCP server on the network. If there is, the DHCP server responds with a broadcast known as a DHCP Offer packet, because the client still has no IP address. Because the packet is a broadcast, the client still processes it even though the client has no configured IP address. If the network has multiple DHCP servers, they all respond with a DHCP Offer, and the client accepts the first offer it receives. The client then broadcasts a packet known as a DHCP Request packet. This serves two purposes. First, it notifies the selected DHCP server that the client has elected to accept the DHCP Offer. Second, it notifies all other DHCP servers that the client selected another DHCP server, allowing them to place that offered IP address back in the pool of IP addresses they can offer to clients. Finally, the DHCP server responds with a final broadcast known a DHCP Acknowledgement packet, which notifies the client that it can use the IP address that it was offered and provides additional configuration information such as subnet mask, default gateway, name servers, and so on. At this point, the client configures itself accordingly and can begin engaging in full TCP/IP communications.

DNS provides for the resolution of host names and fully qualified domain names to IP addresses. The reason for this is simple. Most humans do not know the IP address of the remote hosts that they are trying to communicate with. They know the name, such as www.cisco.com. Unfortunately, the network hosts require the IP address of the remote host to communicate with that host. When an IP host receives a request to communicate with a remote host by name, the host automatically and transparently contacts a DNS server to resolve the name to an IP address, which if successful allows the two hosts to communicate with each other. A detailed discussion of DNS is beyond the scope of this book, but an excellent resource for understanding DNS is *DNS and BIND, Fourth Edition*, by Paul Albitz and Cricket Liu.

Network Time Protocol (NTP) is used to synchronize the time across hosts over the network. Time synchronization is critical for applications such as Windows authentication, Kerberos, IPsec, as well as event logging. NTP functions over UDP port 123 and allows clients to synchronize their time with a master time server, known as a stratum 1 or stratum 2 server.

IP Routing

I have alluded to routing repeatedly in this chapter but have not really explained the routing process in detail and why it is important to us. Routing is nothing more than taking the data from a host and transmitting it across the network to a host on a different subnet. To do this, routers (and firewalls) need to be able to determine what network the data needs to be delivered to. We have already established how an IP address can be configured with different network IDs, which is what routers use to determine what specific subnets exist.

Routers collect this information regarding the subnets that exist and store it in what is known as a routing table. The routing table consists of the following information:

- Network IDs (and thus subnets) that the router is aware of.

- IP address of the gateway or router that can be used to deliver data to the corresponding subnet. This is the actual route to the subnet, and the router may have multiple routes to a given subnet.

Routers can build and maintain this routing table information in one of two methods. The first is for the data to be manually updated and maintained by an administrator. The second is to use routing protocols to actively interrogate the network and determine all subnets, routers, and the routes that exist so that the protocol can use that information to successfully transmit data to the appropriate subnet.

As you would expect, in large networks the process of manually updating and maintaining this routing information is practically impossible. Therefore, in large or complex networks it is recommended to implement routing protocols to automatically take care of all the processes related to the building of the routing table, the maintenance of the routing table, the verification of the routing table, and the determination of which route is the best route to take.

Types of Routing

Fundamentally, there are three types of routing:

- Static routing

- Default routing

- Dynamic routing

Static routing is the process of an administrator manually entering, maintaining, updating, and removing the routes that a router is configured with. Static routing is a time-consuming process and in most cases should not be used. Notable exceptions to this are in small networks or in the network perimeter, as discussed in Chapter 9, "Where Firewalls Fit in a Network."

Default routing, also known as the route of last resort, provides a mechanism to configure a client or router with what is known as its default gateway. Default routing essentially says, "If you cannot figure out how to route this packet to the appropriate network, send it to the default gateway." Default routing is typically implemented on host systems because they generally do not need to know about every subnet on the network. In addition, default routing is commonly used on routers within an organization to point to the router that provides Internet connectivity. This ensures that all data destined for a network that is not defined on the internal network is directed to the Internet, without the organization needing to have routes to the entire Internet on all of their internal routers.

Dynamic routing functions almost exactly like static routing does, but the information is automatically provided through the use of routing protocols. These routing protocols replace all the manual requirements of static routing, which makes dynamic routing the routing method of choice for large or complex network environments. We will look at dynamic routing in more detail in a later section of this chapter.

How the IP Routing Process Works

For all the apparent complexity involved in routing, the routing process itself is a pretty simple and straightforward process. In fact, when you understand the routing process fundamentals, it does not matter how large or small the network is; the process is the exact same. To illustrate the routing process, look at Figure 3-15.

Figure 3-15 *Routing Process*

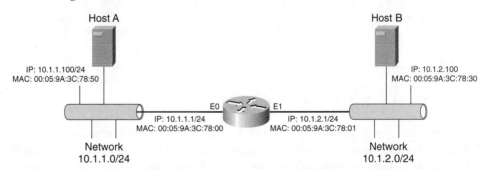

This example shows two hosts, Host A and Host B, on two separate networks. Host A has an IP address of 10.1.1.100 and a MAC address of 00:05:9A:3C:78:50. Host B has an IP address of 10.1.2.100 and a MAC address of 00:05:9A:3C:78:30. When Host A determines that it needs to communicate with Host B it will perform the appropriate name resolution to determine what the

IP address of Host B is. When it receives the IP address of 10.1.2.100, Host A determines that Host B is on a remote network (through a process known as AND'ing) and thus that the data must be routed to Host B.

To do this, Host A builds an IP header with a source IP address of 10.1.1.100 (its own IP address) and a destination IP address of 10.1.2.100 (the IP address of Host B). This allows for each host to be logically identified by any device that receives the packet. When Host A builds the frame at Layer 2, however, it does something different with the source and destination MAC addresses. Physically, Host A cannot communicate directly with Host B. Instead, Host A has to physically communicate with something that can successfully route the data to Host B. In this case, that is the default gateway for Host A, which happens to be the E0 interface of the router. Host A uses the IP address for its default gateway (10.1.1.1) to ARP and resolve the MAC address for the E0 interface (00:05:9A:3C:78:00). After this has been determined, Host A builds the frame with a source MAC address of 00:05:9A:3C:78:50 and a destination MAC address of 00:05:9A:3C:78:00. At this point, the data is put on the network, where it is received by the router.

The router processes the frame, where it discovers that the frame is addressed to it. This causes the router to begin processing the IP header. When it does that, the router discovers that the packet is actually addressed to 10.1.2.100. In most cases, this causes the packet to be dropped, but routers first attempt to determine whether they have a route for the destination network or a default router. In this case, because the router is also connected to network 10.1.2.0/24, it determines that it can directly route the packet to the logical destination (Host B).

The router then rebuilds the frame, but it changes the source and destination MAC address. For the source MAC address, the router uses the MAC address of the interface that is connected to network 10.1.2.0/24 (in this case, 00:05:9A:3C:78:01). Because the router can directly communicate with Host B, it uses the MAC address 00:05:9A:3C:78:30 as the destination MAC address and sends the data across the network to be received by Host B.

When Host B processes the frame, it discovers that the frame is addressed to it. This causes Host B to begin processing the IP header, where it discovers not only that the packet is addressed to it but also the IP address of the source address (in this case, 10.1.1.100, the IP address of Host A). Therefore, Host B knows exactly what IP address it should address any responses to, repeating the routing process to ensure that the data eventually arrives at Host A.

Routing works the exact same way in larger networks, the only difference is the number of hops that a packet may traverse before ultimately arriving at its logical destination. Because the IP address of the packet is never changed, the logical destinations are always able to communicate with each other. The physical address of the frame changes every time a router rebuilds the frame, replacing whatever the source and destination MAC address with its own MAC address for the source and the MAC address of the next router or the final destination as the destination.

Different Classes of Routing Protocols

Although each routing protocol has its own specific functionality, they can all be generally classified as falling into three categories:

- **Distance vector**—Distance vector routing protocols are relatively simplistic in design and tend to use a "distance" to determine the best path. The distance is measured by counting how many times a packet goes through a router, known as a hop, until it arrives at the destination network. The smaller the hop count, the shorter and better the route. Distance vector routing protocols receive routing information from neighbors that they believe to be correct but do not verify. If a neighbor router claims that it can deliver data to a network, it is accepted as being accurate and correct. Because the source router has not independently verified the accuracy of this information, distance vector protocol routing is frequently referred to as "routing by rumor."

- **Link state**—Link-state routing protocols are more complex than distance vector protocols and can take into account information such as the network topology, bandwidth between routers, and congestion. Whereas distance vector protocols know only what they are told, link-state routing protocols typically build routing tables consisting of information about the entire topology, allowing each router to know how every other router is interconnected, thus allowing that information to be used for routing decisions. Because of this additional information, link-state routing protocols are known as being more intelligent than distance vector protocols, but they typically require more CPU and memory resources than distance vector protocols.

- **Hybrid**—Hybrid routing protocols use functionality from both distance vector and link-state routing protocols, attempting to leverage the best aspects of each while eliminating the drawbacks. Hybrid routing protocols are typically proprietary protocols such as the Cisco Enhanced Interior Gateway Routing Protocol (EIGRP).

Common Routing Protocols

There are a number of common routing protocols that most environments use.

Routing Information Protocol

RIP is a distance vector routing protocols that uses the hop count exclusively to make routing decisions. RIP supports a maximum hop count of 15 hops, making any destination that requires more than 15 hops to be unreachable. Therefore, RIP is suited for small and relatively simple network environments.

RIP has two different versions: 1 and 2. RIPv1 is a classful routing protocol, which means that it can only route between networks that are using the default subnet information. Because most networks today implement some form of CIDR, RIPv1 1 is typically no longer used. RIPv2 supports classless routing information, multicasts rather than broadcasts for communications, and provides the ability to ensure that routing data is only exchanged between hosts that can be authenticated. Because of the classless functionality and increased security of RIPv2, if you need to use RIP you should only use RIPv2.

> **NOTE**   RFC 1058 defines RIPv1. RFC 2453 defines RIPv2.

Open Shortest Path First

Open Shortest Path First (OSPF) is a link-state routing protocol that uses the Dijkstra algorithm to determine the shortest path through the network. OSPF is a much more robust and scalable protocol than RIP, taking into account factors such as adjacency, neighbor information, link information, and bandwidth in making routing decisions. Because each router running OSPF has a table that contains the entire topology of the OSPF network, each router can determine the true best route through the network, taking into account things such as network speeds. For example, OSPF can determine that traversing three gigabit hops to access a network is faster than traversing two 1.544-Mbps hops.

Like RIP, OSPF also includes additional authentication mechanisms to ensure that only permitted routers and hosts can exchange routing information. Because of the increased functionality and scalability of OSPF, many networks have elected to use OSPF as the routing protocol.

> **NOTE**   OSPFv2 is defined in RFC 2328. OSPFv1 is defined in RFC 1131, but it never made it to an operational status and therefore was never really used.

Border Gateway Protocol

OSPF and RIP are both routing protocols that were designed to primarily route data among systems that share a common administrative authority, typically referred to as an autonomous system. Autonomous systems tend to be smaller in size and easier to manage. For example, even a global company may only have 200 subnets that need to be routed. For that reason, OSPF and RIP are typically referred to as interior gateway protocols, because they are really designed for routing of data within a given environment, or autonomous system.

Border Gateway Protocol version 4 (BGPv4) provides for the routing of data between autonomous systems and does so on a scale of magnitude that interior gateway protocols cannot touch. For that reason, BGPv4 is referred to as an exterior gateway routing protocol. Because of this, BGPv4 is the standard method of routing data across the Internet. After all, the Internet is really just a collection of independently managed and maintained subnets and autonomous systems. Although OSPF and RIP can be used internally, most companies that need to connect to the Internet and share routing information with other routers on the Internet do so through the implementation of BGPv4.

> **NOTE**   The following RFCs define BGP:
>
> - RFC 1267
>
> - RFC 4271

Applications Using IP

No discussion of TCP/IP would be complete without a look at the applications that use IP. Unlike services, which frequently perform functions that are then used by IP, the applications that use IP are relatively independent of IP and typically interface with the users and are rarely used by other IP processes.

Common Applications Using IP

The most common applications that use IP tend to revolve around access to Internet-based resources such as web servers and mail servers. In addition, file and print services are the most common application that is implemented in most corporate networks.

- Web browsers and web servers allow users to access graphical content using HTTP, which uses TCP port 80. In addition, if secure web browsing is required, the data can be secured using Secure Sockets Layer (SSL), commonly known as HTTPS, which uses TCP port 443.

- Electronic mail is delivered via two primary mechanisms: SMTP and POP3. SMTP uses TCP port 25 and serves to primarily transmit e-mail messages to the mail server (or between mail servers) because it has a limited ability to queue e-mail messages on the client side. This is where POP3 (which uses TCP port 110) comes in. It does a much better job of queuing e-mail messages and therefore is typically used by the client to receive e-mail messages from the mail server.

- File and printer sharing typically, but not always, occurs over TCP ports to provide for a reliable and connection-oriented delivery mechanism. A notable exception to this is Network File System (NFS), which is typically used by UNIX-based hosts and typically uses UDP port 2049. Microsoft file and print services typically use TCP port 139 or TCP port 445.

Less-Common Applications Using IP

Some less-common, but still frequently used, applications that are based on IP include the following:

- **Telnet**—Telnet is used to provide remote console connections over TCP port 23. Telnet is an insecure protocol, which means that the data being transmitted is not encrypted, rather it is done so in cleartext.

■ **FTP**—FTP is used to transmit and receive files between hosts. Although this may seem similar to file sharing, the key difference is that file sharing tends to be an interactive session within the operating system itself (unlike FTP, which tends to operate as a distinct client application). FTP operates in two primary modes: active FTP and passive (PASV) FTP. Active FTP commonly uses two TCP ports for communication. TCP port 21 is used for connection establishment and control information, and TCP port 20 is used for the transmission of data. Passive FTP uses TCP port 21 for connection establishment and control information, and the client and server negotiate a random high port or a preconfigured port for the transmission of data. Like Telnet, FTP transmits all data in cleartext.

■ **TFTP**—Although it is common to think of TFTP and FTP as practically the same because of the names, nothing could be further from the truth. TFTP is a completely self-contained protocol in no way associated with FTP. Whereas FTP can navigate directory structures and authenticate access, TFTP is unauthenticated and requires exact paths to transmit or receive data. In addition, TFTP uses UDP port 69 for connection establishment, and then performs the file transfer using two random UDP high ports. Because of the unreliable nature of TFTP, as well as the lack of authentication or robust file system navigation capabilities, TFTP tends to be used for small or specialized forms of file transfer such as transferring router and firewall configurations and operating systems.

■ **Syslog**—Chapter 12, "What Is My Firewall Telling Me?," covers syslog in much greater detail; however, as a brief introduction, syslog is used by network devices to transmit event log information from a host to a server where the event is typically stored and reported upon. Because these messages can be extremely large in volume, syslog is typically configured to use UDP port 514 for the transport mechanism. This reduces the overhead involved in maintaining a syslog session, freeing up that memory and processor usage for other applications, programs, and services. The downside of this, of course, is that if UDP is used, there is no guarantee that the syslog data was successfully transmitted and received. To address this, some firewalls and syslog servers can be configured to use TCP port 514 (Cisco defaults to using port 1470), thereby using the native reliability characteristics of TCP to ensure that the syslog data is successfully delivered. Syslog is also an insecure protocol, requiring no authentication and delivering the data in cleartext.

Protocols Used to Implement Security

In addition to general protocols that are used on IP networks, a few specialized protocols were developed with security and/or secure methods of communication in mind. Some of the more commonly known protocols that are used for security on an IP network are as follows:

■ **Secure Shell (SSH)**—SSH is similar to Telnet, but it provides for remote console connectivity that uses encryption and authentication to ensure that the data that is transmitted is secured and tamper proof and that all connections are authenticated. Therefore, SSH should be used instead of Telnet in all circumstances that allow it. SSH uses TCP port 22 for transport communications.

■ **Internet Protocol Security (IPsec)**—Technically a framework of a number of protocols, IPsec provides security functionality for IP-based communications. This includes encryption, authentication, and nonrepudiation functionality. Unlike most encryption mechanisms that we have discussed at the application or presentation layer (such as SSH or HTTPS), IPsec functions at the network layer. It does this by essentially taking a complete data packet and encapsulating it with the corresponding IPsec-specific header information and then transmitting the data over IP. This procedure allows IPsec to be used to secure virtually any data transmitted over an IP network, regardless of the actual application source. Consequently, IPsec can be used to secure insecure protocols such as SNMP, NTP, or syslog by encapsulating that insecure data within a secure IPsec frame.

Summary

Simply put, TCP/IP is the network. Because most networks today run TCP/IP and most firewalls operate using TCP/IP, it is critical for the firewall administrator to understand how TCP/IP functions. The reason for this is simple: Most firewall filtering rulesets and access control lists are written and designed to filter traffic based on information obtained from the TCP, UDP, ICMP, or IP header information. Without an understanding of how these protocols function and the applications, processes, and services that enable these functions, it is almost impossible to effectively protect network resources with a firewall. This is especially true with regard to NAT (which is implemented in almost every major firewall produced today).

Part II: How Firewalls Work

## CHAPTER 4

Personal Firewalls: Windows Firewall and Trend Micro's PC-cillin

Firewall technology has moved both upward into the large enterprise and service-provider space as well as all the way down to the desktop level. Desktop firewalls, also known as personal firewalls, are designed to protect a single system. These firewalls have been around for a long time in the Linux and BSD space but only relatively recently have they made a significant entrance into the Windows desktop. Many computer vendors now bundle a personal firewall with a trial license on every system they sell. In addition, Microsoft now offers a personal firewall, Windows Firewall, enabled by default with every version of Windows XP with Service Pack 2 (SP2). (Prior to Windows XP SP2 it was known as Windows Internet Connection Firewall [ICF].)

This chapter provides an overview of two personal firewall packages for the Windows platform: Windows Firewall and Trend Micro's PC-cillin. The focus of this chapter is not a detailed discussion of these products from the perspective of how secure they are as a firewall product but rather on a general level how you can use them, as examples of the many personal firewall solutions, to improve the security of an endpoint system.

Windows Firewall and Windows XP

The ICF, now dubbed Windows Firewall, is a simple stateful firewall that is part of the Windows XP operating system. In essence, Windows firewall provides the same core functionality that other personal firewall products on the market provide, such as stateful connection management and configurability for specific traffic that is desired.

Windows Firewall does come bundled with every new version of Microsoft's operating systems. The firewall capabilities can also be utilized in Windows Server 2003 Standard and Enterprise editions.

Essentially, Windows Firewall is the next version of Microsoft Windows ICF. It provides basic filtering capabilities on all Windows XP and 2003 Server platforms so that an administrator or end user can limit the traffic reaching the system (it does not filter traffic coming from the system). It's limited in that it is not a stateful firewall but rather a simple access list type of filter. Also, it only looks at the network and transport layers of the ISO protocol stack (Layers 3 and 4). This firewall is mostly useful for end users who do not require complex firewall capabilities to protect their systems and are looking for a simple packet filter to block typical Windows services such as NetBIOS, Remote Procedure Call (RPC), and others.

How Windows Firewall Works

By default, Windows Firewall comes with an assigned security profile. This profile provides what are termed as "exceptions" for Print and File Sharing as well as Remote Assistance and Universal Plug-and-Play (UPnP) with the local subnet. The local subnet is defined as the local network that the system is connected to. If the system is connected to multiple networks (for example, if the system has multiple interfaces), these network ranges are considered part of the local subnet. These services allow the ports listed in Table 4-1 to connect to the system.

Table 4-1   *Default Windows Firewall Profile Exceptions*

Service	TCP Ports	UDP Ports	Program
File and Printer Sharing	139,445	137,138	—
Remote Assistance	—	—	C:\Windows\system32\sessmgr.exe
Remote Desktop	3389	—	—
UPnP Framework	2869	1900	—

Note that by default only the Remote Assistance exception is enabled. Although the other exceptions are created in the profile, they are not enabled. Figure 4-1 shows the default configuration for the Windows Firewall.

Figure 4-1   *Windows Firewall Default Configuration*

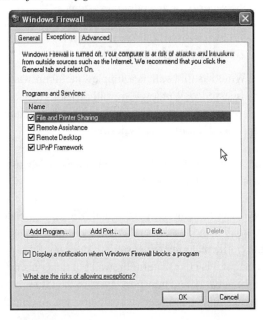

After Microsoft released XP SP2, Windows Firewall was turned on by default. Third-party firewall vendors enable users to turn off Windows Firewall during the installation of their software.

Configuring Windows Firewall

Configuring Windows Firewall is fairly straightforward. To open Windows Firewall, go to **Start** and choose **Control Panel**. This will open the Control Panel window as shown in Figure 4-2.

Figure 4-2   *Windows XP Control Panel*

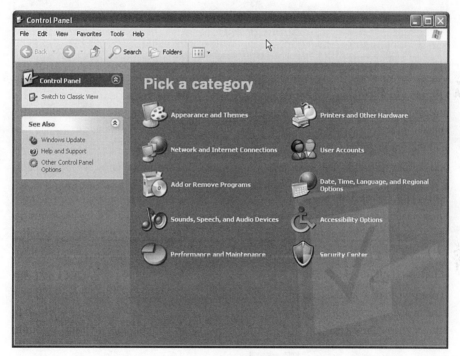

Choose **Security Center** at the lower-right corner of the window to open the Windows Security Center window. Choose **Windows Firewall** at the lower-left corner, as shown in Figure 4-3.

This opens the Windows Firewall window. The settings on the General tab determine whether the firewall is on or off. As mentioned earlier, Windows Firewall is on by default since the release of Windows XP SP2. You have three options with the Windows Firewall: on, on without exceptions, and off (as shown in Figure 4-4).

Figure 4-3 *Windows Security Center*

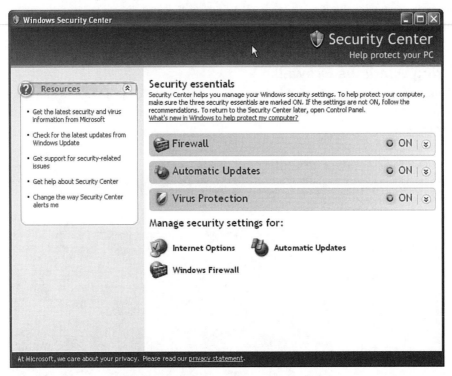

Figure 4-4 *General Tab of the Windows Firewall*

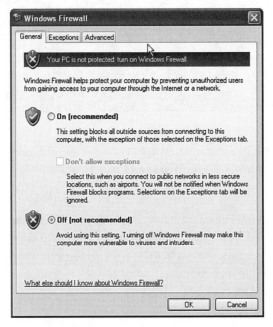

When the firewall is turned on, the user is offered the possibility of running the firewall with exceptions as specified in the Exceptions tab or with no exceptions at all. Microsoft recommends that when accessing a network such as a public wireless network (say at Starbucks or a T-Mobile hotspot in an airport) that the firewall should be set to on without exceptions. This setting blocks other users on the public wireless network from accessing system shares or other resources on the firewall-protected system.

When the system is on a safer network (such as a home office or a local office LAN), you can set the firewall to on with exceptions to allow for file sharing and remote assistance. These default exceptions are activated in the Windows Firewall policy on the Exceptions tab, as shown in Figure 4-5. The need to provide these exceptions is to allow the end system to participate in a Windows network environment and for folder and file shares to be made available to other systems on the local network. Remember that exceptions should be turned on only in known, secure networks. Such a network may be a home network or a corporate LAN and cannot be precisely defined in all cases. When in doubt, consult the network administrator regarding the security of the local network or simply do not allow exceptions.

Figure 4-5 *Default Exceptions for Windows Firewall*

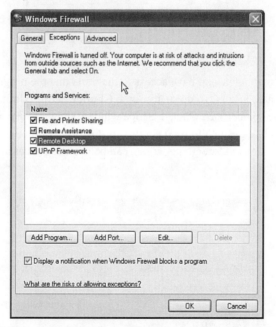

Adding an exception to the default Microsoft policy is relatively simple. Exceptions can be added either as specific network ports or as programs that are to be provided access to the network. To add a program to the exception list, click the **Add Program** button in the lower left of the Exceptions tab. Doing so opens a new window with a list of programs that are to be added to the exceptions list, as shown in Figure 4-6. Choose the specific program to be added.

There is a difference between specifying a program in the exceptions list and statically opening a TCP or UDP port. The difference comes from the fact that specifying a specific application in the exceptions list means that the port that the application listens on will be allowed through the firewall only if the defined application opens the port. The disadvantage to specifying the application in the exceptions is that if the port is used by another application, the firewall will not permit traffic through to the application because it is not the program defined in the exception list.

Figure 4-6   *Program Exception List*

To specify which computers can have access to the ports that the program listens on, change the scope of the permitted access. To do so, click the **Change Scope** button at the lower-left corner of the window. Doing so opens the Change Scope window shown in Figure 4-7. Here you can add a custom list of IP addresses to allow exceptions for the program in the firewall. Alternatively, the entire local subnet, or even foreign networks, can be provided access.

Figure 4-7   *Changing Scope*

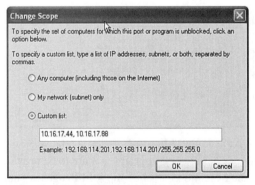

To add a port to the exceptions list, click the **Add Port** button on the Exceptions tab. Doing so opens the Add a Port window. As shown in Figure 4-8, here the user can enter the name of the service as well as a comma-separated list of ports that the service requires to be open in the firewall in order to be accessible to other systems. The **UDP** or **TCP** button on the window must be selected to define the specific transport protocol, too.

Figure 4-8 *Add a Port Window*

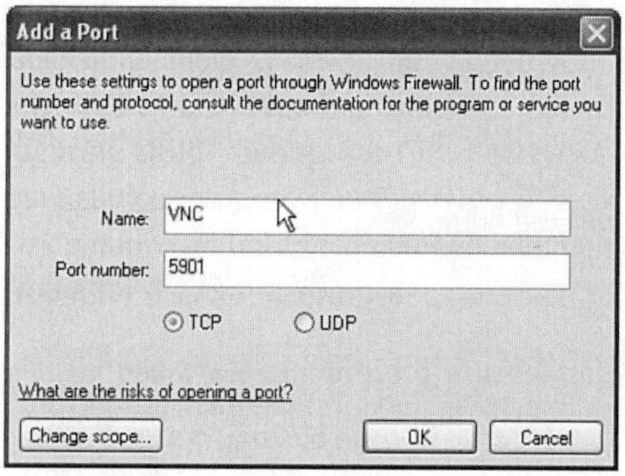

For home use, the typical ports that may need to be accessible by the local network include TCP/135, UDP/137, TCP/139 (traditional NetBIOS ports), and TCP/445 (NetBIOS over TCP/IP). It may be desirable to open TCP/3389 (for Microsoft Remote Desktop).

Finally, the Advanced tab allows the user to determine on which interfaces the Windows Firewall will be enabled as well as define a log file to store the firewall logs. In addition, specific Internet Control Message Protocol (ICMP) messages can be specified to be allowed to traverse the firewall in order to ease debugging of connection problems. A last-resort capability is also available, allowing the user to restore the Windows Firewall service to its default settings. Figure 4-9 shows the Advanced tab.

Figure 4-9 *Windows Firewall Advanced Tab*

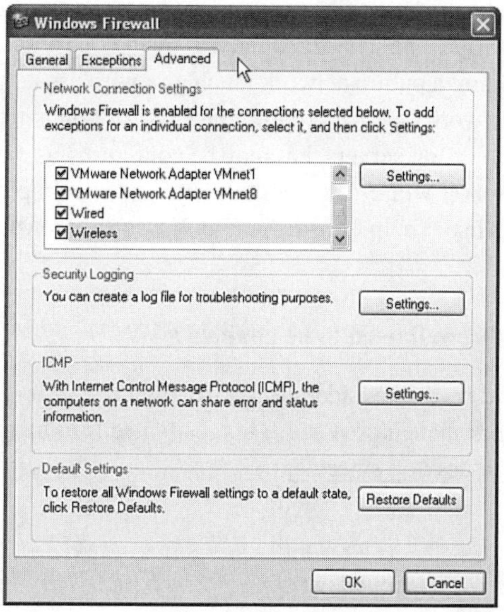

Windows Firewall Features

The Windows Firewall software builds on top of the ICF/Internet Connection Sharing software that is now deprecated in Windows XP SP2. Essentially, Windows Firewall provides the following features over the ICF:

- The ability to specify options on a global level so that they apply to all connections.

- An operating mode that does not allow exceptions.

- Startup security (covered below).

- IPv4 traffic scoping. The end user can specify that the firewall accept traffic from specific IP addresses.

- The ability to specify exceptions by service or by program.

- IPv6 support.

Of particular interest is the new startup security. Whereas ICF was active after the system had booted up and the ICF service was successfully started by the Windows kernel, Windows Firewall is active from the very start. During system boot, the Windows Firewall applies a default stateful filter to the system to allow basic networking functionality such as Dynamic Host Configuration Protocol (DHCP), Domain Name System (DNS), and communication with domain controllers, but blocks all other traffic until the system boot process has completed. Only then are the settings configured by the user applied to the firewall.

Windows Firewall Checklist

When configuring Windows Firewall, you must configure several features depending on the system role in the network. The answers to the following questions will depend on whether the system will connect using a public network (such as a wireless network in a coffee shop or a library) or a private network (such as a corporate LAN or home network) or both. Additionally, Windows Firewall settings on servers that may be configured as a web server, an authentication server, or a database server will differ from the settings on a simple desktop or laptop system. You can use this checklist to help ensure that the Windows Firewall settings are appropriate for a given system.

- **Does Windows Firewall need to be enabled?**

  This is determined by the consideration of whether the system will be exposed to a less-secure network than anticipated. This really needs to be considered more for laptops rather than desktop systems.

- **What exceptions (if any) should be configured in the Windows Firewall policy?**

  — **Remote Desktop?**

  To allow an external user to access the system using Microsoft Remote Desktop Client.

  — **File and Printer Sharing?**

  This is necessary to share files with other users and systems as well as print documents.

  — **Other services?**

  Should other services such as Remote Assistance, Virtual Network Computer (VNC), or Internet Information Server (IIS) be accessible through the firewall?

- **Should the exceptions be configured as programs or as services?**

  If you configure exceptions as programs, the firewall only allows the traffic through if the specified program is active. Otherwise, the traffic is blocked. However, if the program is a set of services, such as Windows File and Printer Sharing, it may be easier to configure the exceptions as a range of network service ports rather than programs.

- **For which interfaces should Windows Firewall be configured?**

  The end user or administrator needs to decide whether all network interfaces will have the firewall active or just those that may be exposed to "insecure" networks. This typically applies to desktops with multiple interfaces but can also apply to laptops with both a wired and a wireless interface. In some cases (such as a laptop with a built-in wireless interface), it is best to apply the firewall to all interfaces to ensure that attackers cannot slip by through an active wireless connection.

- **Which ICMP types should be allowed through the firewall?**

  At the very least, ICMP echo reply packets, ICMP destination unreachable packets, and ICMP Time-To-Live (TTL) Exceeded packets should be allowed through the firewall for debugging potential network connectivity problems.

- **Should logging be configured?**

  Logging can cause a degradation in system performance. Turn logging on only when it is needed to debug a problem with the firewall.

After you have answered all of these questions, you can appropriately configure the firewall for the system. One item to consider is that if logging is configured, who will be reading the logs and how often? It is of little value to configure logging if no one actually looks at the logs.

Trend Micro's PC-cillin Firewall Feature

One of many third-party antivirus/Internet security suites, Trend Micro's PC-cillin includes a personal firewall that you can use to protect the system. The Trend Micro PC-cillin suite is a combination of a personal firewall, an antivirus system, an antispyware system, an antispam filter, and an identity-theft protection system through blocking of phishing and pharming attacks. This product is ideal for end-user, home or small office customers who need an all-in-one package to defend against a wide variety of threats from the network. It is not really targeted to the enterprise user because centralized management and configuration are not available. This section focuses only on the firewall portion of PC-cillin security suite. Like Windows Firewall, PC-cillin firewall is configurable and provides protection against a wide variety of network threats.

PC-cillin Requirements

Trend Micro's firewall supports Windows systems going all the way back to Windows 98 and 98 SE. This backward compatibility is a rare feature for many personal firewalls because vendors typically consider those systems so old that they are no longer on the market. Microsoft no longer supports Windows 98 or 98 SE, but you can still find these systems in use. PC-cillin requires systems to meet the specifications described in Table 4-2.

Table 4-2 *Trend Micro's PC-cillin System Requirements*

Operating System	Minimum Processor	Minimum Memory	Free Disk Space Required	Browser
Windows 98/98 SE Windows ME	Intel Pentium 233 MHz	128 MB	120 MB	Microsoft Internet Explorer 5.5 SP2 or higher Netscape 7.1 and above AOL 7.0 and above Firefox 1.0
Windows 2000 SP4 Windows XP Home Edition or Professional SP2	Intel Pentium 300 MHz	128 MB	120 MB	

How the Trend Micro Firewall Works

The Trend Micro firewall works as a blend of a traditional stateful firewall and intrusion detection system (IDS). An IDS monitors the traffic in and out of the protected system for attacks and upon detection of an attack it can alert the user. Most IDSs detect attacks by matching the network traffic against a signature of the attack. A signature is like a fingerprint. It identifies an attack by matching the network traffic ("the evidence") against a known signature describing the attack ("the fingerprint"). When the traffic matches the signature, an attack has been detected. As in the case of real evidence, however, this method is not foolproof and leads to false positives sometimes. A false positive is a case where benign network traffic is mistakenly categorized as an attack and an alert is generated for the user.

A stateful firewall not only examines the various headers of a packet but also ensures that the connection is active by tracking each connection in a state table. Most stateful firewalls, such as PC-cillin, can also dynamically open secondary ports for protocols that require more than one network port to complete a connection. PC-cillin's firewall also inspects the contents, too, using a rudimentary built-in IDS. Filtering decisions made by the firewall are based on defined rules as well as the context that has been established and stored in a state table by previous packets that have already passed through the firewall.

The Trend Micro firewall comes with a preset series of policies that end users can modify to accommodate their specific requirements. The firewall can filter HTTP strings from server to server to prevent hybrid attacks such as Nimda and Code Red and to identify and stop Trojan attacks. Finally, the firewall uses its built-in IDS capabilities to identify and stop common firewall attacks such as oversize packet fragments, overlapping fragment attack, ping of death, and others. Unfortunately, the IDS signatures are not user updateable or configurable. If Trend Micro determines that a new IDS signature needs to be released for the firewall, users can only update the system when Trend Micro incorporates that signature into the product. They cannot configure new signatures on their own.

Configuring the Trend Micro Firewall

Configuring the Trend Micro firewall is straightforward and easy. When the firewall software, which is a part of Trend Micro's PC-cillin Internet security suite, has been installed, the main control panel should be opened. This can be done either by right-clicking the Trend Micro Internet security suite icon in the notification area at the lower right of the Windows taskbar and then choosing the **Open Main** option or by just double-clicking the icon. Alternatively, the user can open PC-cillin's main panel by choosing **Start > Programs > Trend Micro PC-cillin > Trend Micro PC-cillin Internet Security 2005**. To verify that PC-cillin has registered properly in Windows XP's security center, you can launch the security center by choosing **Start > Control Panels > Windows Security Center** (which brings up the Windows Security Center window displayed in Figure 4-10). From here you can see that the Trend Micro PC-cillin software has registered itself as both the firewall for the system (effectively disabling the built-in Windows Firewall) and the antivirus suite for this system.

Figure 4-10   *Trend Micro PC-cillin Registration in Windows Security Center*

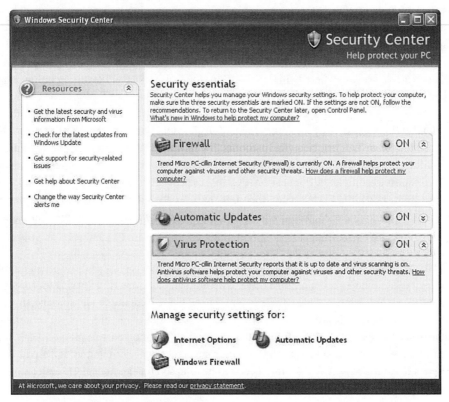

When the Trend Micro Internet Security window is open, you can choose the firewall configuration controls by clicking the **Firewall** button near the lower right of the control panel, as shown in Figure 4-11.

From this window, the user can modify the firewall profiles by clicking the **Firewall Profiles** button in the middle of the window. This opens up the profile selection window shown in Figure 4-12. At this window, users can choose to enable or disable the firewall as well as choose the specific profile they want to apply to the firewall. Additionally, they can add and configure a new profile if the default profiles are insufficient to meet their needs.

Figure 4-11 *Trend Micro Internet Security Window*

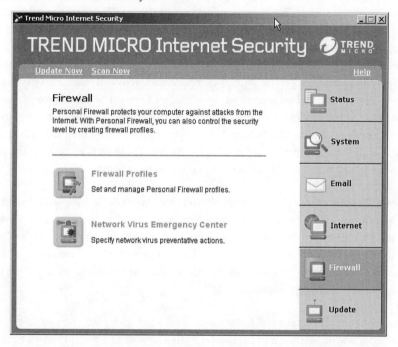

Figure 4-12 *Trend Micro Firewall Profiles*

The default profiles include an office network connection, a home network connection, a wireless network connection, and a direct connection to the Internet. Each one has specific exceptions to the firewall policy for various services. The office network, wireless network, and direction connection profiles each have a list of specific exceptions for various services such as HTTP, Secure Shell (SSH), DNS, and others in the firewall profile. The home network profile, however, has no preconfigured exceptions. Not all exceptions are active. By default, only the NetBIOS (for Windows file sharing and printing) and the Windows Domain Services protocols are enabled by default in the office network and the wireless network profiles. In the direct connection profile, these two services are disabled, but the AOL Connection service is enabled. It is up to the end user to enable additional exceptions to the various profiles. These profiles provide the end user with a quick way of allowing specific services in and out of the system.

Unlike the Windows Firewall, the Trend Micro firewall only deals with services and not programs. From a conceptual point of view, this means that programs that open dynamic ports (for example, many instant messenger programs) for listening are not easy to configure in the Trend Micro firewall because the ports they use will vary. To accommodate this issue, a range of ports needs to be opened, which leaves the system more vulnerable. The Home Network profile is analyzed for the purpose of this configuration example.

When a profile has been selected, the security level needs to be set. You can do this in the Firewall Profiles Editor window shown in Figure 4-13. To access the Firewall Profiles Editor window, choose a specific profile in the Firewall Profiles panel and click the **Edit** button in the middle of the Firewall Profiles panel.

Figure 4-13   *Trend Micro Firewall Security Level*

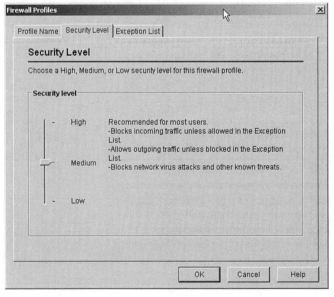

The security level feature of the Trend Micro firewall enables the end user to adjust the overall protection provided by the firewall. There are three security levels defined in the Trend Micro firewall product: Low, Medium, and High. The Low security level is recommended for users who do not need a great deal of protection, such as those who are on a LAN that is considered secure or for home users who do not directly connect to the Internet without another device such as a Linksys router or other device. This profile allows both incoming and outgoing network traffic but blocks viruses and other known threats through the firewall's rudimentary IDS capabilities.

The Medium security level, designed for most users who use a wireless network or some sort of public LAN, blocks incoming traffic unless specifically listed in the exception list but allows all outgoing traffic unless it's specifically blocked in the exception list. It also blocks network virus attacks and other known threats as in the Low security level.

Finally, the High security level blocks both incoming and outgoing traffic unless specifically provided for in the profile exception list. It also blocks, as in the Medium and Low security levels, network virus attacks and other threats, but it also provides alerts for outgoing traffic. This level is meant for users who require a high degree of security on their system, such as those who are directly connected to the Internet through a broadband connection where the connection is always active.

To change the security level in the policy, open the **Security Level** tab in the Firewall Profiles window, as shown in Figure 4-13. Slide the slider either up (towards High) for greater security or down (towards Low) for lower security. By default, the slider is set to Medium, which is sufficient for most users.

With the security level for the firewall set, the next step is to define the exception list to the policy. Open the **Exception List** tab in the Firewall Profiles window. Remember that an exception is designed to allow a particular service in or access to a particular service on the outside of the firewall. Because the Trend Micro firewall is a stateful firewall, many of the more common services such as DNS and DHCP work because the system generates the initial traffic outbound and the firewall knows that a response is expected from a server to the initial traffic. Adding exceptions to the firewall depends on what specific traffic should be allowed inbound to the system or, as in the case of the High security level, what traffic should also be allowed outbound from the system. For example, in many cases, exceptions in the firewall profile for the Windows Domain Services and NetBIOS are needed to allow the system to authenticate to Windows domain controllers as well as participate in file sharing and printing in a Windows network environment. If a web server is running on the system, an exception should be added to allow other systems access to the web server port. It all depends on the role and on what software is installed on the system. To add exceptions to the firewall policy, click the **Add** button, as shown in Figure 4-14.

This opens a new window where a wide variety of information about the exception can be entered, such as the protocol to use, the direction of traffic, the port number(s) the traffic uses, whether to allow the traffic or deny it, and a name for the service.

Figure 4-14 *Trend Micro Firewall Exception List*

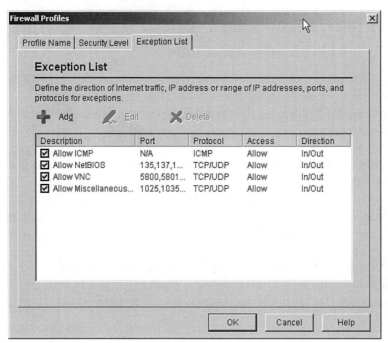

One final feature to review in Trend Micro's firewall is the Network Virus Emergency Center. To access this panel in the Internet security suite, go back to the main window (Figure 4-11) and click the **Network Virus Emergency Center** button. This will open the window shown in Figure 4-15.

You can configure this part of the firewall to respond to a wide variety of network viruses, as shown in the list in the middle of the window. The response is limited to one of two possibilities: a simple pop-up window indicating that the firewall has responded to a detected virus or completely severing the network connection upon detection of a virus. This allows the user to configure the firewall to help prevent the spread of the virus or worm immediately upon detection.

Figure 4-15 *Trend Micro Network Virus Emergency Center*

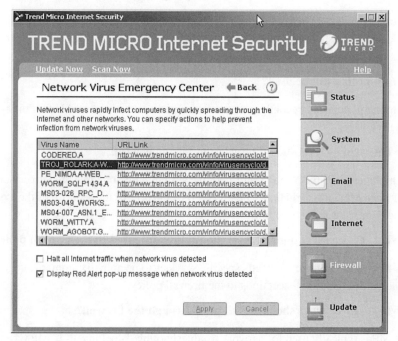

Trend Micro Firewall Features

Like the Windows Firewall, the Trend Micro firewall is a stateful firewall that keeps track of outbound packets and allows inbound response packets to reach the destination host. In addition, the firewall security level can easily be set according to a predefined level of Low, Medium, or High. Coupled with the IDS and antivirus features in PC-cillin, the firewall can identify and stop a network virus or worm before it damages the underlying host operating system and spreads to other systems.

Trend Micro Firewall Checklist

Like the Windows Firewall, you must configure several features depending on the system role in the network. One of the key differences is that the Windows Firewall should be disabled. Fortunately, the Trend Micro Internet security suite installer checks the status of the Windows Firewall before installing the Trend Micro product to ensure that no conflict exists between the two firewalls.

You can use the following checklist to help ensure that the Trend Micro firewall settings are appropriate for a given system:

■ **Is the Windows Firewall disabled?**

Windows Firewall should be disabled to register Trend Micro's PC-cillin as the firewall.

- **What profile and security level should be set?**

  This depends on where the system is located. On a public network, the profile and security level should be set to High. On a trusted network, the security level can be set to a lower value.

- **What profile will be used?**

  This helps define a preconfigured set of exceptions that can be enabled for the system if necessary.

- **What security level should be selected for the firewall?**

  This determines the overall security of the system based on three predefined settings of Low, Medium, and High. The greater the concern for the security of the system, the higher the security setting should be.

- **What service exceptions (if any) should be configured in the firewall policy?**

  If the system provides or needs specific services to be able to communicate, they should be entered as exceptions to the firewall policy.

- **Which ICMP types should be allowed through the firewall?**

  ICMP is typically used for network troubleshooting. Blocking all ICMP types may make it difficult to conduct such troubleshooting. It is recommended that ICMP echo reply packets, ICMP destination unreachable packets, and ICMP Time-To-Live (TTL) Exceeded and possibly ICMP echo request packets from the local network be allowed in order to make network troubleshooting more effective.

- **Should the Network Virus Emergency Center disable network connectivity upon detection of a virus?**

  The Network Virus Emergency Center can disable network connectivity of the system upon detection of a network virus. This helps prevent the spread of viruses and worms but may result in the system becoming disconnected due to false positives, too.

After you have answered these questions, you can appropriately configure the firewall for the system.

Summary

The Windows Firewall and the Trend Micro firewall are examples of personal firewalls that are part of an overall effort to provide security all the way down to the system endpoint. Like all network security devices, they require some level of maintenance and monitoring to ensure that they are current and appropriately configured for the system environment. The ease of use of the Windows Firewall and the Trend Micro firewall make them especially well suited for the entry-level user.

## CHAPTER 5

Broadband Routers and Firewalls

Depending on the report you want to accept, between 53 percent and 62 percent of Internet access in the United States is provided by broadband connections. Outside the United States, broadband access percentages can exceed 75 percent of all Internet access methods (http://www.websiteoptimization.com/bw/0511/).

Although broadband Internet access provides for increased download speeds and an explosion of Internet-based services and resources, it also introduces some unique problems to the small office/home office (SOHO) and home user markets. With dialup connections, the need to protect the resources accessing the Internet is not considered as critical, because systems are rarely left connected to the Internet all the time. Rather, users dial the computer into a service provider, do what they need on the Internet, and then hang up the modem, thus protecting the system with the most secure of "firewalls" by disconnecting it from the network.

With most broadband connections, however, the Internet connection is always on; and if the computer is left on, the computer remains always vulnerable to attack. Of course, this scenario is nothing new to the corporate arena, where always-on Internet connections are normal, but it presents a whole new issue of how to secure environments that are often out of the control of the IT department and frequently do not have people with the technical expertise to deal with security issues at the location where the resources are.

Many home users and hobbyists also want to take advantage of the increased speed and better functionality that a broadband connection provides, but want to ensure that their systems are as secure as possible. They have neither the technical expertise nor desire to secure their computers properly, but at the same time they want something that they can place between their computer and the network and be relatively certain that their computer will be protected.

How Broadband Routers and Firewalls Work

Many broadband routers and firewalls function primarily through the use of Network Address Translation (NAT) to hide the internal systems behind a single external IP address. These so-called "NAT routers" or "NAT firewalls" do an adequate job of hiding resources from casual attack methods, but they do not perform advanced firewall functions; therefore, it is really a bit of a misnomer to call them firewalls, at least in the sense that firewalls such as the Cisco

Secure PIX Firewall, Microsoft ISA Server, and Check Point Firewall-1 products are considered firewalls. Rather, many broadband routers and firewalls are just NAT-based packet-filtering routers providing a degree of privacy, but they typically lack advanced firewall features such as stateful packet inspection (SPI), proxying of data, or deep packet inspection.

Figure 5-1 shows the NAT process.

Figure 5-1   *How NAT Works*

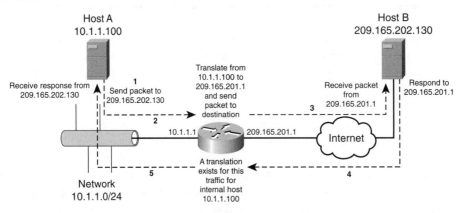

The steps numbered in Figure 5-1 can be further explained as follows:

1. The client initiates a connection to an external host (HostB).

2. The broadband router/firewall receives the request and translates the request from the internal IP address to the address of the router/firewall's external interface. The router/firewall keeps track of this translation in a translation table.

3. The packets are delivered to the external destination (HostB), which believes that the packets originated from the external IP address of the router/firewall. The external host (HostB) responds accordingly to the external IP address of the router/firewall.

4. When the router/firewall receives the response from the external host, it checks its translation table for a matching outbound request.

5. If it finds one, the router/firewall repackages the packet and delivers it to the internal host (HostA), which thinks that the response is from the external host (HostB).

In addition, most broadband routers/firewalls are designed not to permit any unsolicited packets from an external host to be delivered to an internal host.

Although this is generally an adequate level of protection for most home environments, it is important to understand that reliance on NAT alone to protect hosts is a false sense of security because NAT does not guarantee security in and of itself, as noted in RFC 2663 Section 9.0. For example, NAT devices are as susceptible to targeted attacks, such as denial-of-service (DoS) attacks, as non-NAT devices. NAT also provides for no actual filtering of packets leaving the internal network; instead, it permits all outbound traffic as long as it can be translated accordingly. Although it is a subtle difference, NAT provides more privacy than it does security.

Therefore, only when used in conjunction with other technologies can NAT serve as an effective security mechanism. The best broadband routers/firewalls (for example, many of the Linksys broadband firewalls) include application-level filtering, deep packet inspection, SPI, firewall hardening, and NAT.

Linksys Broadband Routers/Firewalls

Linksys makes a number of broadband routers (with basic firewall functionality) and broadband firewalls (with advanced firewall functionality) for both wired and wireless networks. Most of the wired products begin with a model number of BEF; most of the wireless products begin with a model number of WRT. The Linksys broadband routers/firewalls are designed with the home user in mind, and therefore are designed with simplicity of implementation in mind. All function as NAT routers, and some models and versions also provide stateful packet inspection in addition to NAT; unfortunately, Linksys does not do a good job of specifying which models and versions of firmware have this functionality. This difficulty is compounded by the fact that SPI was removed from some versions of firmware, so literally the same hardware with different versions of firmware may or may not support SPI.

This chapter examines the Linksys BEFSR41v4 EtherFast Cable/DSL Router with 4-Port Switch. The BEFSR41v4 is designed primarily for the home and small office user, and as a result has a relatively basic and simple-to-implement feature set. For ease of review, the features have been categorized as follows for the discussion that follows:

- Security and filtering features

- Routing features

- Management and administration features

- Miscellaneous features

Security and Filtering Features

The BEFSR41v4 is a basic NAT router (with firewall functionality) that can perform basic port filtering to allow traffic both coming into and going out of the protected network to be filtered. Unlike many firewalls that take a "block all, permit only" minimalist approach to filtering outbound traffic, the Linksys is just the opposite, instead taking the approach of "permit all outbound, block only." The idea is that it is easier to block a couple of ports or IP addresses than it is to identify the ports or IP addresses that should be permitted.

Inbound traffic still adheres to the minimalist filtering policy, blocking all traffic to all ports unless you otherwise configure the router to permit the traffic. Unfortunately, filtering incoming traffic can only be done based on the destination port number, so it is not possible to permit only certain external hosts to access the protected resources. Either the entire Internet can access the resources or none of the Internet can.

The BEFSR41v4 also supports the concept of a demilitarized zone (DMZ) system. The DMZ functions by effectively taking a host from the internal network and using NAT to expose it in an unfiltered fashion to the Internet. This exposure allows any Internet host to fully connect to and access the host in an unrestricted and nonfirewalled manner. In general, a DMZ is a bad idea; however, some circumstances, particularly when attempting to run gaming applications and such, require connectivity to the system that the Linksys filtering rules are not capable of easily or properly supporting. Consequently, a DMZ provides a simple, albeit entirely insecure method of making sure that the host can be accessed by Internet hosts.

Because Linksys routers utilize NAT, some protocols such as IPSec, PPP over Ethernet (PPPoE) passthrough, and Point-to-Point Tunneling Protocol (PPTP) fail to function properly. This failure results because NAT changes the source address of packets that are translated through the router, causing the destination host for those packets to believe that the data has been compromised (which strictly speaking, it has). To facilitate using these protocols through a Linksys router/ firewall, Linksys supports what is known as virtual private network (VPN) passthrough. VPN passthrough allows traffic in a VPN tunnel to pass through the router/firewall by essentially encapsulating the entire VPN packet in another packet, typically User Datagram Protocol (UDP). The router can then perform the NAT translation on that UDP packet, never actually changing the contents of the VPN packet. If you want to allow VPN traffic to pass through the router, you must enable VPN passthrough.

Routing Features

Because the BEFSR41v4 is targeted at the small office as well as the home user market, it supports some basic routing capabilities to allow it to be deployed in an environment with multiple internal subnets. In addition to being able to configure static routes, the router also supports RIP versions 1 and 2. Although RIP can prove adequate for small environments, the implementation of RIP on the router is extremely basic and lacks any kind of security functions; therefore, you should strongly consider whether this router is the appropriate firewall solution for you if you need the firewall to provide advanced routing functionality. In such cases, a more robust firewall such as the Cisco Secure PIX Firewall might be a better solution.

Management and Administration Features

Most Linksys network devices use a web-based management interface that uses HTTP as the transport protocol. Unfortunately, HTTP does not provide for encryption or security of the data being transported, so you should use caution with regard to the passwords you configure for the router, because they can relatively easily be captured using a network sniffer. By default, the router does not allow management access to the external interface, and although it can be permitted, it is generally a bad idea to do so.

The security model employed by Linksys is a simple shared password security model. All users log in using the same username and password to perform any management functions, and all authenticated users have the same rights.

The Linksys routers also typically provide basic syslog functionality, allowing the router to send events to a syslog server on the same subnet as the internal interface, as well as their own internal log-viewing software known as Log Viewer (which you can find at ftp://ftp.linksys.com/pub/befsr41/).

Miscellaneous Features

Because most home users do not have a Dynamic Host Configuration Protocol (DHCP) server on their home network, most Linksys routers feature DHCP server functionality built in to the router and enabled by default. This functionality allows a user to simply plug a computer into one of the router's switch ports, obtain an IP address that is valid for the router (typically on the 192.168.1.0/24 subnet), and then connect to the router using a web browser on the computer to configure the router accordingly (typically, the router internal interface IP address is 192.168.1.1).

Another feature of newer Linksys routers that can be enabled but is typically disabled by default is Universal Plug-and-Play (UPnP). UPnP allows hosts on the internal network that are using UPnP-capable operating systems to automatically configure the router to allow traffic from the external network to access the corresponding internal network resource. As a general rule, unless this functionality is required, you should disable UPnP on your router.

To facilitate connectivity to various broadband providers, most Linksys routers support multiple Internet connection types. The default setting is just to use DHCP to obtain an external IP address from the service provider, but static assigned IP addresses and PPPoE are supported, as well as solutions specific to certain areas of the world, such as Remote Access Service (RAS), PPTP, and Heart Beat Signal. Because many service providers provide only a dynamic IP address for use on the external interface, most Linksys routers also support dynamic Domain Name System (DNS) through either DynDNS (http://www.dyndns.org) or TZO (http://www.tzo.com). This support allows the router to automatically update the DNS entries for hosts that are protected by the router but need to be Internet accessible (such as websites). In both cases, you need to have a valid account with either DynDNS or TZO for this functionality to work properly.

Linksys Requirements

Most Linksys routers have an extremely small requirements list. Because the assumption is that the router will be connected to a small or home network that lacks any kind of DHCP server, the routers ship with the internal interface configured with the IP address of 192.168.1.1 and are configured to act as a DHCP server to provide IP addresses to any host on the internal network. Therefore, connecting internal hosts to the router for the purpose of configuring the router is very much plug and play. Just plug a host into the internal network of the router (either through the integrated switch on models that feature it, or through a separate hub or switch for models that do not contain a built-in switch), turn the router on, and then turn the computer on. The computer should obtain an IP address, allowing it to communicate with the router.

To provide for the external connectivity, you need to coordinate with the service provider to determine what the requirements are to connect to their network. If the service provider supports DHCP clients, the router will automatically obtain the proper IP address information. If your service provider requires the use of PPPoE or something similar, they will provide you with the appropriate information, and you just configure the router accordingly.

At this point, the router will allow all internal hosts unrestricted access, while allowing no external hosts to initiate access to internal resources.

How the Linksys Router/Firewall Works

Most Linksys routers/firewalls rely on simple NAT routing and basic port filtering to control the flow of traffic through the router. Depending on the direction of the traffic flow, a different filtering methodology is applied.

Filtering Traffic from External Sources

Linksys adheres to the minimalist approach to filtering when it comes to filtering traffic from external sources. By default, all traffic that originates from an external host is blocked by the router/firewall unless it is specifically permitted. This policy ensures that only the traffic you explicitly permit is allowed to access protected resources. Linksys provides three methods of explicitly permitting traffic:

- Port-range forwarding

- Port triggering

- DMZ forwarding

Port-Range Forwarding

Port-range forwarding is the classic port-forwarding configuration that most firewalls and routers implement. With port-range forwarding, you enter the starting and ending port that should be permitted, select the appropriate transport protocol (TCP, UDP, or both), and specify the IP address of the internal host that is providing the specified service. Doing so causes the router to take all traffic received on the external interface that is destined to the specified ports and forward the traffic to the internal host. Unfortunately, there is no way to specify which external hosts should be allowed to access the internal resources, so you are forced to allow all external resources access, or allow none at all. In many cases (for example, a Simple Message Transfer Protocol [SMTP] server), you want all external hosts to be able to access the server, so this is not a problem. If you have an FTP server that you only want certain external hosts to access, however, you really need to implement a firewall other than the Linksys router. Figure 5-2 illustrates how port-range forwarding works with an internal host running a web server.

Figure 5-2 *Port-Range Forwarding*

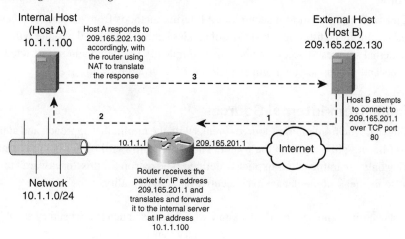

In Figure 5-2, the router is configured to allow port forwarding for TCP port 80 to the internal web server (HostA) located at IP address 10.1.1.100. The process works like this:

1. The router receives a packet destined to its external IP address using TCP port 80.

2. The router forwards the response to the internal web server (HostA), keeping the source IP address of the original external host (HostB) unchanged.

3. This allows the web server (HostA) to know that it needs to respond to the external host (HostB), the reply to which the router will then translate using NAT, causing the external host (HostB) to think it has been communicating with the router the whole time.

Port Triggering

Port triggering forwards traffic to internal hosts in a similar manner to how port-range forwarding works, with one important difference. Port triggering does not forward any traffic to an internal host until that internal host has initiated some form of traffic for an external destination. When that occurs, the port triggering mechanism automatically allows traffic to be forwarded to the host that initiated the trigger condition.

Port triggering is used primarily to support applications that attempt to communicate with hosts using different ports than what they were contacted on. A common example of this is many gaming applications. For example, Unreal Tournament uses UDP ports 7777 through 7779 to communicate between hosts, but uses port 27900 to communicate with the central game server. Using port forwarding, you would need to potentially permit all of those ports, all the time, to allow a host to run the application. With port triggering, you can configure the router to open ports 7777 through 7779 only after an internal host has attempted to connect to something on the external network using port 27900.

DMZ Forwarding

DMZ forwarding is the most insecure of all filtering methods from external sources because it applies absolutely no filtering. The host still resides behind NAT, but the router will allow all traffic from external sources to access the host in a completely unfiltered and unrestricted manner. For all intents and purposes, you might as well not even have a firewall.

Filtering Traffic from Internal Sources

Filtering of traffic from internal sources breaks with the minimalist approach and applies a terribly flawed filtering philosophy to the router. The router allows all traffic from internal sources, blocking only the traffic that is explicitly defined. The reason for this "backward" implementation speaks to the heart of the debate over security and functionality.

The vast majority of home users do not know what a port is, much less what they should or should not be filtering. By allowing all traffic by default, Linksys ensures that the router/firewall is easy to set up, with little to no configuration required to allow access to external resources. This easy setup dramatically saves technical support costs. Unfortunately, this insecure method of implementation allows all traffic to exit the network (for example, allowing a back door that has been installed on the user's computer to send sensitive information to a host on the Internet or allowing a virus/worm to propagate to external hosts). Because it is so easy to implement, however, ease has won out over security.

Linksys generally supports three levels of filtering of traffic from internal sources:

- By IP address

- By port range

- By MAC address

In all instances, any IP addresses, destination port numbers, or MAC addresses specified will not be allowed to access external hosts.

Configuring Linksys

Linksys uses a web-based interface to perform all configuration functions. This interface is accessible by default from any internal host and is accessed using a web browser such as Microsoft Internet Explorer. Upon accessing the web-based interface, you are prompted with a Username/Password dialog box. Refer to the user guide of your appropriate router for the relevant information, but typically the username/password combination of admin/admin is the default user account. You can change the password from the Management screen, which is discussed later in this chapter. In the case of the BEFSR41v4, the interface is separated into five main tabs:

- Setup

- Security

- Applications & Gaming

- Administration

- Status

No configuration settings are accessible from the Status tab. As shown in Figure 5-3, it merely displays the status of the router.

Figure 5-3 *Linksys Status Tab*

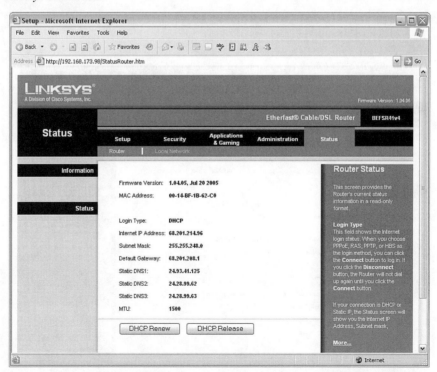

Configuring Basic Setup

The BEFSR41v4 Setup tab consists of four screens:

■ Basic Setup

■ DDNS

■ MAC Address Clone

■ Advanced Routing

On the Basic Setup screen, you can configure how the router connects to the service provider (for example, using DHCP or PPPoE). Depending on which connection type you specify, additional options will be made available on the screen. You can also specify the host and domain name as well as the maximum transmission unit (MTU) for the router, if it is required by your service provider.

The Basic Setup screen is also where you configure the local network settings for the router (such as the internal interface IP address, and the DHCP server settings for the router). In the DHCP settings, you can specify the DNS servers to use; if you leave the values empty, the router automatically uses the values that it obtained from the service provider as the DNS server for the internal clients. Figure 5-4 shows the Basic Setup screen.

Figure 5-4 *Basic Setup Screen*

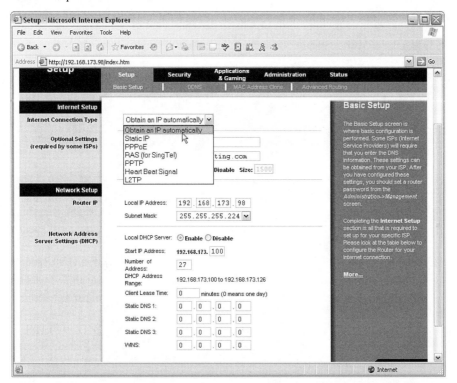

The DDNS screen is where you can configure the router with the appropriate settings to enable it to dynamically update the DNS settings with either DynDNS or TZO when the external IP address of the router changes. Just enter the username (DynDNS) or e-mail address (TZO) that you registered with, along with the appropriate password and domain name, and the router will automatically update DNS anytime the router's external IP address changes.

On the MAC Address Clone screen, you can configure a specific MAC address (for example, if your ISP requires a specific MAC address to be used by your router).

On the Advanced Routing screen, you can configure whether to use NAT as well as configure RIP or static routes, as shown in Figure 5-5.

Figure 5-5 *Advanced Routing Screen*

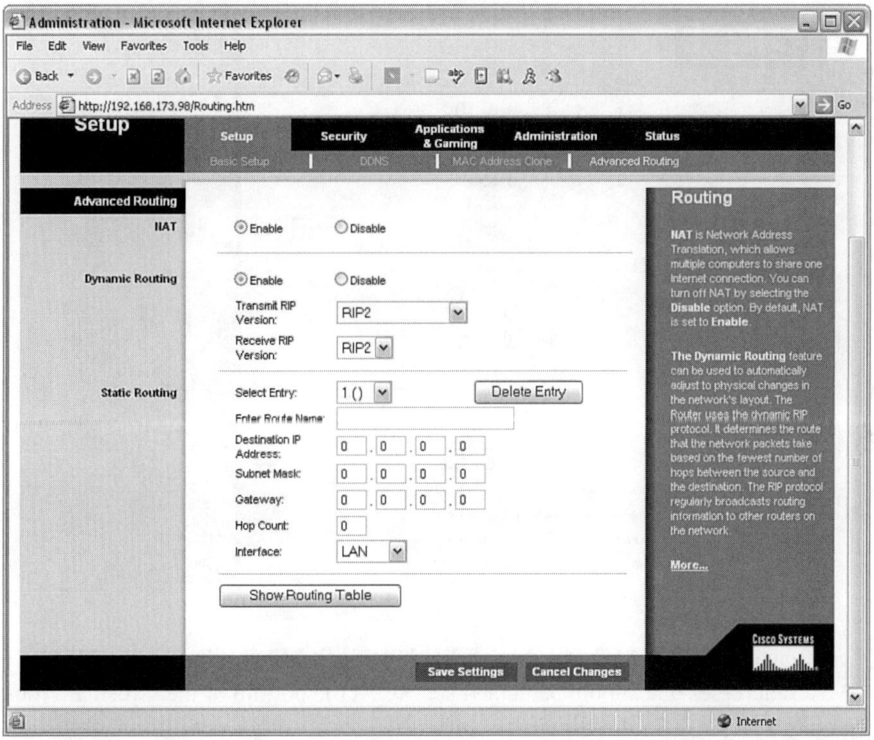

NAT configuration is a simple enable/disable toggle. To enable RIP routing, just select **Enable** and then select the transmit and receive RIP versions from the drop-down boxes. To enter a static route, fill in the appropriate information and specify the interface that the route uses as the exit interface.

Configuring Security

The Security tab consists of two screens, Filter and VPN Passthrough. In both instances, the configuration applies to traffic from the internal network accessing external resources (egress filtering).

The Filter screen is where you can configure IP address, port, and MAC address filtering of internal hosts. For example, if you want to prevent host 192.168.173.115 from accessing the Internet, you can specify that IP address in the Filter IP Address Range fields, and the router will not allow that host to access external resources. Similarly, if you want to prevent certain port numbers from being accessed by internal hosts (for example, instant messenger software or gaming ports), you specify them, too. Keep in mind that the router only supports five entries for either IP address range or port range, so you need to be judicious about what you filter. Figure 5-6 shows the filter screen.

Figure 5-6 *Filter Screen*

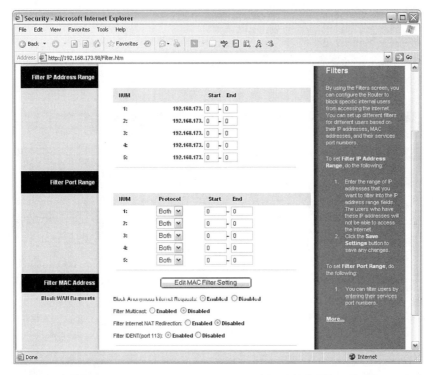

If you want to filter by MAC address, just click the **Edit MAC Filter Setting** button and specify the MAC addresses that should be denied access. At the bottom of the screen are four radial selections with the default setting in parenthesis:

■ **Block Anonymous Internet Requests** (**Enabled**)—This setting prevents the router from being able to be pinged or otherwise connected to on the external interface, unless you have defined a port-forwarding filter. This should be enabled, but keep in mind that not being able to ping the router can make it more difficult to troubleshoot.

■ **Filter Multicast** (**Disabled**)—This setting allows multicast traffic to be forwarded to the appropriate destination. Multicast traffic is traffic destined to multiple hosts. This allows the traffic to be sent one time, while allowing multiple registered hosts to receive it, which it more efficient than sending the traffic individually to each host (which is a process known as unicast). A host registers to receive this multicast traffic by virtue of the fact that it is running an application that is configured to listen on the corresponding multicast IP address. Multicast is frequently used for the transmission of multimedia and streaming data. Multicast traffic is frequently filtered when it is either unnecessary (for example, because no applications that utilize multicast are running on the network) or to prevent multicast-based attacks from being initiated (for example, to prevent an attack that uses multicast traffic to saturate a network with bogus traffic, thus effecting a DoS on the network). Although somewhat counterintuitive, you want to disable filtering if you want to permit multicast traffic.

- **Filter Internet NAT Redirection (Disabled)** — This setting enables you to configure the router to block access to local resources from other local computers that are attempting to access the local resource via the external (NAT) address.

- **Filter IDENT(port 113) (Enabled)** — IDENT allows hosts to query the device, and thus discover information about the host. Unless applications specifically require this degree of access, you should always filter IDENT traffic.

On the VPN Passthrough screen, you can configure the router to transparently pass IPSec, PPPoE, and PPTP traffic from internal hosts to external resources. All three settings are enabled by default, and if you are going to use NAT and need to access remote resources using any of the three protocols, you should enable these settings.

Configuring Applications & Gaming

The name of the Applications & Gaming tab is somewhat misleading because although the settings are typically going to be implemented by home users to support their gaming applications, in function the Applications & Gaming tab is where the configuration of filtering from external sources to internal resources is performed. This tab has five screens:

- Port Range Forwarding

- Port Triggering

- UPnP Forwarding

- DMZ

- QoS

On the Port Range Forwarding screen, you can configure the router to permit certain types of traffic from all external hosts over the specified ports to the specified internal destination. Thus, you can protect servers behind the router/firewall, while still allowing access to the applications and resources on the server from external hosts. For example, if you were running an SMTP server on the internal server located at 192.168.173.115, you would configure the router as shown in Figure 5-7.

Figure 5-7   *Configuring Port-Range Forwarding*

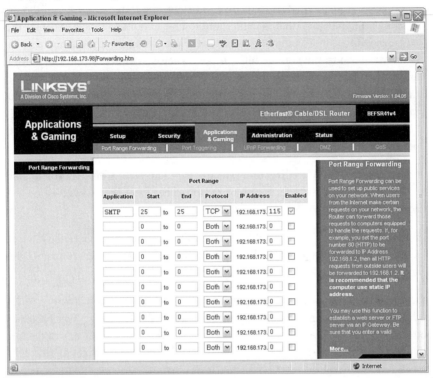

On the Port Triggering screen, you can define a port or range of ports that, when the router detects an internal host attempting to connect to, causes the router to dynamically permit a port or range of ports to be forwarded to the internal host. In this fashion, applications that are running on external servers and that attempt to connect to the internal host over ports other than the one the internal host originally used can be configured to be permitted. This is typically done to support gaming applications, which frequently work by having a computer initiate a connection to a central server on one port and then communicate with any number of other servers using a different set of ports. For example, to support Unreal Tournament, you configure the router as shown in Figure 5-8. In this case, when the router detects an internal host attempting to connect to an external resource using TCP or UDP port 27900, the router automatically configures a forwarding rule to allow all external hosts to connect to the internal host over TCP or UDP ports 7777 through 7779.

On the UPnP Forwarding screen, you can configure port forwarding to UPnP-based devices. Unless you require UPnP, it is recommended to use basic port forwarding, which is more secure because it cannot be manipulated by hosts running the UPnP protocol.

On the DMZ screen, you can identify a single host that will be treated as a completely unfiltered and unprotected host by the router. Although the internal host still uses NAT for communications with external resources, the router/firewall allows all solicited and unsolicited traffic from external sources to the server specified as being in the DMZ.

Figure 5-8   *Configuring Port Triggering*

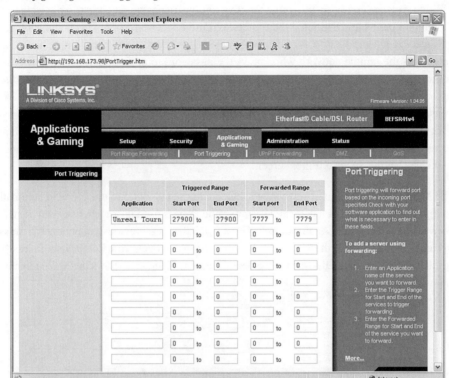

On the QoS screen, you can define specific levels of service and priority for different types of network traffic. Such distinctions are typically done to ensure that latency-sensitive applications such as videoconferencing and Voice over IP (VoIP) are given priority and preferential treatment by the router. On this screen, you can configure the router to essentially place the defined traffic in front of any other traffic, to ensure that the specified traffic is allowed to pass instead of being delayed by other less-important traffic.

You can specify quality of service (QoS) priority by either the device MAC address, the Ethernet switch port that the traffic came from, or the application port in question. For example, if you are running an Internet-based phone, you can specify the MAC address to ensure that all traffic coming from the phone is given preferential treatment by the router. There are two priorities, low and high, allowing you to decide how the traffic should be treated.

Configuring Administration

On the Administration tab, you can define how the router will be managed and how logging should be configured. You can also perform software upgrades and reset the router to the factory defaults.

The Management screen is used to specify what the router password is. Keep in mind that all users will access the router web-based interface using the same password, so you should consider using a unique password for the router and sharing the password with as few people as possible. In addition, you can configure the router to allow remote management access, which can prove handy if your company has distributed the routers to remote locations, but expects the routers to be managed by a central entity. As a word of caution, however, permitting remote access allows anyone on the remote network who knows the password to potentially be able to access and configure the router; therefore, unless you really need this functionality, you should disable it. Also, keep in mind that because the router uses HTTP as the access protocol, all the data being transmitted—including passwords—is sent in an unencrypted format, which means anyone with a network sniffer can capture and obtain that information. As a general rule, remote management access should not be permitted, and you should ensure that Block Anonymous Internet Requests is enabled on the Security|Filter screen.

The Management screen is also where you can configure the router to use UPnP to automatically configure the router to open ports and permit traffic. This is used in conjunction with the UPnP Forwarding screen of the Applications & Gaming tab that was previously mentioned in this chapter. Because UPnP allows for the automatic configuration of the router from UPnP hosts, unless you require UPnP it should be disabled, which is the default setting. Figure 5-9 shows the Management screen.

Figure 5-9 *Management Screen*

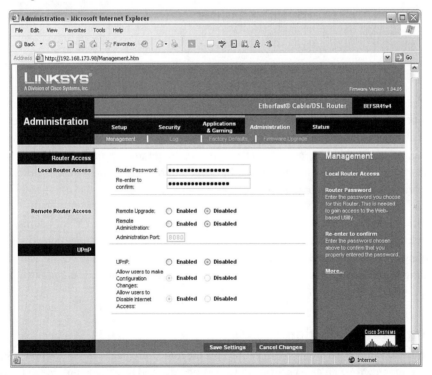

On the Log screen, you can specify the IP address of a syslog server and enable logging from the router. The Factory Defaults screen contains a simple toggle selection that enables you to reset the router to the factory defaults.

If you need to upgrade the software on the router, you can do so on the Firmware Upgrade screen. You can browse for an upgrade file on the local computer that is managing the router and click the button to upgrade. When the router has been upgraded, it reboots to begin running the new code.

Linksys Checklist

To implement a basic Linksys router, perform the following tasks:

Step 1   Obtain the connection information required by your ISP.

Step 2   Plug the router into the service provider device or network jack using the external/WAN interface of the router.

Step 3   Connect a computer that is configured to be a DHCP client to one of the switch ports on the router.

Step 4   Turn the router on.

Step 5   Turn the computer on. The computer should automatically obtain an IP address from the router, allowing it to connect to the router.

Step 6   Using a web browser, connect to the router's internal network interface IP address, typically http://192.168.1.1. When prompted, enter the default username (admin) and password (admin).

Step 7   At the Setup tab, configure the router using the information from Step 1.

Step 8   At the Management screen of the Administration tab, enter a new password.

Step 9   At this point, the router should allow all traffic to external destinations, while blocking access to all internal resources from external sources.

Step 10   If you require filtering, define the appropriate port-range forwarding (for ingress filtering) or filtering (for egress filtering) rules as needed.

Step 11   Test connectivity to external resources from internal systems, and to internal systems as defined by the port-forwarding rules from external systems.

Summary

Linksys broadband routers provide a simple, NAT-based packet-filtering router solution (some of which include stateful packet inspection) for small office environments as well as for home-based networks and users. Although some broadband router models lack the robustness of stateful packet-inspecting firewalls and lack granularity for configuring port forwarding, you can use them in simple environments where the security risk does not justify a substantial investment. If you require granular filtering rules, or if you require more advanced filtering mechanisms than simple NAT and port forwarding, you should consider implementing a more advanced firewall such as the Cisco Secure PIX Firewall, Microsoft ISA Server, or NetFilter over Linux.

CHAPTER **6**

Cisco PIX Firewall and ASA Security Appliance

One of the most widely deployed firewalls on the Internet is the Cisco PIX Firewall. The PIX, along with the new Cisco Adaptive Security Appliance (ASA), is poised to improve Cisco's market share of the firewall and virtual private network (VPN) marketplace by providing advanced security, increased performance, and more robust functionality. Originally acquired from a company called Network Translations back in the early to mid-1990s, the PIX has undergone significant development and improvements so that it has become one of the best firewalls on the market today. The PIX not only provides firewall capabilities but also VPN services and basic intrusion detection system (IDS) features. The ASA builds upon the PIX firewall base to include full-featured VPN and intrusion prevention system (IPS) capabilities. The firewall features of the PIX and ASA are implemented using what Cisco terms an adaptive security algorithm (ASA—not to be confused with the Cisco Adaptive Security Appliance, which is also termed ASA) to provide stateful firewall functionality. This chapter covers PIX and ASA model options for a network as well as how the PIX/ASA firewall works, how to configure for network connectivity and to access the PIX Device Manager (PDM) (for 6.x versions of software) and the Adaptive Security Device Manager (ASDM) (for 7.x versions of software), and a checklist of the things to consider when implementing a Cisco PIX or ASA in the network.

PIX/ASA Features

The PIX/ASA is a powerful stateful packet-inspection firewall with some basic application-inspection capabilities. One of the nice things about the PIX/ASA firewall is that fundamentally all hardware models run pretty much the same software (with the notable exception being the PIX 501 and PIX 506E, which will not run the newest PIX 7.x software, as discussed in the section "Cisco PIX Firewall and ASA Models"). For the PIX firewall, these features include the following:

- Failover functionality whereby two PIXs can provide high-availability services to a network. This functionality is only supported in PIX 515E or larger firewalls and is supported in both active/passive or active/active (for PIX software 7.x or newer) modes of operation.

- Zero-downtime software upgrades.

- DHCP server. The PIX now has a built-in DHCP server to provide address allocations for remote office or branch offices.

- Object grouping. Administrators can now group network objects (such as devices, networks, and services) into logical groups to simplify access control list (ACL) definition and maintenance.

- ACLs for controlling traffic access both inbound and outbound. The PIX can also "precompile" the ACLs using turbo ACLs, which provides for enhanced performance.

- Command-level authorization for role-based access control.

- Network Address Translation (NAT)—both unidirectional as well as bidirectional to support overlapping private address ranges.

- Network Time Protocol (NTP) support for clock synchronization to a time server.

- Simple Network Management Protocol (SNMP) monitoring with CPU monitoring using SNMPv2.

- Virtual firewall services (PIX software 7.x).

- Layer 2 transparent firewall (PIX software 7.x).

- Software and configuration updates via HTTP and HTTPS.

- HTTPS-based command-line interface (CLI) access.

- VPN services providing both LAN-to-LAN and remote-access VPN services.

- PPP over Ethernet (PPPoE) support for users connecting the PIX to an xDSL interface (not supported in PIX software 7.x).

- Quality of service (QoS) (PIX software 7.x).

- Tunneling application control to block and prevent applications that tunnel through web application ports such as instant messaging, peer-to-peer file share, and other applications such as GoToMyPC.

- IPv6 networking.

- Secure Shell Version 2 (SSHv2) and SNMPv2C (PIX software 7.x).

- Multicast support for multimedia applications.

- Port Address Translation (PAT) for H.323 and Session Initiation Protocol (SIP) for voice applications.

- Deep packet inspection for services such as HTTP, FTP, Extended Simple Mail Transfer Protocol (ESMTP), and more.

- Intrusion detection signatures for packet inspection.

- VLAN support.

These are just some of the features available in the PIX firewall. For a complete listing of features, refer to http://www.cisco.com/go/pix and http://www.cisco.com/en/US/products/hw/vpndevc/ps2030/products_data_sheet0900aecd80225ae1.html.

The ASA Security Appliance shares many of the same features as the PIX firewall, as well as a few additional ASA-specific features, including the following:

- IPS

- Network antivirus, antispam, and antiphishing capabilities

- Dedicated out-of-band management interfaces

For a complete listing of features, refer to http://www.cisco.com/go/asa and http://www.cisco.com/en/US/products/ps6120/prod_models_comparison.html

Choosing Between the PIX and the ASA

One of the first questions to answer when trying to determine what Cisco firewall your environment requires is what the difference between the Cisco PIX Firewall and the Cisco ASA is. The ASA is essentially the latest version of the Cisco firewall solution and is based largely on the PIX software. In fact, the Cisco ASA and enterprise versions of the PIX (PIX 515E and larger) actually run the same firewall software starting with the 7.x code base. In the case of the PIX, this firewall software is commonly known as PIX version 7.x. In the case of the ASA, this firewall software is commonly known as ASA version 7.x. Versions of software prior to 7.0 are not supported on the ASA.

The major difference between the Cisco PIX Firewall and the ASA does not lie in the firewall functionality itself, but rather in the additional features that the ASA provides in an integrated solution. Although the PIX can perform some basic IDS functions, it is really not an effective IDS solution in and of itself. The ASA addresses this PIX deficiency by incorporating a fully functional and feature-complete IPS solution as a component of the ASA. In essence, the ASA not only runs the PIX firewall software, it is also capable of running the complete Cisco IPS software to provide an integrated firewall and IPS solution. This is commonly referred to as deep packet inspection. In conjunction with the advanced IPS capabilities, the ASA also provides for content security and control for antivirus, antispam, and antiphishing (commonly referred to as anti-X) scanning through the use of the Content Security Control and Control Security Services Module

(CSC SSM). The ASA also supports Secure Sockets Layer (SSL)-based VPN connections and VPN clustering to provide for load balancing of VPN clients. Finally, the ASA tends to provide for much better performance than the PIX at a similar price point due to the fact that the ASA uses newer-generation processors and application-specific integrated circuits (ASIC) than the PIX does.

So the question of whether you should select a PIX or an ASA comes down largely to whether you need the additional functionality of the ASA, because fundamentally they both provide the exact same basic firewall functionality. If you do need the additional IPS functionality that the ASA provides, or think you will in the near future, the ASA is the appropriate choice. If you do not, the PIX firewall is the appropriate choice.

Cisco PIX Firewall and ASA Models

To implement a Cisco PIX or ASA in a given network, you need only purchase the PIX or ASA hardware and software from Cisco. Cisco PIXs come in all sizes—from small office/home office (SOHO) models to large enterprise or service provider models. The trick is to know what size PIX or ASA is appropriate for your network. In general, you can classify the PIX or ASA products into three solutions:

- SOHO solution

- Medium- to large-office solution

- Enterprise office and service provider solution

SOHO Solution

The PIX 501 is the model designed for the SOHO market and comes with a built-in four-port switch. The PIX 501 is primarily intended for offices of fewer than 10 internal users (although it can be licensed for 10, 50, or unlimited users) and for use as the termination point for a single VPN connection, typically to a central office or a small number of remote clients. The next model up is the PIX 506E, which is designed for the small office/remote office market and comes with two Fast Ethernet ports. The PIX 506E is primarily intended for offices of fewer than 100 internal users and for use as the termination point of no more than 25 VPN connections (either remote users or remote office connections). Both the PIX 501 and 506E can only run PIX software in the 6.x code branch (latest version is 6.3(5) at the time of this writing).

Medium- to Large-Office Solution

The first model designed for medium-sized to large offices is the PIX 515E. This model comes in a 1U form factor with two built-in Fast Ethernet ports and two PCI expansion slots that can accommodate additional Fast Ethernet ports or an optional VPN acceleration card (VAC) (this is standard on unrestricted, failover [active/passive] and failover [active/active] models). The PIX 515E can be used simultaneously to terminate up to 2000 VPN tunnels (either terminating connections from remote locations or remote users). The PIX 515E can also be configured to support active/active and active/passive failover and redundancy for high-availability requirements. It is difficult to quantify users that a PIX 515E can support. Instead, the performance of the PIX 515E (and larger firewalls) is quantified in throughput and concurrent connections. The PIX 515E supports a cleartext throughput of 190 Mbps and 130,000 concurrent connections.

The medium- to large-office market is also the market segment that the Cisco ASA is initially targeted at. Both the ASA 5510 and the ASA 5510 Security Plus are effective solutions. The ASA 5510 Security Plus product is essentially a software upgrade that permits more users, network interfaces, and VLANs, and that introduces high availability to the ASA 5510. The ASA 5510 supports three Fast Ethernet ports (five with the Security Plus). The ASA 5510 supports a cleartext throughput of 300 Mbps and 50,000 concurrent connections; the ASA 5510 Security Plus increased the concurrent connections to 130,000 (throughput remains the same).

Enterprise Office and Service Provider Solution

The next two models of the PIX firewall are designed specifically for large enterprises and service providers: the PIX 525 and 535. The 525 is produced in a 2U form factor and can accommodate up to ten Fast Ethernet or two Fast Ethernet and three Gigabit Ethernet interfaces. The PIX 535 also comes in a 2U form factor and can accommodate 14 Fast Ethernet or 9 Gigabit Ethernet interfaces. Both models provide all manner of high-availability functionality such as zero-downtime upgrade and VPN stateful failover as well as all the features of previous PIX models. The PIX 525 supports a cleartext throughput of 330 Mbps and 280,000 concurrent connections. The PIX 535 supports a cleartext throughput of 1.7 Gbps and 500,000 concurrent connections.

For the ASA, the ASA 5520 and 5540 were designed with the enterprise and service provider market in mind. Both build upon the basic features of the ASA 5510 and support 4 10/100/1000 and 1 10/100 interfaces. The ASA 5520 and 5540 also support a greater number of VLANs and the use of security contexts (if licensed). The ASA 5520 supports a cleartext throughput of 450 Mbps and 280,000 concurrent connections; the ASA 5540 supports a cleartext throughput of 650 Mbps and 400,000 concurrent connections.

> **NOTE**   Because of the fundamental similarities between the PIX and ASA in the context of firewall functionality, the remainder of this chapter uses the term *PIX* to refer to both PIX and ASA functionality and features for simplicities sake. In cases where there is something unique about the ASA, it will be called out individually.

How the PIX/ASA Firewall Works

> **NOTE**   With the implementation of the PIX and ASA software starting with version 7.0, many of the features and functionality of the firewall were changed dramatically. Version 7.0 was truly a major design shift. This chapter is written to include the 6.x software because, in addition to the new 7.x software, that is the version of software that most Cisco PIX firewalls are running. Where possible, we point out the new/changed features, commands and functionality that is provided via the 7.0 code. If no note specifies which version of software a command functions on, that means that the command is the exact same regardless of whether the firewall is running 6.x or 7.x software. For more detailed information about PIX 7.0 code, refer to the *Cisco ASA and PIX Firewall Handbook* (Cisco Press).

Fundamentally, the PIX/ASA firewall functions by filtering traffic that is transmitted through the firewall across the firewall interfaces. This allows the PIX/ASA to protect hosts and networks from unauthorized access while still permitting access that is deemed (and defined) by the administrator as acceptable. The firewall functionality performs these tasks by parsing a security policy, functioning in a firewall mode of operation, and performing stateful inspection of the data.

Firewall Security Policy

The firewall security policy (not to be confused with the general security policies discussed in Chapter 10, "Firewall Security Policies") on the PIX firewall is what determines the traffic that will be permitted or denied by the firewall. To facilitate this, the PIX implements a combination of the following elements to assist in making filtering decisions:

- Separate the network into zones based on security levels

- Use ACLs to permit or deny traffic

- Apply Network Address Translation (NAT)

- Apply authentication, authorization, and accounting (AAA) for through traffic

- Apply web or FTP filtering

In addition, the Cisco ASA can perform the following:

- Use the Advanced Inspection and Prevention Security Services Module (AIP SSM) to perform deep packet inspection on the data. The AIP SSM is beyond the scope of this book.

- Use the CSC SSM to perform threat protection and content control for antivirus, antispyware, antispam, antiphishing, URL blocking, content filtering, and file blocking. The CSC SSM is beyond the scope of this book.

- Apply QoS policies to give priority to certain types of network traffic. QoS is beyond the scope of this book.

Separate the Network into Zones Based on Security Levels

The PIX separates a network into separate zones based on their security level. These security levels range from 0 (completely untrusted) to 100 (completely trusted). Depending on the number of interfaces on a given PIX, there are at least two zones: 0 (outside interface) and 100 (inside interface). If there are additional interfaces on the PIX, they can be assigned a security level value from 1 to 99. Traffic from higher-security zones is allowed to pass to lower-security zones provided a translation rule is in place (the translation rule is optional for 7.x). Traffic between zones of equal security is also allowed to pass unimpeded, provided that the connections between resources have been enabled.

Use ACLs to Permit or Deny Traffic

A fundamental aspect of almost all firewalls, including the PIX and ASA, is the use of ACLs to define the list of traffic permitted or denied by the firewall. The PIX can use multiple ACLs that can be applied independently to each interface on the firewall. For PIX 6.x, the ACLs are always applied to inbound traffic on an interface. With PIX/ASA 7.x, this functionality has been expanded to allow the ACL to be applied to both inbound and outbound traffic on an interface.

It is important to understand that the concept of inbound and outbound traffic in the context of an ACL is based on the traffic direction on the given interface, not the network that the traffic may have come from. For example, it is easy to think of an outbound ACL as applying to traffic that is coming from the internal network (after all, the traffic is going out of the network). This is not correct, however. From the perspective of the firewall, that traffic would actually be *inbound* traffic on the internal network interface and would be most effectively filtered by using an ACL that is applied to inbound traffic on the internal network interface. An example of an ACL applying to outbound traffic is the traffic permitted to exit an interface to a demilitarized zone (DMZ) segment.

Apply NAT

PIX firewalls can also use NAT to facilitate the use of private IP addresses on the internal network, hide the local address of resources, and resolve IP routing problems due to overlapping IP address ranges on connected networks. NAT is typically used any time that traffic from a lower-security level interface is allowed to pass to a higher-security level interface. This implementation typically requires the use of both an address translation *and* an ACL.

The PIX uses two types of translation:

- **Static translation**—An external address is assigned on a 1:1 basis to an internal address. This is commonly referred to as traditional NAT.

- **Dynamic translation**—An external address (or address pool) is assigned to an internal address range (or ranges) and an address from that pool is dynamically assigned on a first-come, first-serve basis. If all addresses in the pool are taken then the PIX can dynamically switch to PAT, where a single external address can provide translation to multiple internal addresses by mapping TCP and UDP port numbers to unused port numbers on the translated address. In addition, PAT can be configured without a NAT address pool, allowing a single external IP address to perform all translations.

Two primary exceptions apply to this situation. First, if the hosts on the different networks are not using NAT at all, as is typically the case with VPN connections, translations are not required. Instead, the command **nat 0** *acl* is used to specify the traffic (based on the ACL) that should not be translated and rather should be directly transmitted through the firewall.

The PIX 7.x code also changes this functionality in that translations are no longer required; however, an ACL is still necessary. In this case, the traffic is either permitted or denied as determined by a corresponding ACL.

Apply AAA for Through Traffic

Certain types of traffic, in particular HTTP traffic, can also require authentication and authorization of the user attempting to initiate this traffic. This can be used to ensure that only permitted users are able to pass the traffic in question through the firewall. In addition the PIX can be configured to forward accounting information to a RADIUS or TACACS+ server for reporting of usage.

Apply Web or FTP Filtering

The PIX and ASA can perform some rudimentary filtering of web (HTTP and HTTPS) and FTP traffic by default. This functionality can be greatly enhanced through the use of third-party content-filtering systems, allowing for granular filtering and control of access to specific websites, FTP server, and many other Internet-based applications (such as instant messenger and peer-to-peer file-sharing applications). In particular the following Internet filtering products are supported for seamless integration with the PIX/ASA:

- Websense Enterprise

- Secure Computing SmartFiler (formerly Sentian by N2H2)

- CSC-SSM (although it is not as feature rich as the previous two solutions are and is really tailored more to the small/medium environment that needs basic filtering functionality)

Firewall Modes of Operation

Traditionally, PIX firewalls operated in a single mode of operation, known as routed mode. This is the most common firewall mode of implementation and treats the firewall as a router hop on the network. Devices on one side of the firewall are considered to be on different subnets than devices on the other side of the firewall.

With the advent of PIX/ASA 7.x and the ASA security devices, a new mode of operation known as transparent mode was implemented. In transparent mode, the firewall operates more like a bridge than a router, transparently allowing traffic to traverse the firewall without requiring additional router hops or manipulation of the data. Essentially, the same network exists on both sides of the firewall. Because the firewall interfaces do not have IP addresses assigned to them (at least not in the conventional sense, you still need to assign an IP address to perform remote management of the firewall), the firewall is commonly referred to as operating in stealth mode (because it is not easily detectable).

For most implementations, the firewall will be configured to operate in routed mode (and this is the default operating mode). Some notable exceptions that lend themselves to transparent mode are instances where you want a firewall that can filter traffic that would be otherwise blocked by routed mode (for example, unsupported routing protocols or multicast traffic). In addition, transparent mode firewalls can use EtherType ACLs to allow the firewall to filter some types of non-IP traffic. Transparent firewalls can also be used in situations where you do not want or need to re-IP address devices on each side of the firewall, instead of leaving them as previously configured with no additional configuration required.

Stateful Inspection

Stateful packet inspection lies at the heart of how PIX/ASA firewalls function. This functionality is provided through a process known as the Cisco adaptive security algorithm (ASA). The ASA uses a stateful approach to security. Every inbound packet is checked exhaustively against the ASA and against connection state information in memory. The ASA applies the following default rules (although this is by far not an exhaustive list) to traffic coming into the PIX:

- Allow any traffic connections that originate from the inside, higher-security, network to an external, lower-security network unless specifically denied by an ACL.

- Allow any traffic for which application inspection has been configured and the traffic has been determined to be acceptable traffic.

- Drop and log attempts to initiate connections to a translation slot (for example, a server protected by the firewall) from the outside unless there is an ACL that permits that connection.

- Drop and log source routed IP packets.

- Deny all Internet Control Message Protocol (ICMP) traffic from lower-security interfaces through the firewall except if explicitly permitted. This prevents responses to outbound ICMP traffic from being able to be successfully delivered (for example, if an external host is pinged using an ICMP echo, the result will appear to be a request timed out because the ICMP echo-reply packet will be blocked on the external interface and never reach the original source host).

- Permit all ICMP traffic to the firewall itself (this can be disabled or controlled with ICMP inspection).

- For PIX 6.x traffic may not exit the PIX firewall on the same network interface it entered. For PIX 7.x, this is a configurable option.

The ASA allows connections from a higher-security interface to a lower-security interface without an explicit configuration for each internal system and application, as shown in Figure 6-1.

Figure 6-1 *Cisco PIX ASA Operation*

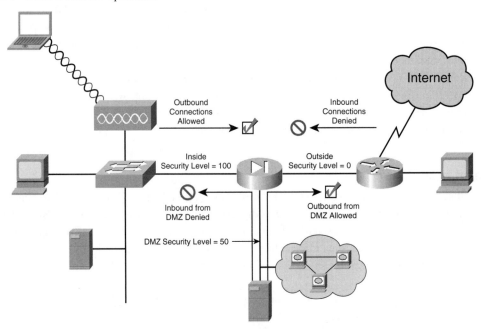

The ASA is always in operation and monitors all return packets to ensure they are valid. This is done by checking the state table to determine whether the packet in question is a response to a legitimate outbound connection. If it is, the packet is automatically permitted (this is the definition of stateful packet inspection). In addition, the ASA actively randomizes the TCP sequence numbers while ensuring that they stay within an acceptable range to minimize the risk of TCP sequence number attack.

The ASA can also perform application inspection for certain types of traffic to determine whether it should be permitted or denied.

Application Inspection

Application inspection is provided on the PIX firewall as a component of the ASA through the use of fixups or inspections. For PIX/ASA 7.0, the **fixup** command has been replaced by the use of the **policy-map** command. Functionally, the process is similar between a fixup and a policy map.

Application inspection allows the firewall to perform additional inspection of certain types of applications. In doing so, the firewall can make filtering decisions based not on the protocol in use (for example, SMTP) but on the actual application (for example, only allowing **HELO**, **MAIL**, **RCPT**, **DATA**, **RSET**, **NOOP**, and **QUIT** commands for SMTP traffic).

Application inspection is performed on the following protocols/applications (PIX/ASA versions older than 7.1 may not support all of these applications):

- **ctiqbe**—This inspection allows for Cisco IP Softphone and other Cisco Telephony Application Programming Interface/Java Telephony Application Programming Interface (TAPI/JTAPI) applications to work across the firewall.

- **dns**—This inspection allows you to define the maximum Domain Name System (DNS) length. The default value is 512, which can cause issues with some Microsoft DNS servers (http://support.microsoft.com/kb/828263).

- **esmtp**—This inspection enables you to define the commands that will be allowed for SMTP and ESMTP applications functioning across the firewall. Microsoft Exchange servers can experience problems with certain ESMTP inspection configurations (http://support.microsoft.com/?kbid=895857).

- **ftp**—This inspection will prepare secondary channels for FTP data transfer, track the FTP command-reference sequence, and generate and audit trail and NAT-embedded IP addresses.

- **gtp**—This inspection performs application inspection for the GPRS Tunneling Protocol (GTP) that is used for providing secure access over wireless networks.

- **h323**—This inspection provides support for H.323-compliant applications such as Cisco CallManager and VocalTec Gatekeeper. This allows it to NAT embed IP addresses and dynamically allocate negotiated connections over different ports than the initial connection was established.

- **http**—This inspection provides for enhanced HTTP inspection (for example, ensuring compliance with RFC 2616). It also allows the firewall to use URL screening through third-party content-filtering software such as Websense or Secure Computing. Finally, it provides for the ability to perform Java and ActiveX filtering.

- **icmp**—This inspection allows the firewall to perform stateful inspection of ICMP traffic in a manner similar to how TCP and UDP traffic are inspected (for example, by ensuring that only one response is generated for one request and that the sequence numbers used are correct). Without this command, it is recommended that ICMP traffic not be permitted through the firewall.

- **icmp error**—This inspection allows the firewall to create xlates for intermediate hops that send ICMP error message.

- **ils**—This inspection provides NAT support for Microsoft NetMeeting, SiteServer, and Active Directory products that use Lightweight Directory Access Protocol (LDAP) to communicate with an Internet Locator Server (ILS).

- **mgcp**—This inspection is used to support Call Agent and other media gateways.

- **netbios**—This inspection performs inspection of NetBIOS traffic on UDP ports 137 and 138.

- **pptp**—This inspection inspects PPTP protocol packets and dynamically creates the generic routing encapsulation (GRE) connections and xlates required to permit the PPTP traffic.

- **rsh**—This inspection allows for RSH clients and servers to negotiate port numbers for communications with each other.

- **rtsp**—This inspection allows the firewall to permit RTSP packets such as those used by RealAudio, RealNetworks, Apple QuickTime 4, RealPlayer, and Cisco IP/TV.

- **sip**—This inspection is used to allow SIP Voice over IP (VoIP) calls to function through the firewall by allowing the dynamic embryonic connections required by SIP to be created.

- **skinny**—This inspection is used to allow Skinny Client Control Protocol (SCCP) VoIP services to function through the firewall.

- **snmp**—This inspection is used to implement SNMP inspection in conjunction with the use of the **snmp-map** command. You can also use this inspection to change the ports that SNMP is listening on.

- **sqlnet**—This inspection is used to ensure that the data stream for Oracle applications is consistent on either side of the firewall and inspects the packets to determine which embedded ports need to be opened for SQL*Net Version 1.

- **sunrpc**—This inspection can be used to change the port that the firewall is listening for Sun Remote Procedure Call (RPC) traffic and allows for the creation of dynamic ports that are required for Sun RPC communications.

- **tftp**—This inspection is used to create the dynamic connections and translations required to facilitate TFTP file transfers.

- **xdmcp**—This inspection is used to allow the dynamic connections and X Window System sessions required to permit X Display Manager Control Protocol (XDMCP) communications.

Configuring the Cisco PIX/ASA

Complete configuration of the Cisco PIX is beyond the scope of this book. However, we can cover some of the initial steps required to set up the PIX and to allow an administrator access to the graphical user interface (GUI), the Adaptive Security Device Manager (ASDM) (previously known as the PIX Device Manager [PDM] for software versions previous to 7.0).

To initially configure a PIX out of the box, connect a serial connecter to the console port of the PIX (which is typically outlined with a light blue color). Use the blue serial port cable that came with the PIX. If you cannot find that cable, you may also use a null modem or a rollover cable. The serial port settings in the terminal emulation software on the PC should be as listed in Table 6-1.

Table 6-1   *Serial Port Setting for PIX Console*

Setting	Value
Baud	9600
Parity	None
Number of Bits	8
Number of Stop Bits	1

After the console connection has been established, start up the terminal emulation software (Microsoft Windows typically comes with HyperTerminal, and you can alternatively use TeraTerm Pro) with the settings in Table 6-1. The PIX command prompt should immediately appear (if not press the **Enter** button on the keyboard):

```
pixfirewall>
```

Next, type the **enable** command to access the privileged mode of execution. By default, the enable password on a new PIX is not set:

```
pixfirewall> enable
Password:
pixfirewall#
```

By default, the **enable** command assumes that the user is trying to access privilege level 15 (the highest privilege level). To begin configuring the PIX for basic network access, several actions must be performed:

- Assign IP addresses for the firewall interfaces.

- Configure the firewall name, domain name, and passwords.

- Configure the firewall routing settings.

- Configure the firewall for remote management access.

- Configure the network address translation settings for outbound access.

- Configure the ACLs.

- Configure logging on the firewall.

Assigning IP Addresses to the Firewall Interfaces

To communicate on the network, the firewall needs to have IP addresses assigned to the firewall interfaces. The process of doing this changed between PIX/ASA version 6.x and 7.x, but the fundamental steps are the same: Enable the interface, configure the interface itself, and assign an IP address to the interface.

Assigning IP Addresses in PIX 6.x

To assign IP addresses to the PIX interfaces, the administrator must enter configuration mode. Because the PIX uses a command interface that is similar to IOS, administrators enter configuration mode as they would on a Cisco IOS-based router:

```
firewall# configure terminal
firewall(config)#
```

When in configure mode, the next item is to enable the interfaces. The PIX interfaces are administratively shut down in the default configuration. To enable the interfaces, use the **interface** *hardware-id hardware-speed* command:

```
firewall(config)# interface ethernet0 auto
firewall(config)# interface ethernet1 auto
```

By default, the Ethernet0 (or FastEthernet0) hardware-id is considered the outside interface and the Ethernet1 (or FastEthernet1) hardware-id is considered the inside interface. The configuration of the interface itself is performed by the **auto** command word. This specifies that the interface speed should automatically be determined by the PIX rather than be specified by the administrator. You can also manually define the hardware speed (for example, 10 or 100).

The next step to configuring the interface is to assign a name and security level to the interface. By default, the outside interface has a security level of 0; the inside interface has a security level of 100. The name that you assign is the name that you can use throughout the configuration to easily identify a given interface. For example, this allows you to use **inside** to refer to the Ethernet1 interface. You can use the command **nameif** *hardware-id if-name security-lvl* to configure the interface name and security level:

```
firewall(config)# nameif ethernet0 outside security0
firewall(config)# nameif ethernet1 inside security100
```

With the interfaces now active and configured, the IP addresses can be assigned (it is just as possible to assign the IP addresses *prior* to enabling the interface, but the interfaces still will not work until enabled).

Assigning IP addresses is performed at the global configuration mode. The firewall supports static IP addresses on all interfaces and can also be configured to use DHCP or PPPoE-assigned addresses on the outside interface only. To assign a static IP address, use the **ip address** *interface-name ip-address subnet-mask* command:

```
firewall(config)# ip address outside 10.19.24.1 255.255.255.0
firewall(config)# ip address inside 192.168.122.1 255.255.255.0
```

To make sure that the PIX can communicate with devices on both sides, ping the address of a system on either interface:

```
firewall(config)# ping 10.19.24.100
        10.19.24.100 response received -- 0ms
        10.19.24.100 response received -- 0ms
        10.19.24.100 response received -- 0ms
firewall(config)# ping 192.168.122.226
        192.168.122.226 response received -- 0ms
        192.168.122.226 response received -- 0ms
        192.168.122.226 response received -- 0ms
firewall(config)#
```

Assigning IP Addresses in PIX/ASA 7.x

For the PIX/ASA 7.0 software, the commands that need to be run have changed, but the necessary steps are the same: Enable the interface, configure the interface itself, and assign the interface IP address. From the global configuration mode, access the interface configuration mode for the interface that you want to configure by running the **interface** *interface-name interface-number* command:

```
firewall(config)# interface ethernet 2
firewall(config-if)#
```

When you are in the interface configuration mode, you can perform all the interface configuration and IP address assignments. To enable the interface, run the **no shutdown** command. To name the interface, run the **nameif** *name* command. To assign the security level, run the **security-level** *number* command. To configure the speed and duplex settings on the interface, run the **speed** {**auto** | **10** | **100** | **1000** | **nonegotiate**} command and the **duplex** {**auto** | **full** | **half**} command. Examples of these commands follow:

```
firewall(config-if)# no shutdown
firewall(config-if)# nameif dmz01
firewall(config-if)# security-level 50
firewall(config-if)# speed auto
firewall(config-if)# duplex auto
```

Configuring the IP address is a matter of running the **ip address** *ip-address* [*mask*] or the **ip address** *dhcp* [**setroute**] command. The **setroute** option enables you to configure the firewall to use the route assigned by the DHCP server as the default route for the firewall. Unlike previous versions of software, PPPoE is no longer supported, and DHCP addresses can be assigned to any interface (not just the outside interface). In most cases, you need to assign a static IP address, as shown here:

```
firewall(config-if)# ip address 10.21.67.17 255.255.255.240
```

Repeat these commands for all interfaces that need to be configured.

> **NOTE**   Like most Cisco devices, changing the configuration only changes the running configuration. For the changes to be considered permanent and committed to memory, they must be saved to NVRAM. For PIX software running 6.x and earlier, this is done by running the **write memory** command at the privileged mode of execution:
>
> ```
> firewall# write memory
> ```
>
> For PIX/ASA software running 7.x and newer, this is done by running the **copy running-config startup-config command:**
>
> ```
> firewall# copy running-config startup-config
> ```
>
> You need to do this anytime you are finished running commands and are ready for the firewall configuration to be made permanent.

Configuring the Firewall Name, Domain Name, and Passwords

Now that the firewall has been assigned IP addresses and the interfaces are functioning properly the next step is to configure some basic firewall configuration values such as the firewall host name, domain name, and passwords. The commands to perform these configurations are the same for all versions of the PIX/ASA software. You can configure the host name by running the **hostname** *name* command, and the domain name is configured by running the **domain-name** *domain* command from the global configuration mode:

```
firewall(config)# hostname houqepixfw01
houqepixfw01(config)# domain-name houqe.lab
```

There are two passwords that the PIX/ASA uses by default (and you are not using any form of AAA authentication). The first is known as the login password and is used to authenticate remote access via Telnet or SSH. The command to set the login password is **passwd** *password:*

```
houqepixfw01(config)# passwd ReallyDifficultPassword
```

The second is known as the enable password and is used to access the global configuration mode and to provide ASDM/PDM access. The command to set the enable password is **enable password** *password* level *level* and is shown here. The **level** syntax is not required, and if left blank defaults to privilege level 15. You can set multiple passwords, each granting access to a different privilege level.

```
houqepixfw01(config)# enable password DifferentPasswordThanPasswd
```

At this point, the firewall is able to authenticate administrative access and remote management access connections (although it still needs to be configured to allow remote management access).

Configuring the Firewall Routing Settings

With IP connectivity established, the next step is to configure routing for the firewall. The firewall supports both static routes and dynamic routing using Open Shortest Path First (OSPF; for more information about configuring OSPF routing, see *Cisco ASA and PIX Firewall Handbook* [Cisco Press]). You can configure static routes on all software versions by running the **route** *interface-name ip-address netmask gateway-ip* [*metric | tunneled*] command. This same command can be used to set the default route for the PIX as follows:

```
houqepixfw01(config)# route outside 0.0.0.0 0.0.0.0 10.21.67.2 1
```

The value **1** at the end of the **route** command specifies the metric to the next hop and is optional. In general, the default route will point to the next-hop router for the firewall on the internet, for example pointing to the Internet service provider router.

Configuring the Firewall for Remote Management Access

The PIX/ASA firewall supports three primary methods of remote management access:

- Telnet

- SSH

- ASDM/PDM

Both Telnet and SSH are used to provide CLI access to the firewall, whereas the ASDM/PDM provides an HTTPS-based GUI management console.

Configuring Telnet Access

Telnet remote management is the simplest, yet least secure, method of remotely managing the firewall. The reason for this is that Telnet does not encrypt the data in transmit and in fact sends the data in cleartext. This makes it easy for a malicious user to capture the data and learn things like the usernames and passwords required to gain access to the firewall. Because of this deficiency, it is not possible to access a PIX/ASA firewall over the outside interface using Telnet alone (although PIX/ASA does support Telnet to the outside interface if it is protected by IPsec).

The configuration to allow Telnet access is the same for all PIX/ASA software versions. This is done by running the **telnet** {*hostname | ip-address mask interface-name*} command at the global configuration mode:

```
houqepixfw01(config)# telnet 10.21.120.15 255.255.255.255 inside
```

You can restrict Telnet access to certain IP addresses or hosts by defining the appropriate subnet mask. For example, in the preceding command, only the host with IP address 10.21.120.15 is allowed to connect to the firewall. You can also define the interface that the Telnet access will be permitted to by using the appropriate interface name (for example, inside or dmz01, if you named an interface dmz01).

Because of the general insecurity of Telnet, and because SSH provides the same functionality to the firewall, use SSH instead of Telnet.

Configuring SSH Access

Configuring SSH is a little more involved than configuring Telnet access because for a connection to be established using SSH the target host needs to have an RSA key pair for identity certificates. Therefore, configuring SSH access is actually a series of smaller steps that must be performed:

Step 1   Assign a host and domain name to the firewall.

Step 2   Generate and save the RSA key pair.

Step 3   Configure the firewall to allow SSH access.

The procedure for assigning the host and domain name for the firewall was covered previously in this chapter. The reason why it is important to do this is that the RSA key pairs use the host and domain name in the key-generation process.

Generating and saving the RSA key pair is performed in one of two methods depending on whether you are using PIX 6.x or PIX/ASA 7.0. For PIX 6.0, you can generate the RSA key pair by running the **ca generate rsa key** *key-size* command from the global configuration mode:

```
houqepixfw02(config)# ca generate rsa key 1024
For <key_modulus_size> >= 1024, key generation could
  take up to several minutes. Please wait.
Keypair generation process begin.
.Success.
houqepixfw02(config)#
```

One of the bigger deficiencies of the PIX 6.x software is that, unlike every other configuration setting, the RSA keys are not saved when you issue the **write memory** command. Instead, they need to be saved separately using the **ca save all** command from the global configuration mode:

```
houqepixfw02(config)# ca save all
```

For the PIX/ASA 7.x software, generating the RSA keys requires the use of the following command:

```
crypto key generate rsa [usage-keys | general-keys] [label key-pair-label]
    [modulus size] [noconfirm]
```

As a general rule, the only syntax required is the following:

```
houqepixfw01(config)# crypto key generate rsa modulus 1024
INFO: The name for the keys will be: <Default-RSA-Key>
Keypair generation process begin. Please wait...
houqepixfw01(config)#
```

You can specify a modulus size of 512, 768, 1024 (the default size), or 2048. Unlike previous software versions, the RSA keys are saved when you save the firewall configuration (for example, by running the command **copy running-config startup-config**).

After the RSA keys have been generated, the step to actually permit SSH access to the firewall is the same for all software versions and is similar to how Telnet access is permitted. Just run the command **ssh** *ip-address mask interface* command:

```
houqepixfw01(config)# ssh 10.21.120.15 255.255.255.255 inside
```

Like Telnet, SSH can be restricted to subnets or hosts. Unlike Telnet, SSH can also be configured for remote access to the outside interface.

PIX/ASA 7.x also supports running SSHv1 or SSHv2 (previous software versions supported a variant of SSHv1 1 known as version 1.5). In general, SSHv2 is considered more secure, and the firewall can be restricted to only supporting SSHv2 by running the **ssh version 2** command.

Configuring ASDM/PDM Access

In addition to the CLI management methods, PIX/ASA firewalls support a GUI for remote management. For PIX 6.x, this management interface is known as the PIX Device Manager (PDM). For PIX/ASA 7.x, this management interface is known as the Adaptive Security Device Manager (ASDM). Both are extremely similar to each other, with the ASDM being the logical upgrade and replacement for the PDM. The ASDM/PDM functions as a web-based management interface using a small web server running on the firewall and Java plug-ins on the client computer to function. Configuring the ASDM/PDM requires a couple of steps that are the same for all software versions. First, you must ensure that you have downloaded and installed the ASDM/PDM software on the firewall (by default, it is included with the firewall). Second, you need to enable the HTTP server on the firewall by running the **http server enable** command. Third, you need to permit HTTP access in a manner similar to Telnet and SSH by running the **http** *ip-address mask* command:

```
houqepixfw02(config)# http server enable
houqepixfw02(config)# http 10.0.0.0 255.0.0.0 inside
```

Historically, access to the ASDM/PDM is performed by connecting to the web server using a web browser such as Microsoft Internet Explorer. The ASDM also can use a Java-based application that allows you to launch ASDM without needing to start a web browser, as shown in Figure 6-2.

Figure 6-2 *Cisco ASDM Launcher*

Just enter the IP address or host name of the firewall and the appropriate username and password. If you do not use any form of AAA, leave the username blank and enter the enable password to connect to the firewall. The ASDM will parse the running configuration of the firewall and display the General Device Information screen, as shown in Figure 6-3. The ASDM is an intuitive GUI interface that you can use to configure the firewall in lieu of the CLI.

Figure 6-3 *General Device Information Screen*

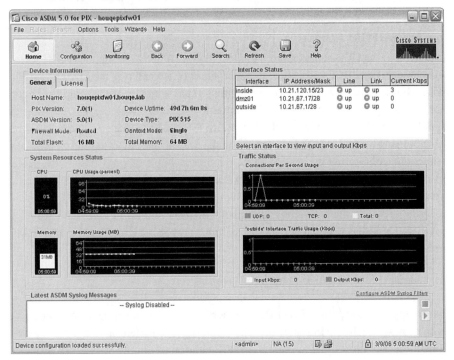

Configuring NAT Settings for Outbound Access

After the default route has been set, the PIX/ASA is almost ready to pass traffic between the inside, higher-security interface and the outside, lower-security interface. In most situations, to provide for this outbound traffic functionality you need to configure NAT because the firewall will typically be hiding the internal network IP addresses from the external network resources using NAT. This is not a requirement, however (although it is generally recommended), and the PIX/ASA 7.0 in particular does not require NAT for outbound communications. The configuration (or lack thereof) for NAT differs depending on whether you are using PIX 6.x or PIX/ASA 7.0.

Configuring NAT for PIX 6.x

Outbound access for the PIX firewall generally requires the configuration of two policies. First, define the translation method that is going to be used for the outbound requests. Second, ensure that if an ACL exists for the given network interface that an access rule is defined to allow the traffic in question. By default, the PIX firewall allows all traffic from a higher-security interface to a lower-security interface, by virtue of the fact that there is not a default ACL on any interface.

There are two primary methods of performing translation: a static translation or a dynamic translation. Static translations are essentially a one to one mapping of internal addresses to external addresses. Therefore, they require that the internal address not change and consequently do not tend to be an effective method of providing outside access to a bunch of hosts. Instead, they tend to be used in conjunction with ACLs to provide access to internal resources from external sources (we address this configuration later in this chapter).

Dynamic translation uses NAT/PAT to dynamically assign addresses (or ports) to internal hosts that require external access. The firewall keeps track of which communications sessions belong to each internal host and allows the firewall to perform the required translations.

To configure dynamic NAT, you need to build a NAT rule. The simplest way to do this is to specify what traffic is to be translated using the **nat** command and then set up a global pool using the **global** command. The **nat** command is used to define what local addresses will be included for NAT. The syntax of the command is this:

```
nat [(local-interface)] id local-ip [mask [dns] [outside | [norandomseq]
    [max_conns [emb_limit]]]
```

The *id* and *local-ip* syntax are used to define the local IP addresses that will be included in the corresponding NAT translation (defined by the ID). A notable exception to this is the **nat 0 access-list** *acl-name* command, which configures the firewall to *not* use NAT for any addresses that match the corresponding ACL. This is typically used for access across VPN connections. In most other cases, you would define the NAT addresses as follows:

```
houqepixfw02(config)# nat (inside)1 0.0.0.0 0.0.0.0
```

In this case, we have specified to use NAT for all addresses. If we only wanted NAT to be used for addresses on the 10.1.1.0/24 subnet, we could have replaced the *local-ip* and *mask* with 10.1.1.0 and 255.255.255.0. After you have defined what local addresses should use NAT, the next step is to configure the global pool.

The **global** command is used to define the pool of global addresses that will be used by the translation rule. The easiest way to think of the global addresses is that these are the external addresses that the internal clients will appear to be coming from when they access external resources. You can specify one or more global addresses in the pool. If you specify a single address instead of performing NAT, the firewall will automatically perform PAT instead. The syntax of the command is this:

```
global [(if-name)] nat-id {global-ip [-global-ip] [netmask global-mask]} | interface
```

The **interface** syntax can be used to specify to use the interface IP address for PAT instead of defining an additional IP address for the global pool. This is particularly useful in cases where there is a single address available for use (for example, when using a PIX firewall in a SOHO environment over a broadband connection such as digital subscriber line [DSL] or cable modem). The following command configures a global pool on an outside interface to use addresses 10.21.67.40/28-10.21.67.45/28:

```
houqepixfw02(config)# global (outside)1 10.21.67.40-10.21.67.45 netmask
   255.255.255.240
```

When all the IP addresses are being used by NAT, the firewall will automatically switch to using PAT (assuming that a PAT statement has been configured) to allow more addresses out. Alternatively, if you only have the IP address that is assigned to the interface, you can simplify the global command as follows:

```
houqepixfw02(oonfig)# global (outside)1 interface
outside interface address added to PAT pool
houqepixfw02(config)#
```

Assuming that there is not an ACL that needs to be configured, the hosts defined by the NAT translation rule will have outbound access.

Configuring NAT for PIX/ASA 7.x

A major difference between the PIX/ASA 7.x software and previous versions is that by default the firewall does not require NAT and will allow outbound access with no additional configuration required. Of course, if your environment requires NAT (which most Internet-connected firewalls require), you must execute the appropriate NAT configuration commands on the firewall.

To require NAT for communications, you must first run the **nat-control** command (no additional syntax). When NAT control is disabled (the default), the firewall allows communications with outside hosts without the configuration of a NAT rule. When NAT control has been enabled, the next step is to run the **nat** and **global** commands. For the PIX/ASA 7.x, the **nat** and **global** syntax differs slightly:

```
nat (real-ifc) nat-id real-ip [mask [dns] [outside] [[tcp] tcp-max-conns
   [emb-limit]] [udp udp-max-conns] [norandomseq]]
global (mapped-ifc) nat-id {mapped-ip[-mapped-ip] [netmask mask] I interface}
```

In this particular case, however, the actual commands are the exact same command syntax for previous versions of software. Therefore, running all three commands might look like this:

```
houqepixfw01(config)# nat-control
houqepixfw01(config)# nat (inside)1 0.0.0.0 0.0.0.0
houqepixfw01(config)# global (outside)1 10.21.67.10-10.21.67.14 netmask
   255.255.255.240
```

In this case, NAT control is enabled, a NAT pool for all internal addresses is configured, and a global pool from 10.21.67.10 through 10.21.67.14 is configured. At this point, internal hosts can access external resources using NAT.

Alternatively, if you only have the IP address that is assigned to the interface, you can simplify the global command as follows:

```
houqepixfw01(config)# global (outside)1 interface
INFO: outside interface address added to PAT pool
houqepixfw01(config)#
```

Configuring the ACLs

Controlling traffic is the cornerstone of all firewalls, and the PIX/ASA controls the flow of traffic through the firewall by implementing ACLs. PIX/ASA ACLs are essentially linked lists of values known as ACL entries (ACEs) that are parsed in a top-down manner with entries at the top of the ACL being processed before entrees further down the ACL are processed. This processing is performed in a first-match manner, which means that as soon as the data being processed by an ACL is matched to an ACE, the ACL stops being parsed and the action defined in the matching ACE is performed. Therefore, ensure that when you build your ACLs you place entries to permit traffic ahead of entries that deny traffic; otherwise, as soon as the data matches an ACE that denies the traffic, the traffic will be blocked, and the ACE that permits the traffic will never be processed.

The configuration and implementation of ACLs is a two-step process:

1. Define the ACL and implement the ACEs.

2. Assign the ACL to an interface.

Defining the ACL and Implementing the ACEs

The PIX/ASA supports a number of different types of ACLs:

- **Access list EtherType**—This ACL is used to filter traffic based on the EtherType value.

- **Access list extended**—This is the most commonly implemented type of ACL and is used for general-purpose filtering of TCP/IP-based traffic.

- **Access list standard**—This ACL is used to identify the destination IP addresses that will be used in a route map for OSPF route redistribution.

- **Access list webtype**—This ACL is used for WebVPN filtering and is only supported on PIX/ASA 7.1 and newer.

You can configure multiple types of ACLs on a PIX firewall and define multiple ACLs of the same type. Doing so enables you to define purpose-based ACLs. A purpose-based ACL means that the ACL is defined for a given purpose and the ACEs in the ACL have been written explicitly for that purpose. Doing so enables you to use different ACLs to control and filter traffic in multiple situations. For example, you might build one ACL to control traffic coming from the Internet to a DMZ segment and then build another ACL with different ACEs to control traffic coming from the DMZ to the internal network.

Building an ACL is a pretty straightforward procedure that typically requires defining the following elements:

- What action should be taken for traffic that matches the ACE in the ACL?

- What protocol is being used?

- What is the source for the traffic?

- What is the destination for the traffic?

- What application port/ports are being used?

ACLs are built on all software versions by running the **access-list** command with the appropriate parameters. Table 6-2 shows the parameters available for an extended ACL.

Table 6-2   *access-list Parameters*

Parameter	Description
default	(Optional) Sets logging to the default method, which is to send system log message 106023 for each denied packet.
deny	Denies a packet if the conditions are matched. In the case of network access (the **access-group** command), this keyword prevents the packet from passing through the security appliance. In the case of applying application inspection to a class map (the **class-map** and **inspect** commands), this keyword exempts the traffic from inspection. Some features do not allow deny ACEs to be used, such as NAT. See the command documentation for each feature that uses an ACL for more information.

Table 6-2   *access-list Parameters (Continued)*

Parameter	Description
dest_ip	Specifies the IP address of the network or host to which the packet is being sent. Enter the **host** keyword before the IP address to specify a single address. In this case, do not enter a mask. Enter the **any** keyword instead of the address and mask to specify any address.
disable	(Optional) Disables logging for this ACE.
icmp_type	(Optional) If the protocol is **icmp**, specifies the ICMP type.
id	Specifies the ACL ID, as a string or integer up to 241 characters in length. The ID is case sensitive. Tip: Use all capital letters so you can see the ACL ID better in your configuration.
inactive	(Optional) Disables an ACE. To reenable it, enter the entire ACE without the **inactive** keyword. This feature lets you keep a record of an inactive ACE in your configuration to make reenabling easier.
interface *ifc_name*	Specifies the interface address as the source or destination address.
interval *secs*	(Optional) Specifies the log interval at which to generate a 106100 system log message. Valid values are from 1 to 600 seconds. The default is 300.
level	(Optional) Sets the 106100 system log message level from 0 to 7. The default level is 6.
line *line-num*	(Optional) Specifies the line number at which to insert the ACE. If you do not specify a line number, the ACE is added to the end of the ACL. The line number is not saved in the configuration; it only specifies where to insert the ACE.
log	(Optional) Sets logging options when a deny ACE matches a packet for network access (an ACL applied with the **access-group** command). If you enter the **log** keyword without any arguments, you enable system log message 106100 at the default level (6) and for the default interval (300 seconds). If you do not enter the **log** keyword, the default logging occurs, using system log message 106023.
mask	The subnet mask for the IP address. When you specify a network mask, the method is different from the Cisco IOS Software **access-list** command. The security appliance uses a network mask (for example, 255.255.255.0 for a Class C mask). The Cisco IOS mask uses wildcard bits (for example, 0.0.0.255).
object-group *icmp_type_obj_grp_id*	(Optional) If the protocol is **icmp**, specifies the identifier of an ICMP-type object group. See the **object-group icmp-type** command to add an object group.
object-group *network_obj_grp_id*	Specifies the identifier of an network object group. See the **object-group network** command to add an object group.

continues

Table 6-2   *access-list Parameters (Continued)*

Parameter	Description
object-group *protocol_obj_grp_id*	Specifies the identifier of a protocol object group. See the **object-group protocol** command to add an object group.
object-group *service_obj_grp_id*	(Optional) If you set the protocol to **tcp** or **udp**, specifies the identifier of a service object group. See the **object-group service** command to add an object group.
operator	(Optional) Matches the port numbers used by the source or destination. The permitted operators are as follows: • **lt** (less than) • **gt** (greater than) • **eq** (equal to) • **neq** (not equal to) • **range** (an inclusive range of values. When you use this operator, specify two port numbers, for example, **range 100 200**.)
permit	Permits a packet if the conditions are matched. In the case of network access (the **access-group** command), this keyword lets the packet pass through the security appliance. In the case of applying application inspection to a class map (the **class-map** and **inspect** commands), this keyword applies inspection to the packet.
port	(Optional) If you set the protocol to **tcp** or **udp**, specifies the integer or name of a TCP or UDP port. DNS, Discard, Echo, Ident, NTP, RPC, SUNRPC, and Talk each require one definition for TCP and one for UDP. TACACS+ requires one definition for port 49 on TCP.
protocol	Specifies the IP protocol name or number. For example, UDP is 17, TCP is 6, and EGP is 47.
src_ip	Specifies the IP address of the network or host from which the packet is being sent. Enter the **host** keyword before the IP address to specify a single address. In this case, do not enter a mask. Enter the **any** keyword instead of the address and mask to specify any address.
time-range *time_range_name*	(Optional) Schedules each ACE to be activated at specific times of the day and week by applying a time range to the ACE. See the **time-range** command for information about defining a time range.

The syntax that the parameters are input in an extended ACL is as follows:

```
access-list id [line line-number] [extended] {deny | permit} {protocol |
    object-group protocol_obj_grp_id} {src_ip mask | interface ifc_name |
    object-group network_obj_grp_id} [operator port | object-group
    service_obj_grp_id] {dest_ip mask | interface ifc_name | object-group
    network_obj_grp_id} [operator port | object-group service_obj_grp_id |
    object-group icmp_type_obj_grp_id] [log [[level] [interval secs] | disable
    | default]] [inactive | time-range time_range_name]
```

Although this may seem like a lot of information, many of the values are optional and not necessary in most cases. Most **access-list** entries use an abbreviated syntax:

```
access-list id {deny | permit} protocol source destination operator port
```

For example, if you wanted to define an **access-list** entry to permit HTTP traffic from any host to a web server, you would run the following command:

```
houqepixfw01(config)# access-list out_in_01 permit tcp any host 10.21.67.2 eq http
```

In this example, we defined an ACL ID of "out_in_01" and configured it to permit TCP port 80 (HTTP) from any source to the destination 10.21.67.2. If you want the same ACL to also permit SMTP traffic to a different server, run the following command:

```
houqepixfw01(config)# access-list out_in_01 permit tcp any host 10.21.67.3 eq smtp
```

You can view the ACL to see that both lines have been added to the same ACL by running the following command (the implicit deny ip any any rule at the end of all ACLs is not shown, which is a good reason to explicitly add it to all ACLs):

```
houqepixfw01(config)# show access-list out_in_01
access-list out_in_01; 2 elements
access-list out_in_01 line 1 extended permit tcp any host 10.21.67.2 eq www (hitcnt=0)
access-list out_in_01 line 2 extended permit tcp any host 10.21.67.3 eq smtp (hitcnt=0)
```

The hitcnt value displays whether any packets have matched the ACE, which can assist in troubleshooting connectivity through the firewall. For example, if you do not see the hitcnt value increasing when traffic that is supposed to be matching the ACL is being transmitted, it might mean that the ACL is misconfigured. A common example of that happening would be accidentally specifying the wrong protocol for the ACL (for example, using TCP when you should have used UDP).

After the ACL has been defined, the firewall still is not using the ACL. For that to occur, you must assign the ACL to an interface.

Assigning the ACL to an Interface

Fundamentally, there are two methods of filtering traffic: ingress filtering and egress filtering. Ingress filtering defines filtering traffic that is coming into a trusted network from an untrusted network. Egress filtering defines filtering traffic that is coming from a trusted network to an untrusted network.

For PIX software version 6.x and below, all ACLs were applied to traffic coming into an interface. So, for example, if you wanted to apply an ACL for traffic coming from the internet to a DMZ segment, you would apply the ACL to the outside interface of the firewall, thus allowing it to filter traffic coming into the firewall on the outside interface. This would be an example of an ingress filter. To build an egress filter (for example, to filter traffic from the inside network to the outside network), you would apply the appropriate ACL to the inside interface.

With the PIX/ASA software 7.x and above, the concept of applying ACLs became a little bit more complex, but at the same time more flexible. Rather than only being able to apply an ACL to inbound traffic on a given interface, with the 7.x software you can apply an ACL to an interface and define whether it applies to traffic entering the interface (in) or exiting the interface (out). This flexibility allows you to do things such as define an egress filter and apply it to outbound traffic on the outside interface.

Regardless of which software the firewall is running, ACLs are applied to an interface by running the **access-group** command. The only real difference between 6.x and 7.x is the ability to specify in or out in the syntax as follows:

```
access-group access-list {in | out} interface interface-name [per-user-override]
```

For example, if you want to apply the ACL that was previously defined (ACL out_in_01) to the outside interface on the firewall, you run the following command:

```
houqepixfw01(config)# access-group out_in_01 in interface outside
```

At this point, assuming that you have your translation rules configured accordingly, the traffic that has been permitted or denied in the ACL out_in_01 will be filtered on the outside interface accordingly.

Configuring Logging on the Firewall

One of the most valuable capabilities of any firewall is the ability to log events so that the administrator can be informed of and aware of what is going on with the firewall. Cisco PIX/ASA firewalls use syslog for the logging of all events on the firewall (syslog and logging in general is discussed in much greater detail in Chapter 12, "What Is My Firewall Telling Me?"), which allows an administrator to be able to read/parse the logs for important events or events that may require additional action (for example, events that indicate a misconfiguration of the firewall may be occurring).

In general, PIX/ASA firewalls support the following commonly used logging destinations:

- Console

- Monitor (Telnet and SSH sessions)

■   ASDM (PIX/ASA 7.x only)

■   Remote syslog server

Regardless of the logging method implemented, it is important to ensure that the firewall has the correct date and time (either by manually entering the date and time or using NTP to automatically configure the date and time) to ensure that the logs can be easily interpreted. For more information about configuring the date and time on PIX/ASA firewalls, see the *Cisco ASA and PIX Firewall Handbook* (Cisco Press).

Configuring Console, Monitor, or ASDM Logging

Console, monitor, and ASDM logging all function in a similar manner in that they are all designed to output the logging results to the management interface (the CLI in the case of console and monitor logging or the ASDM GUI in the case of ASDM logging). Consequently, they all use similar variations of the **logging** command. Before you can enable any particular method of logging, the first step is to enable logging in general on the firewall by running the command **logging on** from the global configuration mode of execution. This command is the same command for all versions of PIX/ASA software.

To enable console logging run the command **logging console** [*logging-list* | *level*]. The *logging-list* syntax enables you to refer to a list of defined logging level, event class, and message IDs that have been previously defined by the **logging list** *name* {**level** *level* [**class** *event-class*] | **message** *start-id*[*-end-id*]} command. The level syntax defines the maximum level of system log messages to log. For example, if you want to log debug level and below, you run the following commands:

```
houqepixfw01(config)# logging on
houqepixfw01(config)# logging console debug
%PIX-5-111008: User 'enable_15' executed the 'logging console debug' command.
%PIX-3-710003: UDP access denied by ACL from 10.21.120.178/137 to
inside:10.21.121.255/137
```

This command causes the firewall to display all log messages to the console session of the firewall. If you are using Telnet or SSH to connect to the firewall and you want to have the log messages display in the Telnet or SSH session, run the **logging monitor** [*logging-list* | *level*] command. This causes the firewall to log all messages to Telnet or SSH sessions, but they will not actually be displayed to the active Telnet or SSH session until you also run the command **terminal monitor.** Terminal monitor enables the display of the syslog messages to the current Telnet or SSH session. For example, if you want to log debug level and below and display the syslog messages on the current SSH session, run the following commands:

```
houqepixfw01(config)# logging on
houqepixfw01(config)# logging monitor debug
houqepixfw01(config)# terminal monitor
%PIX-5-111008: User 'enable_15' executed the 'terminal monitor' command.
```

```
%PIX-3-710003: UDP access denied by ACL from 10.21.120.178/137 to
    inside:10.21.121.255/137
```

You can stop the display of syslog messages, while still having the firewall perform monitor logging, by running the command **terminal no monitor**. These commands are the same for all versions of the PIX/ASA software.

> **CAUTION** Although logging at debug level can assist in troubleshooting a problem, it should be strongly cautioned before implementing on a production firewall (because of the volume of data that will be logged). Debug logging can cause events to be lost from the logging buffer due to volume of data and in extreme circumstances can have a negative impact on the performance of the firewall due to the amount of logging messages. In some cases, the only method of recovering from logging debug messages is to reboot the firewall.

You can configure ASDM logging either at the CLI using the **logging asdm** [*logging-list | level*] command or through the ASDM interface. To use the ASDM, you need to launch the ASDM and login to the firewall. When you are at the default home screen, as shown in Figure 6-3, click the **Configuration** button in the toolbar. In the Features pane, click the **Properties** button and then navigate through the feature tree to select **Logging Filters**, as shown in Figure 6-4.

Figure 6-4 *Logging Filters Screen*

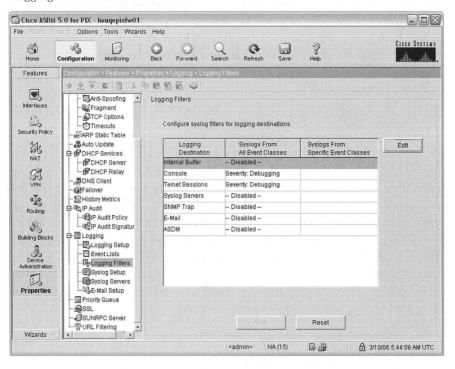

Figure 6-5 *Edit Logging Filters Screen*

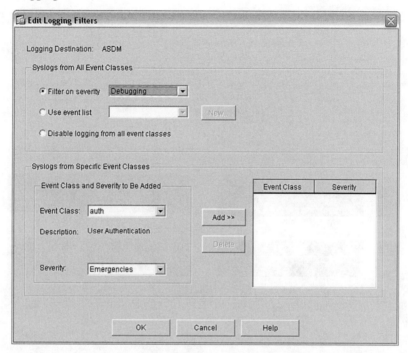

As you can see, the previous commands we ran are shown in this screen, and you can edit or change any of the depicted logging settings. To enable ASDM logging, click **ASDM** and then click the **Edit** button to display the Edit Logging Filters screen, as shown in Figure 6-5. Click the **Filter on severity** button and select the appropriate severity level from the drop-down list (in this case, **Debugging** was selected). When you have finished, click **OK.**

The last step is to save the configuration changes to the firewall to cause the firewall to use the updated configuration. You can do that by clicking **Apply** in the Logging Filters Screen shown in Figure 6-4. If you return to the home screen (by clicking the **Home** button in the taskbar), you will now see the syslog messages being displayed in the ASDM interface in the Latest ASDM Syslog Messages group box, as shown in Figure 6-6.

Figure 6-6 *ASDM Log Messages*

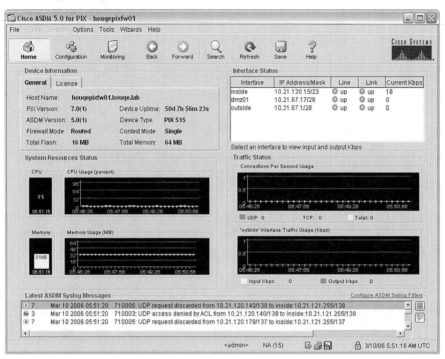

Configuring Logging to a Remote Syslog Server

Although logging to the console, monitor or ASDM can be handy for troubleshooting problems and viewing log messages while logged in to the firewall, if you need to store logs for long-term archive or auditing purposes, you need to configure the firewall to transmit the syslog messages to a remote syslog server. Like the previous logging methods, you must first enable logging in general by running the **logging on** command. Then, you need to define what syslog server the firewall should transmit the syslog messages to by running the **logging host** *interface-name syslog-ip* [**tcp**/*port* | **udp**/*port*] [**format emblem**] command. At a minimum, you need to define the interface that the syslog server is connected to (typically the inside interface) and the IP address of the syslog server. After you have done this, you need to define the level of syslog messages that will be logged by running the **logging trap** [*logging-list* | *level*] command. For example, if you want to transmit syslog messages to the syslog server running on 10.21.120.10 and you want to transmit logging levels errors or above, you run the following commands:

```
houqepixfw01(config)# logging host inside 10.21.120.10
houqepixfw01(config)# logging trap errors
```

At this point, the firewall will transmit the syslog messages to the syslog server (in this case, using the default port UDP 514).

PIX/ASA Checklist

As with configuring any firewall, administrators should develop a checklist that they can use during the installation and implementation of the PIX/ASA firewall in the network. There are really two components to this checklist. First, you want to define the implementation requirements and determine how the firewall should be configured and what options will be enabled. In essence, design and plan your firewall implementation before you configure and implement the firewall. To help with the planning of your PIX/ASA firewall implementation, consider the following items (although not an exhaustive list, it is a good basic checklist for many environments):

- Determine how many interfaces will be required.

- Determine how the interfaces will need to be configured (for example, interface speed and duplex).

- Determine the IP addresses that will be assigned to the firewall interfaces and how the addresses will be assigned (for example, static IP addresses or DHCP configuration).

- Determine what type of routing will be used (dynamic or static) and define any static and default routes.

- Determine how NAT will be used (for example, static, dynamic, no NAT at all, or any combination of the three).

- Define which internal hosts will need to be accessed from the outside, and whether that access will be handled by static NAT or without NAT.

- Define which ACLs (both inbound and outbound) will be required.

- Define how authentication and command authorization on the PIX will be handled (for example, will a AAA server be required?).

- Define the firewall administrator roles and the corresponding access levels that will be required.

- Will remote-access or LAN-to-LAN VPNs be configured on the PIX/ASA? If so, define the VPN configuration settings.

- Define the passwords that will be used on the firewall.

- Define how the PIX will be managed (for example, using Telnet, SSH, ASDM) and from what networks or hosts remote access will be permitted.

- Define how logging will be handled (for example, will the PIX/ASA log to a remote syslog server?).

After you have completed your planning and defined the requirements and determined how the firewall should be configured and what options will be enabled, the second step of the PIX/ASA checklist is to list out the specific configuration steps required to configure the firewall. Whereas the preceding checklist focused on the planning and design, this checklist uses that information to define what actually needs to be done for the actual firewall configuration. A good configuration checklist for the PIX/ASA firewall consists of the following:

1. Configure the firewall interfaces.

2. Configure the firewall passwords.

3. Configure the firewall name and domain name.

4. Assign addresses to the firewall interfaces.

5. Configure the appropriate routing.

6. Configure the appropriate remote management settings.

7. Configure AAA as required.

8. Configure the firewall time settings

9. Configure the appropriate logging settings.

10. If required, configure NAT and any other translations.

11. Build and implement the appropriate ACLs and apply them to the appropriate interfaces in the appropriate direction.

12. Configure application inspection.

13. Configure advanced features such as failover, VPN, or IPS.

14. If the firewall is an ASA, configure the advanced antivirus, antispyware, and antiphishing settings.

Summary

This chapter provided a brief overview of the workings and capabilities of the Cisco PIX and ASA firewalls. Both firewalls provide stateful packet inspection as well as deep packet-inspection firewall capabilities in models designed to protect environments from the SOHO to the largest of enterprises and service providers. With the implementation of many of the features that the 7.x firewall software provides, the PIX/ASA can meet the security needs of virtually any environment or organization. The PIX has a long and distinguished history in the firewall marketplace, and although the ASA is newer, it builds upon the PIX history and functionality, allowing either firewall to be implemented as the cornerstone of an organization's network security architecture.

## CHAPTER 7

Linux-Based Firewalls

Linux-based firewalls come in a variety of flavors. Originally, Linux-based firewalls were based on the *ipfw* code (which itself was taken from the Berkeley Software Distribution [BSD] of UNIX). This code comprised the original version of firewall capabilities within the Linux kernel. The next evolutionary step beyond ipfw was the ipfwadm utility (which was actually a rewrite of BSD's ipfw utility). This firewall code and utility began to be available in Linux kernels in the 1.0 series and provided significant flexibility by allowing the administrator to do the following:

- Change the default policies for all firewall categories

- Automatically add the necessary extra rules when the named hosts have more than one IP address

- List and reset packet/byte counters atomically for setting up a reliable accounting scheme

- List the existing rules in a number of formats

Additionally, the ipfwadm utility provided support for the following:

- Specifying the interface address and/or name for the rules.

- Bidirectional rules, TCP ACK, and TCP SYN matching

- Packet redirection (used for transparent proxying)

- Masquerading

With the release of Linux kernel 2.2, a new filtering system came into place, *ipchains*. The ipchains filter was an expansion of the ipfwadm capabilities as well as a significant rewrite of the underlying filter code. Like the ipfwadm firewalls, ipchains firewalls are not stateful and must be configured to accept TCP packets with the ACK bit set to allow for return traffic from a remote server. As a result, ipchains-based firewalls rely on the packet itself to determine whether it is part of an existing connection. This is inherently a less-secure method because packets can easily be forged to bypass such filtering.

The Linux 2.4 kernel series witnessed another, more extensive rewrite of the Linux filtering and firewall capabilities, NetFilter. However, this rewrite resulted in a more mature stateful firewall with more powerful inspection and logging capabilities. An advantage this provides is the fact that Linux firewalls are inexpensive to put together because they can be installed on commodity hardware and there is a great deal of support in the open source community for them. Some companies have even begun to package Linux-based firewalls in a commercial format and provide commercial technical support for the product.

This chapter provides an overview of how NetFilter and its utility, iptables, work.

NetFilter Features

You can find some of the key NetFilter features at the main website for NetFilter development, http://www.netfilter.org. These features include the following:

- Stateless packet filtering for both IPv4 and IPv6

- Stateful packet filtering for IPv4 traffic

- Network Address Translation (NAT) and Network Address Port Translation (NAPT)

- Flexible and extensible infrastructure

- Multiple layers of application programming interfaces (APIs) for third-party extensions

- Large number of plug-ins/modules

Another benefit of NetFilter is that it is open source, so any modifications that end users want to make can be done without waiting for a vendor to provide new code for their firewall. In addition, NetFilter can support as many interfaces as the hardware that is running it can support. This support allows for multiple demilitarized zones (DMZs) to be created, which you can use to increase the granularity of security for various systems based on their needs.

NetFilter Requirements

The more formal name of iptables is NetFilter. NetFilter requires the use of a Linux kernel version 2.4 or greater and was designed as the replacement for the previous firewall code in the Linux kernel prior to 2.4. In addition to the kernel modules for the NetFilter code, the iptables utility is needed to configure and manipulate the firewall rules. These two elements are the only items required for getting a firewall and NAT device based on NetFilter's working under Linux.

How NetFilter Works

NetFilter, or more commonly known by the name of the manipulation utility, iptables, works, on the surface, similarly to the ipchains firewall code of earlier Linux kernels. The first thing you need to understand about NetFilter is the concept of tables, chains, and rules. Tables are used to provide certain types of functionality, which are defined in more detail through this chapter. Chains define the path in which a packet can travel. The chains are made up of rules, which define what action should be taken on packets that match the rule. An easy way to think about it is that chains simply contain a list of the rules, and tables contain the different types of chains.

NetFilter has five built-in chains, which are grouped into the following three tables:

- Filter

- NAT

- Mangle

The filter table has three built-in chains that function in a similar fashion to the three primary chains of ipchains. The function of the chains in the filter table is to test the payload of the packets (as well as other characteristics) and to accept or reject the packets based on the results of that evaluation. The three built-in chains found in the filter table are as follows:

- INPUT

- FORWARD

- OUTPUT

The INPUT chain evaluates packets that are destined for the firewall itself. The OUTPUT chain evaluates packets that originate from the firewall. The FORWARD chain evaluates packets that are traversing the firewall from one network interface to another. One of the key differences between the chains in NetFilter and ipchains is that in ipchains all packets going from one network interface to another traverse all three of the main chains (INPUT, FORWARD, and OUTPUT). In NetFilter, however, they need only traverse the FORWARD chain because that one is the one involved in forwarding packets between interfaces. Figures 7-1 through 7-3 show the chain traversal.

In Figure 7-1, the packet from the source host 192.168.45.10 is directed to the firewall itself. To reach the firewall, the packet must traverse the rules that are in the INPUT chain of the filter table.

Figure 7-1 *NetFilter INPUT Chain Processing*

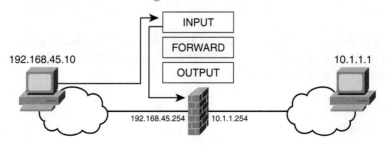

In Figure 7-2, the traffic from host 192.168.45.10 is directed to the server at 10.1.1.1. Typically, this also requires NAT to be present so that the server 10.1.1.1 has an external address assigned to it, but this is beyond the scope of the current discussion. To reach the system 10.1.1.1, the traffic must traverse the rules in the FORWARD chain of the filter table because the traffic is going from one interface to another on the firewall.

Figure 7-2 *NetFilter FORWARD Chain Processing*

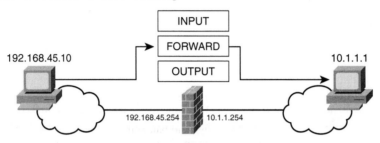

In the final example of Figure 7-3, a process on the firewall is communicating with the host 192.168.45.10. The traffic must traverse the rules in the OUTPUT chain of the filter table on the firewall before reaching its destination. Typically, unless the firewall is filtering traffic in both directions, the OUTPUT chain is empty and all traffic is allowed out from the firewall (which could be considered a security risk in certain environments).

Figure 7-3 *NetFilter OUTPUT Chain Processing*

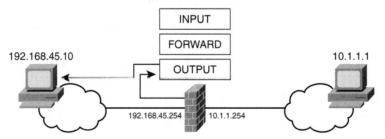

One of the key features that NetFilter has over ipchains is that NetFilter is a stateful packet filter. Instead of requiring a specific inbound rule for every outbound connection, the NetFilter code can identify return traffic that is related to previously seen outbound traffic. This identification provides for a more efficient and secure firewall than is possible with ipchains.

The NAT table performs Network Address Translation (and Port Address Translation) functions on packets. This includes destination NAT (DNAT), source NAT (SNAT), and masquerading. This table consists of three built-in chains:

■ PREROUTING

- POSTROUTING

- OUTPUT

The PREROUTING chain processes packets before the local routing table is consulted, and is used primarily for destination NAT. Destination NAT is where the destination address of the IP packets is modified as they traverse the NAT device. DNAT can be used to accomplish the following capabilities:

- Port forwarding

- Load balancing

- Transparent proxying

Port forwarding is where the firewall accepts packets for a destination host behind it and forwards the packet unchanged to the destination. Load balancing is where the firewall accepts packets destined for an externally visible IP address but distributes the connections across multiple servers behind it to ensure that no one server gets overloaded. Load balancing proves particularly useful in a web farm situation where multiple web servers serve identical content; to ensure consistent performance or high availability, the firewall directs connections to the various servers based on their current connection load. Although this is not the only way that you can accomplish load balancing, it is one of the more popular ways. Finally, transparent proxying is similar to port forwarding, but instead of allowing the connection from the client to the server to go unaltered, the firewall intercepts the connection. Although the client believes that it is communicating with the destination server, it is actually communicating with a firewall that is inspecting and potentially altering the packets before redirecting them to the destination system. Although the NetFilter code does not perform the proxying itself, this capability is possible using the Squid proxying software package.

Because the DNAT occurs in the PREROUTING chain of the NAT table, the INPUT and FORWARD chains in the filter table see the real address of the destination system.

The POSTROUTING chain processes packets after the routing decision has been made, and is primarily used for source NAT. This version of NAT modifies the source IP address in the packets as they traverse the NAT device. Whereas the INPUT and FORWARD chains see the modified IP address of a packet having undergone DNAT, all three chains—INPUT, OUTPUT, and FORWARD—see the unmodified IP address of packets undergoing SNAT.

Masquerading is a simple version of SNAT in which packets receive the IP address of the output interface of the firewall as their source address. This functionality is the same as NAT overload in Cisco IOS code as well as the **global** command in the PIX.

The final table in NetFilter is the mangle table. This table enables the firewall to modify numerous packet header fields, including Type of Service, Time To Live (TTL), Differentiated Service Code Point (DSCP) field, TCP Mean Segment Size (TCPMSS), and Explicit Congestion Notification (ECN). Additionally, this table allows for the marking of packets for later processing by user-defined chains in the firewall rules using the MARK match and MARK target. The MARK target is used to set special values on a packet to perform additional operations on the packet. This value could include specific routing considerations based on the MARK (using the iproute2 program) or bandwidth limiting or class-based queuing as well as other operations. For kernel 2.4.18 and later, this table has five built-in chains: PREROUTING, INPUT, FORWARD, OUTPUT, and POSTROUTING. Previous kernel versions have two built-in chains: PREROUTING and OUTPUT.

NetFilter enables administrators to devise chains to extend the capabilities of the built-in chains. Each user-defined chain *must* be associated with one of the three tables in NetFilter. As with ipchains, packets can be diverted to the user-defined chains, and when the processing of the packet in the user-defined chain is complete, the packet processing continues at the first rule after the one that sent the packet to the user-defined chain. The next section covers the full path of packets through the various chains in NetFilter.

Configuring NetFilter

The NetFilter packet filter is configured through the iptables command utility. Like its predecessor, ipchains, iptables enables firewall administrators to control a wide variety of features in the NetFilter packet filter. Chief among these are adding or inserting filter rules within a preexisting set of rules, defining the policy of the various chains in the filter, or creating user-defined chains for specific purposes such as testing for denial-of-service (DoS) attacks or other specific attacks.

The path a packet takes through the NetFilter process depends on whether it is destined for the firewall host itself or whether it is being forwarded to a second interface. For most packets that traverse the firewall, the sequence of tables and chains is as follows:

1. Mangle PREROUTING

2. NAT PREROUTING

3. Filter FORWARD

4. NAT POSTROUTING

As shown in Figure 7-4, the process of forwarding packets to the second interface involves a routing decision by the firewall. If a packet is destined for the firewall itself, it must traverse the filter INPUT chain before reaching the local process on the firewall. Packets sent by local processes on the firewall *must* traverse the filter OUTPUT chain and *might* traverse the NAT POSTROUTING chain but only if some form of destination NAT is being conducted. Overall, the process through the NetFilter tables and chains is very logical in order and efficiency.

Packets need not traverse *every* chain in the NetFilter system. It all depends on the destination of the packet as well as what rules are applicable and whether NAT is involved.

Figure 7-4   *Packet Traversal of NetFilter Tables and Chains*

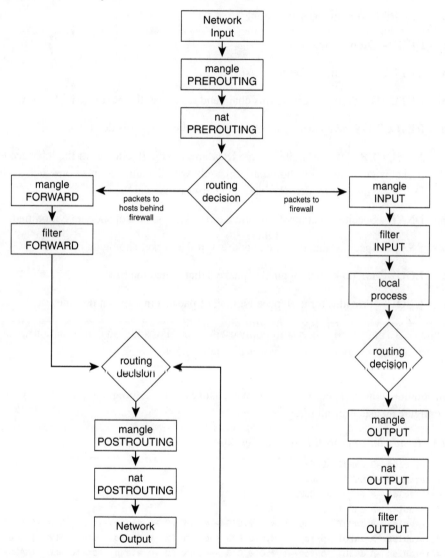

Although the configuration of NetFilter firewalls using the iptables utility may appear to be a daunting task, you can also configure NetFilter through a variety of graphical interface tools such as Firewall Builder, Firestarter, or Webmin. Some examples to follow show how you can configure NetFilter using the iptables utilities as well as these graphical tools. This discussion is not meant to be a detailed method of how to use these tools but rather a brief introduction to these tools. You must further explore and decide which tool you are most comfortable using to manage Linux-based firewalls.

IPTables Command-Line Tool

The iptables command-line tool works very much like the older ipchains tool. The iptables utility provides for several commonly used actions (known as targets) for packets that match the filter rules:

- **ACCEPT**—Let the packet through.

- **DROP**—Drop the packet.

- **QUEUE**—Pass the packet to userspace.

- **RETURN**—Stop processing this chain and resume at the next rule in the previous chain.

- **REJECT**—Send an error packet when a matched packet is detected.

- **MASQUERADE**—Map the source IP address to the IP address of the interface that the packet is going out. You should use this only with dynamic connections such as dialup or a DHCP-assigned provider IP address. Otherwise, use SNAT.

- **DNAT**—Specifies that the destination address of the packet should be modified.

- **SNAT**—Specifies that the source address of the packet should be modified.

- **LOG**—Turn on kernel logging of packets that match the rule.

- **ULOG**—Provides for userspace logging of packets that match the rule.

> **NOTE**   These are the most commonly used targets. For additional information about these and other targets, check out http://www.netfilter.org.

In addition, you can specify a user-defined chain as a target, too. Example 7-1 shows how you can configure a basic firewall filter.

Example 7-1   *Basic Linux Firewall Filter Configuration*

```
# iptables -P INPUT ACCEPT
# iptables -P OUTPUT ACCEPT
# iptables -P FORWARD ACCEPT
# iptables -A INPUT -i lo -j ACCEPT
# iptables -A INPUT -p tcp -s 0.0.0.0/0 --dport 22 -m state --state NEW -j ACCEPT
# iptables -A INPUT -p tcp -s 0.0.0.0/0 --dport 25 -m state --state NEW -j ACCEPT
# iptables -A INPUT -p tcp -s 0.0.0.0/0 --dport 80 -m state --state NEW -j ACCEPT
# iptables -A INPUT -p tcp -s 0.0.0.0/0 --dport 5900 -m state --state NEW -j ACCEPT
# iptables -A INPUT -p tcp -s 0.0.0.0/0 --dport 5901 -m state --state NEW -j ACCEPT
# iptables -A INPUT -m state --state ESTABLISHED,RELATED -j ACCEPT
# iptables -A INPUT --reject-with icmp-host-prohibited -j REJECT
```

Firewall Builder, Firestarter, and Webmin also come in handy when configuring NetFilter.

Firewall Builder

You can find the Firewall Builder software at http://www.fwbuilder.org. Unlike other firewall management software, Firewall Builder provides a policy compiler for Linux's NetFilter firewall as well as for FreeBSD's and OpenBSD's packet filter (pf) firewall, the IPFilter (IPF) firewall, and the Cisco PIX Firewall. IPF is another open source firewall software package that can be built in to a variety of operating systems, including Sun Solaris, NetBSD, FreeBSD, OpenBSD, HP's HP-UX, and SGI's IRIX operating systems. Building a firewall policy with Firewall Builder is exceptionally easy and flexible. You can build a simple packet filter using Firewall Builder much more easily than with the iptables command-line utility, as shown in Figure 7-5. The filter in Figure 7-5 is partially based on the filter given in Example 7-1. The services allowed in are Secure Shell (SSH:TCP/22), Simple Mail Transport Protocol (SMTP:TCP/25), Hypertext Transfer Protocol (HTTP:TCP/80), two Virtual Network Computing connections (VNC-0:TCP/5900, VNC-1:TCP/5901), and TCP traffic that is part of a previously established connection. All other traffic is denied.

Figure 7-5 *Using Firewall Builder to Define Firewall Policy*

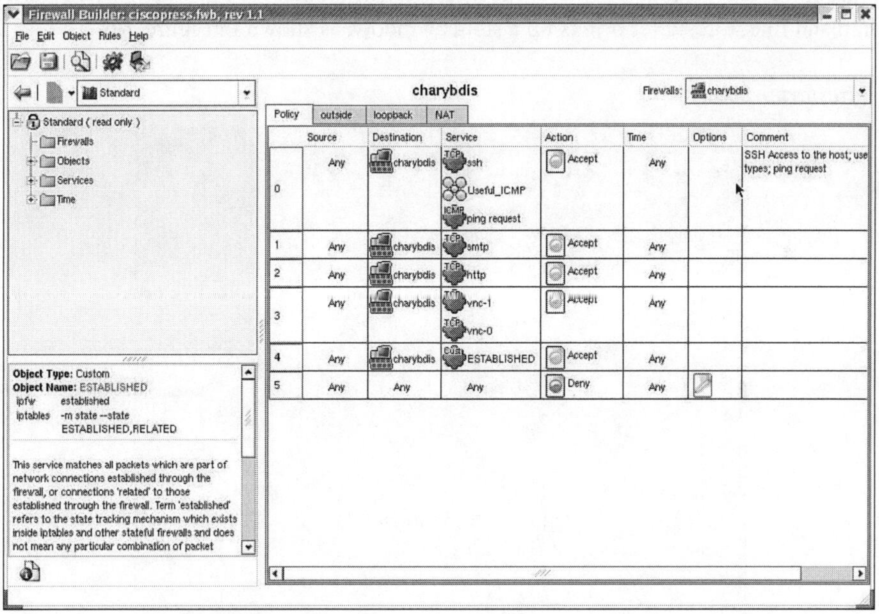

Firewall Builder is available as packages for a variety of operating systems, including Red Hat 9, Fedora Core 3 and 4, Slackware Linux, MacOS X, and Windows 2000 and XP. Firewall Builder uses a dual-license model. The software is available under the GNU Public License (GPL) for operating systems that are available under GPL (such as Red Hat and other Linux derivatives—this list also includes the BSD-derived operating systems, too, even if they are not strictly available under GPL). The software is available under a commercial license for commercial operating systems (this includes Sun Solaris, HP's HP-UX, and SGI's IRIX).

Firewall Builder stores the configuration of the firewall and its policy in an XML file titled *firewall_name*.fwb. In addition, when the firewall policy is compiled, it creates a file called *firewall_name*.fw. This is a shell script that is uploaded to the firewall to apply the changes to the filter policy.

Firestarter

Firestarter is an open source visual firewall policy compiler similar to Firewall Builder. Like Firewall Builder, Firestarter provides the administrator with a graphic interface to build a filtering policy. However, unlike Firewall Builder, Firestarter cannot group items into objects or provide control over multiple firewalls. Firestarter is focused on the policy of a single firewall. Firewall Builder, on the other hand, can manage the policies of multiple firewalls from a central server. Firestarter is to Firewall Builder as the PIX Device Manager (PDM) or Adaptive Security Device Manager (ASDM) is to the CiscoWorks Management Center for Firewalls. When started from the command line, Firestarter brings up a status window, as shown in Figure 7-6.

Figure 7-6   *Firestarter Status*

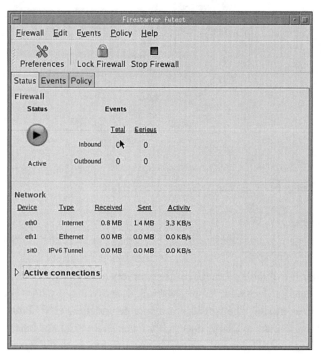

You can use Firestarter to build both an inbound as well as an outbound policy on the firewall, as shown in Figure 7-7. Like its Firewall Builder counterpart, the policy can be detailed or it can be as sparse as needed. After the policy has been defined, it can be saved and is stored in flat text files and shell scripts in /etc/firestarter.

Figure 7-7   *Firestarter Policy Definition*

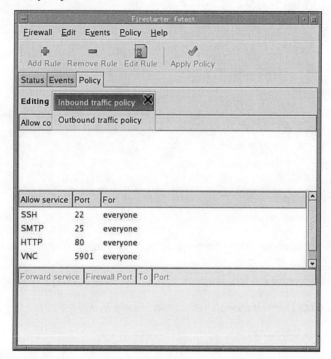

Figure 7-7 shows the same policy for TCP-based traffic as defined earlier using the iptables utility and the Firewall Builder software.

Webmin

The final method for managing NetFilter on a Linux system covered in this chapter is Webmin. This software is available at http://www.webmin.com. Webmin is more than just a firewall management system. Webmin can manage users, network configuration, system configuration, and much more, as shown in Figure 7-8.

Figure 7-8 *Webmin*

By default, Webmin comes with two methods of managing NetFilter, as shown in Figure 7-9:

■ The Linux Firewall module

■ The Shoreline Firewall module (otherwise known as Shorewall)

Figure 7-9 *Webmin Firewall Modules*

The focus during this discussion is on the Linux Firewall module because the Shoreline Firewall module requires the installation of additional files from the Shorewall project (http://www.shorewall.net).

Webmin enables administrators to control all three tables in NetFilter—filter, mangle, and NAT—through either the Linux Firewall Webmin module or the Shorewall Webmin module, as shown in Figure 7-10.

Figure 7-10 *Webmin NetFilter Tables*

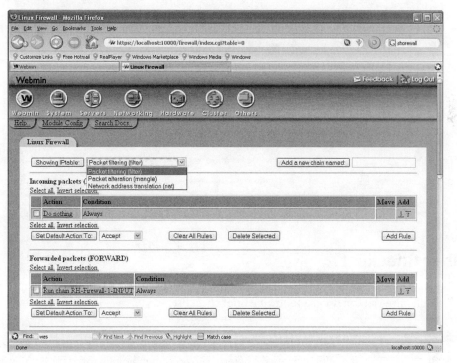

Figure 7-11 shows the configuration of a simple firewall example.

Figure 7-11 *Webmin Configuration of a Simple Firewall*

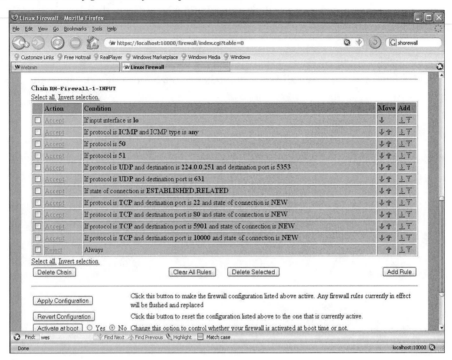

NetFilter Checklist

Building a NetFilter-based firewall is not difficult. End users interested in setting up their own NetFilter firewall can use the following brief checklist:

Step 1 Select a system to be used as the firewall.

Step 2 Install additional network interfaces (minimum number of required interfaces is two).

Step 3 Install at least the minimum recommended memory (preferably more if the firewall will be providing more than just filtering services).

Step 4 Select a Linux version to install (Debian, Fedora Core, Red Hat, Gentoo, and so on).

Step 5 Install the operating system.

Step 6 Configure the operating system (assign addresses to interfaces, either by using Dynamic Host Configuration Protocol [DHCP] or static assigned addresses).

Step 7 Define which services will be allowed through the firewall.

Step 8 Define which hosts will be translated by the firewall.

Step 9   Using the iptables utility, Firewall Builder, Firestarter, Webmin, or another utility, create the firewall filter ruleset.

Step 10   Apply the ruleset to the external interface (that is, the public interface) of the firewall.

Step 11   Test connectivity through the firewall.

Step 12   If desired, define what outbound traffic is to be filtered.

Step 13   Apply the outbound filter to the internal interface of the firewall.

Step 14   Retest connectivity through the firewall.

Summary

NetFilter is an extremely flexible and modern firewall filter. It provides many advantages over previous Linux filtering code, with the most important advantage being that it is a true stateful firewall. In addition, the ability to translate individual hosts on a network through the firewall allows for significant benefits over the previous masquerading done by ipfwadm/ipchains-based firewalls. Although requiring more effort than a packaged firewall from a vendor such as the Cisco PIX or a Linksys firewall in terms of administration, the Linux NetFilter-based firewall provides a powerful firewall at a reasonable price for the user.

Application Proxy Firewalls

Application proxy firewalls are perhaps the most complex firewalls to implement. This complexity is due in large part to the fact that unlike other firewall technologies, application proxy firewalls can make filtering decisions based on the actual application data, which requires that firewall administrators better understand the applications that will traverse the firewall. Practically speaking, two elements comprise an application proxy firewall:

■ Application layer filtering

■ Proxy server functionality

This chapter looks at those two elements to an application proxy firewall and then specifically examines how the Microsoft ISA Server 2004 firewall functions.

Application Layer Filtering

Application proxy firewalls are the most intelligent firewall architecture. By intelligent, we mean that an application proxy firewall can perform the most detailed inspection on data before making a filtering decision. An application proxy firewall can decode and process at the application layer the data contained in packets. Consequently, application proxy firewalls can filter based on the actual application data content. For example, with a packet-filtering firewall, the firewall can merely permit or deny traffic based on data such as the IP protocol in use. So a packet-filtering firewall merely knows whether it should permit or deny HTTP traffic, for example, and processes the traffic accordingly. With an application proxy firewall, however, it not only knows whether it should permit or deny HTTP traffic, it can also be configured to filter based on the type of HTTP traffic. Such a configuration allows an application proxy firewall to interrogate the data and identify malicious web traffic, such as being able to distinguish between normal HTTP traffic and Code Red HTTP traffic, and filter accordingly. This capability gives firewall administrators a tremendous amount of flexibility and control over exactly what traffic will and will not be permitted.

How Application Filtering Works

Application filtering typically functions through the use of processes known as application proxies, application gateways, service proxies, application filters (Microsoft ISA Server 2004 term), or fixups (Cisco term). These application filters typically provide stateful application layer filtering of the data that is traversing the firewall. Generally, the application filters perform two functions:

- **Protocol access**—Protocol access provides a means of permitting secondary connections for protocols and applications that use multiple protocols (for example, FTP, which uses separate and distinct control [TCP port 21] and data (TCP port 20] protocols).

- **Protocol security**—Protocol security is the meat of application filtering and provides the mechanisms by which the application filter protects and inspects the protocols that are traversing the firewall.

Most application filters required dedicated filters to provide for the protocol security functionality. For example, if the firewall is going to filter HTTP traffic, it has to know how to process HTTP traffic at an application layer level. Some common application filters are Simple Mail Transport Protocol (SMTP), Domain Name System (DNS), POP, FTP, HTTP, and Remote Procedure Call (RPC). These filters are, for all intents and purposes, fully functioning processes that can act, function, and process data as if they were actually the SMTP, DNS, POP, FTP, http, or RPC application in question. For example, an application-filtering firewall that is configured for SMTP can typically not only process SMTP traffic, but you can also control the SMTP functions that will or will not be allowed. You could, for instance, allow only **HELO**, **MAIL**, **RCPT**, **DATA**, **RSET**, **NOOP**, and **QUIT** commands per RFC 821. And, potentially, you could provide advanced application filtering on SMTP traffic such as spam and antivirus filtering of the SMTP traffic.

In addition, many application layer firewalls provide a generic filtering process that allows for rudimentary configuration for any application that is being filtered. The problem with these generic application filters is that although they may be able to effectively filter any given application, they may not be able to perform all the required functions to adequately filter the given application (because they were not specifically designed for the given application).

The Difference Between Application Filtering and Deep Packet Inspection

Deep packet inspection is sometimes referred to in the same context as application filtering, but some subtle differences force us to treat each method as a separate and distinct method. Whereas application filtering can truly masquerade and provide the application functionality, deep packet inspection is more of an integration of intrusion detection system (IDS) and intrusion prevention system (IPS) functionality into a stateful packet-inspecting firewall. Deep packet inspecting firewalls typically contain a database of attack signatures and attack patterns, just like an IDS/IPS would. In fact, to be brutally honest, deep packet inspection is merely a good marketing term to describe integrating IDS/IPS functionality into the firewall. After all, because the firewall is going to see all the traffic anyway, why not just let it handle the IDS/IPS functionality? This is the thought process behind newer firewalls such as the Cisco Adaptive Security Appliance (ASA) and Juniper Networks Integrated Security Gateways (ISG).

The most important distinction to remember about deep packet inspection is that the firewall typically is not really application aware. Sure, it can determine what constitutes a bad application or protocol (such as HTTP) from its database of signatures, but it cannot actually act and function like an HTTP server, which is what an application-filtering proxy firewall can do.

Proxy Server Functionality

In the context of firewalls, proxy servers (proxies) have a couple of primary functions:

■   Act as an intermediary between hosts

■   Cache data to reduce the time and external bandwidth required to service requests

Proxies act as an intermediary by literally intercepting and responding to requests between hosts, as shown in Figure 8-1.

Figure 8-1   *Communication Process Between Hosts Through a Proxy*

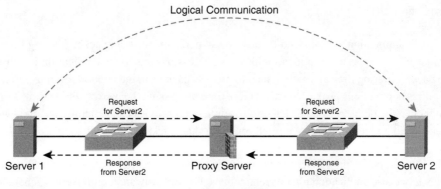

In this case, Server1 and Server2 are attempting to communicate with each other. The proxy resides between the two hosts and responds to all communications and requests between the two hosts. This ensures that the two hosts never actually communicate directly with each other. Logically, Server1 and Server2 are communicating with each other, even though physically the communication process is occurring through a proxy. This function is completely transparent to the end user/system, which means that Server1 has no idea that it is not actually communicating directly with Server2 and vice versa.

Many proxies, in particular proxies that support the HTTP protocol, can also cache data, which in turn allows the proxy to service subsequent requests for the same data from cache, instead of needing to forward the request to the external source. This allows the proxy to help reduce Internet bandwidth requirements, because the first request for the data uses Internet bandwidth whereas all subsequent requests are services from the proxy's cache. This has the additional effect of reducing the time that it takes to display the data because many proxies are connected to the clients that use them over faster connections.

These two elements, application filtering and functioning as a proxy, are the two elements that really identify an application proxy firewall from other types of firewalls such as deep packet inspecting firewalls.

Limitations of Application Proxy Firewalls

Because of how effective application proxies can be at filtering traffic, one might wonder why everyone does not use an application proxy firewall. There are a few good reasons for this.

First, application proxies are only effective at proxying requests for applications that the proxy has defined. Unfortunately, most proxies can handle only a relatively small number of applications. This limitation means that the other applications are not permitted, or that you have to use a generic service proxy (which may not provide the required functionality), or that the proxy handles the additional traffic as a packet-filtering firewall (making the firewall a hybrid application proxy firewall).

Second, application proxies tend to have worse performance than packet-filtering firewalls. This stands to reason because application proxies process packets to the application layer (in contrast to packet-filtering firewalls, which tend to process packets to the network or transport layer). This requires applications proxies to spend more time processing the packet, which results in increased latency in the delivery of data. Therefore, application proxies can generally handle fewer packets per second and a smaller maximum throughput than packet-filtering firewalls.

Finally, application proxies tend to be more expensive than corresponding packet-filtering firewalls. This is because application proxies tend to have higher hardware requirements (generally needing faster processors and more memory) as well as higher development costs, because the application intelligence enabling the proxy to function requires more development and maintenance than a packet-filtering firewall. Consequently, application proxies tend to be used as more specialty firewalls, whereas packet-filtering firewalls tend to be a more general-purpose firewall.

Microsoft ISA Server 2004 Firewall

Microsoft ISA Server 2004 is a hybrid stateful packet-inspecting, circuit-filtering, and application layer proxy firewall. By hybrid, we mean that it can provide any of those functionalities at any given time based on the traffic it is receiving. If it has an application filter for the given protocol or application, it will function as an application proxy firewall for that traffic. If it does not, it will resort to either stateful packet inspecting or circuit filtering as required. In addition, ISA Server 2004 includes virtual private networking (VPN) and caching capabilities, allowing it to function as an all-in-one device that, as one would expect, integrates pretty cleanly with Microsoft-centric environments.

Before we look at the features of Microsoft ISA Server 2004, let's talk about the elephant in the room, namely the perception that ISA Server 2004 is not a "real" firewall. This perception is largely the result of misinformation, lack of education regarding the product, and simple dislike/disregard of anything Microsoft being remotely considered as a security solution. When you look at ISA Server 2004 with an honest and skeptical eye, it is relatively easy to cut through many of the fallacies and realize that Microsoft ISA Server 2004 is an effective and practical firewall solution.

First on the list of misconceptions is the statement that any firewall running on a Windows platform cannot be secure. This is just not factually accurate. All firewalls run on some operating system. In the case of firewalls such as the Cisco PIX Firewall or Check Point SecurePlatform, the operating system is specialized and hardened for use on a firewall. Windows, out of the box, is not designed to be run on a firewall, but it can be effectively secured and hardened following the principles of running the minimum required services and functionality necessary to operate as a firewall alone. Some excellent resources detail how to effectively secure the underlying Windows operating system:

- **NSA Security Configuration Guides**

  http://www.nsa.gov/snac/downloads_all.cfm?MenuID=scg10.3.1

- **Hardening the Windows Infrastructure on the ISA Server 2004 Computer**

  http://www.microsoft.com/technet/prodtechnol/isa/2004/plan/
  hardeningwindows.mspx

- **Windows Server 2003 Security Guide**

  http://www.microsoft.com/technet/security/prodtech/windowsserver2003/
  w2003hg/sgch00.mspx

- **ISA Server 2004 Security Hardening Guide**

  http://www.microsoft.com/technet/prodtechnol/isa/2004/plan/
  securityhardeningguide.mspx

> **NOTE**   Keep in mind that many of the procedures for Windows 2000 are applicable to Windows 2003 and vice versa, so do not hesitate using both the Windows 2000 and 2003 guides regardless of your actual operating system

Another frequent misconception is that ISA Server 2004 is "just" an upgrade to Microsoft Proxy Server 2.0. Although ISA Server 2004 is indeed the logical upgrade to Proxy Server 2.0 (technically, ISA Server 2000 is the direct upgrade to Proxy Server 2.0), that is not to say that ISA Server 2004 is just a proxy server. Proxy Server 2.0 had absolutely no advanced firewall features. It was primarily a caching engine with basic packet-filtering capabilities. Microsoft ISA Server 2004 is a fully featured firewall, capable of performing stateful packet inspection as well as application layer filtering and proxying. In addition, it can function as a caching engine. Simply put, trying to claim that because ISA Server 2004 is an upgrade to Proxy Server it is therefore not a "real" firewall has absolutely no technical merit.

Microsoft ISA Server 2004 Features

Microsoft ISA Server 2004 consists of two editions: Standard Edition and Enterprise Edition. The predominant differences between the Standard and Enterprise editions relate to scalability. Table 8-1 summarizes the differences between the Standard and Enterprise editions.

Table 8-1   *Comparison of ISA Server 2004 Standard and Enterprise Editions*

Feature	Standard Edition	Enterprise Edition
Networks	Unlimited	Unlimited, with the addition of enterprise networks (networks that can be applied to any firewall array anywhere in the enterprise)
Scale up	Up to 4 CPUs and 2-GB RAM	Unlimited (per operating system)
Scale out	Single server	Up to 32 nodes using Microsoft Network Load Balancing (NLB)
Caching	Single server store	Unlimited (through the use of Cache Array Routing Protocol (CARP))
High availability	None	Yes (using NLB)
Management	Local management and configuration	Array and enterprise-level configuration
Underlying operating system	Microsoft Windows Server 2003 (Standard or Enterprise Edition), Microsoft Windows 2000 Server or Advanced Server with Service Pack 4 (SP4) or later, or Windows 2000 Datacenter Server	Microsoft Windows Server 2003 (Standard or Enterprise Edition)

As you can see, if you need multiple ISA servers working in tandem, or need additional memory and processors, you need to use the Enterprise Edition. Similarly, if you need a high-availability solution, use Enterprise Edition.

In general, Microsoft ISA Server 2004's firewall features can be categorized as follows:

- Security and filtering features

- Firewall clients and authentication

- Web caching server functionality

- Network services publishing

- VPN functionality

- Management and administration features

- Miscellaneous features

Security and Filtering Features

The Microsoft ISA Server 2004 firewall is a hybrid firewall capable of performing the following:

- **Stateful packet inspection**—ISA Server 2004 can perform full stateful packet inspection and filtering of all traffic passing through the firewall.

- **Circuit filtering**—ISA Server 2004 can perform application-transparent circuit filtering to a host of protocols, including Telnet, RealAudio, Windows Media technologies, and Internet Relay Chat (IRC). This filtering occurs at the transport or session layer as opposed to the application layer. This proxy functionality works in conjunction with the stateful packet-inspection functionality.

- **Application filtering**—ISA Server 2004 can act as an application proxy and filter traffic for a number of protocols including HTTP, FTP, and Gopher. This allows Microsoft ISA Server 2004 to act on behalf of clients, hiding and protecting the client from external resources and threats.

Microsoft ISA Server 2004 can perform these filtering functions in a multidirectional method, supporting as many network interfaces as the physical hardware can contain. This allows for the creation of multiple demilitarized (DMZ) segments, allowing for the creation of unique filtering rulesets on a per-DMZ segment basis. Of course, filtering of traffic for/from the internal and external networks is also available.

Microsoft ISA Server 2004 also supports basic intrusion detection functionality, although full intrusion detection system (IDS) functionality is best provided through the integration of third-party products such as ISS RealSecure or similar products. Currently, ISA Server 2004 can natively detect the following intrusion/attack attempts:

- WinNuke

- Ping of death

- Land attack

- IP half scan

- Port scan

- UDP bomb

- POP3 buffer overflow

- SMTP buffer overflow

- DNS zone transfer

- DNS length overflow

- DNS host name overflow

Firewall Clients and Authentication

Microsoft ISA Server 2004 supports the following three types of firewall clients for systems that are attempting to access resources outside the protected network:

- SecureNAT client

- Firewall client

- Web proxy client

SecureNAT Client

The SecureNAT client is effectively any device that attempts to communicate through the ISA Server 2004 firewall without being configured as one of the other firewall types. For all intents and purposes, this is the traditional "point to the firewall as the default gateway to communicate" type of a client. Therefore, practically any type of TCP/IP network host can communicate through the firewall as a SecureNAT client. Although easy to implement (there is no special configuration required beyond just enabling network communications on the host), the SecureNAT client is the least secure and capable of the firewall clients. SecureNAT clients cannot be configured to authenticate with the firewall to determine what access should be permitted, nor can they access resources requiring complex protocols (protocols that require multiple connections; for example, standard FTP [port] mode connections) without the use of application filters installed on the firewall itself.

Firewall Client

The ISA Server 2004 firewall client is one of the components to an ISA Server 2004 solution that really separates it from the competition in terms of the kind of control over access that can be managed. The firewall client software can be installed on any Windows-based client, which is a limitation in environments that use Linux, Sun, UNIX, or Mac computers. Once implemented, however, the firewall client enables you to define access to external resources based on users and groups and authenticate all access requests to ensure that only the users you have specified are allowed to communicate. It also enables you to define how they can communicate. This authentication information is stored in the firewall log files, making it easy to perform a forensic analysis to determine what sites, protocols, and applications the user was running or accessing.

Perhaps the most powerful feature of the firewall client is the ability to enforce security controls on the client itself (for example, allowing only applications that you explicitly permit to function on the client or allowing only certain ports on the client to be used for communications). For example, a relatively difficult task to perform with most firewalls is to prevent instant messaging and peer-to-peer applications from being used by the users. Instant messaging applications can almost all use HTTP (or any other protocol) as the transport protocol, making it difficult to effectively block at the firewall. Similarly, many peer-to-peer applications can do the same thing. With the firewall client, you can define the names of applications that should not be allowed to run; they will be blocked by the firewall client software. Keep in mind that if the users can rename the application executable, they can bypass these restrictions.

Web Proxy Client

The web proxy client is used anytime a computer is configured via its web browser to use a proxy, and the ISA Server 2004 server is specified as the proxy. Although web browsers are the most commonly implemented applications that use proxies, instant messaging software and other applications that support using a proxy can also be configured as web proxy clients.

The web proxy client enables you to improve the performance of web access because the data can be cached by the firewall and served to the clients out of cache. This also reduces bandwidth requirements, as discussed in the next section. The web proxy client also supports using authentication for access, similar to the firewall client, thus providing a mechanism to control and track access on a user basis.

Web Caching Server Functionality

Although technically not a firewall or security feature, the ISA Server 2004 server provides full caching server functionality. This allows the server to transparently cache web request and then service subsequent requests out of cache, thus reducing the amount of bandwidth that is used for client web browsing. This also allows the ISA Server 2004 server to function as a proxy, retrieving content on behalf of clients.

Network Services Publishing

To provide access to protected resources, ISA Server 2004 implements what are known as publishing rules. These rules are used to provide inbound/ingress filtering functionality to resources that are being protected by the firewall. For example, if you have a web server that needs to provide services to external clients, you would use network services publishing (specifically web server publishing rules) to "publish" or provide access to the protected web server resource. There are four types of publishing rules:

- Web server publishing rule

- Secure web server publishing rule

- E-mail server publishing rule

- Server publishing rule

As you would expect, the first three rules are specialized to handle the corresponding types of network services. The server publishing rule is the generic catchall rule type for any and all other publishing requirements.

VPN Functionality

Microsoft ISA Server 2004, like many other firewalls, also provides integrated VPN functionality, allowing you to use the ISA Server 2004 both as a component in a site-to-site VPN as well as a termination point for remote access VPN services. Although previous versions supported Point-to-Point Tunneling Protocol (PPTP) and Layer 2 Tunnel Protocol / IP Security (L2TP/IPsec) VPN protocols, ISA Server 2004 also supports native IPsec tunnel mode VPN implementations.

Because the VPN functionality is integrated with the firewall, ISA Server 2004 can also perform stateful packet filtering and inspection on VPN traffic that is passing through the firewall, providing additional security and control of all traffic that is entering or exiting the protected network. Doing so enables you to perform actions such as limiting your remote sales users to a subset of servers and services on the protected network.

Management and Administration Features

Arguably some of the most deficient aspects of previous versions of ISA Server were the fact that the management interface was not intuitive, the access rule management methodology was contrary to almost every other product out there, and the monitoring and reporting capabilities left a lot to be desired. ISA Server 2004 has gone a long way toward improving these deficiencies.

Management Interface

As shown in Figure 8-2, ISA Server 2004 takes advantage of the Microsoft Management Console to provide a management interface. This management console can either be accessed locally on the ISA server by using Terminal Service (TS) or Remote Desktop (RDP) to start a terminal session, or can be installed on a remote system (such as the administrators desktop) to allow for remote management of all ISA Server 2004 resources in the environment. In the case of TS or RDP, the TS/RDP process handles protection and encryption of the data over the network. In the case of installing the management console on a remote system, Microsoft is intentionally vague as to what if any encryption or protection of the data that is transmitted between the management console and the ISA Server 2004 server occurs. Like all Microsoft products, administrative access is granted through the use of Microsoft users and groups, as well as by defining individual or ranges of IP addresses that are allowed to make management connections.

Figure 8-2 *ISA Server 2004 Management Console*

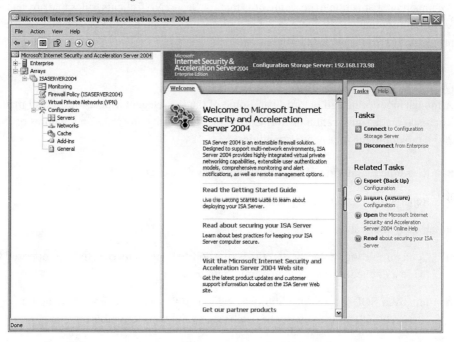

In addition, some third-party web-based management interfaces can be implemented, allowing for the management of the ISA server to be performed via a web browser, thus eliminating the need to install a management client for remote management.

Access Rule Management

Access rule management has also been greatly simplified, following well-defined conventions that have been long established for firewall rule management. Unlike server publishing rules, which are designed for defining inbound/ingress filters, access rules are used to define outbound/egress filters to protect traffic that is sourced from a protected network. Rules have the following components that can be defined in a wizard-driven fashion:

- Rule name

- Rule action (permit/deny)

- Protocol the rule applies to

- Source traffic

- Destination traffic

- Users to which the rule applies

An important distinction to be aware of is that for SecureNAT clients, rules that are set to apply to all IP traffic actually only apply to defined protocols, so you need to ensure that you define any protocols that you want to filter based on.

Monitoring and Reporting

Although monitoring and reporting are some of the less-elegant aspects of firewall management, Microsoft made significant improvements to the monitoring and reporting features of ISA Server 2004, providing the following capabilities:

- Real-time monitoring of log entries and firewall sessions

- Report customization and publishing

- E-mail notification

- Configurable log summary start times (the ability to pick any start time, as opposed to having to use a defined start time such as midnight everyday)

- Improved SQL logging (the ability to log to a SQL server, thereby allowing for the use of advanced SQL tools to query the database and build custom reports)

- Microsoft Data Engine (MSDE) logging capabilities

Miscellaneous Features

Although the ability to support multiple networks may sound like a given, multinetwork support is actually a new feature of ISA Server 2004, allowing it to be implemented in enterprise environments that contain multiple networks (both internal and perimeter networks such as DMZ segments). In conjunction with this, you can define the relationships between the networks and then use this information during rule creation. By default, ISA Server 2004 supports the following networks:

- The internal network (this is the subnet directly connected to the internal interface of the firewall)

- The external network (any IP addresses that do not belong to another network)

- The VPN clients network (any IP addresses which are assigned to VPN clients)

- The local host network (the IP addresses of the firewall itself)

Remote VPN users represent one of the bigger security risks for most environments. These users typically connect to all sorts of networks that are outside of the control of the IT department and then attempt to connect to their corporate network. This allows the VPN client to become a carrier of viruses, worms, and other malicious software and content, thereby spreading it to the corporate network when they establish their VPN connection. To help mitigate this risk, ISA Server 2004 includes VPN Quarantine Control. With VPN Quarantine Control, ISA Server 2004 can be configured to enforce policies on the VPN clients, including the following:

- All security updates and service packs defined by the administrator must be installed.

- The client must have antivirus software installed and enabled.

- The client must have personal firewall software installed and enabled.

If these conditions are not met, the VPN client will not be connected to the VPN and gain access to the full network resources; instead, they will be connected to a limited-access network where they can download and apply any required patches and updates. Although this does not remove any malicious software from the VPN client computer, by requiring only patched and updated systems to connect you can help ensure that the VPN client computer is less susceptible to threats.

Microsoft ISA Server 2004 Requirements and Preparation

ISA Server 2004 can be a relatively complex product to implement. A number of system requirements and recommendations should be implemented before installing and configuring ISA Server 2004. Table 8-2 details the system requirements as well as my recommendations beyond the system requirements.

Table 8-2   *System Requirements*

Component	Minimum	Recommended
Processor	Single Pentium III 550 MHz	Single or dual Xeon 3 GHz
Memory	256 MB	2 GB
Disk space	150 MB	Mirrored or RAID5 36-GB capacity with separate disks for caching (if implemented)
Network	At least two 10/100-Mbps network adapters	At least two 100/1000-Mbps network adapters
Operating system	Microsoft Windows 2000 Server or Advanced Server with SP4 or later	Microsoft Windows Server 2003 (Standard or Enterprise Edition)

In addition to the system requirements, you need to harden the operating system prior to installing ISA Server 2004 on the system. Use the guides mentioned early in the "Microsoft ISA Server 2004 Firewall" section as a basis for securing the underlying operating system as well as the Microsoft ISA Server 2004 software.

Of particular importance is to harden the external network interface (at a minimum) to remove all clients, services, and protocols except TCP/IP itself, as shown in Figure 8-3.

Figure 8-3   *External Network Interface Configuration*

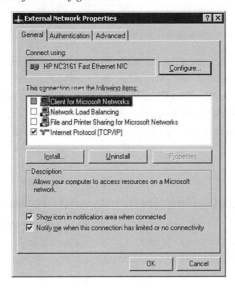

In addition, you also need to configure the routing table on the ISA server accordingly to support all the networks it will need to reach, or you will need to install and configure Routing and Remote Access on the firewall to enable routing protocols such as OSPF or RIPv2.

Finally, ensure that you disable any network services or applications that are not explicitly required by ISA Server 2004. Table 8-3 lists the core services that are required by ISA Server 2004, including the startup mode that should be used. All other services should be disabled.

Table 8-3   *Service Requirements*

Service Name	Function/Purpose	Startup Mode
COM+ Event System	Core operating system	Manual
Cryptographic Services	Core operating system (security)	Automatic
Event Log	Core operating system	Automatic
IPSec Services	Core operating system (security)	Automatic
Logical Disk Manager	Core operating system (disk management)	Automatic
Logical Disk Manager Administrative Service	Core operating system (disk management)	Manual
Microsoft Firewall	Required for normal functioning of ISA Server 2004	Automatic
Microsoft ISA Server Control	Required for normal functioning of ISA Server 2004	Automatic
Microsoft ISA Server Job Scheduler	Required for normal functioning of ISA Server 2004	Automatic
Microsoft ISA Server Storage	Required for normal functioning of ISA Server 2004	Automatic
MSSQL$MSFW	Required when MSDE logging is used for ISA Server 2004	Automatic
Network Connections	Core operating system (network infrastructure)	Manual
NTLM Security Support Provider	Core operating system (security)	Manual
Plug and Play	Core operating system	Automatic
Protected Storage	Core operating system (security)	Automatic
Remote Access Connection Manager	Required for normal functioning of ISA Server 2004	Manual
Remote Procedure Call (RPC)	Core operating system	Automatic

continues

Table 8-3   *Service Requirements (Continued)*

Service Name	Function/Purpose	Startup Mode
Secondary Logon	Core operating system (security)	Automatic
Security Accounts Manager	Core operating system	Automatic
Server	Required for ISA Server 2004 Firewall Client Share	Automatic
Smart Card	Core operating system (security)	Manual
SQLAgent$MSFW	Required when MSDE logging is used for ISA Server 2004	Manual
System Event Notification	Core operating system	Automatic
Telephony	Required for normal functioning of ISA Server 2004	Manual
Virtual Disk Service (VDS)	Core operating system (disk management)	Manual
Windows Management Instrumentation (WMI)	Core operating system (WMI)	Automatic
WMI Performance Adapter	Core operating system (WMI)	Manual

How the Microsoft ISA Server 2004 Firewall Works

Almost all management functions for ISA Server 2004 firewalls are performed with the ISA Server management console. This is a Microsoft Management Console (MMC)-based management console that is either run on the ISA server itself (and typically accessed via RDP/TS) or must be installed separately on the remote management workstation (via the ISA Server 2004 installation program). Figure 8-4 shows the ISA Server 2004 management console.

To perform remote administration of ISA Server 2004 firewalls using the management console, the management workstation must be added to the Enterprise Remote Management Computers (to manage all firewalls in the enterprise) or the Remote Management Computers (to manage a single firewall in the enterprise) computer set, and then remote management must be enabled. The easiest way to do this is to right-click the **Firewall Policy** object in the management console and choose **Edit System Policy**. Under the **Remote Management** configuration group, select **Microsoft Management Console** and ensure that **Enable** is checked on the **General** tab. Next, click the **From** tab and choose the appropriate group that you want to update, as shown in Figure 8-5, and then click **Edit**.

Figure 8-4 *ISA Server 2004 Management Console*

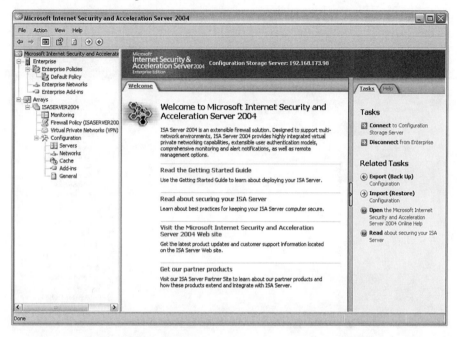

Figure 8-5 *Modifying Remote Management Rules*

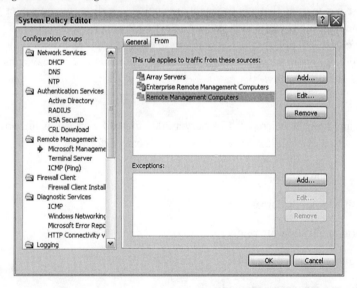

At the Properties screen, add, edit, or delete systems that will be allowed to perform remote management on the firewalls. When you have finished, click **OK** to close any open windows, returning to the management console. Before *any* configuration changes are actually performed on the ISA servers, the last task is to select to either apply or discard the changes, as shown in Figure 8-6.

Figure 8-6 *Applying Configuration Changes*

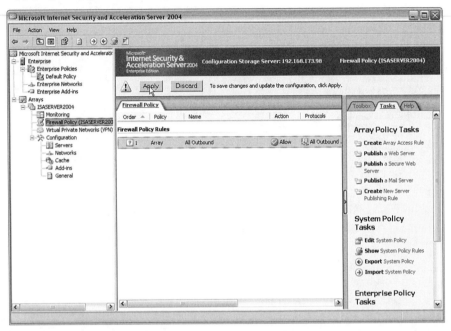

> **NOTE** Keep in mind that any time you are applying or discarding changes you make, if you have made multiple changes then you are selecting to apply or discard all of the changes, or in the event of firewall policy changes, you are selecting to apply or discard the entire firewall policy. Make sure you are comfortable with any and all changes you have opted to make before you decide to click **Apply**.

To understand how the Microsoft ISA Server 2004 firewall works, it is important to identify the specific functions that an ISA Server 2004 firewall can perform:

- Filter outbound access

- Publish internal resources

- Perform application filtering

- Configure system policy rules

- Configure client access methods

- Cache web data

Filtering Outbound Access

ISA Server 2004 manages and applies all rules in what is known as a firewall policy. Two general classifications of rules, publishing rules, are used to define access from external sources to internal/protected resources, to external destinations.

Access rules consist of the following policy elements:

- **Rule action**—This defines whether traffic should be allowed or denied when the rule conditions are met.

- **Protocols**—This is where you specify the protocols to which the rule applies. These can be any Layer 3 (IP level) protocol, any Layer 4 (transport layer) port number, or any ICMP properties.

- **Source**—This is where you define the source of the traffic that the rule will apply to, typically an internal network.

- **Destination**—This is where you define the destination of the traffic that the rule will apply to, typically an external network.

- **User sets**—This is where you define the users that the rule will apply to. To take advantage of user sets, you cannot be using the SecureNAT firewall client because it has no means of performing authentication.

- **Content types**—This is where you define the Multipurpose Internet Mail Extensions (MIME) types and file extensions that the rule will apply to. Content types can only be specified and used with rules for the HTTP and tunneled FTP (FTP that is handled by the Microsoft ISA Server 2004 web proxy filter) protocols, allowing you to define what specific content will be permitted (for example, denying .exe extensions in URL requests).

- **Schedules**—This is where you define the schedule during which the rule will be applied. Schedules only apply to new connections; existing connections that are in place outside of the hours that the schedule has defined are not disconnected automatically.

Building the access rule is a largely wizard-driven process, with the exception of configuring the content types and schedule, which must be done by editing the properties of an existing rule. Just right-click the firewall policy and choose **New > Access Rule**, as shown in Figure 8-7.

Figure 8-7 *Creating an Access Rule*

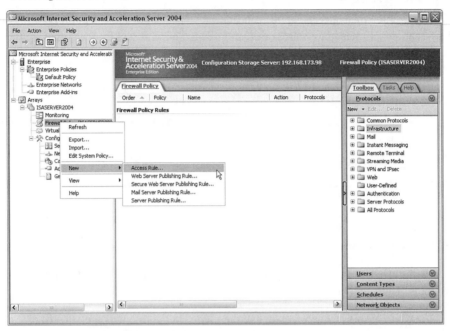

This will begin the New Access Rule Wizard. At the Welcome screen, assign an appropriate access rule name and click **Next**. At the Rule Action screen, select to **Allow** or **Deny** the traffic as appropriate and click **Next**. At the Protocols screen, you can select to apply the rule to **All Outbound Traffic**, **Selected Traffic**, or **All Outbound Traffic Except Selected Traffic**. If you choose the latter, you must click **Add** to specify the protocols that the rule applies to. For example, Figure 8-8 shows a rule being created that applies to the HTTP protocol only.

Figure 8-8 *Protocols Screen*

When you have finished, click **Next** to be presented with the Access Rule Sources screen. Click **Add** to specify the traffic source that this rule will apply to. Figure 8-9 shows the Add Network Entities screen that is accessed by clicking **Add**.

Figure 8-9 *Add Network Entities Screen*

After you have specified the appropriate source, click **Next** to be taken to the Access Rule Destinations screen. Once again, click **Add** and specify the destination traffic that the rule will apply to. When you have finished, click **Next**. At the User Sets screen, specify the users that the rule will apply to. Keep in mind that only web proxy clients and firewall clients perform authentication; so if you want the rule to apply to everyone, including unauthenticated users, just accept the default value of **All Users**, as shown in Figure 8-10.

Figure 8-10 *User Sets Screen*

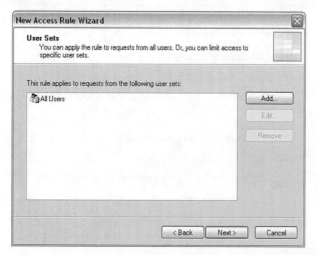

Review the rule configuration and click **Finish**. At this point, the rule has been created but not applied to the firewall. Just click **Apply** in the MMC as previously discussed.

If you need to change any of the rule settings, including editing the content type or schedule configuration, just right-click the rule and choose **Properties** or **Edit System Rule** as appropriate for the corresponding rule.

Publishing Internal Resources

Publishing internal resources follows largely the same process as creating an access rule. It is a wizard-driven process, but the focus of a publishing rule is allowing access *to* protected resources, as opposed to access rules (which allow access *from* protected resources).

Regardless of which type of publishing rule you need to create, the process is fairly similar. The first step is to right-click the firewall policy and select to create a new publishing rule (for example, a web publishing rule) and follow the wizard. At the Welcome screen, enter the appropriate rule name and click **Next**. At the Select Rule Action screen, specify whether traffic that matches the rule should be permitted or denied and click **Next**. Figure 8-11 shows the Define Website to Publish screen. This is where you specify the information for the internal server that is hosting the website. Enter the appropriate information and click **Next**. For example, if you use host headers to allow multiple websites to exist on the same physical server, you will want to check the box to **Forward the original host header instead of the actual one (specified above)**. This will cause the ISA server to actually keep the host header information, instead of just routing all web requests to the default website on the internal web server. One of the nice features of the web publishing rule is the ability to specify individual folders on the website that the rule will apply to. When you have finished, click **Next**.

Figure 8-11 *Define Website to Publish Screen*

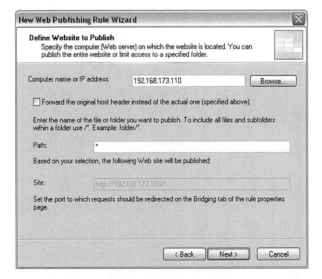

At the Public Name Details screen, you enter the information that the website will be known to the public as (for example www.cisco.com). You can also define the public path that the Microsoft ISA Server 2004 server will advertise. Figure 8-12 illustrates this screen.

Figure 8-12 *Public Name Details Screen*

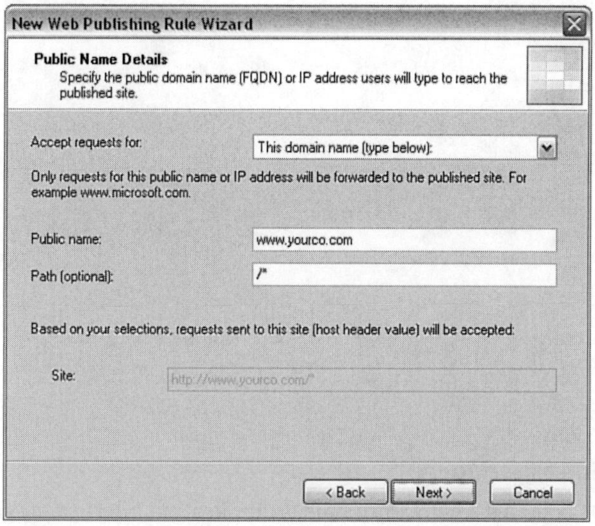

When you have finished, click **Next**. Doing so brings you to the Select Web Listener screen. The web listener allows you to define the external IP address and port number that the firewall will listen for requests for this rule on. If you do not already have a listener defined, you can click **New** to launch the New Web Listener Definition Wizard. Doing so enables you to define the interfaces and IP addresses as well as the port numbers that the rule will use. You can also define the internal path that the web request will be directed to on the internal web server. In most cases, the internal and external paths will match; if you want the external path to redirect to a different internal path, however, you can specify different settings. For example, if you want http://www.cisco.com/sales.htm to redirect on the internal web server to http://www.cisco.com, you specify an external path of **http://www.cisco.com/sales.htm** and an internal path of **/***. After you have defined the listener, just select it from the Web Listener drop-down dialog box, as shown in Figure 8-13, and click **Next**.

At the User Sets screen, select the users who the rule will apply to and click **Next**. Review the configuration and click **Finish** to create the rule. Once again, if you want to apply the rule to the firewall, you must then click **Apply** in the management console.

Figure 8-13 *Select Web Listener Screen*

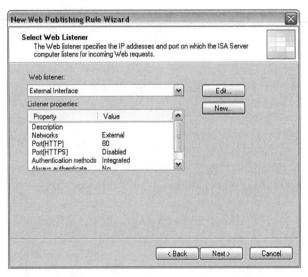

Performing Application Filtering

ISA Server 2004 contains a number of built-in application filters to provide for application layer inspection of the corresponding traffic. Configuring the application filters is performed in various locations within the management console. For web filters, just right-click an HTTP or HTTPS rule and select **Configure HTTP**. By default, Microsoft ISA Server 2004 supports the following HTTP application-filtering options:

- Maximum header length (in bytes)

- Maximum payload length (in bytes)

- URL length and query length protection (in bytes)

- URL normalization and high bit character blocking

- Windows executable blocking

- User defined HTTP method filtering (for example, denying POST methods)

- File extension filtering

- User-defined HTTP header content

- User-defined signature content filtering

For application filters, most can be managed from the add-ins screen, as shown in Figure 8-14.

Figure 8-14 *Application Filters*

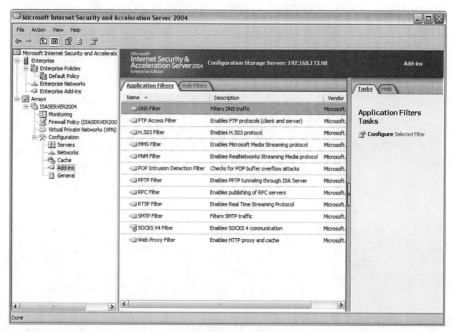

A notable exception to this is the DNS filtering, which is configured under the **General** section of the management console by clicking **Enable Intrusion Detection and DNS Attack Detection** (by default, both intrusion detection and DNS attack detection is enabled).

Configuring System Policy Rules

Access rules and server publishing rules control the access to and from networks protected by the firewall. To control access to the firewall itself, system policy rules have been created. These rules do not show up by default when you view the firewall policy, but they can be enabled by selecting the firewall policy and then clicking **Show System Policy Rules**. Doing so causes all system policy rules to display in addition to any access and publishing rules, as shown in Figure 8-15.

You can add, change, and delete the system policy rules manually, or you can edit the system policy via a graphical user interface (GUI) by right-clicking the firewall policy and selecting **Edit System Policy**. Doing so launches the System Policy Editor screen, as shown in Figure 8-16.

Figure 8-15 *Displaying the System Policy Rules*

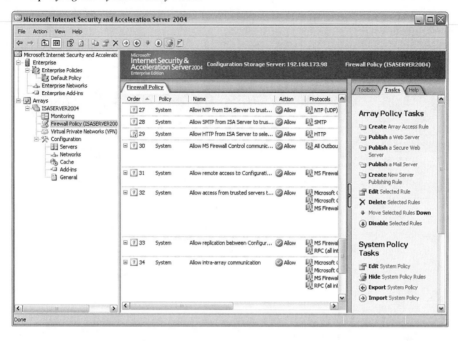

Figure 8-16 *System Policy Editor Screen*

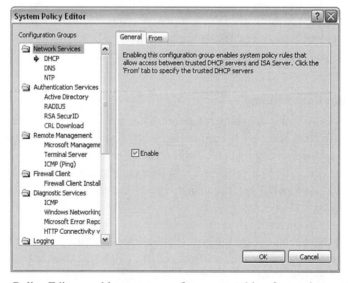

The System Policy Editor enables you to configure everything from what systems are allowed to remotely manage the firewall to how the firewall performs its authentication tasks.

Configuring Client Access Methods

As previously mentioned, Microsoft ISA Server 2004 supports three firewall clients: the SecureNAT client, the firewall client, and the web proxy client. The SecureNAT client really is not a client at all. Instead, any system that accesses the firewall via TCP/IP that is not one of the other client types is a SecureNAT client.

Configuring the Web Proxy Client

The web proxy client is any system that has been configured to use a proxy for Winsock applications. This is typically done in the client web browser settings, specifying the IP address and port number that should be used to access the proxy server. From the ISA server side, the web proxy configuration is performed by clicking **Networks** in the management console to open the Networks configuration screen and then right-clicking the internal network and selecting **Properties**, as shown in Figure 8-17.

Figure 8-17   *Selecting the Internal Network Properties*

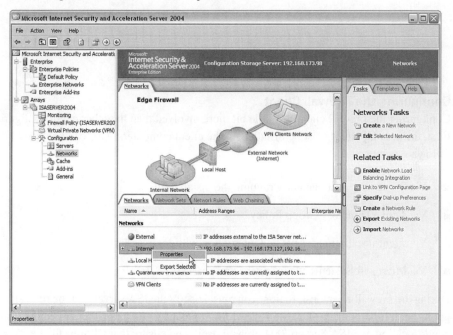

From the Internal Network Properties screen, select the **Web Proxy** tab and specify whether to enable web proxy clients (by default, they are enabled) and define the port number that the clients will connect on. You can click **Authentication** to define which users will/will not be permitted access. Figure 8-18 shows the Web Proxy tab.

Figure 8-18 *Web Proxy Configuration*

Configuring the Firewall Client

Configuring the firewall client is a little bit more involved than the other client configurations. First, the firewall client must be installed on the client computers. This can be done in the following manners:

- Via file sharing and manually running the installation

- Via Active Directory Group Policy

- Via silent installation scripts and integration with login scripts

- Via Microsoft Systems Management Server (SMS)

During the firewall client installation, you must specify the ISA server that the firewall client will get its configuration from. This step allows you to manage the firewall client configuration at a single location, the ISA Server 2004 firewall itself, and ensure that all firewall clients receive the same configuration settings.

On the ISA server itself, two general firewall client configuration tasks need to be performed.

Step 1   Configure the general firewall client configurations settings.

Step 2   Configure the firewall client application settings.

The firewall client general configuration is performed in a similar fashion to the web proxy client configuration. Just right-click the appropriate network in the management console, choose **Properties**, and then select the **Firewall Client** tab, as shown in Figure 8-19.

Figure 8-19 *Firewall Client Tab*

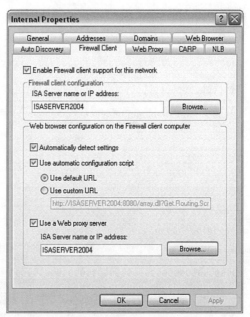

Doing so enables you to define settings such as the configuration script that should be used and whether the client should use a proxy server. In addition, you can specify the names of domains that the firewall client should not apply to by selecting the **Domains** tab and entering the domain name.

The firewall client application settings can be configured by clicking **General** in the management console then clicking **Define Firewall Client Settings**. Doing so launches the Firewall Client Settings screen, as shown in Figure 8-20. On this screen, you can define applications that will or will not be permitted to run on the client computer and how permitted applications will be allowed to communicate on the network. An important thing to keep in mind is that the application name is a constant; so if the users change the name of the application (for example, from kazaa.exe to happy.exe), the firewall client settings no longer apply, because the application name no longer matches the name that was defined. An alternative is to use third-party products that integrate with Microsoft ISA Server 2004.

Caching Web Data

Configuring the firewall to cache web data is a straightforward process. In the management console, navigate to the Cache screen, right-click the server, and choose **Properties** to launch the Server Cache Properties screen, as shown in Figure 8-21. Notice how the Cache icon has a red arrow pointing down, denoting that caching is not currently enabled.

Figure 8-20   *Firewall Client Settings Screen*

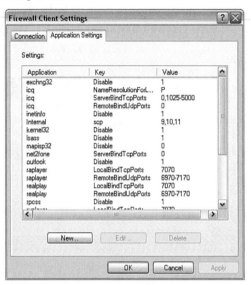

Figure 8-21   *Launching the Cache Properties Screen*

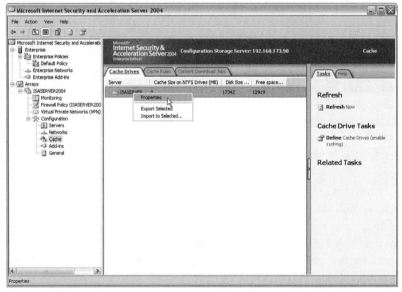

To enable caching, just select the drives and the maximum cache size and click **Set**. When you have finished, click **OK** and then click **Apply** to apply the configuration change to the firewall. You must restart the ISA services before the caching functionality will be enabled.

When caching has been enabled, you can define rules regarding what data should be cached and how it should be cached by selecting the **Cache Rules** tab from the Cache screen and defining an appropriate rule. Like most other tasks in Microsoft ISA Server 2004, this is a wizard-driven process that is relatively straightforward and easy to understand.

Microsoft ISA Server 2004 Checklist

Enabling and configuring Microsoft ISA Server 2004 can be a relatively complex task. It is not something that should be performed without extensive planning and design prior to implementation. To get a basic ISA Server 2004 implementation in place and operational, the following tasks should be performed:

Step 1   Install the underlying operating system.

Step 2   Ensure that network services such as DNS are functioning properly.

Step 3   Configure routing on the firewall as required.

Step 4   Determine the firewall clients that will be implemented.

Step 5   Determine the edition of Microsoft ISA Server 2004 that is most appropriate for your environment.

Step 6   Install ISA Server 2004.

Step 7   Harden the appropriate underlying operating system and applications.

Step 8   Configure the system policy rules.

Step 9   Configure access rules (filter outbound access).

Step 10   Configure server publishing rules (filter inbound access).

Step 11   Enable web data caching.

Step 12   Configure the firewall clients accordingly.

Step 13   Perform application filtering.

Step 14   Configure additional functionality (that is, VPN, remote logging, and so on) as required.

Summary

Application proxy firewalls can perform a specialized role in managing the security of an enterprise by providing for application layer inspection of the data that is being controlled. This allows application proxies to not only make filtering decisions based on the protocol or port that traffic is using, but by looking at the raw data and making a filtering determination based on the application itself, for example differentiating between malicious and non-malicious web traffic.

Microsoft ISA Server 2004 is a fully featured enterprise class firewall that provides for application filtering of many protocols, while implementing stateful packet inspection for all remaining traffic. It can be used as a standalone perimeter firewall but is particularly effective as the interior firewall in a dual-firewall architecture.

NOTE   For more information about Microsoft ISA Server 2004, check out *Dr. Tom Shinder's Configuring ISA Server 2004* (Syngress, 2004).

## CHAPTER 9

Where Firewalls Fit in a Network

Arguably, the most important task of any firewall implementation takes place before the firewall itself is ever configured. For a firewall to be able to successfully protect resources, it is critical to implement a design that lends itself to protecting those resources in the most efficient manner. Although virtually any firewall placed in front of resources will provide some degree of protection, if you implement a design based specifically on how the resources should be protected, and how the firewall itself functions, it will be that much easier to ensure that your resources are as secure and protected as they can possibly be. Simply put, you need to implement a design that places your firewall in the most strategic and effective location.

Different Types of Office Requirements

Although every firewall implementation is truly unique, a couple of fundamental designs from which virtually all firewall designs are created. The first question to ask when implementing a firewall is whether the firewall is going be located at a central location or a remote location. When you have answered that question, you need to examine the resources that need to be protected. With that in mind, the next step is to determine how many demilitarized zones (DMZs), if any, need to be implemented.

Although most of these design questions are based on protecting internal resources, they should be equally applied to the question of how the firewall will screen Internet access for your internal resources, essentially protecting the Internet from your systems, while at the same time enabling you to restrict and filter the kinds of Internet-based traffic that will be allowed from your internal resources.

Central Office

Although referred to as a central office implementation, the key to this implementation is not necessarily that it exists at the central office. Rather, the central office implementation refers to an implementation that has a number of common elements:

■   A concentration of resources must be protected by the firewall.

- A significant number of internal users need access to external resources through the firewall (for example, if the firewall handles the majority of the company's Internet access).

- Technical personnel can actively monitor and manage the firewall because they are physically located at the same location.

As a result, the central office implementation is applicable in any environment that matches these elements. For example, many large companies have multiple locations that would all warrant the central office design, because there may be two or more "hub" locations with a high concentration of users, resources, and administrators.

The central office implementation is highlighted by an implementation that tends to be more complex than the remote office implementation and tends to utilize higher end hardware and software to achieve the objective of protecting resources. For example, the central office may utilize multiple firewalls in a dual-firewall implementation to protect resources and may have multiple firewalls implemented in a task-specific fashion. You might have a separate Internet-screening firewall, web-application firewall, and e-mail-filtering firewall.

Central office implementation are also frequently underpinned by more advanced firewalls—such as Cisco Secure PIX Firewalls, NetScreen, Check Point, or Microsoft ISA Server—as opposed to smaller Network Address Translation (NAT) routers or small office/home office (SOHO) firewall products.

As a general rule, the central office implementation tends to provide for the most hardened and secure firewall implementation.

Remote Office

The remote office implementation tends to revolve around a more simple, point solution design. As opposed to the central office, remote offices typically have few technical resources at the location with the expertise required to effectively manage and maintain a firewall. Remote offices also rarely have internal resources that must be accessed by remote sources, which means that often the firewall implementation is little more than an Internet-screening firewall, keeping all Internet sources from accessing internal resources and restricting Internet access by internal resources.

Although the central office implementation lends itself to protecting literally thousands of users and resources, the remote office implementation is really only effective at protecting a relatively small number of users and resources, generally fewer than 100 users and resources. Consequently, the remote office implementation lends itself to the use of SOHO firewall solutions ranging from lower-end firewalls such as the Cisco PIX 506E, NetScreen 5, or NetScreen 25 all the way down to the basic NAT filtering routers such as some of the Linksys or D-Link product lines.

Single-Firewall Architectures

There are two predominant firewall architectures, the single-firewall and dual-firewall architectures. The single-firewall architecture is simpler because it relies on the use of a single firewall device with which to filter and control the flow of traffic.

If you elect to go with a single firewall for your firewall implementation, you can choose from a few different designs:

- Internet firewall with a single DMZ

- Internet firewall with multiple DMZs

- Internet-screening firewall (no DMZ)

Internet Firewall with a Single DMZ

The Internet firewall with a single DMZ is the most common firewall architecture, because it lends itself to being an all-around general-purpose architecture. With this architecture, the firewall has three interfaces: an internal interface that is connected to the protected network, an external interface that is connected to the Internet, and a DMZ interface that is connected to a screened subnet upon which reside the servers and systems that external users need to access. Because the resources on the DMZ segment have to go through the same interface to access both internal or external resources, this architecture is frequently referred to as a "DMZ-on-a-stick" architecture.

In this architecture, traffic flow is controlled in three directions. Traffic from Internet-based systems is permitted only to resources on the DMZ segment. Internet-based systems can never directly access resources on the internal network. Traffic from DMZ-based systems is permitted both to the Internet as well as to internal resources. In this fashion, the DMZ resources can frequently serve as a proxy in the event that data that resides on the internal network is required by the external system. Finally, traffic from the internal network is permitted to the DMZ as well as to the external network. In all situations, the only traffic that should be allowed is traffic that is explicitly permitted by a corresponding access control list (ACL). Figure 9-1 illustrates a single DMZ implementation with the corresponding traffic flow restrictions.

Internet Firewall with Multiple DMZs

The Internet firewall with multiple DMZs is similar to the single DMZ architecture, the only real difference being that there will be multiple single-homed DMZ segments coming off the firewall. There is no practical limit to the number of DMZ segments, the only real restriction being the number of interfaces the firewall can physically or logically support.

Figure 9-1 *Single Firewall with Single DMZ*

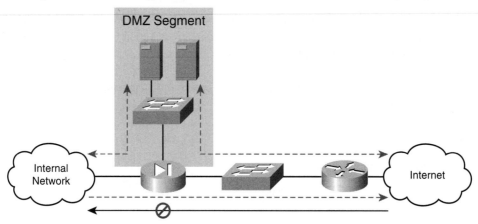

This architecture is typically implemented when the need to separate resources on different and distinct DMZ segments exists. With a single DMZ, all resources that will be accessed from external sources exist on the same DMZ segment, which means that if any one of those systems is compromised, there is nothing to stop the attacker from using that system to compromise more critical servers on that DMZ segment. To mitigate this, you can place systems with differing security requirements in their own DMZ segment, thus reducing the possibility that a compromise of an unrelated system will impact your more critical resources. For example, you may place web servers in one DMZ segment and Simple Mail Transfer Protocol (SMTP) servers in a different DMZ segment, so that if the web servers (which are traditionally more susceptible to attacks) are compromised, the SMTP servers are still safely protected on another DMZ segment where the firewall does not allow traffic between DMZ segments to pass.

Like with the single DMZ architecture, you want to control the flow of traffic in the same manner, preventing all traffic from external sources from accessing internal resources directly and, unless otherwise required, preventing all traffic from traversing from one DMZ segment to another. Figure 9-2 illustrates a single firewall with multiple DMZs architecture.

Internet-Screening Firewall (No DMZ)

A single firewall without a DMZ is really only suited to function as an Internet-screening firewall. This is because without a DMZ segment, any traffic coming from the external network breaks the cardinal rule of firewall design: that no traffic from an untrusted source can directly access internal resources.

An Internet-screening firewall exists to do two things. First, it prevents external hosts from initiating connections to any protected resource. Second, it can be implemented in such a manner as to filter and restrict traffic from internal hosts to external resources, typically through the use of content-filtering software such as Websense or SurfControl.

Internet-screening firewalls are also frequently implemented for remote office scenarios, because it is relatively rare that a remote office contains resources that need to be accessed from external sources.

Figure 9-2   *Single Firewall with Multiple DMZs*

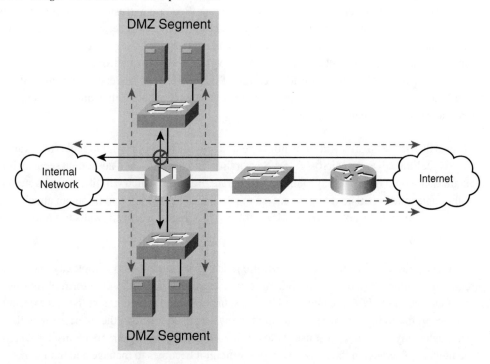

Dual-Firewall Architecture

The dual-firewall architecture is more complex than the single-firewall architecture, but it is also a more secure overall design and provides for a much more granular level of control over traffic traversing the firewalls. This is because the architecture uses two firewalls, ideally of different vendors and models, to act as exterior and interior firewalls providing a DMZ segment between the two firewalls, as shown in Figure 9-3. Like previous designs, traffic is permitted into the DMZ segment as well as from the internal network to the external network, but no traffic from the external network is permitted directly to the internal network.

Figure 9-3   *Dual-Firewall Architecture*

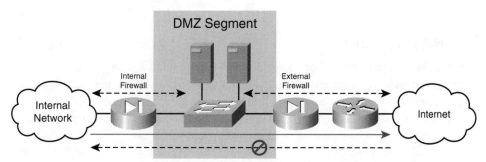

The granular control in a dual-firewall architecture comes from the fact that each firewall controls a subset of all the traffic entering and exiting a network. Because untrusted (that is, external) traffic should never be allowed to directly access a trusted (that is, internal) network, the exterior firewall can be configured specifically to grant access to and from the DMZ segment and external systems. Similarly, the interior firewall can be configured to grant access to and from the DMZ segment and internal resources. This allows for the creation of two distinct and independent points of control of all traffic into and out of all corporate network segments, whether they are DMZ segments or internal network segments.

When a dual-firewall architecture is implemented with different firewall models (for example, a Cisco PIX Firewall and a Microsoft ISA Server firewall), you also gain additional security because an attacker would need to compromise two separate firewalls (which will likely not be susceptible to the same attack methods) to gain access to protected resources. In addition, an attacker also needs to be knowledgeable in the workings of two different types of firewalls to tamper with the configurations.

The downsides of a dual-firewall architecture relate to implementation complexity and cost. With regard to complexity, a dual-firewall architecture frequently requires some form of routing be implemented in the DMZ segment to allow resources in the DMZ segment to send external-destined traffic to the exterior firewall and internal-destined traffic to the interior firewall. Although many companies just use static routing statements on the servers themselves, the larger the number of servers in the DMZ, the more difficult it becomes to manage and maintain so many routing statements. Whereas routers can be used, allowing the administrator just to update the router with new routes, the use of routing protocols should be avoided, because an attacker can potentially use the information provided by the routing protocol to gain insight regarding the internal network topology and structure.

Aside from the obvious costs related to implementing and maintaining multiple firewalls, it is also more expensive to implement and manage a dual-firewall architecture because you need people who understand multiple firewall technologies.

Because of the cost and complexity of the dual-firewall architecture, it is typically implemented in environments with critical security requirements such as banking, government, finance, and larger medical organizations.

The Firewall System

To paraphrase Shrek, the network perimeter is like an onion; it has lots of layers. Historically, a firewall has always been considered a device. It exists on the network perimeter—in many cases, it *is* the network perimeter—and is wholly responsible for controlling traffic entering and exiting a protected network. This philosophy is antiquated and no longer a relevant philosophy.

Instead, a firewall should no longer be considered a device, but a system of devices that work in concert to control the flow of traffic into and out of a protected network. In doing so, the firewall system implements a layered design that eliminates the reliance of any one device to do all the filtering. This has the effect of eliminating many of the single points of failure that exist in traditional "firewall device"–based implementations.

The firewall system layers depend on whether a single- or dual-firewall architecture has been implemented.

Single-Firewall System

With a single-firewall architecture, the firewall system consists of the following layers:

■ External router

■ Network segment between the external router and firewall

■ DMZ segment

Figure 9-4 depicts this architecture.

Figure 9-4   *Single Firewall System*

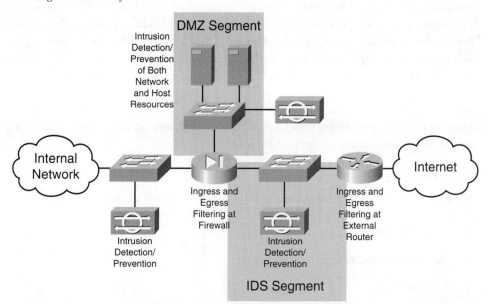

At the outermost layer of the firewall system, the external router should be the first point of control of traffic entering (ingress filtering) and exiting (egress filtering) your network. The only traffic that should be allowed to traverse the router is traffic destined for the firewall or resources being protected by the firewall. This serves two purposes. First, it makes it easier to monitor the traffic on the segment between the router and the firewall because only traffic that should be delivered to the firewall should exist on that segment. Second, it protects the firewall from any nonpermitted traffic, thus helping to ensure that if for some reason the firewall may be vulnerable to an exploit based on that nonpermitted traffic, it is stopped by the router. Keep in mind that in addition to protecting the firewall and protected resources, the router itself should be hardened and protected to ensure that external threats are not able to target the router directly.

The network segment between the external router and the firewall is the first point for implementing intrusion detection and prevention systems (IDS/IPS). Because only explicitly permitted traffic should be allowed to traverse the router, the IDS/IPS can be configured to send an alarm any time it detects nonpermitted traffic. This serves as an alarm that somehow the filtering at the external router has failed.

The firewall itself is the next layer, and it should be configured with ingress and egress filters to permit only traffic required by protected resources on either the DMZ or internal network segments. As previously mentioned, allowing traffic from external sources to internal sources should be prevented at all costs.

Resources in the DMZ segment should be protected by a combination of host-based firewalls and host- and network-based IDS/IPS. Such a setup enables you to permit or deny, at the server itself, exactly which traffic should be allowed. This setup effectively provides for three separate and distinct filtering layers—the external router, the firewall, the host itself—to provide for maximum protection of the resources in the DMZ. In addition to host-based firewalls, Layer 2 security controls such a private virtual LAN (VLAN) and IDS/IPS can protect the servers in the DMZ from being accessed by other servers in the DMZ, helping to ensure that if one server is compromised that it is unable to be used to access another server in an open and unfiltered manner.

Finally, the internal network is protected by filtering at the external router and the firewall and includes IDS/IPS between the firewall and the internal network, allowing you to identify and monitor all traffic that comes from the firewall.

Dual-Firewall System

With a dual-firewall architecture, the firewall system consists of the following layers:

- External router
- Network segment between external router and exterior firewall
- Exterior firewall
- DMZ segment
- Interior firewall

Figure 9-5 depicts a dual-firewall system.

Figure 9-5 *Dual-Firewall System*

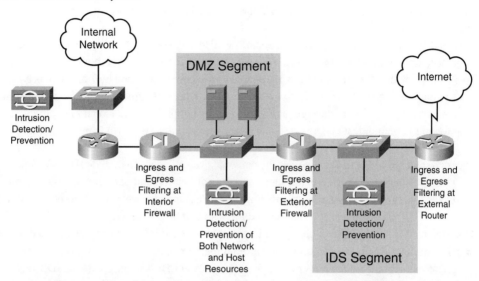

The only real physical difference with the dual-firewall system over the single-firewall system is the implementation of two firewalls. This setup provides for separate and distinct choke points in your network to control the flow of traffic, with the appropriate ingress and egress filtering on the exterior and interior firewalls.

Where Personal/Desktop Firewalls Fit in a Network

Personal and desktop firewalls are frequently overlooked as security devices that should be implemented on a network. BlackHat 2004 had a keynote speaker introduce the concept of the de-perimeterization of the network. The problem he pointed out was that today's applications require so many ports to be opened in the network firewall to function properly that the network firewall almost does not need to exist in the first place. Although I disagree that the network firewall does not need to exist, the basic idea that we cannot rely on network firewalls alone to protect resources is a sound one. After all, a network firewall can only control traffic that passes through it. If an attacker can gain control of a system on the other side of the firewall, he potentially has unfiltered and unrestricted access to launch attacks from the compromised system to all other systems, rendering the network firewall useless as a defense mechanism.

Consequently, it is a good idea to incorporate firewall technologies on the servers themselves, giving you the ability to control traffic at the point closest to the data that you need to protect: the server network interface card (NIC). Because the firewall is running on the server itself, you can implement the most restrictive filtering rules possible, literally permitting only the traffic specifically required by the applications running on the server.

As illustrated in Chapter 4, "Personal and Desktop Firewalls," there are a number of ways to implement personal firewalls, ranging from built-in utilities such as Windows Firewall for

Windows-based systems and IP filter for UNIX- and Linux-based systems to third-party firewall applications such as Trend Micro, ZoneAlarm, and Cisco Security Agent (CSA).

When determining the appropriate personal firewall to use, you must consider a few elements. First, you need to determine whether you need to control both inbound and outbound traffic with the personal firewall. Many built-in firewalls enable you to control inbound traffic, which is typically the most important traffic to manage; however, the ability to control outbound traffic can be an important defense strategy to prevent the spread of worms. For example, if the personal firewall will not allow the worm to communicate on a port, it can effectively prevent the worm from spreading.

Second, you need to consider whether the personal firewall needs to include IDS/IPS functionality. Because the personal firewall exists closest to the application and data that needs to be protected, it makes for a great location to implement an IDS/IPS. One of the biggest weaknesses of network-based IDS/IPS is that the sheer volume of data that must be processed is too great for the IDS/IPS to effectively filter and report on. When implemented as a component of the personal firewall, however, the IDS/IPS can be configured around the very specific traffic that is necessary for the applications running on the server, making it much easier to filter traffic with the IDS/IPS (because only the traffic required by the applications running on the server should be allowed).

Finally, you need to consider what will be necessary to provide for centralized management and reporting on your personal/desktop firewalls. It is one thing to manage a handful of perimeter network firewalls. When you start talking about implementing and needing to manage, maintain, configure and report on thousands of firewalls in an environment, however, the issues around centralized management and reporting become significant problems. Consequently, it is extremely important to look in detail at the enterprise-level capabilities of these products. A good personal/desktop firewall for a home user is not necessarily going to be a good solution for 10,000 desktops in an enterprise.

Where Application Firewalls Fit in a Network

The closer you come to the resource that needs to be protected, the more intelligent and specific you can get in filtering traffic directed at that resource. Because application firewalls enable you to perform deep packet inspection and filter based on the raw application data, they are best suited for implementation close to the resources they protect. There are a couple of reasons for this.

First, many application firewalls cannot filter traffic for which a proxy does not exist. As a result, if an application firewall receives traffic that it cannot proxy, it is forced to drop the traffic. The closer to the resources being protected that the application firewall is implemented, the less the likelihood is that it will have to deal with traffic other than traffic that is actually destined for the protected resource.

Second, because application firewalls typically perform a more detailed inspection of the data, they perform worse than a comparable stateful packet-filtering firewall. By placing the firewall closest to the resources being protected, you reduce the volume of extraneous traffic that the firewall must filter, thus preventing the firewall from becoming a performance bottleneck.

Application firewalls are most commonly implemented in a dual-firewall architecture as the interior firewall. This setup allows the firewall to perform the most in-depth inspection of the traffic that is actually destined for your internal network.

Firewalls and VLANs

One of the most common questions with regard to designing a firewall implementation is how VLANs and firewalls interact with each other. Historically, firewalls and VLANs went together like oil and water. Physical separation of resources for the purposes of security was a sacred cow. It was an untouchable fact in network security. This was reinforced by exploits and security issues that allowed traffic to traverse between VLANs without going through a firewall or router, effectively bypassing any security that was in place. A few things have contributed to a change in thinking regarding firewalls and VLANs.

First, people became very comfortable with VLANs on their internal networks and started using them to segment resources logically throughout their internal network. Second, people started to realize that if they used multiple DMZs to house resources of differing types, they could further segment and secure their perimeter resources by placing resources with common access rules in different DMZ segments, instead of just tossing everything into a single DMZ segment. The problem with creating so many DMZ segments is that doing so required an incredible expenditure in network infrastructure equipment such as switches and firewalls. After all, physically separate DMZ segments required a dedicated switch and firewall interface on each DMZ segment, at a minimum, which frequently made the solution cost prohibitive. To address the cost issues, VLANs were looked at as a viable solution. Finally, switch vendors began securing their software to help prevent the circumstances (typically buffer overflows) that would allow traffic to traverse VLAN segments without going through the firewall or router.

Separate DMZ segments are fundamentally no different than separate subnets on an internal network. On the internal network, VLANs are used to logically separate subnets in lieu of physical separation. The benefits of this are well understood. It is cheaper to implement because you do not need physically distinct switches or routers for each subnet, and it is easier to manage the overall environment because moving resources from subnet to subnet merely requires a change in the VLAN configuration (and, of course, a change of the IP address of the system being moved). This same logic was applied to the network perimeter, which resulted in using VLANs to create distinct DMZ segments. Although using VLANs addressed the cost issue completely, the use of VLANs creates a couple of important issues for folks to consider.

First, whereas logical separation of resources on a trusted network was generally considered an adequate security risk, it is not as secure as physical separation of resources. At the end of the day, a logically separated subnet is still physically connected to other subnets in the same switch fabric. Normally for traffic to go from one VLAN to another, it must go through a router (or firewall and thus can be filtered accordingly); because there is no actual physical separation between the VLANs, however, it is possible for traffic on one VLAN to inadvertently be delivered to another VLAN without using a router or firewall. The most common exploit to take advantage of this logical separation is to create a situation that causes the switch to forward packets across VLANs without going through the corresponding router or firewall. On a trusted network, this might not be a big deal. If the only separation between your internal network and the Internet is a VLAN, however, the risk becomes much more substantial. Traffic from the Internet could wind up on your internal network, completely bypassing the firewall. It's important not to overstate this risk. It is not really a trivial task to accomplish, and when switches have been found to be vulnerable to such an attack the vendors tend to fix the switch software relatively quickly, but the risk does exist.

NOTE   For more information about VLAN security, check out the following white papers:
http://www.sans.org/rr/whitepapers/networkdevs/1090.php
http://www.cisco.com/en/US/netsol/ns340/ns394/ns171/ns128/networking_solutions_white_
paper09186a008014870f.shtml

The second issue to consider when using VLANs is that because there is no physical separation of resources, a server on one DMZ segment may be plugged into the same switch right next to a server in another DMZ segment. This setup can make it very easy to inadvertently plug a server into the wrong VLAN, and thus the wrong DMZ segment (which may create an inadvertent security risk). Although you can mitigate this by paying careful attention to detail and having well-documented and well-followed procedures and policies, the bottom line is that the best technical controls out there cannot prevent every instance of human error. Some examples of good practices to mitigate this problem are as follows:

■   Set trunking to off on all access ports.

■   Enable port fast on all access ports.

■   Implement port security on all access ports.

■   Limit the use of VLAN 1.

■   Configure dedicated native VLANs on trunk ports.

■   Manually configure allowed VLANs on trunk ports.

■   Shut down all unused ports and place them in an unused VLAN.

Although you can use VLANs in the network perimeter, it is important not to use them to separate resources that have distinctly different security levels. For example, the Internet and the internal network should always be physically separated from every other network or DMZ segment with a firewall physically sitting between the segments and controlling the flow of traffic. Additionally, if you are going to use VLANs, you should implement an IDS/IPS solution that can notify you of traffic that has an incorrect source or destination IP address, indicating that traffic from one VLAN may be incorrectly on a different VLAN or that a server from one VLAN may have been inadvertently plugged into the wrong VLAN. You should also plan on implementing VLAN access control lists (VACLs) to provide a means of filtering traffic at Layer 2, and thus within the VLAN, to further protect resources.

Virtual Firewalls

Virtual firewalls build upon the practice of using VLANs. After all, if you can logically separate a switch into multiple subnets, why not have the ability to use a single interface on a firewall (or a logical interface on a firewall blade in a switch chassis) to filter between those logical subnets. The benefit of this approach is that you further reduce the cost of implementation by removing the need for each VLAN to connect to a physically distinct interface.

Virtual firewalls are most commonly implemented by separating a single firewall into multiple logical firewalls, sometimes referred to as security contexts. Virtual firewalls are also frequently implemented on network devices that support firewall hardware or software as a component of the network device. For example, a Cisco Catalyst 6500 with a Firewall Services Module (FWSM) allows you to create up to 100 virtual firewalls within the switch. The virtual firewall can then be associated with corresponding VLANs, providing the same functionality that would exist if a physical firewall had been used to segment the VLANs from the rest of the network.

Because virtual firewalls can so easily be integrated into many switches, they are a good way to segment and secure internal resources. Virtual firewalls are also commonly used to segment DMZ segments that use VLANs as the segmentation method. This allows multiple VLANs to be secured by multiple virtual firewalls using a single firewall interface.

A big disadvantage of virtual firewalls is the fact that many folks have a hard time conceptualizing virtual devices and objects. This can make it difficult to troubleshoot or diagnose problems. Additionally, each virtual firewall is typically treated as an individually managed and maintained resource, in addition to the system context (or physical device itself), which increases management costs. Finally, not all virtual firewalls can function exactly as if there were a physical firewall. For example, in certain configurations, virtual firewalls may not be able to support technologies such as dynamic routing protocols (such as when using Cisco FWSM and transparent mode configuration).

Using Firewalls to Segment Internal Resources

Perhaps the most overlooked implementation of a firewall is on the internal network. Many companies make the mistake of considering their entire internal network to be a trusted network. Unfortunately, the prevalence of worms and viruses today undermine this philosophy. Companies are repeatedly decimated by worms that spread unchecked throughout the network because there are no firewalls implemented throughout the internal network to segment and control traffic on the internal network. In a number of instances, firewalls should be considered on the internal network:

■   To protect sensitive internal resources

- To protect from WAN or remote-access (VPN, dial-in, etc.) requests

- To protect individual internal resources

Protecting Sensitive Internal Resources

Sensitive internal resources include any servers that contain critical and sensitive data such as human resources (HR) data, financial data, or source code. This could also include segmenting resources based on things such as department or job function. These servers and resources should really only be accessed by certain individuals, and in conjunction with access controls in place on the server itself, a firewall can be used to prevent unauthorized hosts from even being able to access the server in the first place. For example, if the HR server only should be accessed by the HR department, and the HR department resources are on a defined range of IP addresses, a firewall can be configured to only allow those IP addresses to access the server over the network. An even better implementation exists in environments where the firewall can be configured, frequently through the use of VLANS, to place all the HR resources (both the servers and the computers of all the HR users) on the same protected subnet. This enables you to configure the firewall to block all traffic from external sources, while still allowing the HR users to access any resources on the rest of the internal network. Figure 9-6 depicts this kind of segmentation.

Protecting from WAN or Remote-Access Requests

Another overlooked part of the internal network is the remote locations that exist either across the WAN or across a VPN or dial-in connection. Because these are still corporate-owned and -managed networks, the tendency is to treat them as trusted network segments. Unfortunately, small office locations rarely are given the level of technical resources that the corporate or larger office locations are. That makes those remote computers and systems more vulnerable to attack and compromise than the systems at the well managed central office.

To protect against this, all traffic from remote locations should be filtered such that the remote systems only have access to the resources that they require. For example, think of your network as a wheel (the central office) with a bunch of spokes (the remote offices). The odds are in favor that most of the remote offices do not need to communicate with each other. As a result, you should prevent them from being able to do so. This policy has the intentional side effect of also working to prevent the spread of worms throughout your network by ensuring that the remote offices are unable to infect each other directly.

Filtering of the WAN traffic should not be restricted only to preventing the remote offices from communicating with each other, however. Even at the central or main offices, firewalls should be implemented to control the resources that remote offices are allowed to access. For example, if the remote offices only need access to e-mail, implement a firewall to only allow access to the e-mail servers.

Figure 9-6 *Using a Virtual Firewall to Protect Internal Resources*

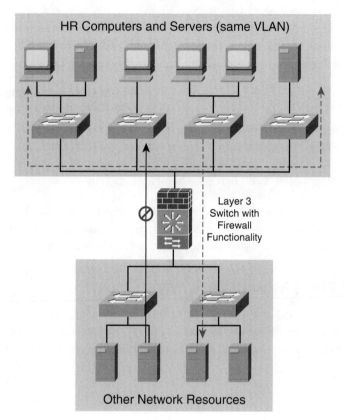

Protecting Individual Internal Resources

Individual internal resources can range from your important servers to every single device on your network. On the surface, it may seem an insurmountable task to protect all of your internal resources. However, through the use of a combination of network and in particular host-based firewalls, it is a surprisingly doable task to implement a filtering strategy throughout your internal network that can effectively protect any individual resource on the entire internal network.

Be Realistic When Implementing Internal Firewalls

It is easy to become overwhelmed with implementing firewalls on the internal network because we have a tendency to think that we need a full-blown firewall everywhere. Unless your company is exceedingly rich, you probably will not get 100 dedicated firewalls to filter traffic from 100 WAN connections. Keep in mind that when we are talking about firewalls, we are talking about everything from simple packet-filtering routers to full-blown application proxies. It is important to select the proper firewall for the correct circumstances, and although a packet-filtering router is probably not a good choice as your only line of defense from the Internet, it can be a great choice for use within the internal network.

Because most of your WAN circuits and subnets have to traverse a router anyway, implementing filtering on the router is an easy thing to do without needing to spend the money necessary to implement a separate and distinct firewall. When you consider the functionality provided by routers that are capable of running firewall code, such as the Cisco IOS Firewall, it becomes easy to implement full-featured firewall filtering throughout the network at a minimal cost.

Also keep in mind the performance implications of implementing firewalls throughout the internal network. Most firewalls do a fine job of performance as it relates to Internet connections. When you start looking at implementing firewalls on internal networks, however, keep in mind that the amount of bandwidth required for internal networks is typically much, much higher (T1 speeds versus Gigabit Ethernet speeds) and that the firewall needs to be able to handle these increased levels of performance or it will become a bottleneck on your network.

Finally, perhaps the best firewall for use on an internal network is a virtual firewall running on the corresponding switch or network device. As previously mentioned, this allows for devices on the switch fabric, regardless of what ports they may be connected to, to be effectively protected from other devices.

High-Availability Firewall Designs

Because firewalls have become critical infrastructure components on the network, it is important to ensure that the firewall, and the functionality that it provides, is always available and accessible. Firewall high availability (HA) and redundancy is typically handled in one of two ways:

- Active/passive failover

- Active/active failover

Regardless of the failover method, firewall HA relies on implementing two firewalls in a parallel configuration. With an active/passive system, one firewall is actively passing traffic while the other firewall is completely passive and does not pass any traffic. If the active firewall fails for whatever reason, the passive firewall becomes the active firewall, allowing for traffic to continue to be transmitted. With an active/active system, each firewall is able to pass traffic that is typically defined by separate and distinct security contexts. A security context is simply the firewall ruleset and functions that a physical firewall is responsible for at any give time. Figure 9-7 shows an active/active system.

In this example, each firewall is the active firewall for their respective DMZ segment, Firewall1 for DMZ1 and Firewall2 for DMZ2. If for some reason Firewall2 were to fail, the traffic destined for DMZ2 would be redirected to Firewall1, which would then deliver it to DMZ2 accordingly. It is important to note that in most cases each firewall in an active/active configuration cannot pass the same traffic at the same time. For example, Firewall1 and Firewall2 cannot both be responsible for the same ruleset that permits traffic to the same DMZ segment. One firewall is the primary, and thus handles all the traffic (such as the case with Firewall1 and DMZ1 in Figure 9-7), and the other firewall is the secondary, and thus only handles the traffic if the primary fails (such as the case with Firewall2 and DMZ1 in Figure 9-7). The primary advantage of an active/active configuration is that you do not have an entire firewall and related hardware sitting unused except in the event that a failure occurs. An active/active configuration also allows you to perform some basic load balancing by placing some of the load on one firewall with the remaining load on the other firewall.

Figure 9-7 *Active/Active Failover Example*

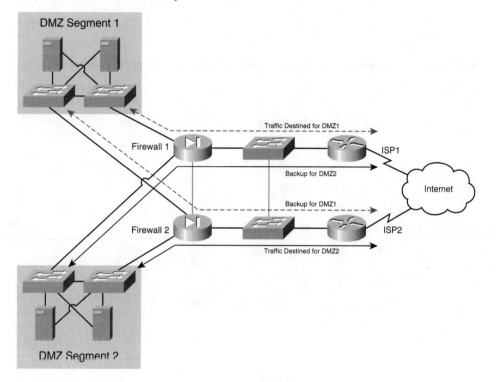

Summary

Perhaps the most important work that can be done to ensure that a firewall can effectively protect the resources it should is done before the firewall is even out of the box: by making the best decision on what it needs to protect and where to place it. It's important to understand which type of firewall design will best protect the resources that need protection. Although a single firewall will do an adequate job of protecting most resources, certain high security environments may warrant using a dual-firewall architecture to minimize exposure and risk.

As important as the design is, it is just as important to determine which firewall best provides the functionality required. Not all firewalls are equal, and an application firewall may be less effective than a transparent firewall in certain circumstances. Similarly, if you require HA from your firewall implementation, you need to ensure that the design solution supports operating in an HA mode.

The most important thing to remember, however, is that a firewall is not a device. It is a system of devices that, if properly implemented, provides multiple layers of defense between the resources you want to protect and malicious users and traffic that want to gain access to them.

Part III: Managing and Maintaining Firewalls

## CHAPTER 10

Firewall Security Policies

The term *security policy* has a number of meanings in the industry. On one hand, it refers to the written policies that dictate how the organization manages the security of their resources. On the other hand, it refers to the actual configuration of the device in question, such as with an access control list (ACL).

This chapter looks at both forms of security policy as they relate to firewalls:

■ The written security policies (sometimes referred to as information security policies) that define what the security objectives for the organization (including their firewalls) are

■ The ingress- and egress-filtering and management policies (sometimes referred to as firewall policies or the firewall ruleset) that define the actual configuration of the device

Written Security Policies

Written security policies exist to provide a high-level roadmap of what needs to be done to ensure that the organization has a well-defined and thought-out security strategy. It is a common misconception that an organization has *a* security policy. In fact, an organization's overall security policy typically consists of numerous individual security policies, which are written to address specific objectives, devices, or issues.

The objective of a security policy is to define what needs to be protected, who is responsible for protection, and in some cases how the protection will occur. This last function is typically separated out into a standalone procedure document such as the ingress-filtering, egress-filtering, or management-access policy documents discussed later in this chapter. In a nutshell, the security policy should simply and concisely outline the specific requirements, rules, and objectives that must be met, to provide a measurable method of validating the security posture of the organization.

To help ensure that your security policies will do this, think of the firewall in terms of security layers, with each layer having a specific realm of operation. Figure 10-1 illustrates this layered view of the firewall. As you can see, the firewall is separated into four distinct components.

Figure 10-1 *Firewall Security Layers*

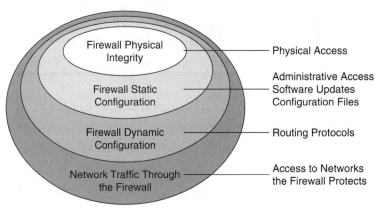

At the center is the firewall physical integrity layer, which is predominantly concerned with the physical access to the firewall. Consequently, you want to ensure that your security policies address issues related to gaining physical access to the device, such as through a hard console port connection.

The next layer is the firewall static configuration, which is predominantly concerned with access to the static configured software the firewall is running (for example, the PIX operating system and startup configuration). At this layer, your security policy needs to focus on defining the controls that will be required to restrict administrative access, including performing software updates and configuring the firewall.

The third layer is the firewall dynamic configuration, which complements the static configuration by being concerned with the dynamic configuration of the firewall through the use of technologies such as routing protocols, Address Resolution Protocol (ARP) commands, interface and device status, audit logs, and shun commands. The objective of the security policy at this point is to define the requirements around what kinds of dynamic configurations will be permitted.

Finally, you have the network traffic through the firewall layer, which is really what the firewall exists to do—protect resources. This layer is concerned with functionality such as ACLs and service proxy information. The security policy at this layer is responsible for defining the requirements as they relate to traffic passing through the firewall.

> **TIP**   When you decide to create your security policies, remember a couple of things:
>
> - The security policy should specify security objectives, not necessarily the actual configuration or commands that need to be run. This allows the policy to be portable across platforms, because all firewalls typically have the same issues and requirements, regardless of the actual commands or configuration required to achieve the requirements.
>
> - In working through your policies, continue to refer back to the layered structure in Figure 10-1 to ensure that the policy addresses all potential issues. Work from the inside (physical security) to the outside. Doing so will reduce the likelihood of overlooking a critical security requirement.

The Difference Between Policies, Standards, Guidelines, and Procedures

One of the more confusing elements of security policies is the interaction between policies, standards, guidelines, and procedures. First, let's define what we mean by each:

- **Policy**—A policy is a document that outlines the requirements or rules that must be met. Policies frequently refer to standards or guidelines as the basis for the existence. The scope of a policy tends to be a broad, high level statement of intent. An example of a policy is an Encryption Use Policy, which might state to the effect of "encryption should be used in these circumstances."

- **Standard**—A standard is a set of requirements, typically system or technology specific, that must be adhered to by everyone. The scope of a standard tends to be to specify the requirements about a given technology or area. An example might be defining that the only acceptable encryption algorithms are Triple DES (3DES) or Advanced Encryption Standard (AES).

- **Guideline**—A guideline is similar to a standard, but it differs in that unlike a standard, a guideline is merely a recommendation or suggestion that should probably be followed but is not necessarily required. Guidelines and standards are largely interchangeable in most cases.

- **Procedure**—A procedure defines the process that is followed to meet the requirements of a policy, standard, or guideline. The scope of a procedure is the specific step-by-step processes and procedures that should be followed for implementing a given standard or guideline. An example of this might be defining the procedures required to implement 3DES or AES encryption on your firewalls.

Figure 10-2 helps to illustrate the relationship between policies, standards, and procedures as a pyramid. Keep in mind that standards and guidelines are interchangeable and occupy the same level in the pyramid. As you go down the pyramid, the documents get more detailed and are more subject to change. So, policies are broad and do not change often. Standards and guidelines are more detailed but more susceptible to change. Procedures are extremely detailed and may frequently change as they incorporate new standards or methods of performing the given tasks.

Figure 10-2   *Policies, Standards, and Procedures Pyramid*

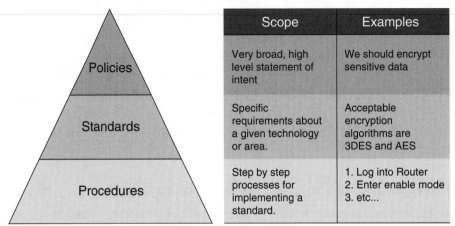

Security Policy Format

To accomplish the goals defined previously, most security policies adhere to a particular format or layout and share common elements. Generally speaking, most security policies share seven sections:

■   **Overview**—The overview section provides a brief explanation of what the policy addresses.

■   **Purpose**—The purpose section explains why the policy is needed.

■   **Scope**—The scope section defines what the policy applies to and defines who is responsible for the policy.

■   **Policy**—The policy section is the actual policy itself.

■   **Enforcement**—The enforcement section defines how the policy should be enforced and the repercussions of not following the policy.

■   **Definitions**—The definitions section contains the definition of any terms or concepts used in the policy.

■   **Revision history**—The revision history section is where the changes to the policy are documented and tracked.

Common Security Policies

Each organization has unique security requirements and therefore their own unique security policies. However, most if not all environments require a number of common security policies, including the following:

■   Management-access policy

■   Filtering policy

- Routing policy

- Remote-access/VPN policy

- Monitoring/logging policy

- Demilitarized zone (DMZ) policy

- Generally applicable policies

Firewall policies (that is, the access policies on the actual firewalls) are covered later in this chapter.

> **NOTE**   For more information about security policies and how to write effective security policies, check out the following resources:
>
> - RFC 2196, *Site Security Handbook* http://www.ietf.org/rfc/rfc2196.txt
>
> - RFC 2504, *Users' Security Handbook* http://www.ietf.org/rfc/rfc2504.txt
>
> - SANS Security Policy Project http://www.sans.org/resources/policies/
>
> - *Hardening Network Infrastructure* (by Wes Noonan, McGraw-Hill Osborne Media), Chapters 2 and 13

Management-Access Policy

As the name implies, the management-access policy exists to define the permissible methods and manner of management access to the firewall. This policy tends to address the firewall physical integrity and firewall static configuration security layers. The management-access policy needs to define which protocols for both remote and local management will be allowed, as well as which users can connect to the firewall and which permissions those users will have to perform tasks.

In addition, the management-access policy should define the requirements for management protocols such as Network Time Protocol (NTP), syslog, TFTP, FTP, Simple Network Management Protocol (SNMP), and any other protocols that may be used to manage and maintain the device.

Filtering Policy

Rather than defining the actual ruleset a firewall will use, the filtering policy needs to just and concisely define the kinds of filtering that must be used and where filtering is applicable. This policy tends to address the firewall static configuration and in particular the network traffic through the firewall layers. For example, a good filtering policy needs to require both ingress and egress filtering be performed with the firewall. The filtering policy should also define the general requirements in connecting dissimilar security level networks and resources. For example, with a DMZ, depending on the direction of the traffic, different filtering requirements may be necessary, and it is the role of the filtering policy to define those requirements.

Routing Policy

The routing policy is typically not a firewall-centric document. However, with more complex perimeter designs as well as the increasing use of firewalls within the internal network, firewalls can easily become part of the routed infrastructure. The routing policy should have a section that specifies including a firewall in the routed infrastructure and defines the method in which the routing will occur. This policy tends to address the firewall static configuration and firewall dynamic configuration layers. In most cases, the routing policy should explicitly prohibit the firewall from sharing the internal network routing table with any external resources. Similarly, the routing policy should define the circumstances in which dynamic routing protocols and static routes are appropriate. The policy should also define any protocol-specific security mechanisms that should be configured, (for example, the use of hashing algorithms to ensure only authenticated nodes can pass routing data).

Remote-Access/VPN Policy

In today's realm of convergence, the difference between the firewall and the VPN concentrator have become more and more blurred. Virtually all major-market firewalls can serve as the termination point for VPNs, and therefore the remote-access/VPN policy needs to define the requirements for the level of encryption and authentication that a VPN connection will require. In many cases, the VPN policy in conjunction with the organization's encryption policy defines the overall VPN methodology that will be used. This policy tends to address the firewall static configuration and network traffic through the firewall layers.

The remote-access/VPN policy also needs to define the protocols that will be used: IP Security (IPsec), Layer 2 Transport Protocol (L2TP), or Point-to-Point Transport Protocol (PPTP). In most cases, IPsec should be used exclusively. Assuming IPsec, the remote-access/VPN policy needs to require the use of preshared keys and extended authentication, with the use of certificates, one-time passwords, and a full Public Key Infrastructure (PKI) for the most secure of environments. Similarly, the remote-access/VPN policy should define what client will be used (that is, the built-in Microsoft VPN client, the Cisco Secure VPN Client, and so on).

Finally, the remote-access/VPN policy needs to define what kind of access and resources will be made available to remote connections and the types of remote connections that will be allowed. For example, if you will allow site-to-site as well as remote client VPN connections, the remote-access/VPN policy needs to define when each type of connection will be used.

Monitoring/Logging Policy

One of the most critical elements of ensuring that a firewall is providing the expected level of security is to implement a firewall monitoring system. The monitoring/logging policy defines the methods and degree of monitoring that will be performed. At a minimum, the monitoring/logging policy should provide a mechanism for tracking the performance of the firewall as well as the occurrence of all security-related events and log entries. This policy tends to address the firewall static configuration layer.

The monitoring/logging policy should also define how the information should be collected, maintained, and reported on. In many cases, this information can be used for defining the requirements of third-party management and monitoring applications such as CiscoWorks, NetIQ Security Manager, or Kiwi Syslog Daemon.

DMZ Policy

The DMZ policy is a wide-ranging document that defines all the elements of not only the DMZ itself but the devices in the DMZ, too. The objective of the DMZ policy is to define the standards and requirements of all devices and connectivity and traffic flow as it relates to the DMZ. This policy tends to address the firewall static configuration and network traffic through the firewall layers.

Because of the complexity of the typical DMZ environment, the DMZ policy is potentially going to be a large, multipage document. To help ensure that the DMZ policy remains functional and effective, typically three broad standards should be defined for all DMZ-related devices, connectivity, and traffic flow:

- Ownership responsibilities

- Secure configuration requirements

- Operational and change-control requirements

Ownership Responsibilities

As illustrated in Chapter 8, "Application Proxy Firewalls," the DMZ has the potential of being the most complex network segment in your entire network, including systems and applications for any number of different groups. Consequently, it is critical to define not only who is responsible for any given system or application but also what those responsibilities entail. Common requirements include the following:

- Full documentation of resources in the enterprise management system

- Appropriate name resolution for all addressable network interfaces

- Immediate access to systems in accordance with the corporate audit policy

- Full adherence to the corporate change control policy

- A 24/7 contact list that ownership groups will make available in the event that systems need to be accessed outside of normal work hours

Secure Configuration Requirements

Because of the unique situation of DMZ systems existing in many cases to allow unknown users to access resources, systems in the DMZ typically must be more secured than would be a typical system on the internal network (for right or wrong, some would contend that all systems should be as hardened as possible, regardless of their location in the network). As a result, it is important to define configuration requirements, such as the following:

- All systems must be patched with vendor updates in a timely fashion.

- All systems and software must be approved by the organizations IT security group.

- All systems must be hardened in accordance with corporate hardening standards.

- All unnecessary software and services must be either disabled or uninstalled if possible.

- Service access must be restricted through the use of ACLs and proxy servers where possible.

- All remote administration must occur over secure channels.

- All systems must be monitored and all events must be saved to an approved log format.

- No administration capabilities will be permitted from external sources.

- All trust relationships between systems will only be permitted if a valid business justification and no alternative workarounds are available.

- Systems will be segmented within the DMZ.

NOTE For more information about industry-accepted hardening guides and recommendations, see the Security Configuration Guides located at http://www.nsa.gov/snac/. These are an excellent resource for using as the baseline from which to develop your own organization-specific hardening recommendations.

Operational and Change-Control Requirements

The operational requirements define what must be done for day-to-day operation and maintenance. The key elements of the operational requirements are to ensure that all systems must adhere to the corporate change-management policy and that all configuration changes must be authorized by the corporate IT security group. Additionally, the operational requirements should stipulate that all adds, moves, and changes must adhere to the corporate DMZ deployment process and procedure.

Generally Applicable Policies

In addition to firewall-specific policies, there are numerous generally applicable policies that although not firewall specific (they have application to many devices, not just firewalls) should nonetheless be applicable to the firewall. These include the following:

- **Password policy**—The corporate password policy should be referred to for not only defining administrative access to the firewall but for use in creating preshared secrets, hashes, and community strings.

- **Encryption policy**—The corporate encryption policy should be referred to for defining all forms of encrypted access, including Hypertext Transfer Protocol, Secure (HTTPS), Secure Sockets Layer (SSL), Secure Shell (SSH), and IPsec/VPN access.

- **Auditing policy**—The corporate auditing policy should be referred to for defining the audit requirements of the firewall.

- **Risk-assessment policy**—The corporate risk-assessment policy should be referred to for defining the methodology that will be used to identify the risks associated with all system add, moves, and changes as it relates to the firewall and network perimeter in general.

Firewall Security Policy

One of the reasons for covering this security policy separately after the other common security policies is that it may well contain or replace elements of any of the previously mentioned security policies. The firewall security policy (sometimes known as the firewall policy) should address all the firewall-specific security requirements, as defined in the layered structure of Figure 10-1. In doing this, the firewall policy may overlap, include, or refer to elements from any of the previous mentioned security policies. In addition, if any other security policies are applicable to the firewall, they should be referenced in this document. A good checklist to ensure complete coverage of your firewall security policy is to build a checklist based on the four layers from Figure 10-1. The following sections cover these four layers.

Firewall Physical Integrity

To ensure that your firewall security policy adequately addresses physical security, make sure that the following elements are components of the security policy:

- Define who is authorized to install, uninstall, and move the firewall.

- Define who is authorized to perform hardware maintenance and to change the physical configuration of the firewall.

- Define who is authorized to physically connect to the firewall, in particular through the console port or physical logon console.

- Define the appropriate recovery requirements in the event of a physical failure or evidence of tampering with the firewall.

Firewall Static Configuration

To ensure that your firewall security policy adequately addresses static configuration security, make sure that the following elements are components of the security policy:

- Define who is authorized to login to the firewall via any connectivity method (local or remote).

- Define the appropriate privileges and users to which the privileges are applicable.

- Define the procedures for performing configuration changes and firewall updates.

- Define the password policy (typically in conjunction with the corporate password policy) for the firewall.

- Define the method of remote login capability, including defining the permitted networks or systems from which remote logins will be allowed (typically in conjunction with the management-access policy).

- Define the recovery procedures for the firewall in the event of a failure.

- Define the audit log policy for the firewall (typically in conjunction with the corporate audit policy).

- Define the encryption requirements for the firewall (typically in conjunction with the corporate encryption policy).

- Define the method of remote management and monitoring (that is, SNMP, syslog, and so on) for the firewall (typically in conjunction with the management-access policy).

Firewall Dynamic Configuration

To ensure that your firewall security policy adequately addresses dynamic configuration security, make sure that the following elements are components of the security policy:

- Define what kinds of dynamic configuration processes and services will be permitted to run on the firewall as well as what networks and devices will have access to those processes and services.

- Define the routing protocols that will be allowed and the security features that will be required.

- Define how the firewall will update and maintain the clock information (that is, NTP).

- Define how one-time password or similar authentication or dynamic encryption and key algorithms will be maintained.

Network Traffic through the Firewall

To ensure that your firewall security policy adequately addresses traffic through the firewall, make sure that the following elements are components of the firewall security policy:

- Define the method by which traffic will be permitted and denied (for example, will traffic be permitted to specific segments and so on).

- Define the process for requesting changes and updates to the firewall ruleset.

- Define the kinds of protocols, ports, and services that will be permitted or denied (this information may be included in more detail in a separate ingress- and egress-filtering document).

This information should be used to build your ingress and egress filters, as discussed in the next section.

Firewall Policies/Rulesets

The previously mentioned policies focus primarily on defining the requirements and expectations of the firewall and interrelated systems. After the requirements have been defined however, you must actually build the configuration and ruleset that the firewall will use. Although somewhat confusing, this is also commonly referred to as the firewall security policy, even though practically the firewall security policy is better defined as a combination of standards, guidelines, and procedures than a policy per se.

For this reason, I like to think of the firewall policy more in terms of the firewall ruleset, to ensure that there is a distinction between the security policies that define the requirements and the security policies (or ruleset) that define the actual rule configuration that adheres to the defined requirements. Generally speaking, three common rulesets need to be defined for the firewall:

- Ingress filters

- Egress filters

- Management-access ruleset

Ingress Filters

Ingress filters are used to restrict traffic coming into an interface or from a given network segment. Ingress filters are commonly applied to traffic coming from an untrusted source (such as the Internet or a DMZ segment) to a trusted source (such as a DMZ or internal network, respectively). To really get comfortable with the concept of ingress filters, it is important to understand that a filter is an ingress filter relative to the direction and source of the traffic being filtered. For example, if you consider a simple single firewall configuration with a one-armed DMZ segment, potentially two ingress filters would apply to the firewall, as pointed out in Figure 10-3.

Figure 10-3 *Ingress Filters*

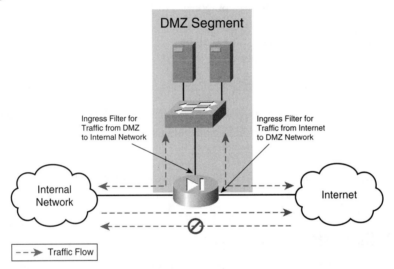

As you can see by the traffic-flow arrows, traffic can flow from the Internet to the DMZ segment, from the DMZ segment to the internal network, from the internal network to either the DMZ or the Internet, and from the DMZ to the Internet (these last two scenarios are technically egress-filtering scenarios, which we discuss in the "Egress Filters" section). Flow is not permitted from the Internet directly to the internal network.

In this scenario, two potential ingress filters will be built. The first will control the access from the Internet to the DMZ. In this instance, the Internet is considered the untrusted network, and the DMZ is considered the trusted network. The second will control the access from the DMZ to the internal network. In this instance, the DMZ is considered the untrusted network, and the internal network is considered the trusted network.

For most commercial firewalls today, the default ingress-filtering methodology is to take a minimalist approach to permitting traffic. This just means that by default all traffic coming in from an untrusted network is denied, except that which is specifically permitted.

Although this is a great out-of-the-box configuration, the reality is that virtually all firewalls that you will implement must be configured to allow some traffic from untrusted to trusted network, most commonly from the Internet to a DMZ and from a DMZ to an internal network. To help in building your ingress filters, follow a systematic approach to ingress filtering.

NOTE   For more information regarding ingress filtering, review these two RFCs:

- RFC 3704, *Ingress Filtering for Multihomed Networks* http://www.ietf.org/rfc/rfc3704.txt

- RFC 2827, *Network Ingress Filtering: Defeating Denial of Service Attacks which use IP Source Address Spoofing* http://www.ietf.org/rfc/rfc2827.txt

---

A Systematic Approach to Ingress Filtering

Perhaps the most effective method of implementing ingress filtering is to use a systematic approach to building your filters. Adhering to the concept of the minimalist approach, an effective method of building your ingress lists is to follow this procedure:

Step 1   Identify the source (untrusted) and destination (trusted) networks or systems that the filter will apply to.

Step 2   Identify the services or applications that will be required.

Step 3   Identify the TCP and UDP ports required for the identified services or applications.

Step 4   Identify the source (untrusted) and destination (trusted) systems that a particular service, port or rule will apply to.

A combination of these first four steps will help you identify what your ingress filter needs to look like to provide access to the services and applications you have decided to make available. In addition to this, however, ingress filtering can be used to protect your network from additional attacks such as denial of service attacks and to some degree IP address spoofing.

Step 5   Identify network source addresses that should not be allowed from the untrusted network. In many cases, this includes the RFC 1918 private address spaces of 10.0.0.0/8, 172.16.0.0/12, and 192.168.0.0/16; the RFC 3330 special-use addresses; and the IP address space of the trusted network and the IP address space of any unassigned addresses, frequently referred to as bogons.

TIP   Although the RFC 1918, RFC 3330, and trusted network IP address space is relatively static and not subject to change, bogons change whenever Internet Assigned Numbers Authority (IANA) assigns someone a new IP address space. Consequently, you will need to update and maintain the bogon list that you will apply to the ingress filter. The list of bogons is maintained at http://www.cymru.com/Documents/bogon-list.html, with a number of different formats that you can reference. Alternatively, you can go directly to http://www.iana.org/ipaddress/ip-addresses.htm, but the list maintained by Team Cymru is generally much easier to dissect and implement.

Step 6   Build and implement the ACL that will apply to your ingress filter and then apply it to the appropriate interface in the appropriate direction.

Step 7   Monitor the ACL to determine whether there is traffic that needs to be permitted which is not being permitted, or more important, if there is traffic that is being permitted that is probably not needed. For example, if the firewall is not reporting any traffic matching a **permit** statement, consider removing the **permit** statement completely.

Adhering to this methodology helps ensure that your ingress filter is complete, adheres to your firewall security policy, and functionally protects the resources intended. This methodology can then be applied to virtually any environment; however, there are really three common situations where ingress filtering is implemented:

■   Access from the Internet to a DMZ segment

■   Access from a DMZ segment to an internal segment

■   Access from the Internet to an internal segment

Access from the Internet to a DMZ Segment

In a perfect world, you would be able to implement a firewall and block all traffic from the Internet, thus protecting your environment from a wealth of external threats and sources. We do not live in a perfect world, however, and more and more it seems that what started as a firewall with relatively few Internet-based access requirements has become a more and more porous situation. Of course, the problem with this is that every time traffic is permitted through the firewall, the firewall becomes less and less effective as a security barrier.

Some folks, particularly at BlackHat 2004, went so far as to declare the network perimeter dead, and although I do not think we are at that point yet, certainly it cannot be argued that firewalls today are in many cases less secure than their counterparts in years past as a direct result of the number of ports that must be opened. With each configuration change, there is also an increase in the likelihood of a mistake or misconfiguration occurring, further reducing the effectiveness of the firewall as a security device.

Although there is no foolproof method of ensuring that mistakes will not happen (indeed, you should plan for and expect mistakes to occur), one can definitely minimize mistakes by implementing an ingress filter for traffic from the Internet to a DMZ segment that is based on a sound baseline or starting template and then takes into account the seven-step method previously described to build the more complex ingress filter required, as seen here:

Step 1   Start by denying everything. Although many systems include an implied **deny** statement at the end of any ACL, it is worth ensuring that there is an explicit **deny** at the end of any ACL. There are a number of reasons for this. First, this will ensure that nothing gets overlooked or that in the event that your firewall does not include an implicit **deny** you are not caught off guard. Second, it will give you the opportunity to configure the firewall to log those denied packets, in the event that you require the information for regulatory reasons, and so on.

Step 2   Evaluate the required DMZ services and corresponding ports that are required for operation. Keep in mind that in most cases ACLs are read top to bottom; so, an entry at the top of the list supersedes one at the bottom of the list.

Step 3   Evaluate the required source and destination IP addresses that correlate with the services and ports that need to be opened. Something to consider is that if everyone on the Internet does not need access to a particular service or port, do not grant everyone on the Internet that access. For example, if you have certain systems that you need to be able to FTP to and from, open your FTP server to those Internet IP addresses only. A service can only be exploited if it is in some way accessible.

Step 4   Review all the rules that you have built in to your ACL and verify the following:

- That services and ports you expect to function do function.

- That services and ports you do not expect to function do not function.

- That you have not opened ports that are not in fact necessary. This can be done by logging the corresponding line in the ACL and testing the application or service in question. If the log shows a permitted connection, it is working. If the log does not show a permitted connection, you might be able to shut that port down. This is historically a problem with services such as FTP that some people mistakenly believe need both TCP port 20 and 21 open inbound to function.

Step 5   Log every ACL line (unless you are certain you do not need the data logged). Although this may seem like an insurmountable amount of data that will be stored, all compliance legislation is pointing to the need for this information to be stored properly. To help manage it, consider implementing third-party security management software such as Cisco CiscoWorks or NetIQ Security Manager.

Step 6   Apply the ACL accordingly on your firewall.

Step 7   Monitor the results of permitted and denied traffic as a result of the ACL until you are comfortable with how the ACL and firewall are functioning.

> **NOTE** The terms *ACL* and *ruleset* are in most cases completely interchangeable. Some firewalls, such as the Cisco Secure PIX Firewall, use ACL to refer to the traffic-filtering list. Other firewalls, such as the CheckPoint series of firewalls, use ruleset to refer to the traffic-filtering list. In truth, the terms are virtually interchangeable in this context, and therefore best practices and recommendations for one are largely applicable to the other, with the technical implementation typically being the only difference.

Access from a DMZ Segment to an Internal Segment

This is perhaps the most important ingress filtering you will implement because it is what truly protects—or exposes—your internal resources to external threats. Today's Internet applications are requiring more and more access to internal resources, and an effective method of mitigating the risks involved in granting that access is to implement a middleware server in the DMZ that is accessed from the Internet, which in turn accesses the back-end data that is typically located on the internal network.

Although this sounds like a relatively simple configuration, the devil is in the details, and in many cases the number of ports that must be opened to facilitate communications can often times cause one to wonder why have a firewall at all! Take, for example, a particularly troublesome DMZ service such as Microsoft Outlook Web Access (OWA). To get an OWA server in the DMZ communicating with the internal Exchange Server and domain controllers, it requires so many ports to be opened that a compelling case can be made that the OWA server might as well be on the internal network anyway. One reason for this is that when you open some ports in the firewall, such as Microsoft Remote Procedure Call (RPC), firewalls cannot distinguish between the RPC communications required for OWA and RPC communications for mapping a drive. From the firewall's perspective, it all is using the same TCP or UDP port, and therefore it is permitted accordingly. Consequently, it is critical when looking at ingress filters from the DMZ to the internal network to take a hard look at what it really means to open up access.

Another issue with ingress filters from DMZ segments is when you have a one-armed DMZ and are using a firewall such as the Cisco Secure PIX Firewall, as shown in Figure 10-4.

Because the DMZ has a single interface for all traffic going to either the Internet or the internal network, building and applying an ACL to that interface will functionally act as an ingress filter to the internal network but as an egress filter to the Internet. This will make the ACL even more complex to design and implement.

The good news is that the same seven steps in building an effective ACL for traffic from the Internet to the DMZ should be applied in this situation, so the methodology remains consistent.

Figure 10-4   *One-Armed DMZ and ACLs*

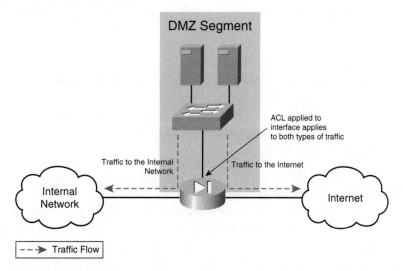

Access from the Internet to an Internal Segment

Building an ACL to control traffic from the Internet to an internal segment is functionally no different from the previously discussed ACL scenarios. What differs, however, is that the traffic is going to come from a completely untrusted network and potentially have direct access to internal resources. Now, the knee-jerk response to this type of implementation is to simply not allow it. I have found that there are few constants in network security, however, and whereas 99 percent of the situations that call for direct access to internal resources can probably be worked around in another fashion, there is always that 1 percent that, for whatever reason, you just cannot do anything about. In those cases, you need to be absolutely certain of what you are allowing through the use of your ingress filter.

Additionally, although technically not an ingress-filtering issue, you should strongly consider using a firewall that does a true application proxy of the service you are advertising to ensure that only the kind of communications at the application layer that you want to permit are indeed being permitted. An example of this is something like the Microsoft ISA Firewall using its application publishing features to grant access to the resource.

Egress Filters

Practically speaking, egress filters are almost identical to ingress filters. The difference lies in what an egress filter applies to. Unlike ingress filters, egress filters apply to traffic that is coming from a trusted network to an untrusted network. As a result, egress filters typically are applied either on firewall interfaces that connect to the internal network or to a DMZ segment. A simple way of thinking of ingress and egress filters is that an ingress filter filters traffic coming in, and an egress filter filters traffic going out.

Unlike ingress filters, however, many firewalls default to allowing all traffic from a trusted source to an untrusted source. This is particularly true when it comes to the Cisco Secure PIX Firewall, which uses the concept of interface security levels to determine which networks will automatically be configured to permit traffic.

The upside of this kind of configuration is that the firewall can be plugged into the network, and then with virtually no configuration, internal hosts can access external (typically Internet-based) resources. From a usability and simplicity perspective, this is a good thing. Unfortunately, from a security perspective it is a very, bad thing because that same simplicity means that even malicious traffic is going to be permitted by default.

Implementing an Egress Filter for Internal Traffic

Perhaps the biggest problem, and reason, that people do not implement egress filters for their internal traffic is that egress filters can be incredibly complex to get right. Ingress filters are relatively straightforward. You know the handful of services and systems that users will need access to, and you configure the ACL accordingly. Because most firewalls today perform stateful packet inspection, the return traffic for connections permitted by the ingress filter is automatically permitted. With an egress filter, there is potentially a much, much larger list of ports that must be opened. Although it is easy to assume that your users really just need HTTP and maybe HTTPS Internet access, the truth is that you probably have users who use all kinds ports to talk to all sorts of legitimate external resources. Similarly, if there are resources in the DMZ that your users need access to, your egress filter is going to need to accommodate those conversations, too.

> **TIP**   Traditionally, egress filtering has always come as an afterthought to ingress filtering. The focus was always on keeping malicious traffic out, not necessarily restricting traffic that is going out. With the types of Internet worms and distributed denial-of-service (DDoS) attacks that have been propagating recently, more companies are looking to egress filtering to prevent their systems from being used to spread worms or participate in DDoS attacks. In addition, more companies are looking to better control the kinds of data that is exposed to the Internet through Trojans and similar programs which can easily be brought into the internal network on a laptop, and then in a completely unrestricted fashion connect back to the malicious user externally. To prevent this, it is a good idea to really approach your egress filter from the minimalist perspective. For example, your employees almost certainly do not need to make Simple Mail Transfer Protocol (SMTP) connections to external resources. Only your Internet gateway mail server does. So in your egress filter, ensure that you block SMTP traffic from all internal hosts except the Internet mail gateway. Although this is a laborious and time-consuming process to build the initial list, and it is painful to implement (because you will almost certainly overlook something), after the egress filter has been implemented it is relatively easy to maintain and provides a dramatic increase in the security posture of your organization.

Once again, the same methodology that is used to build an ingress filter applies to building an egress filter as previously described in this chapter.

Implementing an Egress Filter for a DMZ

As mentioned when discussing ingress filters, if your DMZ is a one-armed DMZ segment, the ingress and egress filter may effectively be the same thing because all communications must go through the same network interface on the firewall. This is particularly true for Cisco Secure PIX Firewalls. When implementing the egress filter portion of your ACL, remember to focus on the traffic that will be permitted from the systems on the DMZ to systems on the Internet. Beyond that, however, the same methodology that applies to your other ingress and egress filters applies here.

> **TIP**   I was performing a security audit in a particular environment and encountered a DMZ situation whereby the ingress filter allowed traffic from a host that was not running the corresponding service, and the egress filter allowed unrestricted HTTP and FTP access to the Internet from DMZ hosts. What I was then able to do, as a result of a security exploit in the web server software it was running, was gain a command shell on the box by which I could run command-line utilities. Next, I was able to use FTP, which the egress filter permitted, to grab the utilities I needed from an FTP server and put them on the server in the DMZ. With everything in place at that point, I was able to launch a different exploit that would grant me a Virtual Network Computing (VNC) session on the server—even though VNC was not installed on the server—and tunnel the display through the firewall over the open port in the ingress filter. This process took approximately 5 minutes to complete from start to finish. Had the egress filter been updated properly to ensure that I could not FTP my utilities to the server, or the ingress filter been updated to account for the fact that the service in question was not running on that server, I would have been nowhere near as successful. As it was, I was able to gain full control of the server in the DMZ, only to discover that it was allowed to make Microsoft RPC connections to the internal network, but that's a story for another day.

Management-Access Ruleset

With ingress and egress filtering sorted out, the next security policy task is to review the management access ruleset. Although some firewalls will include management access in the ingress or egress filter as appropriate, given the nature of access it warrants being called out and given special attention.

The most important thing to remember about management access is that regardless of method, a few rules apply:

- Restrict management access to specific management workstations only.

- Never allow management access from an untrusted network.

> **TIP** Another discovery during the previously mentioned audit was that the firewall in question permitted management connections from the DMZ. Although this was likely done for troubleshooting purposes, when we gained control of a server on the DMZ and put our utilities on it, it was a relatively trivial thing to begin trying to (and eventually succeeding to) crack the passwords on the firewall, thus allowing us to make whatever changes we wanted. Never, ever allow management access from untrusted networks.

■ Always use an encrypted management method.

■ In the event that you cannot use an encrypted management method (for example syslog), consider implementing IPsec to secure the traffic in question.

There are numerous methods of performing remote management and logging of a firewall. Some of the most common methods are as follows:

■ Telnet and SSH

■ SNMP

■ Syslog

■ TFTP and FTP

■ HTTP and HTTPS

■ Proprietary management methods

Telnet and SSH

Telnet is ubiquitous for remote management of firewall appliances; largely due to the fact that it is virtually a de facto standard method of making remote command-line connections to UNIX-based systems and network devices. Unfortunately, Telnet is an unencrypted protocol and should be restricted if at all possible. Instead, use SSH for the same functionality.

SSH allows you to do pretty much the same thing that Telnet does, gain a remote command shell, but SSH traffic is encrypted and thus a secure remote-management method. Even with this, however, you should never configure SSH to be permitted from an untrusted network. Although it is certainly more convenient to be able to SSH into the firewall from home instead of having to drive into the office, exposing SSH on Internet-connected interfaces in particular is asking for a security incident to occur. Instead, consider implementing a VPN configuration that would allow the remote support personnel to VPN into a DMZ from which they could gain management access to the firewall using SSH.

SNMP

SNMP presents a bit of a unique problem with firewalls. On one hand, it is hard to argue the value of SNMP-provided data such as performance statistics. On the other hand, however, SNMP is traditionally an insecure protocol that can be used to completely reconfigure the firewall (assuming that SNMP is not in a read-only mode). In fact, this insecurity is the single biggest reason that organizations decide to completely disable SNMP on their firewalls. Although this is certainly effective, if you want to leverage SNMP you can do some things to make it more secure:

- If SNMPv3 is available on your firewall, use it rather than SNMPv1 or SNMPv2c. SNMPv3 provides for encryption as well as user-based authentication.

- If SNMPv1 or SNMPv2c must be used, consider using IPsec to encapsulate and secure the traffic.

- Do not use the same SNMP community strings on your firewalls that you use anywhere else in your network. This ensures that if the firewall is compromised in some way, the community string is worthless elsewhere in your network.

- If you do not actively intend to use SNMP to make changes to your firewall, implement SNMP in a read-only fashion.

- Restrict SNMP management access to designated management workstations only.

> **NOTE** For more information regarding SNMP and how SNMP functions, review RFC 3411, RFC 3413, RFC 3414, RFC 3415, RFC 3416, RFC 3417, RFC 3418, and RFC 1157. These can all be located at http://www.rfc-editor.org, where you can search for the term "SNMP" and review all 100+ SNMP-related RFCs

Syslog

Syslog differs from most other management methods in that rather than serving as an active method for the administrator to interact with the firewall, syslog simply transmits logging information and data to a syslog server for review, action, and archiving. Because syslog messages can contain information related to potential security exploits, care should be taken to ensure that the firewall can only transmit syslog data to a designated syslog server. Syslog is typically transmitted in an unencrypted fashion over UDP port 514. Consequently, if security is required, you need to implement IPsec for communications between the syslog server and the firewall.

> **TIP**   The Cisco Secure PIX Firewall can transmit syslog over TCP, allowing for connection-oriented communications. This allows the PIX to then be configured to stop permitting all traffic if it is for some reason unable to successfully communicate with the syslog server. In a highly secure environment, this is a good thing because it ensures that only traffic that can be successfully logged will be permitted. However, this can dramatically increase down time and the potential for a denial of service if for any reason the firewall cannot communicate with the syslog server. You need to weigh carefully in your environment the requirements for uptime and availability against the increased security using TCP-based syslog may provide. Although more secure sounds great, the first few times that the firewall stops working because the syslog server was rebooted or crashed may cause you to rethink your syslog policy.
>
> In PIX OS 7.0, this fail-shut behavior can be disabled by running the command **logging permit-hostdown**.

TFTP and FTP

TFTP and FTP are both used primarily for copying files to/from a firewall and updating the system software or configuration. Although FTP provides for authentication mechanisms that TFTP lacks, both protocols transmit the data in an unencrypted fashion and are therefore susceptible to eavesdropping. Given the fact that the traffic frequently will contain configuration data, this is a significant security issue.

To help secure TFTP and FTP traffic, restrict the firewall to only communicate with designated TFTP or FTP servers. Furthermore, if it is possible to encapsulate the TFTP or FTP data in IPsec, do that, too, to ensure that the data in transit is protected accordingly.

HTTP and HTTPS

HTTP and HTTPS are both typically used for web-based remote management. Similar to Telnet and SSH, HTTP uses an unencrypted transmission method (whereas HTTPS uses encryption). Consequently, HTTP should never be used if HTTPS is available.

Because of the nature of HTTPS, providing security for the firewall is largely a process of ensuring that only specified management workstations are allowed to connect to the firewall over HTTPS. Like SSH, HTTPS should also never be configured over an untrusted network such as the Internet.

Proprietary Management Methods

For proprietary management methods such as CheckPoint OPSEC/LEA, connections leave you largely at the mercy of the vendor in terms of ensuring that the protocol itself is secure. The only real options are to ensure that you restrict access only to designated management stations, and if encryption is not provided by the vendor, attempt to encapsulate the traffic in IPsec, similar to SNMP and syslog.

Summary

The key to ensuring that your firewall not only is an effective security measure but is secure in and of itself relies on a well-planned methodology of first defining the security requirements and objectives with a series of written security policies. Then, use those security policies as a guide to build effective and functional ingress and egress filters (and implement secure methods of management access).

Managing Firewalls

This chapter looks at the management of firewalls. From the perspective of the small office/home user, the firewall is a single device that protects the home network from malicious traffic—it keeps out the "bad stuff" and provides the end user a more secure online experience. For the enterprise, the firewall can be both an inbound filter as well as an outbound filter depending on how the security policy calls for enforcing the edge network. Either way, the firewall (or in the case of enterprises, possibly firewalls) must be managed in one fashion or another. Typically, most manufacturers rely these days on a web interface. In the home market, this stems from the fact that a graphical user interface (GUI) is more intuitive to the end user, and therefore ostensibly easier to use, than a command-line interface (CLI). However, for the more daring at heart who so want, there are firewalls (namely the PIX, Linux IPTables, and Solaris IPF to name just a few) that can be managed solely from the CLI. This chapter covers such topics as default passwords, the maintenance of the underlying firewall platform for firewalls such as Linux's NetFilter, and managing firewalls through the CLI as well as a GUI. Finally, a discussion of management interfaces and common firewall management tasks is provided.

Default Passwords

When you purchase a new firewall (or any network device in general) such as a Cisco PIX, a Linksys, a NetScreen, or a SonicWall, out of the box the device has some default passwords set (and in some cases there is no default password). This is because the manufacturer must allow for initial access to the device for the end user to configure it. Most recent documentation for any device admonishes the end user to immediately change the default password to something else. Table 11-1 shows common default passwords for some firewalls.

Table 11-1 *Default Passwords*

Manufacturer	Product	Default Administrative Account	Default Password
Cisco	PIX	None	None
Linksys	BEFSX41	None	admin
NetScreen	(All)	netscreen	netscreen
Netgear	FR314	admin	password

You can find a detailed default password list at either the F/X site (http://www.phenoelit.de/dpl/dpl.html) or at the Nikto site (http://www.cirt.net/cgi-bin/passwd.pl). It is precisely because sites such as these keep lists of default passwords that these passwords are considered detrimental. In some cases, vendors have gotten the hint that although they need to have default passwords for the initial setup, the initial setup should also require the administrator to change the password from the default value. This has been done on some Cisco devices, such as their IDS platform, and is finding more and more acceptance among other vendors.

Maintaining the Underlying Platform

As with any device on the network, firewalls run software (whether it is embedded in an application-specific integrated circuit [ASIC] or runs from Flash memory or runs from a disk file system) to be able to perform their functions. Typically, as in the case of the Cisco PIX and ASA platforms as well as NetScreen and other vendor firewalls, these firewalls run a custom operating system whose source code is not available to the general community for review or tampering. If a bug or vulnerability is discovered by an outside party, it is left to the manufacturer to develop a patch and release a new version of the operating system to be installed by the end user to solve the problem. In addition, any new feature added to the device is done according to the schedule of the manufacturer.

At the opposite end of the spectrum are the open source systems with firewall capabilities. These include Linux, OpenBSD, and Solaris 10, to name a few. Each of these systems' (Linux's NetFilter, OpenBSD's PF, and Solaris 10's IPFilter) firewall source code is available for inspection by outside groups. This does not necessarily mean that the filter code in these operating systems is better, but it can be more easily extended by someone who has the skill set necessary to code the additional capabilities into the software. However, each of these filtering systems runs under a more generic operating system (Linux, OpenBSD, and Solaris, respectively), and therefore the possibility of bugs or vulnerabilities (some tied to the filtering code and others not) may be greater because the underlying operating systems are meant for more general use. Such systems require care, patience, and effort to both maintain and to secure to ensure that the firewall is not compromised. If a bug or vulnerability is discovered in one of these firewalls, the patch for it is likely to be available sooner than a closed source appliance system. Typically, this is because the number of people who may be able to provide a fix for the bug or vulnerability is significantly greater than those involved in the development of commercial closed source systems. This does not mean that vendors such as Cisco, NetScreen, Watchguard, Linksys, and the like do not provide timely patches; in some cases, it depends on the severity of the problem. Statistically, however, Linux and OpenBSD bugs are fixed quickly relative to closed-source vendors (http://csoinformer.com/research/solve.shtml).

Consider the case of a firewall consisting of a simple Intel PC with two interfaces running Fedora Core 4 Linux and NetFilter as the filtering firewall. The number of packages in Fedora Core 4 is on the order of approximately 1500 packages (1806 to be exact). Many packages may contain a bug that could result (however unlikely) in the possible compromise of the system. In addition, the level of effort to secure the system properly or to maintain the system may be beyond the capabilities of most people without a sufficient technical background. For a more novice group of users, a packaged, closed source system may be the better choice. A Linksys router/firewall, a Cisco PIX 501, or a NetScreen 5XP may be better suited for the less-technically-savvy individual or for someone who wants a closed source appliance because of the lower effort required to configure and maintain it. Nevertheless, for those who are willing to make the effort and for those who are skilled, an open source firewall can fit the bill.

Maintaining the underlying platform requires time. The more complex the underlying platform, the more time required. This is where closed source appliances such as PIX, NetScreen, and Linksys have an advantage. They provide a device that, although configured and maintained by the user, eliminates many of the variables inherent in more general operating systems. This makes it much easier for a less-experienced user to be able to maintain the firewall.

Firewall Management Interface

Modern firewalls come with two administrative interfaces:

- The CLI

- The GUI (typically, but not necessarily, web based)

This section provides an overview and some examples of these interfaces.

Managing Firewalls with a CLI

A CLI enables you to use a specific instruction set to configure the firewall. Most firewalls require the end user to do the initial configuration of the firewall (inputting in the basic network information such as IP address, net mask, default gateway, and possibly an administrative password) via CLI *before* the end user can switch over to the GUI. Linux's NetFilter is, for the most part, configured through a CLI, although there do exist several products that allow for configuration of NetFilter-based firewalls through a GUI.

CLIs require knowledge of the command set in the firewall product. For example, to configure NetFilter, use the IPTables CLI to allow inbound Secure Shell (SSH), e-mail, and web traffic (using TCP ports 22, 25, and 80, respectively) and deny all other traffic requires the configuration in Example 11-1.

Example 11-1 *Configuring NetFilter with IPTables*

```
# iptables -P INPUT DENY
# iptables -P OUTPUT ACCEPT
# iptables -P FORWARD ACCEPT
# iptables -A INPUT -i lo -j ACCEPT
# iptables -A INPUT -p tcp -s 0.0.0.0/0 -d 10.16.17.202 --dport 22 -m state --state NEW -
    j ACCEPT
# iptables -A INPUT -p tcp -s 0.0.0.0/0 -d 10.16.17.202 --dport 25 -m state --state NEW -
j ACCEPT
# iptables -A INPUT -p tcp -s 0.0.0.0/0 -d 10.16.17.202 --dport 80 -m state --state NEW -
    j ACCEPT
# iptables -A INPUT -m state --state ESTABLISHED,RELATED -j ACCEPT
# iptables -A INPUT --reject-with icmp-host-prohibited -j REJECT
```

Example 11-2 provides a similar configuration with the PIX command set.

Example 11-2 *Configuring a PIX*

```
gandalf(config)# access-list acl_test permit tcp any host 10.16.17.202 eq ssh
gandalf(config)# access-list acl_test permit tcp any host 10.16.17.202 eq smtp
gandalf(config)# access-list acl_test permit tcp any host 10.16.17.202 eq 80
gandalf(config)# access-list acl_test permit icmp any any
gandalf(config)# access-list acl_test deny ip any any
gandalf(config)# show access-list acl_test
access-list acl_test; 5 elements
access-list acl_test line 1 permit tcp any host 10.16.17.202 eq ssh (hitcnt=0)
access-list acl_test line 2 permit tcp any host 10.16.17.202 eq smtp (hitcnt=0)
access-list acl_test line 3 permit tcp any host 10.16.17.202 eq www (hitcnt=0)
access-list acl_test line 4 permit icmp any any (hitcnt=0)
access-list acl_test line 5 deny ip any any (hitcnt=0)
```

Knowledge of the command set is critical to effectively configure a firewall through a CLI. Many vendors (and third parties) have worked hard to reduce the configuration of a firewall to a more simplistic method. When the initial configuration is done (supplying the firewall software with an IP address and net mask), the end user can immediately switch to a more graphical method of configuring the firewall.

Managing Firewalls with a GUI

A GUI provides a more-user-friendly interface to configure the firewall. Some firewalls are configured through a direct interface on the host, such as Symantec Norton Internet Security shown in Figure 11-1 and Figure 11-2, before the firewall is active. Some come with a preconfigured IP address and an administrative password to be used for access by the end user during initial configuration (such as Linksys or the PIX 501 and 506E series systems).

Figure 11-1 *Symantec Internet Security Configuration*

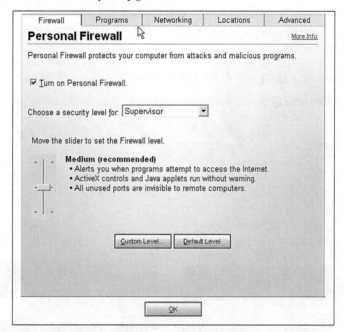

Figure 11-2 *Symantec Firewall Configuration*

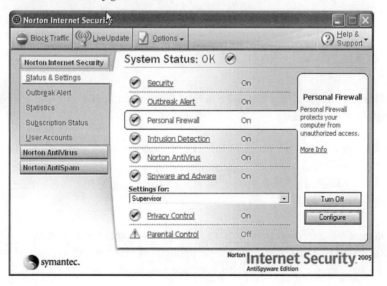

The PIX Device Manager (for PIX operating systems up to versions 6.3(5)), known as the Cisco Adaptive Security Device Manager in PIX version 7.0, is a Java applet that is downloaded from the PIX or ASA device and runs locally through the client browser. Figure 11-3 shows the PIX Device Manager screen.

Figure 11-3 *Cisco PIX Device Manager*

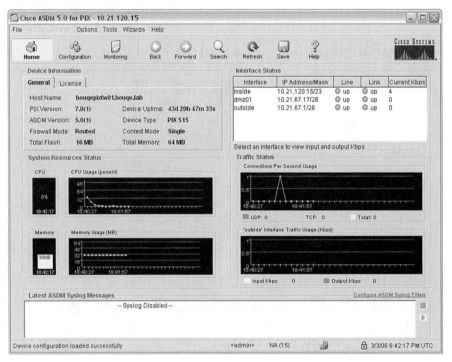

The information is presented in a more natural fashion to the end user in the form of graphics and graphs for performance.

Not to be outdone, there are GUIs for Linux's IPTables firewall software. Some are web based (such as Webmin), and some are applications running on the Linux system itself (such as Firestarter or FW-Builder). Firestarter provides a simple, easy-to-use interface for IPTables, as shown in Figure 11-4.

Webmin provides a method by which the firewall can be managed through a web browser interface, which is more convenient than an application that can only be viewed on an X Windows-enabled server. Figure 11-5 shows this interface.

Figure 11-4   *Firestarter for IPTables*

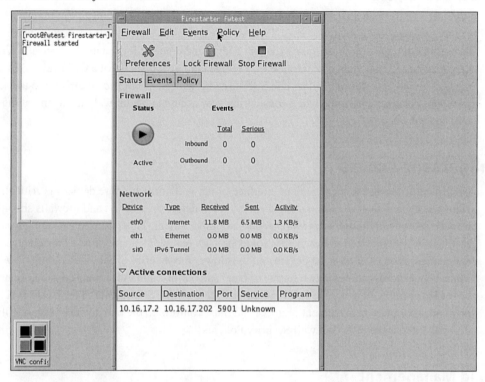

Figure 11-5   *Webmin IPTables Rules Interface*

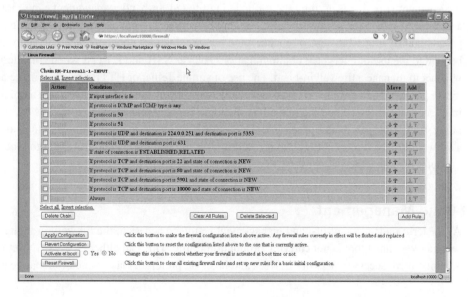

Interface Preference

Whether it is through a CLI or through a GUI, the management of a firewall can range from the highly complex to the relatively easy. Typically, novice users start by administering the firewall through a GUI. Over time, as their experience level and comfort level with the firewall increase, they may find it more convenient to use a CLI. One significant benefit of a CLI over a GUI is that the CLI is available through Telnet and SSH sessions as well as connected directly to the serial port. This becomes important when considering how access to the firewall management interface will be controlled.

Management Access

Control of access to the management interface of network infrastructure devices is critical. Network devices such as routers, switches, intrusion detection sensors, and firewalls should be accessed only by those users who need to administer them. This requirement stems from the fact that an unauthorized user, whether someone with malicious intent or not, may change the configuration or disable the device and thus lower the security of the surrounding network. Management access comes in two forms: in-band and out-of-band. Additional considerations must be made regarding how the firewall is accessed: Telnet, SSH, SNMP, FTP, TFTP, HTTP/HTTPS, or some proprietary management protocol and must conform to the management access policy as discussed in Chapter 10, "Firewall Security Policies."

In-Band Management

In-band management refers to the administrative access to systems and network devices over the same network that is used by the traffic being filtered. In-band management can represent a significant risk to the administrator if certain precautions are not taken. These risks center predominantly around the use of unencrypted communications channels. Specific attention must be paid to the use of encrypted communications such as SSH and HTTPS when considering whether to manage a firewall in-band. The use of simple Telnet or HTTP can result in the administrative password being captured by an attacker who is sniffing the traffic between the administrative interface of the firewall and the rest of the network. In-band management also runs the risk of being susceptible to a denial-of-service (DoS) attack during large-scale outbreaks such as worms. This would make it more difficult to reconfigure the firewall during such an event to block traffic or shut it off altogether if necessary to defeat the attack.

Out-of-Band Management

As the term indicates, out-of-band management results in access to the firewall through a secondary channel that is not carrying production traffic. This can either be a VLAN setup for administrative access to network devices and hosts or, preferably, a completely separate physical network. In addition, out-of-band management can be used to provide access to the serial port of the network device for access should the network fail. Out-of-band management can be more time-consuming to set up and not cost effective for smaller networks, but it represents the most secure and reliable method of administering firewalls and other network equipment.

Telnet vs. SSH

Telnet is an unencrypted network communication protocol that is typically used to provide remote access to systems and other devices. Telnet is originally defined in RFC 854 and was developed long before the Internet was in its current form—when networks were much smaller. Not much consideration was given in the Telnet protocol design to confidentiality in the data being transmitted using the protocol. Therefore, all data transmitted using the Telnet protocol is subject to eavesdropping and susceptible to capture.

SSH provides for cryptographic protection of data as well as authentication and ensures that the integrity and confidentiality of the communication is secured. If a device can support SSH as an access method to the command line, it should be preferred over Telnet. Alternatively, if the device's GUI is accessible within a secure network and it is necessary to remotely manage the device across an insecure network and an SSH connection can be established, it is possible to tunnel the connection through SSH. To establish an SSH tunnel between two hosts, you need to use port forwarding. In the example shown in Figure 11-6 the client establishes an SSH connection through to the SSH server on TCP port 22 (the standard SSH port). However, the client uses the port-forwarding capability to forward his localhost TCP port 1025 and redirects it to the Telnet port of on the router. To access the Telnet port of the router through the tunnel, the client need only telnet to his localhost TCP port 1025 and he will automatically be redirected, through the SSH tunnel, to the router's Telnet port.

Figure 11-6 *SSH Forwarding Across an Insecure Network*

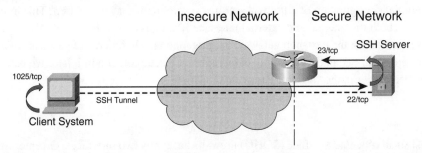

This way the traffic goes through an encrypted SSH session between the client and the SSH server and then the traffic can be forwarded using an insecure protocol such as Telnet.

HTTP vs. HTTPS

A discussion about the use of HTTP versus HTTPS follows a similar line of thought as the previous discussion about Telnet versus secure shell. HTTP is an unencrypted protocol that allows eavesdroppers to view the communication between the client and the server. Although attackers may not necessarily be able to capture the password to the web server, they may be able to capture other information such as specific configuration information or possibly a valid cookie that would then allow the attacker to impersonate a legitimate user and gain access to the firewall's administrative interface.

HTTPS uses Secure Sockets Layer (SSL) encryption technology to encrypt the communication between the client and the firewall web server. This makes it impossible for an attacker to eavesdrop on a management session or intercept any information that could be used to gain access to the firewall or gain information about the firewall configuration.

Common Firewall Management Tasks

One of the first things to accomplish when deploying a new firewall, whether this is for an enterprise deployment or for a deployment in a small office or home office, is to configure some basic aspects of networking. Doing so includes changing the default administrative password, configuring the default gateway, configuring the IP addresses for the internal and external (and possibly other) interfaces, and configuring the logging of messages from the firewall. In addition to these tasks, the firewall administrator must also manage the configuration of the firewall over time. Doing so may require the use of a change control system such as the Revision Control System (RCS), which is available both on the UNIX/Linux platforms as well as the Windows platform. The following sections discuss each of these tasks in more detail.

Initial Configuration

The initial configuration of a firewall requires several items of information. This information includes both the internal and external interface IP addresses (or the use of DHCP on one of those interfaces), the next-hop gateway, logging, and an administrative password. The first three items are discussed in the following paragraphs. A discussion of administrative passwords was provided earlier in the "Default Passwords" section.

Interfaces

Most small office/home office (SOHO) firewalls have only two interfaces. On enterprise firewalls, there can be well over a half dozen interfaces that comprise various demilitarized zones (DMZ) with varying levels of security. In addition, newer enterprise firewalls can also support VLANs and filtering between VLANs while only having a limited number of physical interfaces. All firewalls have at least two interfaces:

- **Inside**—The inside interface is typically assigned a static IP address (and this IP address typically comes from one of the three private IP address blocks—10.0.0.0/8, 172.16.0.0–172.31.255.255, or 192.168.0.0/16—but this is not a hard requirement). This interface serves as a default gateway for systems that are behind the firewall. A default gateway is the gateway of last resort for systems to send traffic to when the other end of the connection (that is, the system being contacted) is not reachable any other way or is not on the client's local network.

- **Outside**—The outside interface can either be assigned a static IP address as provided by the Internet service provider or it can be configured to be assigned an IP address through the Dynamic Host Configuration Protocol (DHCP).

In addition to the IP addresses on the various interfaces, the firewall can also run a DHCP server to provide IP addresses and other configuration information to systems inside the firewall. This server makes the deployment of a SOHO firewall much easier because most vendors also provide some default configuration for the DHCP server, too. Care must be taken to ensure that the scope of the DHCP server does not overlap or conflict with any DHCP scope already in place in the network. Also, in the case of wireless firewall routers (such as the Linksys BEFW11S4 or the WRT54G) that are popular these days, it is extremely important for the administrator of the device to ensure that only authorized users can associate and authenticate to the device. If these devices are not locked down, any user can authenticate and associate to the device, and the DHCP server will provide them with a network address that they can use.

Routing/Gateway

In many cases, where simple firewalls such as the Linksys, the Linux NetFilter, or the PIX 501 or 506E firewalls are used, there is a simple network topology—essentially an internal network behind the firewall and an external network (typically consisting of the external IP address provided by the service provider). These firewalls do not do complex routing but rather just forward packets from the internal network to the external network using a default gateway. The default gateway information is provided either by the administrator or by the service provider's DHCP server when the firewall boots up.

In enterprise networks, however, the firewall can segment multiple networks and DMZs from each other. In this case, the routing can be quite complex and may require the use of a dynamic routing protocol such as the Routing Information Protocol (RIP) or the Open Shortest Path First (OSPF) routing protocol.

To add a default route to a Cisco PIX during initial configuration, you need to use the **route** command as follows:

```
pix(config)# route outside 0.0.0.0 0.0.0.0 172.16.45.1 1
```

This tells the PIX that the default route goes out the outside interface, that the next hop is 172.16.45.1, and that it is only one hop away (that is, it is the next device going outbound).

Logging

Logging is also essential for maintaining and administering a firewall. Logging enables the administrator to see all the traffic blocked by the firewall as well as troubleshoot the firewall configuration when a particular function, such as Network Address Translation (NAT), is not working as expected. Most firewalls such as the PIX 501 or 506E and Linux's NetFilter allow for logging of messages to remote syslog servers.

Syslog's origins are in the UNIX operating system, and syslog is used by a wide variety of processes on many Linux, BSD, and UNIX-derivative operating systems. In addition, many vendors, such as Cisco, have adapted syslog to their products such as IOS and PIX OS. Syslog is defined in the Internet RFC 3164 (available from the Internet Engineering Task Force (IETF) website at http://www.ietf.org/rfc/rfc3164.txt?number=3164). The two primary concepts to understand with syslog is the *message facility* and the *severity*. Each message generated and sent to a syslog server must be sent with a defined facility and severity for the syslog server to understand how to handle the message. The currently defined facilities and severities defined in the syslog RFC (3164) are listed in Table 11-2 and Table 11-3, respectively. There are eight levels of syslog severities possible, as defined in RFC 3164 and shown in Table 11-3 in descending order. One of the confusing aspects of the syslog severity levels is that the lower the numeric value of the severity (with 0 being an Emergency), the *higher* the severity of the message being sent. Also, the "lower" the severity (that is, the higher the numeric value of the severity), the greater amount of information that is generated by the process. So, level 7, Debug, produces a prodigious amount of syslog log messages, whereas level 0, Emergency, produces few messages (but of critical significance). Because syslog originally was developed on the BSD UNIX operating system, many facilities are assigned to specific processes and daemons in UNIX. Processes that have not been explicitly assigned a facility may use one of the "local-use" facilities.

Table 11-2 *Syslog Facilities*

Numeric Value	Facility Name
0	Kernel messages
1	User-level messages
2	Mail system
3	System daemons

Table 11-2 *Syslog Facilities (Continued)*

Numeric Value	Facility Name
4	Security authorization messages
5	Syslog internally generated messages
6	Line printer subsystem
7	Network news subsystem
8	UUCP subsystem
9	Clock daemon
10	Security authorization messages
11	FTP daemon
12	Network Time Protocol (NTP) subsystem
13	Log audit
14	Log alert
15	Clock daemon
16	Local use 0
17	Local use 1
18	Local use 2
19	Local use 3
20	Local use 4
21	Local use 5
22	Local use 6
23	Local use 7

Table 11-3 *Syslog Severities*

Numeric Value	Severity Name
0	Emergency
1	Alert
2	Critical
3	Error
4	Warning
5	Notice
6	Informational
7	Debug

In many cases, syslog servers are kept behind the firewall and, more preferably, in the management network; therefore, there is no need to open up the firewall to allow these messages to reach the server. Example 11-3 demonstrates the commands to configure a PIX 501 or 506E to send its logs to a remote syslog server. The following commands are entered in the configuration or config mode of the PIX device.

Example 11-3 *PIX Logging*

```
logging on
logging timestamp
logging trap informational
logging facility 21
logging host inside 10.16.17.124
```

The command **logging on** tells the device to turn on logging on the device, and the **logging timestamp** command ensures that a date/time field is inserted in each syslog message sent to the remote syslog server. The **logging trap informational** command specifies the level of logging to be conducted. The reason why Informational is a good level to use for logging with the PIX is because it provides enough information to monitor the traffic going through the PIX without overwhelming the administrator with unnecessary information. Level 7, Debug, is typically used only to try and determine a problem with the configuration of the PIX or why some capability of the PIX does not work. The **logging facility 21** syntax specifies which syslog facility is used. The **facility 21** syntax translates, according to Table 11-2, to local use 5. Finally, the last line, **logging host inside 10.16.17.124**, tells the PIX to send its messages to the host on the "inside" of the PIX (that is, the host on the internal network) with the IP address of 10.16.17.124.

No matter how the firewall logs information, it is critical that the logged information be reviewed by an administrator. Administrators can distill the information from firewalls and other sources via a variety of different log analysis tools. These tools range from commercial tools such as CiscoWorks VMS to open source or freeware tools. An excellent resource for log analysis tools is the website http://www.loganalysis.org. Cisco provides detailed instructions on how to set up a syslog server to receive the various messages generated by the PIX firewall. These instructions are applicable to any device that can generate a syslog message and can be found here:

> http://www.cisco.com/en/US/products/hw/vpndevc/ps2030/
> products_tech_note09186a0080094030.shtml#setupsyslogd

Modifying the Configuration

As with any device, from time to time you will need to modify the configuration of the firewall. Whether this is due to a new device brought on line to access the Internet or the addition of a new web server behind the firewall, it will be necessary to change the firewall configuration. The problem with modifying the configuration comes down to change control — ensuring that changes made to a firewall are tracked and logged in case of problems. These items are discussed in the sections that follow.

Change Control

Change control is defined as the process and procedures to manage changes being made to a product or its configuration. For the sake of this discussion, the focus is on the control of changes made to the configuration of a firewall. Change control for firewalls relies on either those changes being logged or a copy of the previous configuration being stored or both. One of the simplest ways to control changes to the configuration of a firewall is to use some sort of revision control system—such as Revision Control Service (RCS) or Concurrent Version System (CVS)—to check the changes and, if necessary, to re-create a previous version of the configuration should a problem arise. This works when the configuration of the firewall is stored as a text file that can be downloaded to a system acting as the RCS or CVS repository. When the configuration of the firewall *cannot* be downloaded as a text file, a running log of the changes made to the firewall should be kept so that changes can be backed out of if necessary. See http://www.cs.purdue.edu/homes/trinkle/RCS for more information regarding RCS, CVS, and other change-control software systems.

To set up a simple change-control system such as RCS (on UNIX, Linux, or Windows) to manage the changes to firewall configurations, it is important to remember that configurations sometimes contain sensitive administrative information such as passwords or access control lists (ACLs). It is important that the RCS (or CVS) system and the directory or folder containing the configuration files be kept secure. In UNIX or Linux, this requires changing the permissions of the RCS repository such that only *root* or others within an administrative group have access privileges, for example:

```
# chgrp wheel configs
# chmod -R 750 configs
```

These commands change the group ownership of the configs directory to the wheel group and then change the permissions on it, as well as all directories beneath it, to read, write, and execute for the owner; read and execute for group members; and no permission for everyone else. This restricts access to the directory, in this example, to just the owner as well as those other users who are members of the wheel group. However, the group members cannot make changes to the files within the directory. They can only view them. Only the owner can make changes to the files in the configs directory.

Under Windows, the process is similar. To restrict access to the administrator only or to the administrative group, the *everyone* group must be removed. This can be accomplished by setting the permissions as shown in Figure 11-7. To set the security permissions on the folder, you must right-click the folder and choose **Properties**. This opens the folder Properties window as shown in Figure 11-7. In the folder Properties window, open the **Security** tab. This opens the Security permissions for the folder, as shown in Figure 11-8.

Figure 11-7 *Folder Properties*

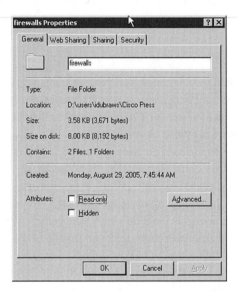

Figure 11-8 *Initial Security Settings for Folder*

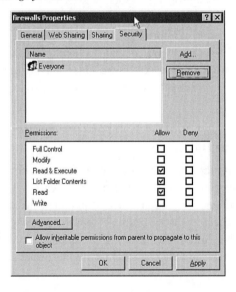

Select the **Everyone** group and click the **Remove** button on the right side of the Properties window. Then click the **Add** button to add the user you want to have ownership of the folder (in this example, the domain administrator has ownership). Figure 11-9 shows the result.

Figure 11-9 *Final Security Settings for Folder*

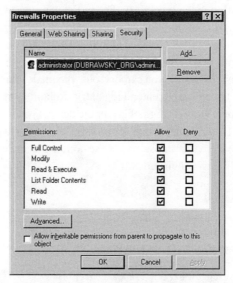

When that is accomplished, access to the folder is limited to only those with the proper credentials, as shown in Figure 11-10.

Figure 11-10 *Access Denied Without Proper Credentials*

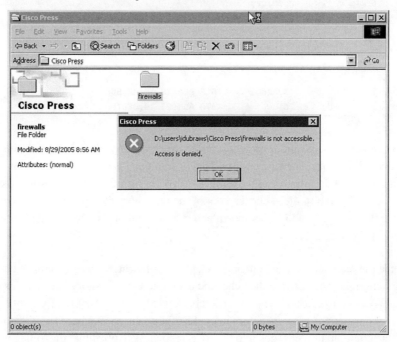

When the configuration repository directory has been secured sufficiently, the next step is to check in the initial configuration to the repository. The initial configuration is the starting point that you will use as a known good configuration for the device. Any changes made after the initial configuration is tracked using the configuration repository. By doing this, you will be able to reconstruct a good configuration in case a specific change is not good or needs to be removed. In addition, by using revision control, you can find out who made what changes and why by requiring the individual making the change to enter a log entry explaining the change and the need for it. To check in the initial, known good configuration for the device, you just use the checkin (**ci**) command as shown in Example 11-4. This example shows how to check in a file to the repository as well as how to check out a file from the repository. These commands are entered on the command line in both UNIX and the Windows environment.

Example 11-4 *Using RCS for Configuration Control*

```
73 # ci -i frodo.cfg
RCS/frodo.cfg,v  <--  frodo.cfg
enter description, terminated with single '.' or end of file:
NOTE: This is NOT the log message!
>> Initial configuration of external/edge router
>> .
done
[root@sauron configs]
126 # co -l frodo.cfg
RCS/frodo.cfg,v  -->  frodo.cfg
revision 1.1 (locked)
done
[root@sauron configs]
127 # ls -l
total 26
drwxrwx---   2 root     sysadmin     512 Aug 29 10:06 RCS
-rw-r-----   1 root     other      11879 Aug 29 10:06 frodo.cfg
```

The **ci** command checks the configuration *into* the repository. The **–i** flag tells the RCS software to create and initialize a new repository. The **co** command is used to check items *out of* the repository. The **–l** flag also locks the repository for the specific user who issued the **co** command. When the configuration file is checked out of the repository, it appears in the local directory (or folder in the case of Windows) as shown above at the end of Example 11-4. The working file in this case is frodo.cfg.

After the file has been checked out and locked, only the current user can make changes to the configuration. When the file is then checked back into the repository, the changes made must be logged. Whenever you check a new revision back into the repository, the RCS software allows you to add a log message to the repository to explain the changes. Example 11-5 demonstrates how to check the configuration changes into the RCS repository. Notice that the **–i** flag was not used because we are not initializing the repository. After the configuration has been checked back into the repository, the working file (in this case, frodo.cfg) is deleted by the RCS software.

Example 11-5 *Checking in Changes to the RCS Repository*

```
[root@sauron configs]
132 # ci frodo.cfg
RCS/frodo.cfg,v  <--  frodo.cfg
new revision: 1.2; previous revision: 1.1
enter log message, terminated with single '.' or end of file:
>> Added new external NAT address, 172.16.45.152 -> 192.168.155.152 - idubraws
>> .
done
[root@sauron configs]
33 # ls -l
total 2
drwxrwx---   2 root      sysadmin     512 Aug 29 10:20 RCS
```

RCS, CVS, and other open source revision-control systems provide an easy, low-cost way of managing and controlling configuration changes.

Change-Control Logging

Change-control logging is the process by which information is entered in the change-control system regarding changes made to a configuration. It is important that information about configuration changes be included when they are made. This provides for easier troubleshooting should a problem occur with the new configuration. When new configuration revisions are checked in to the repository, the RCS software automatically provides for the addition of a log message. The log message should sufficiently reflect the changes made to the configuration so that another person can go in, identify the changes, and be able to back them out if necessary. One way of viewing all the changes made to a particular configuration file through RCS is the use of the rlog program. The rlog program prints log messages and other information about files in the RCS repository. Example 11-6 demonstrates viewing the RCS log for a configuration using the **rlog** command. To view the log file for changes made to the configuration being managed through RCS, the syntax is just **rlog** filename. This displays the log entries for all changes made to the file.

Example 11-6 *Viewing the RCS Log for Configuration Changes*

```
[root@sauron configs]
136 # rlog frodo.cfg

RCS file: RCS/frodo.cfg,v
Working file: frodo.cfg
head: 1.2
branch:
locks: strict
```

continues

Example 11-6   *Viewing the RCS Log for Configuration Changes (Continued)*

```
access list:
symbolic names:
keyword substitution: kv
total revisions: 2;     selected revisions: 2
description:
Initial configuration of external/edge router
--------------------------
revision 1.2
date: 2005/08/29 14:19:59;  author: root;  state: Exp;  lines: +1 -0
Added new external NAT address, 172.16.45.152 -> 192.168.155.152 - idubraws
--------------------------
revision 1.1
date: 2005/08/29 13:51:42;  author: root;  state: Exp;
Initial revision
```

The output in Example 11-6 provides a lot of information. For example, the working file is identified in the Working file line. In addition, it shows how many revisions have been made to the file (in the example, two revisions have been made). A description of the file is provided and below that the revision log entries.

This shows all log entries of the changes made since the configuration file was first checked in to the repository. Note that the name of the user which made the change to the NAT configuration was entered into the log message itself. The user was using the root administrative account however. This is important if the person needs to be contacted regarding the changes he or she made. It is better practice to use individual user accounts to provide accountability for any changes that need to be rolled back out of a configuration.

To view changes made between configurations, the administrator can use the **rcsdiff** command as shown in Example 11-7. The **rcsdiff** command shows the difference between two revisions of a given file in the RCS repository. In the case of Example 11-7, this shows the configuration commands that were entered between the revision levels specified using the **–r** flag on the command line.

Example 11-7   *Viewing Differences in Configuration Revisions*

```
[root@sauron configs]
14 # rcsdiff -r1.1 -r1.2 frodo.cfg
===============================================================
RCS file: RCS/frodo.cfg,v
retrieving revision 1.1
retrieving revision 1.2
diff -r1.1 -r1.2
73a74
> ip nat inside source static 172.16.45.152 66.92.161.152
```

Although RCS is useful for a small site, an enterprise network administrator would be better served by commercial configuration management tools such as the CiscoWorks Management Center for Firewalls. This tool not only provides revision control for the configurations but also a workflow tool that provides for separation of duty among administrators. This prevents a single administrator from making changes and pushing the configuration to the firewall without having another administrator review the changes and approve them.

Updating the Firewall Software

The final topic to consider when managing firewalls is updating the firewall software. There are two primary reasons to update the software. One reason is to take advantage of new capabilities added to newer software versions. The other reason is the need to fix bugs and vulnerabilities in the software. Like all software, firewall software is complicated and contains many lines of code. The code in the firewall may have been rigorously tested, but there will still be corner cases that the software developers did not consider or just outright overlooked. A corner case is a situation that only occurs outside of normal operations. Typically, corner cases arise when multiple conditions occur simultaneously and at an extreme level. For example, a DHCP starvation attack (an attack where the attacker tries to exhaust a DHCP server's ability to provide clients with leases by generating multiple requests for all the IP addresses in the DHCP server's scope) along with a distributed denial-of-service (DDoS) attack. The combination of these two attacks may cause a resource exhaustion on the firewall or trip some other software bug that could make the firewall unusable. These bugs may result in the firewall resetting itself or may result in the firewall allowing invalid traffic through when it should be blocked.

Choosing the Correct Version

The first step in updating a firewall's software is determining the right version. This means determining which version will run on the firewall platform to be upgraded and which version provides all the capabilities desired and for which the firewall is licensed. On SOHO firewalls such as a Linksys device or the PIX 501/506E, the most recent version is typically the correct version to use. However, recently Cisco released PIX OS 7.0 for the PIX platform. This version works on all PIX platforms except for the PIX 501 and the 506E platforms. Take care when a new software version is released by the manufacturer that the requirements for that version are met before attempting to upgrade the firewall. Otherwise, this could result in the firewall being nonfunctional and requiring a software downgrade to a previous version to restore operation.

In the case of Linux NetFilter-based firewalls, the administrator must be careful to ensure that the NetFilter firewall code is compiled into the Linux kernel (either statically or as dynamically loaded modules). In the more recent Linux kernels of the 2.6 series, the NetFilter is automatically included in the kernel configuration as dynamically loaded modules.

Reading the Release Notes

One of the first items to do when deciding with which software release to upgrade a firewall (or any device for that matter) is to read the release notes for that version. The release notes typically include a detailed list of supported devices, new features in the release, and software bugs fixed in the release. In addition, some manufacturers include a list of outstanding bugs that have not been addressed in the release at the time of shipment. The release notes represent a one-stop shop for much, if not all, of the necessary information needed to determine whether the software release being considered is appropriate for the firewall to be upgraded.

Defects and Bugs

Firewall software is complex and contains many subsystems and lines of code. Although the vendors make every effort to identify potential bugs or other errors in the software, not all possible cases can be discovered during testing before the software is released to the general public. Therefore, possible bugs and vulnerabilities in the software may not be detected until after the software has been released.

Vulnerabilities

A vulnerability is a defect that might result in the potential exploitation of the firewall by an attacker to cause either a denial-of-service (DoS) attack or to gain access to the firewall itself. A vulnerability can also be caused by a misconfiguration of the firewall. An example of a vulnerability in firewall software is the Cisco PIX Telnet/SSH DoS attack described on SecurityFocus (http://www.securityfocus.com/bid/6110). This vulnerability, although not providing access to the PIX itself, causes the PIX Telnet/SSH service to become nonresponsive. Cisco immediately released a fix for this problem in PIX OS 6.2.2.111.

A vulnerability due to a *misconfiguration* of the firewall can range from allowing access to Remote Procedure Call (RPC) ports on systems behind the firewall to not setting an access password on the device itself. These types of vulnerabilities are not mitigated by software upgrades but rather by correcting the configuration of the device. One of the quickest ways to find any ports that may be open due to a firewall misconfiguration is to use a network-scanning tool such as Nmap (available at http://www.insecure.org) or Foundstone's Fscan (available from http://www.foundstone.com)

Tracking a Defect

So, a bug or a vulnerability has been discovered in the software version running on your firewall. What do you do now? If the vendor has released a version that resolves the bug or vulnerability, the simplest solution is to download it and apply the patched software. If no fixed software is available, it is important to keep track of the bug and any possible workarounds the vendor has devised. Typically, vendors provide a portal on their websites that include defect information and whether a specific defect has been resolved. For Cisco PIX devices, the Product Security Incident Response Team provides security advisories that can be viewed on the Cisco website at http://www.cisco.com/go/psirt. In addition, for registered users, a database of security-related and non-security-related defects is available. For Linksys devices, this section is part of their technical support website (http://www.linksys.com). Information related to bugs in the Linux kernel is available at the Linux Kernel Archives website (http://www.kernel.org). For Linux kernels 2.6 bugs, there is a specific bug-tracking system, http://bugzilla.kernel.org. For bugs that are NetFilter specific (whether it is the NetFilter code in the kernel or the utilities used to manipulate the NetFilter firewall), there is http://bugzilla.netfilter.org. Regardless of the device, it is important to be aware of bugs and other software issues to be prepared to mitigate any new vulnerabilities that they may introduce into the network.

Summary

Managing firewalls is not much different from managing any other device on the network. However, special care must be taken when managing a firewall because it represents the nexus of security in the any network. In many cases, it represents the *only* security device on the network. Managing a firewall securely is not difficult and does not mean that you are limited only to command-line tools. You can manage many firewalls using SSH (for command-line configuration) and HTTPS (for a browser-based management system) to do such tasks as change default passwords, maintain the platform, make initial configurations, set up logging, modify the configuration, and update the firewall software. Finally, paying attention to potential defects in the firewall software will ensure that a bug or a vulnerability will not sneak up unnoticed and cause a DoS attack or the potential exploitation of devices in the network.

## CHAPTER 12

What Is My Firewall Telling Me?

You have purchased, installed, configured, and are running a firewall. You think it is doing a marvelous job of protecting resources and keeping your network safe and secure. But is it really doing those things? Network and security data and information are arguably the most valuable assets in a firewall administrator's toolbox when combined with the knowledge of how to use them. Firewall data and information greatly increase your ability to identify security compromises and assist in general troubleshooting and maintenance. The challenge, of course, is obtaining this information and knowing what to do with it when you have it.

All mainstream firewalls today provide some method of logging data and information from the firewall. Collecting, reviewing, and understanding what to do with this information will make your job easier. Specifically, you can figure out what your firewall is telling you and with that information you can develop a solution as required.

Firewalls and Logging

The information provided through the use of logging is arguably the most important tool that a firewall administrator has available. Through the use of logging, administrators gain tremendous insight as to the general health and status of their firewalls. I frequently equate the information gained from logging to being similar to how parents know what is going on with their children. Parents spend so much time with their kids that they just know when things are not right, and that allows them to intervene where necessary. Logging provides that kind of insight into the firewall. In fact, logging is really the only method most firewalls can use to inform an administrator what is going on. By collecting—and, most important, by reviewing—the firewall logs, an administrator will rapidly learn the normal and abnormal behavior for the firewall, making it much easier to determine when and how to intervene where necessary to correct the situation.

Generally speaking, there are two methods of logging:

- Syslog logging
- Proprietary logging

The Syslog Protocol

The syslog protocol is the de facto standard method of providing event notification messages across the network. Syslog is defined by RFC 3164 and uses UDP as the default transport mechanism (by default and typically over UDP port 514). By using UDP, syslog gains the advantage of being a low-overhead connectionless delivery method (thus requiring less resources on the systems doing the logging), but that also results in syslog being an inherently unreliable delivery method. Although not common, this can result in messages being lost. To address this deficiency, many devices support using syslog over TCP to provide for reliable data delivery. This process is defined in RFC 3195.

Syslog messages use what is known as a logging facility and severity level to determine where the message should be delivered and the importance of the message. The syslog protocol defines 24 logging facilities, as shown in Table 12-1.

Table 12-1   *Syslog Facilities*

Logging Facility Code	Logging Facility Description
0	Kernel messages
1	User-level messages
2	Mail systems
3	System daemons
4	Security authorization messages
5	Messages generated internally by syslog daemon
6	Line printer systems
7	Network news subsystem
8	UNIX-to-UNIX Copy (UUCP) subsystem
9	Clock daemon
10	Security/authorization messages
11	FTP daemon
12	Network Time Protocol (NTP) subsystem
13	Log audit
14	Log alert
15	Clock daemon
16	Local use 0 (local0)
17	Local use 1 (local1)
18	Local use 2 (local2)
19	Local use 3 (local3)

Table 12-1   *Syslog Facilities (Continued)*

Logging Facility Code	Logging Facility Description
20	Local use 4 (local4)
21	Local use 5 (local5)
22	Local use 6 (local6)
23	Local use 7 (local7)

The easiest way to think of the facility level is to think of each facility as a different pipe, allowing the syslog server to separate and distinguish messages that belong to different systems. The syslog server can then use this information to perform certain actions on messages from one facility while performing completely different actions on messages from other facilities, such as logging messages from each facility into unique files. Although there are 24 facilities, most firewalls use one of the 8 local-use facilities to define where the message originated from and is destined to. For example, the Cisco Secure PIX Firewall defaults to Local4 as the logging facility.

The severity level is used to identify messages of different degrees of importance by grouping them into one of eight categories. Table 12-2 lists the different message severity levels.

Table 12-2   *Syslog Message Severity Levels*

Numeric Code	Level	System Condition
0	Emergency	System is unusable.
1	Alert	Action must be taken immediately.
2	Critical	Critical conditions.
3	Error	Error conditions.
4	Warning	Warning conditions.
5	Notice	Normal but significant conditions.
6	Informational	Informational messages.
7	Debug	Debug-level messages.

The message severity is listed from highest to lowest importance, with Emergency messages being the highest importance and Debug messages being the lowest importance. As a general rule, it is a good idea when first implementing syslog to log only Information-level messages and above, and then restrict the logging even more as you fine-tune the messages that are important to you. For example, as a general rule, Cisco recommends that after the firewall is operational the logging severity level be set to either Warning or Error. The reason for this is that the lower the importance, the more potential messages that will be generated, which can put unnecessary stress and have a negative impact on the firewall performance. The flip side, of course, is that if you are not logging at a severity level that a given event is triggered under (for example, if you have set your logging to Warning but a Notice event occurs), that event will not be logged. You must determine for your environment the appropriate logging severity level.

As shown in Figure 12-1, using syslog requires the implementation of a syslog client on the firewall and a syslog server somewhere on the network.

Figure 12-1   *Delivery of Syslog Messages Across the Network*

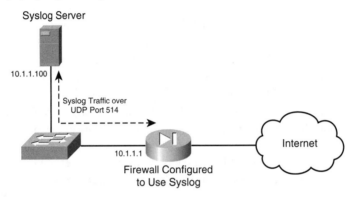

The syslog client is then configured to deliver syslog messages to the syslog server. For example, you can configure a Cisco Secure PIX Firewall to use syslog by running the following basic commands.

For Cisco Secure PIX Firewalls running versions of the PIX OS other than 7.0, the commands are as follows:

```
logging on
logging trap information
logging host inside ip-address
```

For Cisco Secure PIX Firewalls running version 7.0 or later, you need to run the following commands from the configuration mode:

```
logging enable
logging trap information
logging host inside ip-address
```

In addition, I recommend that you log time stamps by running the following command for all versions of PIX OS 6.3 and greater (this only applies to log messages sent to the syslog server):

```
firewall(config)# logging timestamp
```

If you require the firewall to log using a different facility (for example, from the default Cisco PIX logging facility of 20 or local4), you can run the following command to change the logging facility, in this case changing it to Local1 (logging facility code 17, as displayed in Table 12-1):

```
firewall(config)# logging facility 17
```

Configuring the syslog server to receive the syslog message depends largely on the syslog server software that you decide to run. Virtually all versions of UNIX and Linux ship with a built-in syslog server. In addition, a number of freeware as well as commercial syslog server products are available on the market, including the following:

- **Kiwi Syslog Daemon**—This is a popular and relatively inexpensive syslog server for Windows-based systems that can be obtained at http://www.kiwisyslog.com and is shown in Figure 2-2.

- **UNIX syslogd**—Most UNIX and Linux distributions include the syslogd daemon. Refer to your software manufacturer for additional information.

- **CiscoWorks VPN/Security Management Solution (VMS)**—CiscoWorks VMS is a software bundle that includes numerous tools and utilities, including a syslog server for managing and monitoring all aspects of Cisco security devices.

Figure 12-2   *Kiwi Syslog Daemon*

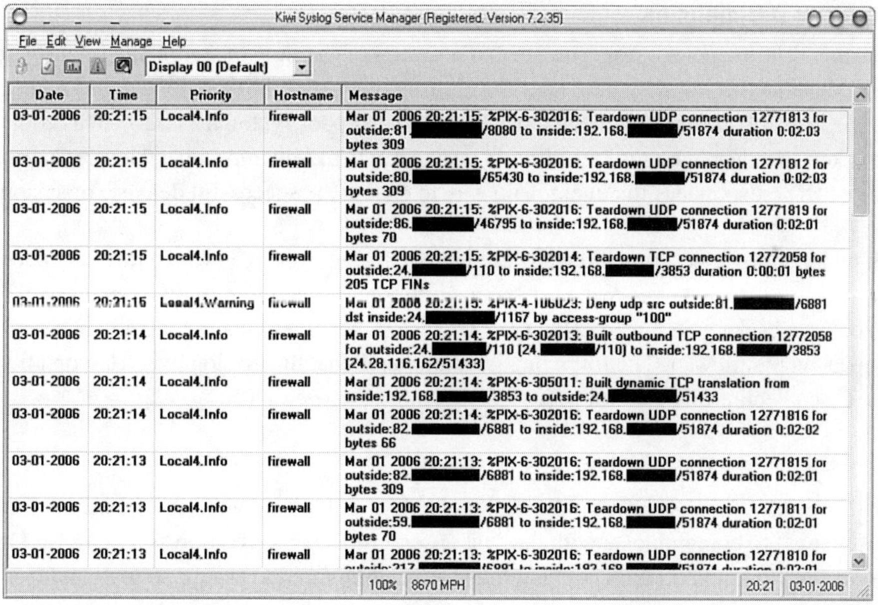

All of these products do a good job at monitoring small- to medium-size environments. If you have an enterprise or large network with a lot of firewalls that generate a large number of syslog messages, however, consider implementing more specialized security incident management (SIM) and log management applications, such as the following:

- **NetIQ Security Manager**—Security Manager is a comprehensive SIM solution that provides real-time security log consolidation, analysis, and reporting of not only syslog but virtually every other logging technology currently in use. Its comprehensiveness allows for the collection of data not only from your firewalls but from your host servers and applications, enabling you to correlate events across the enterprise regardless of what device originally generated the event. This information can then be used for performing forensic analysis and advanced correlation and reporting on the data, helping to identify and eliminate threats and security incidents while ensuring compliance with federal and industry rules and regulations (such as Sarbanes-Oxley and the Health Insurance Portability and Accountability Act). The number of events and the amount of data that Security Manager can handle far exceed the capabilities of any of the previously mentioned syslog server products.

- **Cisco Security Monitoring, Analysis and Response System (CS-MARS)**—CS-MARS appliances provide similar functionality as NetIQ Security Manager, enabling you to perform advanced monitoring, analysis, and threat mitigation and response on not only Cisco-based devices but on a wide range of host systems and applications. This information can be consolidated and reported on, ensuring compliance with federal and industry rules and regulations.

Syslog Security Deficiencies

When you implement syslog, you need to be aware of a couple of significant security deficiencies with regard to how syslog data is delivered across the network. First, by default, syslog uses UDP as the transport mechanism, which makes it easy to spoof syslog messages. This could allow attackers to generate bogus log entries in an attempt to masquerade what they are really doing. The use of UDP also means that there is no way to ensure the successful delivery of syslog message.

To address this issue, some firewalls implement syslog over TCP, which does not necessarily prevent spoofing but does make it a quite a bit more difficult to pull off. Using syslog over TCP also provides for guaranteed delivery of all syslog messages, albeit generally at a performance impact on the firewall. The following is a sample of enabling syslog over TCP on all versions of the Cisco Secure PIX Firewall:

```
firewall(config)# logging host inside 192.168.1.110 tcp/1470
```

In this case, syslog has been configured to use TCP port 1470 (which is the default TCP port that Cisco uses) to communicate with the syslog server located at IP address 192.168.1.110. Keep in mind that your syslog server will also need to be configured to accept syslog messages over TCP. Refer to your syslog server documentation for instructions on how to do this.

> **CAUTION**   When you configure the PIX Firewall to use TCP as the syslog delivery mechanism and the PIX Firewall cannot for some reason communicate with the syslog server (for example, the syslog server is down), by default the firewall will stop delivering all data (not just all syslog data, but all data effectively causing the firewall to fail closed). With PIX OS versions 7.0 and above, you can prevent the firewall from stopping delivering data by running the command **logging permit-hostdown** from the global configuration mode. Unless you require TCP, I recommend not implementing it.

Another security deficiency of syslog is the lack of any method of performing authentication of the message sender, the lack of any method of providing message integrity, and the inability to ensure the privacy of the data through the use of encryption. No native methods within syslog address any of this. Instead, if you require the secure transmission of syslog data, encapsulate the data using a protocol such as IPsec. For more information about encapsulating syslog traffic in IPsec, see Chapter 10 of *Hardening Network Infrastructure* (Osborne/McGraw-Hill).

Proprietary Logging Methods

Proprietary logging is a bit of a misnomer because many firewalls that do not implement syslog use a standard logging methodology developed by Check Point known as Open Platform for Security - Logging Export API (OPSEC LEA). Fundamentally, OPSEC LEA is similar to syslog in that you will need a logging server to retrieve the log information using OPSEC LEA procedure call.

Other firewalls, such as Microsoft ISA Server 2004, use largely proprietary (or rather non-syslog-based) logging methods to log events to a database, typically a Microsoft Data Engine (MSDE) or Structure Query Language (SQL) database. One of the advantages of this kind of logging system is the ability to then be able to build and issue custom queries against the data in the database, providing tremendous functionality and flexibility for building reports. By default, the Microsoft ISA Server 2004 logging data is accessed via the ISA Server Management Console, as shown in Figure 12-3.

Figure 12-3 *Microsoft ISA Server Log Data*

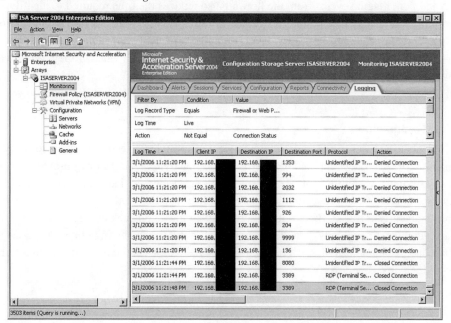

Why Logging Is Important

It is easy to say that you should log events from your firewalls because doing so provides insight as to the status of your firewall, but there are a number of specific and tangible benefits to logging:

■ Improves network administration, troubleshooting, and debugging

■ Establishes a baseline

■ Helps to determine the health of the system

■ Provides intrusion detection and incident containment

■ Facilitates performing forensic analysis

Improved Network Administration, Troubleshooting, and Debugging

If there is one certainty in firewall administration, it is that sooner or later you will need to determine why traffic that should be permitted by the firewall is not being permitted. There are literally dozens of reasons why the firewall may not be allowing the traffic, and the easiest method of determining which reason is the cause is to put the firewall into a debugging mode and then observe the logged data to identify the error or reason why the firewall is not allowing the traffic to pass. Be aware that debug logging can negatively affect firewall performance.

In addition, logging events from the firewall also reduces the time required to identify, troubleshoot, and isolate problems with the firewall. This frees the firewall administrator up to perform other administration tasks. In fact, one of the first troubleshooting steps when working with firewalls is to check the firewall logs to determine whether they can provide any insight on the current issue.

Establishing a Baseline

The only effective method of determining what is normal and secure behavior for a firewall is to monitor the firewall events and identify patterns of activity. Doing so will provide a baseline that makes it much easier to identify when situations are occurring that are outside of the scope of normal operations and functionality. For example, it is quite routine and normal for a firewall to block all sorts of traffic. By monitoring the firewall logs, you can develop a baseline of the kinds of traffic that are typically denied. Doing so makes it much easier to notice exceptions to the baseline, which in turn makes it easier to identify situations and circumstances that warrant additional investigation.

Determining the Health of the System

In conjunction with establishing a baseline, your firewall logs can also be used to determine what the health of the system is. By comparing the current logs to the known baseline, it is much easier to identify conditions that may result in negative performance. Doing so enables you to solve the issues that may be leading to the negative impact in a much more proactive fashion.

Intrusion Detection and Incident Containment

One of the most important reasons for monitoring your firewall logs is that the logs can alert you to potential security compromises and security incidents. I am reminded of a news story I read about a company that discovered their proprietary information had been compromised when they found their internal documentation when performing a search of the Internet. When a legal investigation was launched, it was discovered that the firewall logs contained information relating to the security breach. Because no one was routinely monitoring the logs, however, this information went undetected. Had someone been monitoring the logs, the incident might have been preventable.

Performing Forensic Analysis

The odds are that sooner or later you will have to deal with a security incident in your organization. The simple fact of the matter is that it is impossible to prevent every security incident, all the time. When the security incident occurs, one of the most important questions that will be asked is this: what happened? By collecting and archiving your firewall logs, you greatly increase your ability to determine what occurred so that you can begin the process of recovering from the incident. In addition, this information can be critical evidence in the event that legal action is necessary. To ensure the legal admissibility of your firewall logs, it is critical that your logging system provide a means of demonstrating that the logs have been unaltered and the data contained in the logs is accurate and adheres to the rules of chain of custody (for more information about the chain of custody, see http://www.cert.org/security-improvement/practices/p048.html). Many enterprise logging products provide this functionality as a standard function of their product. If your product does not do this, you can implement third-party solutions such as FSUM (http://www.slavasoft.com/fsum/) to provide file integrity checking and to ensure that the logs have not been altered (especially if the logs are written to a write once, read many [WORM] drive or similar media). Always review all data evidence policies with your organization's legal department to ensure that the process you are following will be admissible in court.

Firewall Log Review and Analysis

After the decision has been made to log events from your firewall, the next step is determining what you should be looking for in the logs and how you should properly perform log analysis. The most important thing to remember is that firewall logs are virtually worthless if no one ever looks at the logs. Logging is merely a means to an end, namely knowing what is going on with your firewalls so that you can respond accordingly. Review of the logs should not be reserved for only when an incident has occurred. It should be a part of the weekly, if not daily, tasks that the firewall administrators perform. To help reduce the time and effort required to review the logs, many of the enterprise security incident management products provide tools and utilities that assist the firewall administrator in separating the wheat from the chaff, allowing the firewall administrator to spend less time reviewing the logs, while still providing the information necessary to help identify situations before they become a problem.

Another aspect of reviewing the logs that should not be overlooked is the need to define a log archive and normalization policy. Too many organizations do not store their firewall logs long enough to adhere to regulations (some of which such as Sarbanes-Oxley are generally accepted to require seven years of log data to be stored). This creates situations where data from the logs may be necessary, but the logs themselves have been destroyed. In conjunction with this, it is important to normalize your log data. Normalization just means converting your logs into a standard format that allows for easier review and correlation of data from different data sources (such as different firewall vendors).

What to Look for in Firewall Logs

After you have collected the firewall logs and begun the process of analyzing the logs, determine the data that you should be looking for in the logs. With that said, it is important to remember not to fall into the trap of looking in your firewall logs only for "bad" events. Yes, firewall logs can be the key element in discovering security incidents and compromises, but that is only one of the reasons for analyzing your logs. You also want to be able to use the log information to assist in defining the baselines and normal operations of the firewall. After all, one of the easiest ways to know whether behavior that has been logged is malicious is to know what the good things are and then note the exceptions.

The simple fact of the matter is that certain events should always raise suspicion when they are detected. Ten of the most common events that warrant further investigation are as follows:

- Authentication allowed.

- Traffic dropped (not addressed to the firewall).

- Firewall stop/start/restart.

- Firewall configuration changed.

- Interface up/down status changed.

- Administrator access granted.

- Connection was torn down.

- Authentication failed.

- Traffic dropped (addressed to the firewall).

- Administrator session ended.

The following sections explain these events in more detail.

Authentication Allowed

Although it may seem rather innocuous at first glance, it is important to look for authentication-allowed events because they can identify situations where access was granted by the firewall when it should not have been allowed. The reasons can range from legitimate administrators logging on when they should not have to malicious users logging on after compromising the account and password that they are using.

In addition, if your firewall is configured to authenticate user access, this event can be used to identify users who have been authenticated for whatever function they are attempting to perform.

Traffic Dropped (Not Addressed to the Firewall)

Most firewalls will have some resources that they are protecting. Traffic addressed to these servers will typically be processed by the firewall and filtered accordingly. Although traffic-dropped messages can indicate that someone is attempting to access a protected resource in a manner other than what the firewall administrator has defined, a common cause of this event is a simple misconfiguration of the ruleset. Therefore, if users cannot access protected resources, it is important to review the logs to determine whether the firewall is dropping the traffic, thereby pointing you in the direction of what may need to be fixed to provide access to the resources requested.

Firewall Stop/Start/Restart

The firewall should never stop, start, or restart without the firewall administrator knowing in advance that the situation is going to occur. This event can be caused by non-firewall-specific issues such as power failures as well as by firewall-specific issues such as the firewall crashing or a high-availability failover, and therefore it should always be investigated in more detail to ascertain the root cause.

Firewall Configuration Changed

Almost all firewall configuration changes should be accompanied with the appropriate change control documentation. This event always warrants further investigation to ensure that the changes that were made are legitimate and in accordance with expected results. In fact, many SIM products can be configured to perform a comparison of the changed configuration against a "known good" configuration when a firewall configuration changed event occurs. In fact, some products such as NetIQ Security Manager can actually use that information to attempt to undo the changes that were made if they are found to be out of compliance with the known good configuration.

Interface Up/Down Status Changed

Firewall interfaces transitioning from an up to a down status and vice versa can indicate problems with the underlying network configuration. This information can prove particularly helpful in situations where redundant firewalls are implemented, because the network interfaces transitioning to a down state could cause the firewall failover process to occur.

Administrator Access Granted

Whenever administrator access is granted, the corresponding event should be investigated. Although similar to monitoring for authentication, in this case we are looking explicitly at gaining administrator access. Most likely the access is expected, and there is nothing suspicious or out of order that warrants further review. However, if that is not the case, this event rapidly becomes an extremely high-priority situation that must be investigated because the implication can be that an administrator account has been compromised.

Connection Was Torn Down

The termination of connections is a relatively routine process that is a part of normal communications. Where this event is particularly important, however, is in listing the reason why the connection was torn down. For example, the connection may have been torn down as a result of SYN timeout, which can be an indicator that someone is attempting to cause a denial of service, especially if there are a lot of events of that nature. In determining the cause of the connection tear down, it is important to review the firewall documentation for the teardown causes. For example, Cisco Secure PIX Firewall version 7.0 message ID 302014 lists the potential reasons for a TCP connection being torn down as shown in Table 12-3.

Table 12-3   *TCP Connection Teardown Reasons*

Reason	Description
Conn-timeout	Connection ended because it was idle longer than the configured idle timeout.
Deny Terminate	Flow was terminated by application inspection.
Failover primary closed	The standby unit in a failover pair deleted a connection because of a message received from the active unit
FIN Timeout	Force termination after 10 minutes awaiting the last ACK or after half-closed timeout.

Table 12-3 *TCP Connection Teardown Reasons (Continued)*

Reason	Description
Flow closed by inspection	Flow was terminated by inspection feature.
Flow terminated by IPS	Flow was terminated by IPS.
Flow reset by IPS	Flow was reset by IPS.
Flow terminated by TCP intercept	Flow was terminated by TCP Intercept.
Invalid SYN	SYN packet not valid.
Idle Timeout	Connection timed out because it was idle longer than timeout value.
IPS fail-close	Flow was terminated due to IPS card down.
SYN Control	Back channel initiation from wrong side.
SYN Timeout	Force termination after 2 minutes awaiting three-way handshake completion.
TCP bad retransmission	Connection terminated because of bad TCP retransmission.
TCP FINs	Normal close-down sequence.
TCP Invalid SYN	Invalid TCP SYN packet.
TCP Reset-I	Reset was from the inside.
TCP Reset-O	Reset was from the outside.
TCP segment partial overlap	Detected a partially overlapping segment.
TCP unexpected window size variation	Connection terminated due to variation in the TCP window size.
Tunnel has been torn down	Flow terminated because tunnel is down.
Unauth Deny	Denied by URL filter.
Unknown	Catchall error.
Xlate Clear	Command-line removal

As you can see, reasons such as "Unauth Deny" or "Flow closed by inspection" can be indicators of malicious traffic and warrant more concern and investigation than a reason such as "TCP Reset—I" (which is a normal method of applications terminating their communications session).

Authentication Failed

Authentication-failed events can be indicators of everything from users making a typo when they enter their password to malicious users making a brute-force attack in an attempt to determine the password. Authentication-failed events should be examined in particular detail when the account in question is a privileged or administrator-level account.

Traffic Dropped (Addressed to the Firewall)

These events are similar to the traffic dropped that is not addressed to the firewall, with the obvious difference being that in this case the traffic is addressed to the firewall. As a general rule, the firewall should not have any traffic addressed directly to it on the external interface; instead, all traffic should be destined for the resources being protected by the firewall. These events can be indicators of malicious users attempting to gain access to the firewall or a misconfiguration of things such as ICMP, IPsec, or management or routing protocols and therefore should be investigated in more detail to determine the exact nature of why the traffic was dropped.

Administrator Session Ended

Similar to administrator access being granted, administrator sessions ending should be monitored to ensure that the administrator who had access was supposed to have access. This type of event can also be used as a time benchmark because only administrators should be able to make changes to the firewall, and therefore the logs should be investigated in more detail for the time preceding the administrator session ending to see exactly what commands may have been run.

Cisco Secure PIX Firewall Syslog Event Baseline

The following syslog events constitute a good baseline of events that should be monitored and paid careful attention to in most environments. In essence, this list is here to answer this question: What specific kinds of events should I look for? It is not meant to be an exhaustive list of all syslog message IDs or the only syslog message IDs that you should be filtering for.

You can use this information to help build filtering rules for your particular logging software—for example, to identify the messages that administrators should get a page or e-mail notification over (for instance, message %PIX-3-201008) versus messages that can just be logged without any special notification occurring. This can be done by using the message ID (for example, %PIX-3-201008) in your logging software's filtering syntax/search strings.

In general, every time Cisco releases a new version of software, syslog events are added/deleted from the list of events. Therefore, your particular version of software may or may not include all of these events, or it may have events that are not listed here.

Obviously, not all events are relevant for all environments, but this list provides a sound starting point of events to be on the look out for, from which you can further customize to meet the logging requirements in your environment. This list can be easily modified to cover both the Cisco Adaptive Security Appliance (ASA) and Cisco Firewall Services Module (FWSM) by just replacing the **%PIX** syntax with either a **%ASA** or **%FWSM**, respectively (in fact, the log messages use %PIX|ASA to mean that either **%PIX** or **%ASA** can be used):

■   All severity level 1 messages (use the string **%PIX|ASA-1** for the filter)

■   **%PIX|ASA-2-106016**: Deny IP spoof from (IP_address) to IP_address on interface interface_name

- **%PIX|ASA-2-106017**: Deny IP due to Land Attack from IP_address to IP_address

- **%PIX|ASA-2-106018**: ICMP packet type ICMP_type denied by outbound list acl_ID src inside_address dest outside_address

- **%PIX|ASA-2-106020**: Deny IP teardrop fragment (size = number, offset = number) from IP_address to IP_address

- **%PIX|ASA-2-201003**: Embryonic limit exceeded nconns/elimit for outside_address/ outside_port (global_address) inside_address/inside_port on interface interface_name

- **%PIX|ASA-2-304007**: URL Server IP_address not responding, ENTERING ALLOW mode.

- **%PIX|ASA-3-316001**: Denied new tunnel to IP_address. VPN peer limit (platform_vpn_peer_limit) exceeded

- **%PIX|ASA-3-201002**: Too many TCP connections on {static|xlate} global_address! econns nconns

- **%PIX|ASA-3-201004**: Too many UDP connections on {static|xlate} global_address! udp connections limit

- **%PIX|ASA-3-201008**: The PIX is disallowing new connections.

- **%PIX|ASA-3-201009**: TCP connection limit of number for host IP_address on interface_name exceeded

- **%PIX|ASA-3-202001**: Out of address translation slots!

- **%PIX|ASA-3-211001**: Memory allocation error

- **%PIX|ASA-3-211003**: CPU utilization for number seconds = percent

- **%PIX|ASA-3-302302**: ACL = deny; no sa created

- **%PIX|ASA-3-304003**: URL Server IP_address timed out URL url

- **%PIX|ASA-3-304006**: URL Server IP_address not responding

- **%PIX|ASA-3-315004**: Fail to establish SSH session because PIX RSA host key retrieval failed.

- **%PIX|ASA-3-317004**: IP routing table limit warning

- **%PIX|ASA-3-322001**: Deny MAC address MAC_address, possible spoof attempt on interface interface

- **%PIX|ASA-3-322002**: ARP inspection check failed for arp {request|response} received from host MAC_address on interface interface. This host is advertising MAC Address MAC_address_1 for IP Address IP_address, which is {statically|dynamically} bound to MAC Address MAC_address_2.

- **%PIX|ASA-3-404102**: ISAKMP: Exceeded embryonic limit

- **%PIX|ASA-3-407002**: Embryonic limit nconns/elimit for through connections exceeded. outside_address/outside_port to global_address (inside_address)/inside_port on interface interface_name

- **%PIX|ASA-3-710003**: {TCP|UDP} access denied by ACL from source_address/source_port to interface_name:dest_address/service

- **%PIX|ASA-4-106023**: Deny protocol src [interface_name:source_address/source_port] dst interface_name:dest_address/dest_port [type {string}, code {code}] by access_group acl_ID

- **%PIX|ASA-4-209003**: Fragment database limit of number exceeded: src = IP_address, dest = IP_address, proto = protocol, id = number

- **%PIX|ASA-4-209004**: Invalid IP fragment, size = bytes exceeds maximum size = bytes: src = IP_address, dest = IP_address, proto = protocol, id = number

- **%PIX|ASA-4-209005**: Discard IP fragment set with more than number elements: src = IP_address, dest = IP_address, proto = protocol, id = number

- **%PIX|ASA-4-401004**: Shunned packet: IP_address ==> IP_address on interface interface_name

- **%PIX|ASA-4-402103**: identity does not match negotiated identity (ip) dest_address= dest_address, src_addr= source_address, prot= protocol, (ident) local=inside_address, remote=remote_address, local_proxy=IP_address/IP_address/port/port, remote_proxy=IP_address/IP_address/port/port

- **%PIX|ASA-4-405001**: Received ARP {request | response} collision from IP_address/ MAC_address on interface interface_name

- **%PIX|ASA-4-405002**: Received mac mismatch collision from IP_address/MAC_address for authenticated host

- **%PIX|ASA-4-407001**: Deny traffic for local-host interface_name:inside_address, license limit of number exceeded

- **%PIX|ASA-4-415012**:internal_sig_id HTTP Deobfuscation signature detected - action HTTP deobfuscation detected IPS evasion technique from source_address to source_address

- **%PIXIASA-4-415014**:internal_sig_id Maximum of 10 unanswered HTTP requests exceeded from source_address to dest_address

- **%PIXIASA-5-111001**: Begin configuration: IP_address writing to device

- **%PIXIASA-5-111003**: IP_address Erase configuration

- **%PIXIASA-5-111004**: IP_address end configuration: {FAILEDIOK}

- **%PIXIASA-5-111005**: IP_address end configuration: OK

- **%PIXIASA-5-111007**: Begin configuration: IP_address reading from device.

- **%PIXIASA-5-111008**: User user executed the command string

- **%PIXIASA-5-199001**: PIX reload command executed from Telnet (remote IP address)

- **%PIXIASA-5-199006**: Orderly reload started at when by whom. Reload reason: reason

- **%PIXIASA-5-304001**: User source address accessed {JAVA URLIURL} dest_address: url.

- **%PIXIASA-5-304002**: Access denied URL url SRC IP_address DEST IP_address: url

- **%PIXIASA-5-415007**:internal_sig_id HTTP Extension method illegal - action 'method_name' from source_address to dest_address

- **%PIXIASA-5-415008**:internal_sig_id HTTP RFC method illegal - action 'method_name' from source_address to dest_address

- **%PIXIASA-5-415010**:internal_sig_id HTTP protocol violation detected - action HTTP Protocol not detected from source_address to dest_address

- **%PIXIASA-5-415013**:internal_sig_id HTTP Transfer encoding violation detected - action Xfer_encode Transfer encoding not allowed from source_address to dest_address

- **%PIXIASA-5-500001**: ActiveX content modified src IP_address dest IP_address on interface interface_name.

- **%PIXIASA-5-500002**: Java content modified src IP_address dest IP_address on interface interface_name.

- **%PIXIASA-5-501101**: User transitioning priv level

- **%PIXIASA-5-502101**: New user added to local dbase: Uname: user Priv: privilege_level Encpass: string

- **%PIXIASA-5-502102**: User deleted from local dbase: Uname: user Priv: privilege_level Encpass: string

- **%PIX|ASA-5-502103**: User priv level changed: Uname: user From: privilege_level To: privilege_level

- **%PIX|ASA-5-612001**: Auto Update succeeded:filename, version:number

- **%PIX|ASA-6-109006**: Authentication failed for user user from inside_address/inside_port to outside_address/outside_port on interface interface_name.

- **%PIX|ASA-6-106012**: Deny IP from IP_address to IP_address, IP options hex

- **%PIX|ASA-6-106015**: Deny TCP (no connection) from IP_address/port to IP_address/port flags tcp_flags on interface interface_name.

- **%PIX|ASA-6-109008**: Authorization denied for user user from source_address/source_port to destination_address/destination_port on interface interface_name.\

- **%PIX|ASA-6-109024**: Authorization denied from source_address/source_port to dest_address/dest_port (not authenticated) on interface interface_name using protocol

- **%PIX|ASA-6-109025**: Authorization denied (acl=acl_ID) for user 'user' from source_address/source_port to dest_address/dest_port on interface interface_name using protocol

- **%PIX|ASA-6-113006**: User user locked out on exceeding number successive failed authentication attempts

- **%PIX|ASA-6-302014**: Teardown TCP connection id for interface:real-address/real-port to interface:real-address/real-port duration hh:mm:ss bytes bytes [reason] [(user)]

- **%PIX|ASA-6-308001**: PIX console enable password incorrect for number tries (from IP_address)

- **%PIX|ASA-6-309002**: Permitted manager connection from IP_address.

- **%PIX|ASA-6-315011**: SSH session from IP_address on interface interface_name for user user disconnected by SSH server, reason: reason

- **%PIX|ASA-6-415009**:internal_sig_id HTTP Header length exceeded. Received length byte Header - action header length exceeded from source_address to dest_address

- **%PIX|ASA-6-415011**:internal_sig_id HTTP URL Length exceeded. Received size byte URL - action URI length exceeded from source_address to dest_address

- **%PIX|ASA-6-605004**: Login denied from {source_address/source_port | serial} to {interface_name:dest_address/service | console} for user "user"

- **%PIX|ASA-6-605005**: Login permitted from {source_address/source_port | serial} to {interface_name:dest_address/service | console} for user "user"

- **%PIX|ASA-6-606001**: ADSM session number number from IP_address started

- **%PIX|ASA-6-606002**: ADSM session number number from IP_address ended

- **%PIX|ASA-6-610101**: Authorization failed: Cmd: command Cmdtype: command_modifier

- **%PIX|ASA-6-611101**: User authentication succeeded: Uname: user

- **%PIX|ASA-6-611102**: User authentication failed: Uname: user

- **%PIX|ASA-6-611311**: VNPClient: XAUTH Failed: Peer: IP_address

- **%PIX|ASA-7-111009**:User user executed cmd:string

- **%PIX|ASA-7-304009**: Ran out of buffer blocks specified by url-block command

> **NOTE**   For an exhaustive list of all Cisco PIX/ASA/FWSM syslog messages, see http:// www.cisco.com/en/US/products/sw/secursw/ps2120/products_system_message_guides_ list.html.

Firewall Forensics

Odds are, you will need to conduct a forensics analysis using your firewall logs at some point. The underlying objective of a forensic analysis is trying to determine what happened and to establish facts that can be used in court. If you have never reviewed the firewall logs previously, this can be a costly and almost insurmountable process because you do not necessarily have any idea what may or may not be a normal event for the firewall.

Performing a forensic analysis is generally an extremely time-consuming and expensive process because in many cases it is much like trying to find a needle in the haystack. You may know what was done, but you do not know necessarily when or how it was done, which can make it tricky indeed to be successful. This is compounded by the fact that you need to gather evidence from the earliest moment possible to establish exactly what transpired.

Because of the potentially sensitive nature of forensic analysis, it is a good idea to use tools that can assist in performing the forensics analysis or to bring in experts who have special training in exactly what should and should not be done. This is where tools like NetIQ Security Manager and Cisco CS-MARS come in particularly handy, because they include built-in correlation, query, and reporting functionality that is particularly suited to this kind of situation. For example, Figure 12-4 illustrates a forensic analysis report from NetIQ Security Manager.

Figure 12-4 *NetIQ Security Manager Forensic Analysis Report*

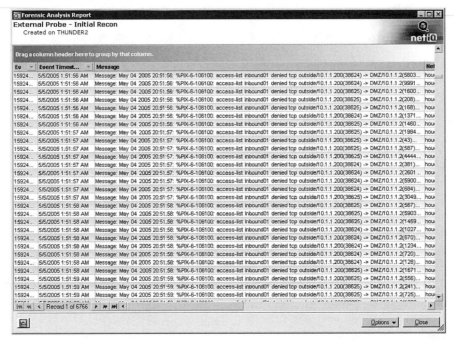

On the surface, the firewall denying traffic is not necessarily something to be concerned about. However, by looking at the data (for example the data in Figure 12-4) with a bit more of a critical eye, the traffic is all originating from the same source (10.1.1.200) to the same destination (10.1.1.2) on a whole slew of different port numbers. This is a classic example of a reconnaissance attack; the attacker is running a port scan in an attempt to determine which ports are open and thereby gain information about the kinds of applications that may be running on those ports. For example, if TCP port 80 is open, it is safe bet that a web server is running on that port, and attackers can begin customizing their attack to determine with certainty that yes indeed a web server is running. This information can then be used to determine the methods of attack that may be successful against the targeted host.

The Value (or Not) of IP Addresses

One pitfall to keep in mind when you review your firewall logs is that just because the logs report that a certain IP address attempted to connect, that does not necessarily mean that IP address was indeed responsible. IP addresses can be spoofed relatively easily. That is not to say that spoofing addresses and actually doing something malicious as a result is a trivial process, which is a frequent misconception regarding IP address spoofing. Although it is easy to spoof an IP address, it is not easy to pull off an attack while spoofing addresses. Think of it like this, if the attacker needs to get some information as a part of the attack, and he is spoofing his IP address, the information is going to be sent to the spoofed IP address—which means that in general it is not going to the attacker. Figure 12-5 illustrates how attackers may spoof their IP address.

Figure 12-5 *How Spoofing Works*

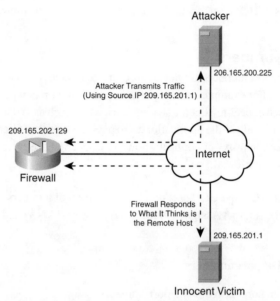

In the example in Figure 12-5, the attacker builds packets with a source IP address of 209.165.201.1 (the IP address of the innocent victim) to transmit to the firewall. When the firewall receives the data, it logs the packets as coming from 209.165.201.1 because that is what the source IP address of the packet is. In reality, the packet came from the attacker, but the firewall has no way of knowing that. In fact, if the firewall needs to respond to any of the traffic that it received, it will actually attempt to connect to the innocent victim, *which could well cause alerts to be generated by the folks who monitor and manage that computer.* This is also a good reason it is a bad idea (and in many cases is illegal) to launch retributive strikes against systems that you think may be attacking your systems. If that were to occur in this case, you have gone from being the good guy to attacking someone who was not even involved in the security incident.

Where spoofing is particularly effective, however, is when the attacker does not necessarily need a response to the data that he sent (for example, when trying to flood the firewall with bogus data), such as when performing attacks that are based on connectionless protocols such as UDP and ICMP. For example, if an attacker attempts to spoof using TCP and is not blocking traffic between the firewall and the innocent victim, when the innocent victim receives a packet based on the spoofed connection, the innocent victim will send a TCP reset because it is not aware of the connection in question. This is one of the reasons that spoofing using TCP (or any connection-oriented protocol) is difficult to successfully pull off.

The bottom line when it comes to the IP addresses that are logged is that after you have what you suspect is the IP address of the system that was involved in the security incident, you still need to perform a more detailed investigation to ensure that the IP address in question was really involved, and that the attacker was not spoofing his IP address in an attempt to mask his trail. One method of identifying this is TCP resets from the innocent victim in your firewall logs.

Deciphering Port Numbers

Like IP addresses, port numbers are not an absolute guarantee of what application or service may have been running. For example, many applications can run on any port that is configured, allowing things such as peer-to-peer file sharing to use a port such as TCP port 80 for communications, which will frequently allow the application to bypass most packet filtering firewalls (but not necessarily application proxy or application-aware inspection) because TCP port 80 is frequently permitted through the firewall.

The lists of default TCP and UDP port numbers, IP protocol numbers, and ICMP message types are managed by the Internet Assigned Numbers Authority (IANA) and can be accessed as follows:

- **TCP and UDP port numbers**

  http://www.iana.org/assignments/port-numbers

- **IP protocols**

  http://www.iana.org/assignments/protocol-numbers

- **ICMP message types**

  http://www.iana.org/assignments/icmp-parameters

Again, although you will need to do additional verification to ensure that the ports logged are actually running the applications and services that are claimed, these lists provide at least an initial starting point from which to begin the investigation.

Securing the Firewall

An important result of performing a forensic analysis is to use that information to determine what needs to be done in the future to secure the firewall. As you identify what transpired and how the incident occurred, use that information to identify flaws in both the written security policy of the organization as well as the actual firewall policy and ruleset. For example, if an attacker was able to compromise a resource on a DMZ segment and then use that resource to gain access to the firewall, that is probably a good indication that access to the firewall from that resource (or from the entire DMZ for that matter) should probably not be permitted.

Summary

In a profession where data and the knowledge of how to use it are critical commodities, firewall logs can provide an incredible degree of insight and information. This information can be used not only to provide help in the day-to-day administration and troubleshooting of the firewall, but can also be used to provide forensics and incident response and containment capabilities.

It is of critical importance that the firewall logs be reviewed on a regular and routine basis and that the logs be normalized and stored for a long duration to ensure that the information contained in the logs is easily deciphered and readily recoverable. Although you want to look for events that denote potential problems, you also want to look for events that are normal and routine, to help develop a feel for what the normal operation and function of the firewall is. This will in turn make it much easier for you to identify events and situations that are abnormal and require additional investigation and response.

## CHAPTER 13

Troubleshooting Firewalls

One of the more difficult skills to cultivate is how to troubleshoot problems related to your firewall or firewall implementation. The reason for this difficulty is that firewalls, by design, tend to do some pretty significant manipulation of network traffic, thus making it difficult to determine whether whatever anomaly you are seeing is an actual problem or a design of the firewall. For example, so many firewalls are designed by default to not respond to Internet Control Message Protocol (ICMP) ping packets. Therefore, if you attempt to ping the firewall to troubleshoot a problem and you do not get a response, it can be difficult to determine whether the lack of a response is indeed a problem or actually is occurring by design.

Although the question of how to troubleshoot a firewall might be unique based on your individual implementation (that is, if your firewall does not allow ICMP you cannot use ICMP as a part of your troubleshooting), a relatively common list of tasks can assist in troubleshooting problems regardless of the firewall vendor or implementation. For example, all firewalls have rulesets to permit/deny traffic. How those rulesets are manipulated is unique to each firewall, but the fact that you need to review them when troubleshooting connectivity issues is true regardless of firewall vendor or implementation. Therefore, it is a good idea to develop a troubleshooting checklist to guide you through the process of troubleshooting your firewalls and firewall implementations.

This chapter presents a troubleshooting checklist and covers techniques when using that list to troubleshoot specific situations.

Developing a Troubleshooting Checklist

There is an old saying that when you practice what you need to do in the time of a crisis, when the crisis occurs the reaction tends to be automatic. When the firewall is down is not the time to try to figure out what you should be looking at to resolve the problem. Instead, develop a troubleshooting checklist in advance. The reason is simple: There will already be enough stress and confusion as a result of the failure; there is no need to increase either by not having a plan. Your troubleshooting checklist is that plan.

Obviously, you cannot plan for every failure that will occur, but you can put together a strategy that, if executed properly, increases the likelihood of being able to isolate the problem more rapidly. The primary objective of the troubleshooting checklist is to provide a methodical and logical approach to troubleshoot the problem. After all, computer systems (including firewalls) are binary devices, they are on or off. The logic is simple, and the devices always do exactly what they are supposed to—even when they fail. A troubleshooting checklist should guide you through that logical troubleshooting process. I often use an analogy of eating an elephant when I talk about troubleshooting. Trying to eat an elephant introduces a big, big problem. If you try to sit down and eat the elephant all at once, you are going to quickly find yourself overwhelmed with the task at hand. Troubleshooting is no different. If you try to troubleshoot the entire problem all at once, you are going to quickly find yourself overwhelmed with the task at hand. However, instead of trying to deal with the whole elephant, if you chop it into smaller, easier-to-manage steak-sized pieces, you will find the task of eating the elephant more manageable. Troubleshooting is no different, and after you have developed a checklist of methodical and logical approaches to troubleshooting a problem, a secondary objective of a troubleshooting checklist is to use the results obtained by following the checklist to narrow down the potential causes of whatever failure is occurring.

Keeping in mind that every firewall, environment, and problem is unique, the following represent a good baseline troubleshooting checklist:

Step 1   Verify the problem reported.

Step 2   Test connectivity.

Step 3   Physically check the firewall.

Step 4   Check for recent changes.

Step 5   Check the firewall logs for errors.

Step 6   Verify the firewall configuration.

Step 7   Verify the firewall ruleset.

Step 8   Verify that any dependent, non-firewall-specific systems are not the culprit.

Step 9   Monitor the network traffic.

Step 1: Verify the Problem Reported

One of the most overlooked steps in troubleshooting is to actually verify that the problem that was reported is occurring as it was reported. Far too often, people report what they suspect the problem is without being for certain that the problem is indeed related to the firewall. I have lost count of how many times I have heard "I cannot access this server, the firewall must be down" only to discover that the server itself was down. So before you begin the actual troubleshooting process, ensure that the problem has been reported accurately and that you understand and if possible can reproduce or see the problem as it is occurring. The old saying "To know where you are going, you need to know where you are at" holds true in troubleshooting. Before you can troubleshoot a problem, you need to make sure you know what the problem is.

Another aspect of verifying the problem is to make sure you treat the problem, not the symptoms. This is similar to treating a medical patient. If a person comes in with a fever and all you do is treat the fever (the symptom), you have done nothing to fix the problem (the illness causing the fever). Accordingly, when the problem is reported, try to distinguish between the symptoms of the problem (which are normally what is reported) and the problem itself. The reason for this is simple. If all you do is treat the symptoms, you may eliminate the cause for the problem being reported, but you have not fixed the problem itself, and a good chance exists that it will reappear at some point in the future. This is particularly true when it comes to dealing with performance-related issues. It is easy to lose sight of the problem, treat the symptom, and move on without ever addressing the root cause of the performance problem.

Step 2: Test Connectivity

In the realm of networking and firewalls, one of the most important and first questions to ask is this: Is the device up? This is where testing connectivity comes into play. Although this step is not applicable to every situation, it is usually a good idea to try to connect to the firewall or system protected by the firewall just to make sure it is up. There are a number of ways to do this.

Using Ping to Test Connectivity

The de facto standard method of testing connectivity is to send a ping to the target host. There are a couple of ways that this can be done that will provide additional information based on the response. To help with understanding the process and the interaction of each step, see the connectivity testing flowchart in Figure 13-1.

The first step is to attempt to ping the target host by its host name. If this succeeds, it validates that everything from name resolution to physical delivery of the data is functioning properly.

If this is not successful, the next step is to attempt to ping the target host by its IP address. This eliminates name resolution as part of the problem. If this succeeds, the problem is likely going to be related to name resolution (either Domain Name System [DNS] resolution or NetBIOS name resolution). Perhaps the DNS server is down or the target host name is not known. If this does not succeed, it is possible that the target host is inaccessible for some reason (regardless, however, the problem warrants more attention).

Figure 13-1 *Connectivity Testing Flowchart*

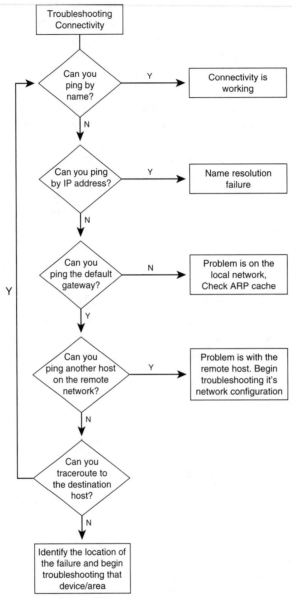

If the target host is remote, the next step is to attempt to ping the default gateway of the source machine as well as another host on the same network as the remote machine (it is a good idea to use the remote machines default gateway as the destination). If you can physically access the target machine, repeat this process in the other direction. These steps validate that both hosts are able to communicate with their local routers as well as validating that you can reach something on the remote network. If they cannot, a good chance exists that the problem exists between the host and its router. It is possible that there is an invalid Address Resolution Protocol (ARP) entry on either the host or the router.

If the hosts can successfully ping their respective routers, and you are unable to ping another host on the remote network, the next step is to perform a traceroute from the source to the target host. This will enable you to determine the approximate location where the problem is occurring. In a complex routed environment, it is generally a good idea to have some baseline results of a functional traceroute because the traceroute is typically unable to provide the IP address of the failing hop. Only by knowing what the next hop from the last successful hop is can you have an idea of what specific router might be the cause.

Testing Connectivity Without Using Ping

One thing to keep in mind when testing connectivity is that many firewalls, by design, do not allow ICMP traffic to traverse the firewall, and thus render the use of ICMP to test connectivity worthless. You have a couple of options in this event. For one, you can permit the ICMP traffic for the purposes of troubleshooting the problem and then disable it again when you are finished. Another option is to use another protocol to determine whether the remote system is responding at all. For example, just telnetting to many TCP ports will either confirm or deny whether a remote host is accessible, as shown in Example 13-1.

Example 13-1 *Telnetting to TCP port 80 to Test Connectivity*

```
C:\Documents and Settings\wnoonan>telnet web server 80
GET /HTTP/1.0

HTTP/1.1 200 OK
Content-Length: 2795
Content-Type: text/html
Content-Location: http://192.168.173.101/Default.htm
Last-Modified: Tue, 23 Nov 2004 05:23:47 GMT
Accept-Ranges: bytes
ETag: "f9fcf19b1cd1c41:336"
Server: Microsoft-IIS/6.0
X-Powered-By: ASP.NET
Date: Thu, 02 Mar 2006 05:29:53 GMT
Connection: close<additional output snipped>
Connection to host lost.
```

By just telnetting to TCP port 80 and typing **GET / HTTP/1.0** and then pressing Enter a few times, I can retrieve the default web page for the server, which at least verifies that the target host is properly connected to and communicating with the network and at best will tell me exactly what web server software is being run as shown on the 5th line from end, "Server: Microsoft-IIS/6.0.

Step 3: Physically Check the Firewall

One of the most common failures on a network is a physical failure. From bumped power cords to incorrectly seated network cables, you can often quickly identify and remedy the problem by paying a visit to the physical machine. In addition, many network devices, including firewalls, provide visual indicators regarding the status of the system. For example, if you do not see a link light on an interface, that is usually a good indicator that the network cable is not plugged in.

In some cases (for example, remote firewalls), it is just not feasible to check the firewall yourself. If you have a trusted person at that remote site, however, you can ask that person to check on the firewall on your behalf. As firewall administrators, many of us have gotten used to being able to do most of our work remotely from our desk. As much of an annoyance as it may be to have to walk over to where the firewall is to check on it, that pales in comparison to spending time trying to troubleshoot a connectivity problem only to find that someone bumped the power cord on the firewall.

Step 4: Check for Recent Changes

Recent changes are not always responsible for problems that occur, but they should always be examined as a potential cause of the problems. The reason for this is simple: Today's networks are so complex that it is difficult to ensure that a change does not cause a problem for a dependent system. Consequentially, it is critical that you have a means of tracking and monitoring the changes that are made in your environment so that you have something that you can refer back to.

Good change control is more than just "busy work." It provides a methodical means of answering the questions of who, what, and when:

- **Who made recent changes**—At the most simplistic, this gives you the name of who to check with regarding the changes to determine whether they can provide insight into the problem.

- **What were the changes that were made**—This is the most important information that your change-control process contains. This information enables you to look at what was changed to make a decision as to whether it looks like the changes could be responsible for the problems. For example, if someone updated the SNMP settings but the problem appears to be with traffic being blocked, a good chance exists that the changes that were made are irrelevant for the problem that is occurring.

- **When were the changes made**—Changes that were made days or weeks ago probably are not responsible for the problems of today. Similarly, however, if the changes were made an hour ago, and the problem showed up an hour ago, it is probably worth investigating the changes in more detail.

It is important to view recent changes as a culprit for problems with a skeptical eye, however. Before spending time undoing the changes, examine the change in the context of the problem and make sure that it makes sense for the changes that were made to be a cause of the problem. For example, one time I watched a company roll back a series of virus Digital Audio Tape (DAT) files because they were the last change made on the network before authentication errors started occurring. Now, anyone who knows anything about DAT updates knows that they have pretty much nothing to do with authentication, and this case was no different. When it was all said and done, the DAT updates were rolled back and the problem still existed, but the company lost hours of time that could have been spent fixing the problem. It was subsequently discovered that a domain controller in error was causing the problems. The point is, make sure that the changes appear to be relevant before devoting full attention to them. Just because there were recent changes does not mean that they are responsible for the problem. This is particularly true with firewalls, where it seems like if a change has been made to a firewall within six months of a problem occurring, someone will immediately question whether the firewall is the problem—even if the problem traffic in question never goes through the firewall.

Step 5: Check the Firewall Logs for Errors

As you saw in Chapter 12, "What Is My Firewall Telling Me?," a wealth of information is available in most firewalls logs and logging systems. Therefore, always review your firewall logs as a routine troubleshooting step. To assist in using the logs as a troubleshooting tool, you can increase the level of logging detail, perhaps changing to informational or even debugging level or selecting to log specific error messages to help isolate the issue. When examining the logs, pay particular attention to the following types of events:

- **Look for state errors**—State errors can be indicators of problems with the firewall translation tables (for example, if the Cisco Secure PIX Firewall has an incorrectly configured static translation value).

- **Look for denied traffic**—Denied traffic is the classic indicator of an incorrectly configured ruleset. Although virtually all firewalls include an implicit **deny** statement at the end of the firewall ruleset, to assist in troubleshooting it can be helpful to include an explicit **deny** and **log** statement to ensure that the denied traffic is logged accordingly.

- **Look for configuration errors**—Often configuration errors will be reported in the firewall logs as error events, allowing you to rapidly identify a configuration error without needing to review the configuration line by line. A good example of this might be speed and duplex mismatch errors, which can cause the firewall to not be able to make a reliable network connection.

- **Look for hardware errors**—Event logs are one of the best sources for discovering hardware-related errors because most firewall vendors log hardware error events in the firewall logs.

Step 6: Verify the Firewall Configuration

There are two elements to verifying the firewall configuration. The first is to compare the current configuration to a known good configuration. The second is to verify that the firewall configuration is accurate with no typos or other errors.

Every time that the firewall configuration is changed (in addition to the first time the firewall is configured), a copy of the new configuration should be saved for archival purposes. This archive represents the last known working configuration. In the event that the firewall is changed, having this archive allows you to compare the current configuration to the archive in an attempt to identify whether any changes have been made to the configuration. If there have been, you can further investigate the changes to determine whether the changes are responsible for the problems that are occurring.

Perhaps the most common source of problems with firewalls, however, comes from simple misconfigurations of the firewall. It is too easy to mistype a line, click the wrong element in a graphical user interface (GUI), or just apply the wrong command to the firewall, thus causing a problem on the network that must be troubleshot. This is particularly true when it comes to troubleshooting the firewall ruleset. It is easy to enter the wrong transport protocol (TCP when you meant UDP), IP address, or port number and thus cause the problem. A great example of this occurred when Cisco released the security advisory "Cisco IOS Interface Blocked by IPv4 Packets." As a workaround, it was recommended that, among other things, protocol 53 be blocked. Unfortunately, so many network administrators see "53" and automatically assume DNS (TCP and UDP ports 53), which resulted in folks implementing rulesets to block TCP and UDP port 53 (thus causing DNS traffic to stop being passed) instead of protocol 53, which is related to Cisco IPv4 Packet Processing Denial of Service (SWIPE).

Step 7: Verify the Firewall Ruleset

As mentioned in the previous section, the firewall ruleset deserves the most scrutiny of anything regarding a firewall during the troubleshooting process. After all, in most cases the firewall exists solely to filter traffic in accordance with the ruleset, which means that if there is a mistake in the ruleset it will almost certainly manifest itself as a problem on the network.

The most common ruleset error is a simple typo. For this reason, I like having someone validate the ruleset other than the person making the changes. The reason for this is simple: The person making the changes generally knows what the changes should be and is more apt to read what he or she thinks the ruleset is supposed to contain, not what the ruleset actually contains. Putting a fresh set of eyes on the ruleset increases the odds that someone will notice that someone inadvertently configured the rule for TCP rather than UDP and so on.

Another common error with rulesets is the processing order of the ruleset. You need to understand in what order your firewall processes the ruleset and then verify that you do not have a rule out of order which is causing the problem. For example, if the rules are processed top down until a match is made and you have a rule that denies traffic before a rule that permits traffic, the firewall is going to process the deny and then exit the ruleset because it found a match, never making it to the line that permits the traffic in question.

Step 8: Verify That Any Dependent, Non-Firewall-Specific Systems Are Not the Culprit

Something else to consider in troubleshooting are the dependent services and systems that are not firewall specific or for which the firewall administrator might not be responsible. This includes the systems that are being protected by the firewall.

Common services to examine are name resolution processes such as DNS and WINS. Many times, someone will attempt to access a resource by name through the firewall and when the request fails assume that the firewall is the problem. However, if name resolution is not working properly, the user may not be able to resolve the name of the resource requested to an IP address, which is the cause of the connection failure.

Another common source of dependent problems are the systems that provide services to users through the firewall, such as web servers. These servers are frequently managed by a completely separate team that may or may not communicate the status of the servers with the firewall administrators. Therefore, the server administrators may take systems down for maintenance and so on without informing the firewall team. When a user attempts to access the resource, the request naturally fails—not because of the firewall but because the server behind the firewall providing the actual service is not online.

External authentication servers such as RADIUS, TACACS+, and Microsoft Windows Domain Controllers can also be a source of problems. For example, if the access to a protected resource behind the firewall requires external authentication and the firewall cannot communicate with the authentication server, it may appear that the firewall is blocking traffic (and in a manner of speaking, it is), but the real problem is not the firewall but a failure of the authentication server.

Step 9: Monitor the Network Traffic

When all else has failed and you are left scratching your head regarding what the problem may be, it is a good time to monitor the actual network traffic and examine precisely how the systems are attempting to communicate to and through the firewall. Doing so can help to identify communications problems that may or may not have shown up in the firewall event logs or may have shown up in the firewall event logs but not have provided enough information to determine a course of action to correct the problem.

As mentioned previously in this book, monitoring the network traffic with something like Ethereal, allowing you to view the raw packets and communications between hosts, is much like having a Rosetta stone to help decipher the network languages and communications processes that hosts are using to talk to each other. For example, a common ruleset error that people implement is to open TCP port 20 to their FTP servers because it has been commonly reported that FTP servers use both TCP port 20 and 21 for communications. Although this is true, most FTP clients and servers can communicate solely using TCP port 21, which can be validated by monitoring the traffic between the client and server. Having access to this kind of information will assist you in identifying and troubleshooting problems that do not exhibit symptoms anywhere else, be it in the firewall logs, configuration, or firewall ruleset.

Basic Firewall Troubleshooting

Three predominant situations with firewalls require some form of troubleshooting:

- Access to protected resources from unprotected networks is not functioning correctly.

- Access to unprotected resources from protected networks is not functioning correctly.

- Access to the firewall itself is not functioning correctly.

Understanding this, you can further narrow down the process to two things:

- Traffic going through the firewall

- Traffic going to the firewall.

To assist in troubleshooting these situations, implement your firewall troubleshooting checklist as it applies to the scenario in question.

Troubleshooting Connectivity Through the Firewall

No matter how well planned, tested, and implemented, sooner or later you will run into problems accessing resources through the firewall. There are any number of reasons for this, but the most common reasons involve problems with the firewall ruleset, problems with the firewall translation tables, problems with Network Address Translation (NAT), or problems with how the application communicates over the network. A good approach to troubleshooting connectivity through the firewall is to use the flowchart in Figure 13-2. The troubleshooting connectivity through the firewall flowchart is based on the general troubleshooting checklist but has been modified for this specific situation.

Figure 13-2   *Troubleshooting Connectivity Through the Firewall*

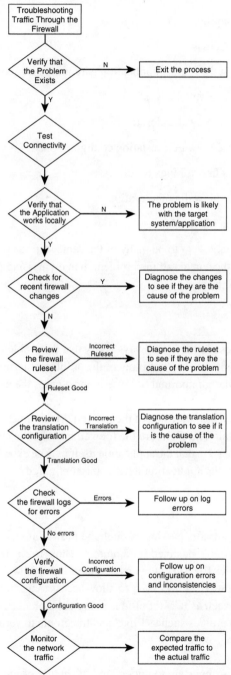

This section covers each step from the flowchart in turn as follows:

Step 1   Verify the problem.

Step 2   Test connectivity.

Step 3   Verify that the remote application is running and accessible locally.

Step 4   Check for recent changes.

Step 5   Review the firewall ruleset.

Step 6   Review the firewall translation configuration.

Step 7   Check the firewall logs for errors.

Step 8   Verify the firewall configuration.

Step 9   Monitor network traffic.

Although these steps may seem to be many of the same steps as previously discussed, it is important to consider the context of the problem, namely passing traffic through the firewall, as you apply each step in the checklist.

Step 1: Verify the Problem

The first step of troubleshooting is to always verify that the problem being reported is the problem that is occurring, and not merely a symptom of the problem. In troubleshooting traffic through the firewall, this is particularly important because in most cases the user or technician reporting the problem likely has a limited understanding of what role the firewall plays in the communication process with the host on the other side of the firewall. Many times, all they know is that the traffic goes through the firewall (and therefore the firewall must be the cause of the problem). In most cases, it never dawns on them that the application itself may be experiencing problems (for example, if the server is down or the application itself is misconfigured).

Step 2: Test Connectivity

Testing connectivity for traffic passing through the firewall is easier said than done, particularly when troubleshooting traffic destined for a protected host from an unprotected network. The reason for this is simple: To protect the host, configure the firewall to provide the minimum required protocols and services necessary to allow access to the protected resource. In most cases, this means that traffic such as ICMP traffic is going to be blocked by the firewall. Consequently, trying to use tools and utilities such as PING and traceroute to verify connectivity can be difficult if not impossible to do.

In these situations, it is important to understand the nature of the application or resource that is being troubleshot and to think outside the box in terms of how to test connectivity. For example, if you are having difficulties accessing a website that is being protected by a firewall, a good idea to verify connectivity is to just attempt to telnet to TCP port 80. Doing so allows you to verify the fundamental ability to access the web server. If you can, it is a good bet that the problem has to do with the application itself, not the firewall. Another option is to attempt to access the server using a different, but permitted, protocol. For example, if the server in question is not only the web server but is also the ftp server, attempt to establish an FTP connection to the server. If that succeeds, you at least know that the host is up and responding to network traffic. Yes, you still do not know whether the firewall or the server is the problem, but you can at least rule out basic networking problems being the cause.

Step 3: Verify That the Remote Application Is Running and Accessible Locally

One of the most important steps of troubleshooting traffic through the firewall is to remove the firewall from the equation and determine whether you can successfully access the resource. I cannot express enough how quickly folks will look at the firewall for being the problem when often the application itself is having problems. Verifying local access is the easiest method of ruling the firewall in or out.

For example, if you have a web server in the DMZ that is not accessible from the Internet, attempt to access the website from a host on the same DMZ segment. If you cannot do that, a good chance exists that the problem has nothing to do with the firewall (because local traffic will not go through the firewall). Conversely, if you can access the resource from a local host, a good chance exists that the firewall is part of the problem in some way, which allows you to then start focusing your resources on the firewall itself.

Step 4: Check for Recent Changes

For the same reasons previously mentioned, it is a good idea to check to determine whether any recent changes have been made to the firewall. The same cautionary statement applies, however: If the changes that were made logically do not make sense as being related to the problem at hand, do not focus on those changes. Keep them in mind, but move on to other more likely causes. Apply the principle of Occam's razor, which just states that all things being equal, the simplest explanation is usually the correct explanation.

For example, if access to a web server is not functioning properly and the last change that was made was to the VPN configuration of the firewall, those changes probably do not have anything to do with the problem at hand, and you should pursue other more plausible explanations. Conversely, if the last change was an update to the static translation statements, that represents a much more likely source of the problem and should be investigated accordingly.

Step 5: Review the Firewall Ruleset

If properly configured, all traffic passing through a firewall should be processed by the firewall ruleset. Accordingly, the firewall ruleset is one of the most common causes of problems for traffic passing through the firewall. When reviewing the firewall ruleset, pay particular attention to the following elements:

■ Ensure that there are no typos in the rules.

■ Verify the protocol and port numbers referenced by the rule.

■ Verify the source and destination addresses referenced by the rule.

■ Verify the processing order of the rules to ensure that the rules are not being applied out of order.

■ Have someone else review the rules to ensure that the rule says what it is supposed to say, not what you think it says. If you have ever seen that e-mail where the entire e-mail is spelled incorrectly to demonstrate how your mind will read what it expects to read, that is what happens here. You know that access to the web server is supposed to occur over TCP port 80, which means that it is easy to look at a rule permitting traffic to UDP port 80 and not catch the problem with that because you expect (and read) TCP.

Although most firewalls today offer stateful translation, allowing return traffic to be automatically permitted by the firewall, some applications such as X Windows return traffic on a port other than what it was sent from. These applications can be particularly difficult to troubleshoot because the ruleset might appear to have what is necessary, only to find that you need an additional rule to explicitly permit the return traffic. In cases such as this, checking the error logs and monitoring the network traffic can quickly illustrate this kind of problem.

Step 6: Review the Firewall Translation Configuration

Because of the prevalence of NAT in most firewall implementations, reviewing the proper configuration of the NAT translation statements can be as critical as verifying the ruleset. After all, if the firewall does not know what systems it should be translating traffic to/from, it does not matter what the ruleset specifies, and therefore the traffic will not be able to reach its destination. Review the translation rules similarly to the firewall ruleset, paying particular attention to the following:

■ Ensure that there are no typos in the translation statement.

■ Verify the protocol and port numbers referenced by the translation statement.

■ Verify the source and destination addresses referenced by the translation statement.

Another area in reviewing the translation rule, especially for outbound connections, is to ensure that the translation pool has an adequate number of addresses for the number of hosts attempting to establish outbound connections. If the translation pool size is too small, hosts will be unable to obtain an IP address that they can use to establish connections to external hosts.

Step 7: Check the Firewall Logs for Errors

As with generic firewall troubleshooting, the firewall logs can provide a wealth of information for you when troubleshooting connectivity through the firewall, allowing you to identify problems with the firewall ruleset, translation statements, firewall configuration, or hardware. Therefore, review the firewall logs for the following:

- **Look for state errors**—State errors can be indicators of problems with the firewall translation tables (for example, if the Cisco Secure PIX Firewall has an incorrectly configured static translation value).

- **Look for denied traffic**—Denied traffic is the classic indicator of an incorrectly configured ruleset. Although virtually all firewalls include an implicit **deny** statement at the end of the firewall ruleset, to assist in troubleshooting it can be helpful to include an explicit **deny** and **log** statement to ensure that the denied traffic is logged accordingly.

- **Look for configuration errors**—Often, configuration errors are reported in the firewall logs as error events, allowing you to rapidly identify a configuration error without needing to review the configuration line by line.

- **Look for hardware errors**—Event logs are one of the best sources for discovering hardware-related errors because most firewall vendors log hardware error events in the firewall logs.

Step 8: Verify the Firewall Configuration

It is always a good idea when troubleshooting traffic passing through the firewall to look at the firewall configuration and confirm that everything is configured accordingly. For example, if the firewall is not configured to route traffic properly, that could prevent traffic passing through the firewall from reaching the intended destination.

Apply the same logic to verifying the configuration as was previously discussed, comparing the current configuration to a known good configuration and verifying that the firewall configuration is accurate with no typos or other errors.

Step 9: Monitor Network Traffic

If you still cannot determine the cause of the problem you are experiencing with the traffic passing through the firewall, the next logical step is to use a sniffer to monitor the network traffic to ensure that the traffic is acting exactly as you expect it is. For example, you can use the sniffer to verify that the traffic is actually using the ports that your firewall ruleset is configured to permit.

Another instance where monitoring the network traffic can assist in troubleshooting a problem is to provide evidence that the firewall is indeed passing traffic between the hosts, as evidenced by the network traffic, and thus any problems accessing the application on the host is likely going to be an application problem.

Troubleshooting Connectivity to the Firewall

Troubleshooting connectivity to the firewall uses the same processes that have been detailed in the chapter, the difference being what the destination of the traffic happens to be. One difference to be mindful of is that unlike traffic that is being passed through the firewall, which typically has a destination that is designed and intended to be accessible, the firewall is not always designed to be accessible. This is particularly true when referring to the external interface of the firewall, which in most cases should not be configured to accept any traffic destined for the actual interface. Consequently, it can be difficult to troubleshoot whether the firewall is accessible using conventional means. By that same token, however, if you can access a resource on the other side of the firewall, by virtue of that success the firewall is online and operational. Beyond these minor changes, however, the troubleshooting process is no different from the process detailed previously in this chapter and in Figures 13-1 and 13-2.

Advanced Firewall Troubleshooting

This chapter has focused primarily on the core tasks of a firewall to process traffic through the firewall and for the firewall to provide for connectivity and access to remote and protected hosts. However, firewalls continue to gain more advanced features and functions, and it is becoming necessary to troubleshoot those advanced features and functions.

Processes such as SNMP, NTP, routing, and authentication all provide ample opportunity for something to fail that you will need to troubleshoot, diagnose, and repair. The key to troubleshooting these advanced features relies on you undertaking a couple of steps:

Step 1   Ensure that you understand the process in question and how it functions. For example, if the firewall is going to use NTP, make sure that you know how NTP functions so that you know how to begin troubleshooting any problems that may occur.

Step 2   Develop troubleshooting checklists that are relevant to the processes and functions in question. For example, although most of the generic firewall troubleshooting checklist steps may be relevant, if you need to troubleshoot SNMP, you need to consider SNMP-specific troubleshooting steps to complement the standard troubleshooting checklist that you will adhere to.

Troubleshooting Example

This section walks through a simple example of troubleshooting a firewall configuration. Troubleshooting starts with the basic connectivity troubleshooting and escalates upward to more complex issues until the specific problem is identified. As mentioned previously, the first step is to verify the problem that is being reported. Consider, for example, the problem shown in Figure 13-3. The web client behind the firewall is attempting to reach a website across the Internet. For the purposes of this example, we use the site http://www.freeciv.org.

Figure 13-3 *Troubleshooting Example Topology*

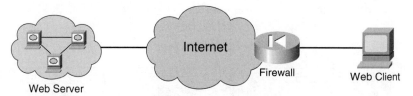

Figure 13-4 shows that the connection has failed. This failure could be for a variety of reasons, but suffices as a simple example of troubleshooting the firewall.

Figure 13-4 *Failed Connection to Website*

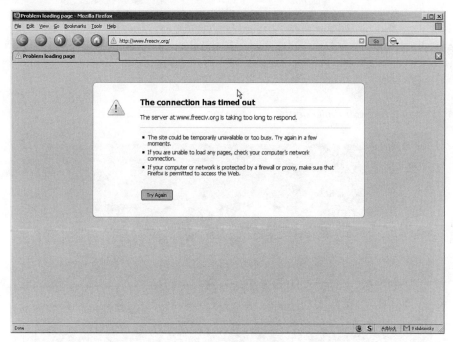

One of the first steps to take is to test the connectivity. Doing so involves verifying that the firewall is up and running as well as verifying that the Internet connection is working.

To verify that the firewall is operational from a hardware perspective requires a physical examination of the firewall device. The firewall power light should be on, and both inside and outside interface indicators should be on. These indicators vary depending on the specific brand of firewall. On the PIX, they are found on the interface ports themselves, as shown by the two arrows in Figure 13-5.

Figure 13-5 *PIX Interface Indicators*

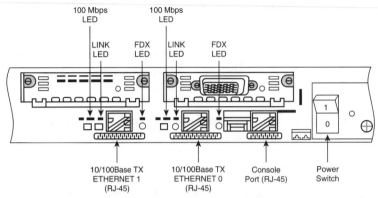

If the firewall is up and functional, the next step is to connect to the firewall and verify that the firewall software has not crashed. You can do so either using the firewall's web interface or by using the command-line interface. Figure 13-6 shows a connection into a firewall and verification that the software is up and running.

Figure 13-6 *Verifying Firewall Functioning*

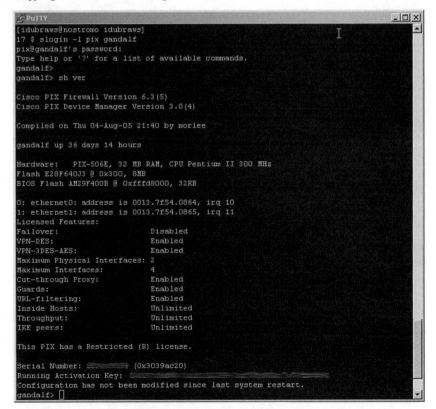

If the firewall is up and running, the next step is to test the Internet connection on the outside interface of the firewall. You can do this by pinging a system out on the Internet. Doing so is somewhat tricky because many networks filter out unsolicited ICMP requests. However, some of the larger search sites such as Yahoo! and Google do allow unsolicited ICMP requests, as shown in Figure 13-7.

Figure 13-7 *Testing Internet Connectivity*

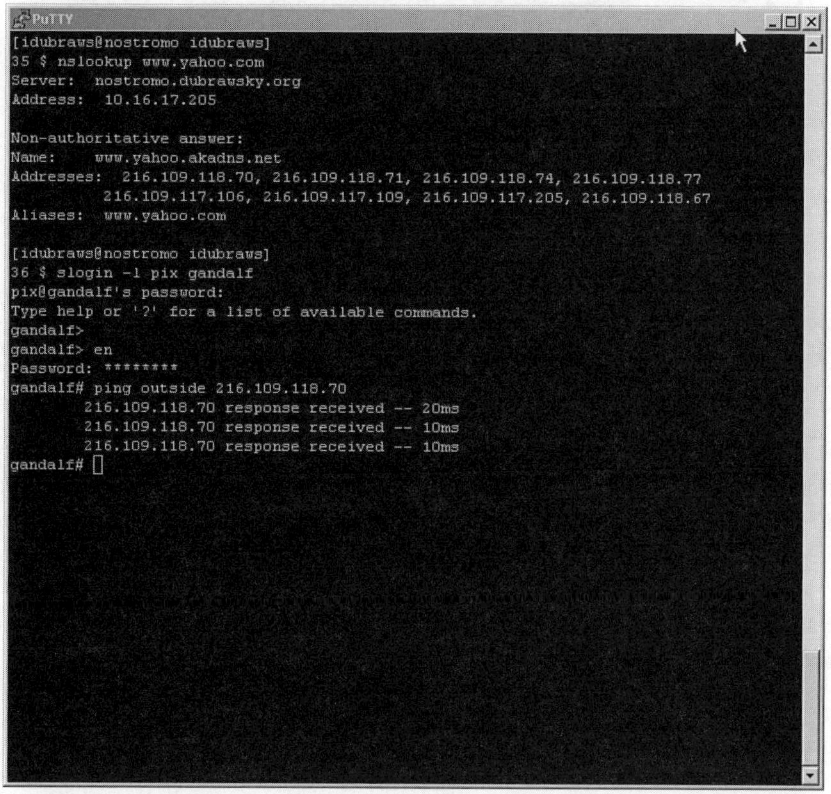

If pinging an external site is possible, the Internet connection is probably working fine, and the problem may be in the configuration of the firewall. However, before going that far, it would be a good idea to verify that the site being contacted is working. To do this, you need only ping the site and, failing that, connect to the specific application port using Telnet or some other connectivity utility. For web servers, the easiest way to check to determine whether the server is up is to telnet to the web server on TCP port 80, as shown in Figure 13-8.

Figure 13-8 *Checking Server Connectivity*

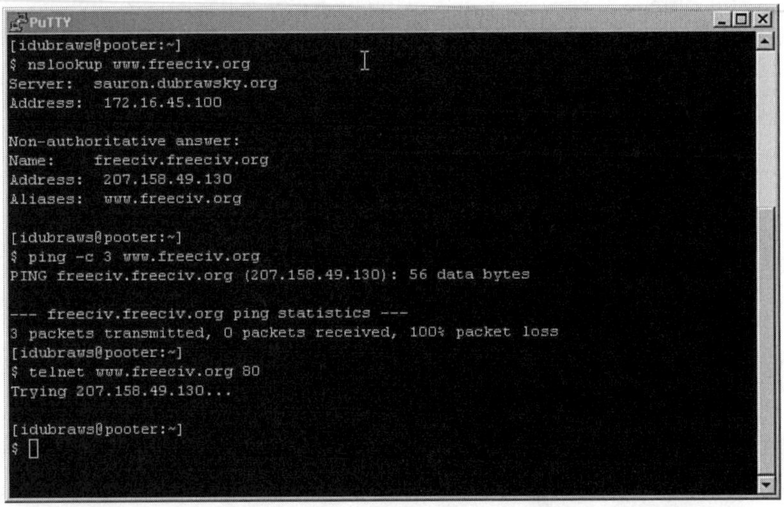

```
[idubraws@pooter:~]
$ nslookup www.freeciv.org                I
Server:    sauron.dubrawsky.org
Address:   172.16.45.100

Non-authoritative answer:
Name:      freeciv.freeciv.org
Address:   207.158.49.130
Aliases:   www.freeciv.org

[idubraws@pooter:~]
$ ping -c 3 www.freeciv.org
PING freeciv.freeciv.org (207.158.49.130): 56 data bytes

--- freeciv.freeciv.org ping statistics ---
3 packets transmitted, 0 packets received, 100% packet loss
[idubraws@pooter:~]
$ telnet www.freeciv.org 80
Trying 207.158.49.130...

[idubraws@pooter:~]
$ []
```

In this example, the assumption is that the web server is not responding because it does not respond to a ping or to the Telnet connection to the web server port, 80.

In more complex cases, you might need to review the firewall configuration to ensure that it is not blocking the traffic unnecessarily. Also, consider that in some cases it is not your end of the connection that may be problematic but the other end. In many cases, you might need to search the vendor's documentation to ensure that the firewall is configured properly or how to turn on the debugging features of the firewall. Like troubleshooting any other problem, troubleshooting a firewall is much an iterative problem. You start with the simple and obvious and work toward the more unique and esoteric if necessary.

Summary

In this industry, anyone can maintain a properly functioning firewall. What separates the good firewall administrators from the okay firewall administrators is the ability of the firewall administrator to step into a problem situation, identify the source of the problem, identify a resolution to the problem, and then execute the resolution to the problem, all in a timely fashion.

Firewalls are too complex for one person to be expected to know everything that should be considered when trying to troubleshoot the problem. Therefore, it is a good idea to develop a troubleshooting checklist to serve as a guide while you attempt to diagnose the problem.

As a part of building a troubleshooting checklist, ensure that at a minimum you consider including the following elements (in no particular order) in your checklists:

- Verify the problem reported.

- Test connectivity.

- Physically verify the firewall is working.

- Verify that the remote application is running and accessible locally.

- Verify that any dependent, non-firewall-specific systems are not the culprit.

- Check for recent changes.

- Review the firewall ruleset.

- Review the firewall translation configuration.

- Check the firewall logs for errors.

- Verify the firewall configuration.

- Monitor network traffic.

CHAPTER 14

Going Beyond Basic Firewall Features

Modern firewalls provide a wide variety of significant services to the end user, whether it is a personal firewall or a network firewall used to protect an enterprise network. Firewall capabilities have increased dramatically over the past few years, and they have quickly become a nexus of security services to a network (or an individual machine). This increase of capabilities has caused firewall administrators to reevaluate and in some cases redefine the expectations of what a firewall can do. At the same time, however, firewalls are not complete solution, and there are limits to how effectively a firewall can provide many advanced features. This chapter explores many of the advanced features that firewalls can provide, while at the same time illustrating the limitations of firewalls in providing these advanced features.

Content Filtering

Many enterprises are beginning to concern themselves with the use of the corporate Internet connection by their employees. The unmanaged access to inappropriate or distracting web content can involve significant legal risk and may well jeopardize network security. Additionally, unmanaged access to web content typically results in significant reduction of employee productivity. These issues cannot be easily ignored by many companies.

One of the newer features being required of firewalls is the capability of filtering the content that passes through them. This filtering typically is defined as URL filtering, whereby the firewall is used either by itself or in conjunction with another appliance or software suite to control which websites users are allowed to visit. However, given that web content can range from the simple to the complex, firewalls typically offload the detailed evaluation and decision making to other devices, which is an excellent example of the limitations of a firewall being a self-contained content-filtering device. Rather, the firewall becomes a control point where the decision made by the evaluation device (whether it is a content engine or a filtering software suite) is applied to user traffic.

Implementing a URL Filter

Implementing URL filters is relatively straightforward. There are two typical ways to implement a URL filter. The first is to maintain a list of URLs that will be blocked on the firewall, typically in the format of an access control list (ACL). This can be a time-consuming process for both the implementation and maintenance of the URL list. Additionally, because ACLs are typically stored in a flat file format, the firewall can be subjected to latency in permitting or denying traffic while a large ACL is being processed.

The second method is to utilize a third-party content-filtering application running on a separate server from the firewall or on a content engine that is separate from the firewall to handle the actual building, maintaining, and configuring of the URL filter list. As previously mentioned, this allows the firewall to offload the processing and evaluation of traffic to the content-filtering device, which enables the firewall to do what it does best, to serve as a control point for traffic, blocking content as defined by the content-filtering device. Because this is the most efficient and effective way to perform content filtering with most firewalls, this is the situation that we detail in this chapter.

For most firewalls to be able to block specific content, they must have access to a database that contains a list of URLs that are prohibited; whenever a user opens a connection to one of these sites, the firewall blocks the connection. Given that the list can be quite extensive and that the enterprise's management may want to deny access to sites that are considered wasteful in terms of time, many higher-end firewalls provide for the use of an external URL database system that can decide whether the connection should be permitted. Thus a specialized device—for example, a content engine or a content-filtering server—performs all the processing of the traffic, which in turn allows the firewall to just provide the necessary enforcement by either permitting or denying the traffic as determined by the content-filtering system.

The Cisco PIX Firewall can work in conjunction with two web-filtering software suites: WebSense and N2H2.

> **NOTE** In 2003, Secure Computing acquired N2H2 and integrated the N2H2 filtering software into their SmartFilter product. The Cisco documentation and command syntax still refers to N2H2, however, and for the sake of simplicity this book uses the term *N2H2* to refer to both products, because the configuration for either is exactly the same.

To configure the PIX to enforce URL filtering, the administrator needs to first configure the PIX to work with the URL-filtering software suite by configuring the PIX with the IP address of the filtering server. For a WebSense server, the command is as follows:

```
gandalf(config)# url-server (inside) vendor websense host 172.28.230.44 protocol TCP
    version 1
```

You can specify either TCP or UDP for the protocol (TCP is recommended) as well as Version 1 or Version 4. The default for TCP is Version 1, whereas UDP only supports Version 4. For an N2H2 server, the command is as follows:

```
gandalf(config)# url-server (inside) vendor n2h2 host 172.28.230.45 port 4005 protocol
    tcp
```

For N2H2, you can define the port and protocol to use. The default values are port 4005 and protocol TCP.

After you have identified the filtering server and defined how the firewall should connect to the filtering server, the next step is to configure the PIX firewall to actually filter URL traffic by running the following command:

```
gandalf(config)# filter url http 0 0 0 0
```

In this case, the PIX firewall will filter all traffic that passes through the firewall. You can also configure the firewall to filter only specific subnets. For example, if you want to filter traffic from network 172.28.238.0/24 to any network, you run the following command:

```
gandalf(config)# filter url http 172.28.238.0 255.255.255.0 0.0.0.0 0.0.0.0
```

When the PIX sees the outbound connection, it does not allow the return traffic from the web server back to the client until it has received a response from the URL-filtering server. When the filtering server approves the connection, the PIX allows the connection to complete back to the client. If the filtering server denies the request, the user is redirected to a block page indicating that access was denied and possibly the reason it was denied. Figure 14-1 shows this filtering.

Figure 14-1 *URL Filtering with the Cisco PIX Firewall*

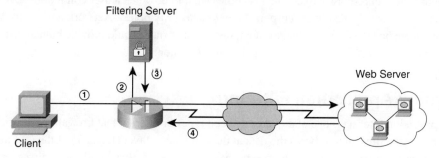

The following is a description of the process in Figure 14-1:

1. The client sends the initial connection to the web server, which replies back as expected. This reply is held at the firewall, however, until a filtering determination has been made.

2. At the same time, the firewall connects to the filtering server using connection 2 to query the filtering server about whether the traffic should be permitted.

3. The filtering server replies to the firewall with whether the traffic should be permitted or denied.

4. If the filtering server approves the URL, it notifies the PIX firewall, and the firewall allows the return traffic to reach the client system. If the filtering server denies the URL, it notified the PIX firewall, and the firewall drops the return traffic, preventing it from reaching the client.

Maintaining URL Filters

One of the biggest problems with URL filtering is the maintenance required of the URL database. To help network administrators maintain their URL filters and keep them as up-to-date as possible, many vendors turn to a subscription service whereby the filtering server at the client site connects to a web server at the vendor's location and downloads a database of URLs with default settings associated with each URL. This service conveniently allows administrator to keep relatively current with new sites that they want to block as soon as possible. Additionally, administrators can configure the system to automatically download new URL databases periodically.

The only difficulty presented by these systems is that they rely on a third-party vendor to determine whether a URL is to be included in the database. In some cases, this reliance can lead to the blocking of legitimate websites that would not necessarily fall into the category of inappropriate during business hours or as a waste of employee time. Additionally, some URL lists may include one website but completely neglect the mirror located in another country. Administrators should use caution when deciding what category of URLs to block and what to allow through.

What to Do If. . .

Many of the more powerful URL-filtering software systems such as WebSense and N2H2 provide detailed reports of which user went to a particular URL or set of URLs. The problem, which is really a human resources issue, then becomes what to do when a user continuously violates the web policy as specified in the corporate network security policy. Network administration staff should not have to deal with the problem; instead, that staff should provide human resources with the necessary information to make an informed decision.

Performing Application Filtering

Application filtering is one of the most difficult types of filtering that firewalls perform, because it requires the firewall to process the data at the application layer (Layer 7) of the OSI model. Application filtering is one of the two primary components of an application proxy firewall, the other being the proxy functionality provided by the firewall. Chapter 2, "Firewall Basics," and Chapter 8, "Application Proxy Firewalls," discuss application proxy firewalls in more detail.

The purpose of application filtering is to enforce a specific security policy on various services provided through the firewall. Whereas network firewalls enforce policy-based on information between Layers 3 and 4, an application firewall goes further. Consider that an attacker can compromise a web server behind a firewall by attacking *through* the web service. Attacks such as Structured Query Language (SQL) injection, cross-site scripting, and viruses and worms represent significant problems because they attack the end host through the specific port that is required to be open in the network firewall. To solve this problem, many vendors and some open source efforts have developed firewalls that can inspect the data payload of the packets passing through the firewall and determine whether they violate the security policy of the end host. If they do violate the policy, these devices can prevent the attacks from affecting the target system.

Applications That Are Hard to Firewall

The difficulty with application firewalls stems from the fact that the transaction between the client and the server is complex and can be made more so if the protocol or the data in the communication expands or increases the complexity of the transaction. Protocols such as eXtensible Markup Language (XML) and Simple Object Access Protocol (SOAP) make web application firewalls especially tricky. To provide proper web application security, the application firewall must have a detailed understanding of legitimate transactions, including the use of URLs; different HTTP methods such as GET (retrieving data from a web server), POST (transmitting data to a web server), and other HTTP methods; session IDs and session cookies; XML and SOAP schemas; SQL queries; and much more.

Many vendors have focused on developing web application firewalls because of the wide array of difficulties faced in providing security to such a ubiquitous protocol as HTTP. Other applications that use protocols such as Simple Mail Transport Protocol (SMTP) and Secure Shell (SSH) also require significant filtering to prevent an attacker from compromising a service that is open in a network firewall.

Web Applications (XML, SOAP, WSDL, CGI)

Consider web applications. These applications may use a wide variety of protocols from simple HTML to XML to Web Service Definition Language (WSDL) and a whole range of Common Gateway Interface (CGI) programs. Many end users believe that the simple solution to web security is Secure Sockets Layer (SSL). When they want to "secure" their web application, they simply use an SSL-capable web server and restrict the traffic to TCP port 443. However, this belief is certainly a misconception. An attacker need have access only to the web server port to attack the *application* running on the server, not the web server itself. In the case of SSL, it just means that the attack happens to be encrypted, because the application (the web server software) is what is being attacked. How can this be? An example illustrates this point.

An attacker finds a web server running on the Internet with a particular application. The server is only accessible through TCP port 443 (HTTPS). Example 14-1 shows using Telnet to access a server on TCP port 443 (HTTPS).

Example 14-1   *Using Telnet to Access a Server on TCP Port 443 (HTTPS)*

```
4 $ telnet 10.16.17.223 443
Trying 10.16.17.223...
Connected to 10.16.17.223.
Escape character is '^]'.
GET / HTTP/1.0
<!DOCTYPE HTML PUBLIC "-//IETF//DTD HTML 2.0//EN">
<html><head>
<title>400 Bad Request</title>
</head><body>
```

continues

Example 14-1 *Using Telnet to Access a Server on TCP Port 443 (HTTPS) (Continued)*

```
<h1>Bad Request</h1>
<p>Your browser sent a request that this server could not understand.<br />
Reason: You're speaking plain HTTP to an SSL-enabled server port.<br />
Instead use the HTTPS scheme to access this URL, please.<br />
<blockquote>Hint: <a href="https://www.innocentvictimcompany.com/"><b>https://
  www.innocentvictimcompany.com/</b></a></blockquote></p>
<hr>
<address>Apache/2.0.52 (Unix) mod_ssl/2.0.52 OpenSSL/0.9.7d DAV/2 PHP/4.3.9 Server at
  www.innocentvictimcompany.com Port 443</address>
</body></html>
Connection to 10.16.17.223 closed by foreign host.
```

A simple connection is clearly not understood by the server. To get around this, the attacker uses OpenSSL, as shown in Example 14-2.

Example 14-2 *OpenSSL*

```
3 $ openssl s_client -connect 10.16.17.223:443
CONNECTED(00000003)
depth=0 /C=US/ST=Maryland/L=Silver Spring/O=dubrawsky.org/OU=IT/CN=Ido Dubrawsky/
emailAddress=idubraws@dubrawsky.org
verify error:num=18:self signed certificate
verify return:1
depth=0 /C=US/ST=Maryland/L=Silver Spring/O=dubrawsky.org/OU=IT/CN=Ido Dubrawsky/
emailAddress=idubraws@dubrawsky.org
verify error:num=10:certificate has expired
notAfter=Oct  6 01:35:00 2005 GMT
verify return:1
depth=0 /C=US/ST=Maryland/L=Silver Spring/O=dubrawsky.org/OU=IT/CN=Ido Dubrawsky/
emailAddress=idubraws@dubrawsky.org
notAfter=Oct  6 01:35:00 2005 GMT
verify return:1
---
Certificate chain
 0 s:/C=US/ST=Maryland/L=Silver Spring/O=dubrawsky.org/OU=IT/CN=Ido Dubrawsky/
emailAddress=idubraws@dubrawsky.org
   i:/C=US/ST=Maryland/L=Silver Spring/O=dubrawsky.org/OU=IT/CN=Ido Dubrawsky/
emailAddress=idubraws@dubrawsky.org
---
Server certificate
-----BEGIN CERTIFICATE-----
MIICqTCCAhICAQAwDQYJKoZIhvcNAQEBBQAwgZwxCzAJBgNVBAYTAlVTMREwDwYDVQQIEwhNYXJ5bGFuZDEWMBQG
 A1UEBxMNU2lsdmVyIFNwcmluZzEWMBQGA1UEChMNZHVicmF3c2t5Lm9yZzELMAkGA1UECxMCSVQxFjAUBgNVBAM
 TDUlkbyBEdWJyYXdza3kxLTAjBgkqhkiG9w0BCQEWFmlkdWJyYXdzQGR1YnJhd3NreS5vcmcwHhcNMDQxMDA2MD
 EzNTAwWhcNMDUxMDA2MDEzNTAwWjCBnDELMAkGA1UEBhMCVVMxETAPBgNVBAgTCE1hcnlsYW5kMRYwFAYDVQQHE
 w1TaWx2ZXIgU3ByaW5nMRYwFAYDVQQKEw1kdWJyYXdza3kub3JnMQswCQYDVQQLEwJJVDEWMBQGA1UEAxMNSWRv
 IER1YnJhd3NreTElMCMGCSqGSIb3DQEJARYWaWR1YnJhd3NAZHVicmF3c2t5Lm9yZzCBnzANBgkqhkiG9w0BAQE
 FAAOBjQAwgYkCgYEAwpCwIAhfnPvq9Q+2Y+CuPZoaKMROeUbEV8GcPlFfJOCrR0CwcQISGfZVQvgUPVNoBiRavu
 9amk4tV6l1bJHZlgRD5bk0tmYRTdvjFUyXPJrcGk493vpqUqYKYX4Nhz7UIm9JIbJ1SlSo5XhW47rS5QRDrfKVL
 PHK4viuX7C56JsCAwEAATANBgkqhkiG9w0BAQQFAAOBgQC4huUgw9ahmLYLPiuBqrGfSbov1OfeIVB83SJQiUlY
 vzVaL/ANaAzcGcPQTobJJ9mgbnCU0C5y1khsX+Y060Ji/
 afJP0KSJu45WKXUw87Dty93Baj4+pTzS0Cyh+0dB6t89dpUnq3AABSClsmCb2J//50EdA2ESnOedpHULQKWQ==
-----END CERTIFICATE-----
```

Example 14-2 *OpenSSL (Continued)*

```
subject=/C=US/ST=Maryland/L=Silver Spring/O=dubrawsky.org/OU=IT/CN=Ido Dubrawsky/
  emailAddress=idubraws@dubrawsky.org
issuer=/C=US/ST=Maryland/L=Silver Spring/O=dubrawsky.org/OU=IT/CN=Ido Dubrawsky/
  emailAddress=idubraws@dubrawsky.org
...
No client certificate CA names sent
...
SSL handshake has read 1249 bytes and written 346 bytes
...
New, TLSv1/SSLv3, Cipher is DHE-RSA-AES256-SHA
Server public key is 1024 bit
SSL-Session:
    Protocol  : TLSv1
    Cipher    : DHE-RSA-AES256-SHA
    Session-ID: E6F3E3D7B5CCBBFF64C00930A0EE9D056F82ED55F483E0682215EF37342D37EE
    Session-ID-ctx:
    Master-Key:
DCE5F0E40DAB7ADF26EEA55A17DAA0E722213B64F229A81ED0CD2E2207CD9D34A9650D4737AAF33855FD946
  2E7E3B5A7
    Key-Arg   : None
    Start Time: 1133540279
    Timeout   : 300 (sec)
    Verify return code: 10 (certificate has expired)
...
HEAD / HTTP/1.0

HTTP/1.1 401 Authorization Required
Date: Fri, 02 Dec 2005 16:23:50 GMT
Server: Apache/2.0.52 (Unix) mod_ssl/2.0.52 OpenSSL/0.9.7d DAV/2 PHP/4.3.9
WWW-Authenticate: Basic realm="SnortIDS ACID"
Connection: close
Content-Type: text/html; charset=iso-8859-1

Closed
```

As you can see, the attacker can get more information from the server this time using OpenSSL. To run a web scanner against an SSL-enabled server, the attacker need only set up an SSL tunnel to the server and then scan through that tunnel. The attacker can easily do so by using the open source utility Stunnel.

This scenario is where web application firewalls work. The precise methods of blocking applications differ from firewall to firewall and application to application. However, by inspecting the traffic more deeply than a network firewall and by applying specific, defined (typically by the firewall or security administrator or by the vendor that provides the application filtering capabilities) security policies to that traffic, the application firewall can identify attacks and prevent them before they ever reach the server. This inspection requires intimate knowledge of the protocol being used

(XML, SOAP, WSDL, and so on) as well as the capability to identify attack strings. If, as in the web server example, the server requires authentication using a username and password combination, but the programmer did not bother to check to make sure the length of the username or password did not exceed a specific value, an attacker can try to overflow a value in the application by sending a large string of characters to the CGI:

```
perl -e 'print "GET /cgi-bin/login?user=ido&password=","A"x2050," HTTP/1.0\n\n"'
```

This attempt may have no effect or it may cause the CGI to return a value that the attacker can then use to further try to refine the attack.

For complex protocols such as XML, SOAP, and WSDL, the problem becomes more onerous because the attack may be embedded within the XML schema or in the SOAP transaction. The application firewall must be able to understand these protocols and compare them against a specific security policy developed by the administrators and the application developers to ensure that any part of the protocol that is outside the policy is blocked from reaching the protected application/server.

Simple Mail Transport Protocol

SMTP is another protocol that presents problems for firewalls. SMTP uses a small command set to transmit e-mail from one server to another. But the data in the e-mail, the payload, can provide a significant problem. One of the most troublesome byproducts of SMTP is spam, or unsolicited e-mail that most folks do not want. Examples of spam include simple unsolicited commercial e-mail (UCE); e-mail with malicious content, such as viruses, Trojans, and worms; and e-mails that attempt to scam or otherwise rip off an unsuspecting reader, such as the Nigerian lottery scam e-mails. Today, spam accounts for approximately 40 percent of all e-mail on the Internet.[1] By the end of 2006, it is estimated that 80 percent of the e-mail on the Internet could be spam.[2]

Antispam and e-mail-filtering capabilities in firewalls are adding to the overall defense against spam. Many vendors have dedicated e-mail or spam "firewalls" that are designed to stop the inflow of unwanted bulk e-mail. Unlike traditional network firewalls, these devices only filter SMTP traffic. In addition, these vendors frequently provide antivirus capabilities in such devices to provide customers with an all-in-one solution to the problems of e-mail spam and viruses. However, network firewall vendors are also adding capabilities to their offerings to identify spam and viruses that pass through their network firewall devices, providing for a single device that performs all network traffic and e-mail filtering. The difficulty remains that e-mail scanning for spam and viruses requires intensive operations that are best left to dedicated application firewalls whereas traffic filtering at Layer 2 and Layer 3 is handled by the network firewall, typically in a complementary fashion to each other.

In addition to commercial offerings, there are many antispam and antivirus open source projects—such as SpamAssassin, MailScanner, MIMEDefang, ClamAV, and many others—for those individuals or organizations who choose to go that route.

Intrusion Detection and Prevention

Because network traffic must cross the firewall to reach the end systems, the firewall has also become a point where the inspection of this traffic is appropriate. For many years, firewall vendors such as Cisco Systems, Inc. and Check Point have been including intrusion detection system (IDS) capabilities to their firewalls. These devices were the first "in-line" IDS systems long before in-line IDS-dedicated appliances ever existed.

Overview of IDS

Intrusion detection is an aspect of security whereby a device detects the fingerprint of an attack within the network. Modern IDSs use a variety of techniques to ensure that the alarms they raise are of actual attacks being conducted rather than a false alarm. Many IDSs connect to the network through a port on a switch, and the interface that connects to that port captures traffic to a particular system or subnet, as shown in Figure 14-2.

Figure 14-2 *Intrusion Detection*

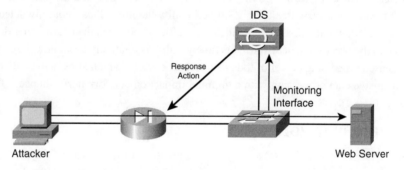

The Firewall as an IDS Sensor

As firewall hardware has become more and more powerful, vendors have sought to use the additional computing power by adding features to the firewall code. Many vendors have offered IDS capabilities in their firewalls for quite some time and have made the firewalls the first true in-line intrusion prevention systems (IPSs). However, the IDS code in the firewall was, until recently, not on par with the IDS code used in the dedicated IDS appliance. For example, the Cisco PIX Firewall integrated IDS capability was really an incredibly small subset of the capabilities of their dedicated IDS/IPS offerings. The IDS capabilities of the firewall did not fully mimic those of the dedicated appliance because of concerns about the impact of those capabilities on firewall performance. However, the firewall does make an excellent sensor in that it is directly in-line with the traffic flow and has the capability to capture *all* traffic destined for target hosts located behind the firewall.

Combined with other IDS devices, such as dedicated appliances, the firewall makes an effective line of defense with these capabilities. In addition to the use of dedicated IDS appliances, the use of host IPS agents helps significantly improve the deterrent capabilities and the defenses of a network. With alarms from firewalls, dedicated IDS appliances, and host IPS agents, a strong correlation can be made in identifying a real attack versus a false positive. This, in turn, can allow the administrator to better conduct countermeasures such as having the dedicated appliance issue TCP resets or use shunning or even allow the firewall to drop the offending traffic. Overall, the role of firewalls in intrusion detection is still being defined as vendors migrate more and more IDS code into the firewall appliance.

The Firewall as the IPS

With the increased market desire to go beyond simple intrusion detection to intrusion prevention, more vendors have begun using the firewall not just as an IDS sensor but as an actual IPS device in and of itself (particularly true of devices such as the Cisco Adaptive Security Appliance [ASA]).

The logic behind this is relatively sound. Because the firewall is a natural control point for network traffic, and because all traffic entering or exiting a network through a firewall must be processed by the firewall anyway, with added IPS functionality the firewall can not only detect intrusion attempts on its own, it can also then block the traffic without requiring any other devices to be involved in the processing decision. This functionality is relatively new and is largely the result of the increased processing power of today's microprocessors, which allow a firewall to perform this more intensive data processing with a minimal impact on network performance.

Virtual Private Networks

Virtual private networks (VPNs) are another feature that firewalls have quickly adopted. Firewalls, by the very nature of their placement in the network design, represent a natural device to provide termination for LAN-to-LAN and in some cases remote-access VPNs. The firewall separates a public network from a private network and provides network administrators with a policy-enforcement point. As with IDSs, vendors include the ability to set up VPNs on a firewall as a common feature for any firewall device available on the market. All open source firewalls also provide accommodations for VPN traffic.

To deal with VPNs, firewalls must take into account a variety of new protocols. For IPsec-based VPNs, the firewalls must provide for the capability of handling the two types of IPsec traffic: Authentication Header (AH) and Encapsulated Security Payload (ESP), although AH is relatively obsolete and rarely used as a VPN transport. Each provides distinct challenges to firewalls to allow an IPsec VPN to be set up either to the firewall itself or through it to a dedicated VPN appliance. Other types of VPNs that many firewalls support include Layer 2 Tunneling Protocol (L2TP) as well as the Point-to-Point Tunneling Protocol (PPTP). Finally, many firewalls now also offer the ability to support an SSL VPN. Each is discussed in the following sections.

IPsec VPNs

IPsec-based VPNs have quickly become one of the most prevalent VPN technologies on the market. The IPsec RFCs call for two protocols: AH and ESP. Both of these protocols can be used in one of two ways: transport mode or tunnel mode.

Authentication Header

The AH protocol is used to provide connectionless integrity and data origin authentication for IP datagrams. In addition, AH provides for protection against replay attacks. AH protects a variety of fields within the IP header, and the modification of those fields by a firewall can result in the destination host discarding the packets because of an invalid AH integrity check. AH does not actually encrypt the data itself, however, and provides for no confidentiality of the data being transmitted. Figure 14-3 shows the general format for an AH header.

Figure 14-3 *IPsec Authentication Header*

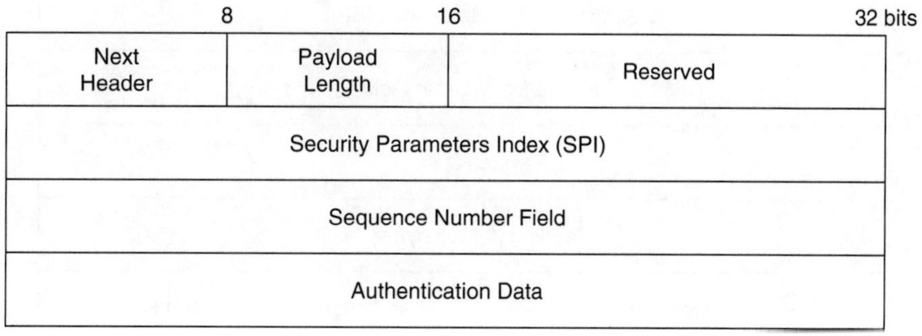

The fields in the AH header are as follows:

- **Next Header**—This 8-bit field identifies the type of payload after the AH.

- **Payload Length**—This 8-bit field specifies the length of the AH. This is calculated as the number of 32-bit words minus 2.

- **Security Parameters Index (SPI)**—This pseudo-random value identifies the security association for this traffic.

- **Sequence Number**—This monotonically increasing counter identifies the sequence of this packet within the connection. This is used to prevent replay attacks.

- **Authentication Data**—This variable-length field contains an integrity check value (ICV). This value is computed over the following:

  — IP fields that are immutable or predictable in value upon arrival at the endpoint

  — The AH header itself

  — The upper-level protocol data in the payload

Encapsulated Security Payload

The ESP protocol seeks to provide protection for the entire IP data packet rather than just parts of the packet as AH does. ESP is typically implemented in one of two fashions. In the transport mode, the ESP header is inserted after the IP header and before the upper-layer protocol data. In the tunnel mode, the ESP header is inserted before the IP header and surrounds the IP packet with a new header and trailer and then optionally encrypts the original IP packet. A new IP header is then added for routing to the destination system.

ESP can provide confidentiality and integrity to the communication and can be used to protect just the transport layer segment (Layer 4 and above) or the entire IP data packet (Layer 3 and above). Figure 14-4 shows the format of the ESP header.

Figure 14-4   *IPsec Encapsulated Security Payload Header*

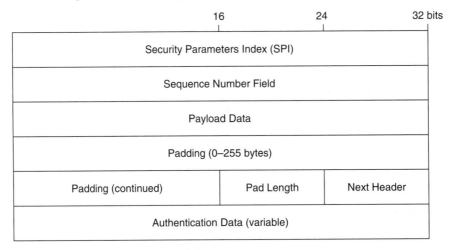

The fields in the ESP header are as follows:

- **SPI**—This pseudo-random value identifies the security association for this traffic.

- **Sequence Number**—This monotonically increasing counter identifies the sequence of this packet within the connection. This is used to prevent replay attacks.

- **Payload Data**—This variable-length field contains data that is described by the Next Header field.

- **Padding**—These null bytes are used to ensure that the fields fall on 8-byte boundaries.

- **Pad Length**—This 8-bit field identifies the number of padding bytes immediately preceding it.

- **Next Header**—This 8-bit field identifies the type of payload contained in the Payload Data field.

- **Authentication Data**—This variable-length field contains an ICV of the ESP data but not including the authentication data.

IPsec Modes

IPsec VPNs can operate in one of two modes: transport mode or tunnel mode. IPsec in transport mode can only be used by the device that generates the original data packet and protects only the upper-layer protocols of the IP packet and not the original IP header, as shown in Figure 14-5. In tunnel mode, the entire original IP packet is encapsulated within a new IPsec header and protected. Tunnel mode must be used for VPN devices that encapsulate packets that other devices (such as a computer on a network) generate. This new header includes new IP information outside the IPsec header, as shown in Figure 14-6.

Figure 14-5 *IPsec ESP in Transport Mode*

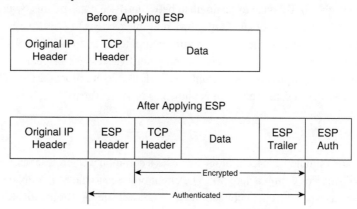

Figure 14-6 *IPsec ESP in Tunnel Mode*

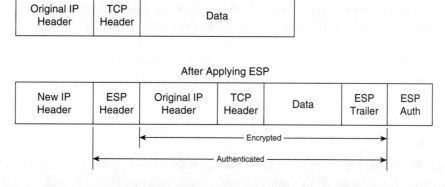

When configuring a firewall to either terminate or to allow IPsec traffic to pass, you must consider the mode. Most firewalls perform some Network Address Translation (NAT) function on the IP packets flowing through them. The modifications, namely the change of the source IP address, made by the NAT process in the firewall can impair the ability of IPsec traffic to travel through the firewall because any changes to the headers of the IP packets may result in the termination point of the VPN determining that the packets were modified en route (and rightly so) and therefore invalid. This is a result of the fact that a component of IPsec, the Internet Key Exchange (IKE) protocol, embeds the source IP address in its payload. When the source address of the packet (which will be the NAT device) does not match the address in the IKE payload, the destination system (the VPN termination point) drops the packet. To work around this issue, many vendors chose to encapsulate the VPN traffic in another packet via a process known as NAT Traversal (NAT-T).

NAT-T typically adds a UDP header (although TCP can be used) that encapsulates the ESP header shown in Figure 14-6. This UDP header allows a NAT device to perform two primary tasks. First, it allows the NAT device to distinguish between IPsec data streams by using UDP ports to identify one stream from another. This allows multiple devices to use IPsec behind the NAT device. Second, NAT-T puts the original source computer IP address into a NAT Original Address (NAT-OA) payload, allowing the receiving computer to access the original source IP address information for the purposes of performing the IKE checksum process. This allows IPsec traffic to traverse NAT devices, hence why it is known as NAT Traversal.

SSL VPNs

SSL VPNs are a simple VPN technology that uses a common web browser as a means of accessing systems and services within a network. The client browses to the SSL VPN device (using TCP port 443, just as when the client connects to a secure website) and authenticates to access the SSL VPN connection. This type of VPN requires no special considerations in terms of the firewall because all traffic occurs over TCP port 443. Therefore, this is the simplest type of VPN that you can deploy behind a firewall and is not affected by the NAT process of the firewall. However, SSL VPNs typically require that the back-end applications and systems support this method of access, which tends to limit the use of SSL VPNs to specialized situations (for example, used in conjunction with Citrix or Microsoft Outlook Web Access).

Few firewalls support SSL VPN functionality, which is a limitation of using firewalls as SSL VPN termination points. In conjunction with the application limitations previously discussed, this lack of support has limited the adoption of SSL VPNs in many environments.

Summary

Although firewalls do provide significant protection for systems, they do not necessarily represent the entire suite of defense that today's systems require. Many traditional firewalls do not stop data-driven attacks that use ports that are configured to pass through the firewalls. To offset such attacks, many vendors' firewalls now include the capability to conduct packet payload inspection like a dedicated IDS appliance. Additionally, some vendors are coupling their firewall offerings with other point-defense products such as content- and SMTP-filtering applications and devices. This coupling allows an IDS device or another detection device to instruct the firewall to block traffic deemed to be an attack against a system or the network. Even more compelling are integrated devices such as the Cisco ASA that combine firewall, IPS, and VPN functionality in a single device to provide a turnkey solution.

Firewalls can also require some additional effort on the part of network administrators to ensure that all services work properly through them. Firewall effects must be considered when deploying IPsec VPNs, primarily because the impact of NAT on these types of VPNs.

You need to be aware of some limitations when implementing these advanced features. You must consider the processing impact that these additional functions place on the firewall. A firewall that is expected to filter network traffic, perform application inspection, filter e-mail, filter web content, and decrypt IPsec VPN traffic will not be able to perform as well as a firewall that does not need to perform as many functions. Additionally, by integrating multiple functions into a single device, you increase not only the impact of a failure of any one component, but also create a potential single point of failure in your network security. For example, if the hardware that provides the VPN functionality in the firewall (for example, the processor) fails, you will need to take the entire firewall down to repair it (as opposed to if the functionality were being provided by distinct devices, in which case only the VPN device would be effected).

Endnotes

[1] "Spam Mushrooms Despite a New Federal Law," http://www.sfgate.com/cgi-bin/article.cgi?file=/chronicle/archive/2004/09/02/BUGVJ8I4AS1.DTL&type=printable

[2] Peterson, Patrick, http://www.dmnews.com/cgi-bin/artprevbot.cgi?article_id=34757&dest=article, November 15, 2005

Part IV: Appendixes

Firewall and Security Tools

The nature of firewalls and how they can be used to manipulate and control network traffic can make it difficult to troubleshoot network problems where firewalls are involved. Similarly, firewalls can introduce some unique and special requirements for managing and maintaining the firewall and the firewall configuration.

This appendix examines some common tools and tool usage to assist in troubleshooting, managing and maintaining firewalls.

Common Troubleshooting Tools

The most fundamental troubleshooting technique for network devices is to merely determine whether a device is reachable. Simply put, is the device up or is it down. To this end, the Packet Internet Groper (PING) utility was developed to provide a simple way to determine the reachability of a device.

Determining Reachability

PING is built upon the Internet Control Message Protocol (ICMP) and uses a system of echo and echo-reply messages to indicate whether a host is reachable. When a source host attempts to determine whether a destination host is reachable, it generates an ICMP echo packet for the destination host. When the destination host receives the echo packet, it responds with an echo-reply packet, allowing the source host to ascertain that the destination is reachable. If for some reason the destination host does not respond, the assumption is that it is unreachable. It is important to note that this is an assumption, because there are any number of reasons a host might not respond to an echo packet even though it is actually up and accessible. Therefore, it is important to understand that the failure to receive a response to an echo message does not necessarily provide any information regarding what, if anything, might be wrong. It simply means that the source host did not receive a response to the echo message.

In the event that a host fails to respond to an echo request, two common messages may be generated. The first is a "request timed out" response. This typically indicates that the destination network was able to be reached but that the destination host did not respond (which indicates a problem with the destination host itself). The other response is "destination network unreachable." This message indicates that the destination network was unable to be located and typically indicates a problem with the network interconnectivity or a routing problem, not necessarily a problem with the destination host.

As mentioned in Chapter 3, "TCP/IP for Firewalls," because of the nature of ICMP traffic, it is a best practice to restrict ICMP through the firewall to prevent ICMP-based attacks from being directed against hosts protected by the firewall. The obvious side effect is that if ICMP is blocked, PING cannot be used through the firewall to troubleshoot potential network problems. A commonly implemented workaround for this is to allow certain types of ICMP traffic through the firewall. These workarounds include allowing echo-reply, time-exceeded, and unreachable messages from untrusted hosts, while allowing echo messages to untrusted hosts. This allows you to ping external hosts and provides a means for the firewall to allow the three common echo message responses to return. This can be done on the Cisco Secure PIX Firewall by applying the commands in Example A-1 as a component of an access list.

Example A-1 *ACL to Permit Only Certain ICMP Message Types*

```
access-list 100 permit icmp any any echo-reply
access-list 100 permit icmp any any time-exceeded
access-list 100 permit icmp any any unreachable
```

As a best practice, your external firewall interface (and all corresponding IP addresses) should not allow any other ICMP traffic. This will prevent someone from being able to ping the firewall external IP address to determine whether it is accessible and will also protect against malicious ICMP-based traffic such as a "ping of death."

Another aspect of reachability is to show how the device was reachable. In other words, what path through the network was taken to the destination host? To answer this question, the traceroute utility (in Windows, the command is **tracert**) was developed. Traceroute functions by sending messages that are designed to exceed the time-to-live value of the next routing hop. This causes the router to respond with a time-exceeded message. Traceroute then increments the time-to-live value (starting at 1, then 2, and so on) and generates a new packet for the destination host, allowing the source host to determine each hop that is traversed on the way to the destination host.

As previously mentioned, PING does not necessarily provide any information regarding where a failure occurred that prevented a host from being reachable. As a result, traceroute is commonly implemented in conjunction with a failed PING test in an attempt to determine where in the network between the source and destination hosts that a failure might have occurred. For example, if you know that there are seven hops between the source and destination, and the destination fails to respond to an echo message, if the traceroute fails to respond after the fourth hop, you know that you should start looking at the network between the fourth and fifth hops as the likely cause of the reachability failure.

Unlike PING, traceroute typically uses UDP datagrams for the transport mechanism. An exception to this is the implementation on Windows, which uses ICMP PING packets. In both cases, however, the IP time-to-live value and the corresponding ICMP time-exceeded responses are the key to how traceroute functions. For example, in Example A-2 a traceroute is issued against the remote destination 10.21.120.43, showing the three routers that are located between the source and destination hosts.

Example A-2 *Traceroute to Remote Destination*

```
C:\Documents and Settings\wnoonan>tracert 10.21.120.43

Tracing route to 10.21.120.43 over a maximum of 30 hops

  1    31 ms    31 ms    31 ms  10.1.1.1
  2    31 ms    32 ms    32 ms  10.2.1.2
  3    45 ms    33 ms    32 ms  10.2.10.19
  4    32 ms    45 ms    31 ms  10.21.120.43

Trace complete.
```

Determining Which Physical Addresses Are Known

A fundamental aspect of network communications is the need for two hosts to be able to physically identify and communicate with each other. This is handled in TCP/IP by the Address Resolution Protocol (ARP). ARP builds and maintains a table of MAC address to IP address associations, allowing a host to be able to physically identify local hosts and address them accordingly. If the host has the wrong physical address, however, the data will not be successfully delivered. This mis-addressing is similar to having the wrong street address on a postal letter.

You can display a list of MAC addresses that a host knows about by running the **arp** command. For Windows hosts, you run **arp -a** to show the contents of the ARP cache, as displayed in Example A-3.

Example A-3 *Displaying the ARP Cache on Windows*

```
C:\Documents and Settings\wnoonan>arp -a

Interface: 192.168.1.114 --- 0x5
  Internet Address      Physical Address      Type
  192.168.1.97          00-0c-ce-e5-56-71     dynamic
  192.168.1.100         00-01-02-29-f4-28     dynamic
```

For many Linux-based hosts, just run **arp**, as shown in Example A-4.

Example A-4 *Displaying the ARP Cache on Red Hat Linux*

```
[wnoonan@keoland wnoonan]$ arp
Address          HWtype   HWaddress           Flags Mask        Iface
192.168.1.114    ether    00:0B:DB:21:C7:81   C                 eth0
192.168.1.101    ether    00:11:11:AF:E4:85   C                 eth0
192.168.1.97     ether    00:0C:CE:E5:56:71   C                 eth0
```

Windows-Specific Tools

In a GUI world, the command-line utility IPCONFIG is the best and most accurate way to
determine the IP address that a Windows computer is running. The reason for this is simple:
dynamically assigned IP addresses and IP address information is not shown in the GUI network
properties of an interface.

In addition to simply providing information regarding the IP address of the host, IPCONFIG can
also provide Domain Name Server (DNS) information, local MAC addresses, name resolution
server information, and Dynamic Host Configuration Protocol (DHCP) server, and DHCP lease
information. You can obtain this information by running the command **ipconfig /all**, as shown in
Example A-5.

Example A-5   *Windows IP Configuration*

```
C:\Documents and Settings\wnoonan>ipconfig /all

Windows IP Configuration

        Host Name . . . . . . . . . . . : host01
        Primary Dns Suffix  . . . . . . : mydom.local
        Node Type . . . . . . . . . . . : Hybrid
        IP Routing Enabled. . . . . . . : No
        WINS Proxy Enabled. . . . . . . : No
        DNS Suffix Search List. . . . . : mydom.local
                                          cisco.com

Ethernet adapter Local Area Connection:

        Connection-specific DNS Suffix  . : mydom.local
        Description . . . . . . . . . . . : 3Com 3C020 Integrated Fast Ethernet
Controller (3C905C-TX Compatible) #2
        Physical Address. . . . . . . . : 00-0B-DB-21-C7-81
        Dhcp Enabled. . . . . . . . . . : Yes
        Autoconfiguration Enabled . . . . : Yes
        IP Address. . . . . . . . . . . : 192.168.1.14
        Subnet Mask . . . . . . . . . . : 255.255.255.0
        Default Gateway . . . . . . . . : 192.168.1.1
        DHCP Server . . . . . . . . . . : 192.168.1.10
        DNS Servers . . . . . . . . . . : 192.168.1.10
                                          192.168.1.11
        Primary WINS Server . . . . . . : 192.168.1.10
        Secondary WINS Server . . . . . : 192.168.1.11
        Lease Obtained. . . . . . . . . : Monday, September 19, 2005 19:12:34
        Lease Expires . . . . . . . . . : Monday, October 03, 2005 19:12:34
```

Linux- and UNIX-Specific Tools

Similar to the Windows IPCONFIG command, IFCONFIG is used to display IP addressing configuration information on UNIX- and Linux-based hosts. In addition to merely displaying the IP addressing configuration, you can use IFCONFIG to actually configure the appropriate IP settings for an interface. Example A-6 shows this IP information.

Example A-6 *Red Hat Linux IP Configuration*

```
[wnoonan@keoland wnoonan]$ ifconfig -a
eth0      Link encap:Ethernet  HWaddr 00:D0:09:DC:B4:2B
          inet addr:192.168.1.118  Bcast:192.168.1.127  Mask:255.255.255.224
          inet6 addr: fe80::2d0:9ff:fedc:b42b/64 Scope:Link
          UP BROADCAST RUNNING MULTICAST  MTU:1500  Metric:1
          RX packets:2443 errors:0 dropped:0 overruns:0 frame:0
          TX packets:201 errors:0 dropped:0 overruns:0 carrier:0
          collisions:0 txqueuelen:1000
          RX bytes:224572 (219.3 Kb)  TX bytes:30513 (29.7 Kb)
          Interrupt:11 Base address:0xe000
```

Packet-Analysis Tools

As mentioned in Chapter 3, "TCP/IP for Firewalls," TCP/IP is the "language" that most network-connected hosts use to communicate with each other. Packet-analysis tools enable you to view the raw transmitted data, providing an incredibly valuable troubleshooting technique. Through the use of tools such as Ethereal, Microsoft Network Monitor, and TCPDump, you can observe all aspects of network communications between hosts, allowing you to detect and identify network-based problems and communications errors. Packet-analysis tools also enable you to answer the question of how, exactly, hosts are communicating with each other.

A common caveat regarding packet-analysis tools is how to implement and use them in a switched network. Because of the nature of switches, packets are only delivered to a switch port if they are physically addressed to a host connected to that switch port. Consequently, if you want the packet-analysis tool to be able to capture all the traffic on the network, you need to configure the switch to forward all packets to the switch port that the packet analyzer is connected to. This configuration is commonly referred to as port mirroring or port spanning. Keep in mind that even without this, a packet analyzer will capture all broadcasts and all traffic that is directed to/from the host that it is installed on.

To allow for the monitoring of traffic from switch ports, Cisco implements a technology known as Switched Port Analyzer (SPAN). With SPAN, you can define a port (or VLAN) that the traffic will be monitored from as well as a port that will be used to perform the monitoring. The switch will then forward all traffic for the monitored port to the monitoring port, allowing for packet-analysis tools to read and process the data. The commands to configure SPAN on Cisco Catalyst 29xx, 35xx, or 37xx series switches are as follows:

```
Switch(config)# monitor session 1 source interface fastEthernet0/1
Switch(config)# monitor session 1 destination interface fastEthernet0/10
```

Just specify the source interface, which is the interface that you want to capture traffic from, and the destination interface, which is the interface to which the packet analyzer is connected.

Most graphical packet-analysis tools can decode the captured network traffic, enabling you to view in plaintext the contents of a packet. There are three commonly implemented packet-analysis tools:

- Ethereal

- Microsoft Network Monitor

- TCPDump

Ethereal

Ethereal is an open source packet-analysis tool that is available from http://www.ethereal.com/. You can install Ethereal on both Windows and UNIX/Linux-based hosts; it has a common interface and functionality regardless of which type of host you install it on.

You can install Ethereal on most hosts without a reboot, which makes it a good tool to install on a system that you are troubleshooting because it requires no downtime for the install. Figure A-1 shows Ethereal in action.

Figure A-1 *Ethereal*

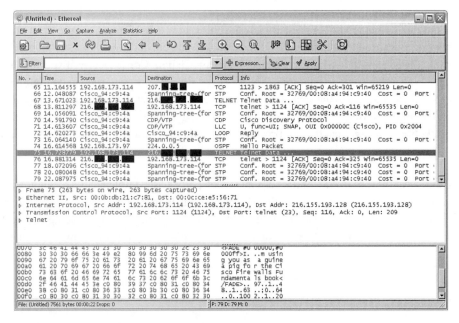

Ethereal uses three window panes to display data: the packet list (top pane), the packet details (middle pane), and the packet bytes (bottom pane). The packet list pane displays all packets that were captured, including basic elements such as the packet number (based on the capture), the time the packet was captured, the source and destination addresses, the protocol in use (if known), and a brief information field to provide additional information (typically a summary of the higher-layer data that was captured).

The packet details pane displays the details of the highlighted packet (in Figure A-1, frame 75) separated by communications layers. For example, in this case, the packet details pane enables you to determine that the packet in question is data from the Yahoo! Messenger application and that it uses TCP and IP for network communications. An interesting note that really underscores how difficult it can be to block instant messenger traffic is that instead of using the normal TCP port 5050 for communications, the application decided to use TCP port 21, causing Ethereal to incorrectly display that the traffic is Telnet traffic. In fact, the reason why this traffic showed as being Telnet traffic is because the person I was communicating with was actually using an application to bypass his corporate firewall, thus enabling him to use instant messenger software. This information is valuable because it allows you to identify ports that should be permitted or denied at the firewall based on the corporate security policy, although applications that can masquerade as other ports (such as Yahoo! Instant Messenger did in this case) can make the building of the firewall ruleset extremely difficult.

The packet bytes pane can be the most interesting pane to view, provided Ethereal knows how to decode the packet. The reason for this is that the packet bytes field enables you to view the actual content that was transmitted. In this case, you can see the actual message that was transmitted via Yahoo! Messenger: "I'm using you as a guinea pig for the Cisco Firewalls Fundamentals book."

Another useful feature of Ethereal is the ability to follow the TCP stream, which enables you to follow the entire TCP conversation between two hosts with a simple click of the mouse. You use this feature by highlighting a TCP packet in the packet list pane, right-clicking the packet, and then choosing Follow TCP Stream from the menu. Ethereal then uses the TCP header information that has been captured to rebuild the communications session as best as it can. Figure A-2 shows a captured TCP stream.

The Yahoo! Messenger IDs have been removed to protect the innocent, but you can still see that the entire communications stream has been rebuilt, which means you can see exactly what was transmitted and what was received. Although it is kind of cool to do this for a Yahoo! Messenger session, imagine if you were capturing Telnet, SMTP, or POP3 communications and thus gaining access to usernames and passwords. Remember that although Ethereal (and other packet-analysis tools) can be great troubleshooting tools, they can also present a security risk, and therefore you should only install them when they are needed and should remove them from hosts when they are no longer needed. Otherwise, attackers can use the tool on a compromised host to gain information to allow them to compromise other systems.

Figure A-2 *Displaying a TCP Communications Stream*

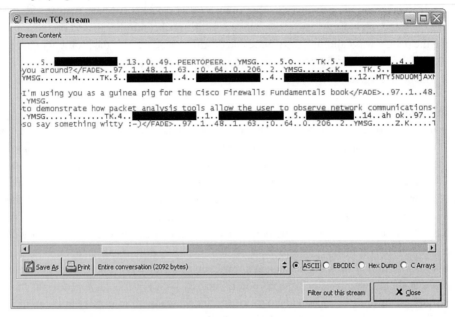

Microsoft Network Monitor

Microsoft Network Monitor is similar to Ethereal, but it only runs on Windows-based hosts. Microsoft Network Monitor has two versions: a free version shipped with some Windows Server operating systems that is capable of monitoring only traffic to the host on which it is installed, and a version that is a component of Microsoft Systems Management Server (SMS) that is a full-featured packet-analysis tool that is capable of capturing traffic destined/from all hosts. The biggest disadvantage of Microsoft Network Monitor over Ethereal is the inability to display captured packets in real time. With Microsoft Network Monitor, you must capture the traffic and then stop capturing to view what you captured (a process that makes it difficult to troubleshoot issues in real time). As you would expect, however, it has a relatively intuitive and easy-to-use interface, as depicted in Figure A-3.

TCPDump

TCPDump is a command-line-based packet-capture tool that is used primarily in Linux/UNIX-based environments. TCPDump is also available for use on Windows-based hosts (Windump), but requires the installation of the WinPCap driver (as does Ethereal). TCPDump has a number of command-line options for use, allowing the user to log the captured packets for review as well as specify relatively complex filtering requirements. In fact, TCPDump and Ethereal use the same filtering language; so after you have learned the proper syntax on one, it is fully portable to the other. At it is simplest, you can run TCPDump with no options, which causes it to capture all packets, as shown in Example A-7. You need to be logged in as "root" on Linux/UNIX systems to use TCPDump.

Figure A-3 *Microsoft Network Monitor Capture Window*

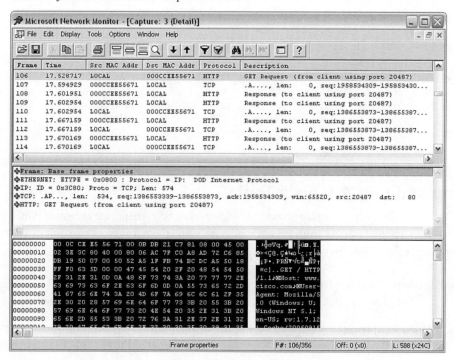

Example A-7 *Running TCPDump to Capture Data*

```
[root@keoland wnoonan]# tcpdump
tcpdump: verbose output suppressed, use -v or -vv for full protocol decode
listening on eth0, link-type EN10MB (Ethernet), capture size 96 bytes
08:39:28.375994 IP 192.168.1.114.1620 > linuxhost.myco.local.ssh: . ack
  189711522 win 64448
08:39:28.416215 IP linuxhost.myco.local.ssh > 192.168.1.114.1620: P 1:225(224)
  ack 0 win 8576
08:39:28.414651 IP linuxhost.myco.local.32769 > windowshost.myco.local.domain:
  28200+ PTR? 118.173.168.192.in-addr.arpa. (46)
08:39:28.414855 IP windowshost.myco.local.domain > linuxhost.myco.local.32769:
  28200* 1/0/0 (85)
08:39:28.415502 IP linuxhost.myco.local.32769 > windowshost.myco.local.domain:
  28201+ PTR? 114.173.168.192.in-addr.arpa. (46)
08:39:28.415641 IP windowshost.myco.local.domain > linuxhost.myco.local.32769:
  28201 NXDomain* 0/1/0 (136)
08:39:28.416732 IP linuxhost.myco.local.32769 > windowshost.myco.local.domain:
  28202+ PTR? 101.173.168.192.in-addr.arpa. (46)
08:39:28.416859 IP windowshost.myco.local.domain > linuxhost.myco.local.32769:
  28202* 1/0/0 (84)
```

continues

Example A-7   *Running TCPDump to Capture Data (Continued)*

```
08:39:28.576472 IP 192.168.1.114.1620 > linuxhost.myco.local.ssh: . ack 225 win
    65520
08:39:28.576549 IP linuxhost.myco.local.ssh > 192.168.1.114.1620:
    P 225:1281(1056) ack 0 win 8576
08:39:28.612847 IP 192.168.1.114.1620 > linuxhost.myco.local.ssh:
    P 0:48(48) ack 1281 win 64464
08:39:28.612902 IP linuxhost.myco.local.ssh > 192.168.1.114.1620:
    P 1281:1521(240) ack 48 win 8576
08:39:28.777119 IP 192.168.1.114.1620 > linuxhost.myco.local.ssh: . ack
    1521 win 65520
```

Logging and Log-Analysis Tools

Most firewalls can log events related to traffic that has been permitted or denied. Unfortunately, the sheer volume of data from even a moderately sized environment can quickly become unmanageable. Most firewalls use one of two types of logging methods:

- **Syslog**—Implemented by most firewalls and uses a relatively simple UDP-based (although the Cisco Secure PIX Firewall also supports TCP) client/server logging method.

- **Open Platform for Security Log Export Application Programming Interface (OPSEC LEA API)**—Implemented by Check Point for Firewall-1, OPSEC LEA is an API-based logging format, similar in function to syslog.

Syslog requires a server and a client component. The client typically runs on the firewall itself; the server is installed on a Windows, Linux, or UNIX host. Syslog server functionality on Linux and UNIX is built in to the operating system. For Windows hosts, however, you must install a third-party syslog server. A popular Windows-based syslog server is the Kiwi Syslog Daemon available at http://www.kiwisyslog.com/. Kiwi Syslog allows not only for the logging of events from the firewall but also provides advanced functionality such as implementing hashing on the logs for chain of custody and legal reasons, event filtering, and event notification via e-mail and pager for specified events.

Syslog uses a combination of facilities and severities to identify the source and type of message that is being generated. Although there are 24 total facilities, most firewalls are configured to use facilities local0 to local7. Message severity consists of the following severity levels:

- **Emergency (0)**—System is unusable.

- **Alert (1)**—Action must be taken immediately.

- **Critical (2)**—Critical conditions.

- **Error (3)**—Error conditions.

- **Warning (4)**—Warning conditions.

- **Notice (5)**—Normal but significant conditions.

- **Informational (6)**—Informational messages.

- **Debug (7)**—Debug-level messages.

In most cases, you should log debug-level severity messages only for the purposes of troubleshooting. A good default setting is to log all messages between Emergency and Informational level and then reduce the information logged accordingly after you have established what information you can obtain from more restrictive logging levels (that is, Notice or Warning).

In the case of the Cisco Secure PIX Firewall, configuring the firewall to log to a syslog server is a relatively trivial task. Example A-8 shows a sample of the commands to be executed.

Example A-8 *Configuring a Cisco Secure PIX Firewall to Use Syslog*

```
firewall(config)# logging on
firewall(config)# logging host inside 192.168.1.101
firewall(config)# logging trap informational
firewall(config)# logging timestamp
```

A valuable component of logging events is the ability to perform log analysis. Whereas most syslog servers enable you to log events, few enable you to perform event correlation or event analysis. In addition, it quickly becomes an insurmountable task for a human being to review the logs in a timely fashion to identify security events or negative trends. Therefore, it is typically necessary to implement a complex scripting environment to parse and correlate the logs that are collected or to use third-party log-analysis tools such as Cisco Security Monitoring, Analysis, and Response System (CS-MARS), Net IQ Security Manager, LogLogic, Network Intelligence, and SenSage. These tools all provide for the archival, parsing, and reporting of huge amounts of data, shifting the burden from the security staff and firewall admins to an automated and intelligent system of review and notification.

Security-Testing Tools

No discussion of firewall and security tools is complete without a brief discussion regarding security-testing tools. Firewall administrators should make regular use of two primary tools to perform basic testing of the firewall ruleset and the firewall's ability to protect hosts and networks: port-scanning tools and vulnerability-scanning tools. To be sure, for an in-depth review of security, other tools such as password-cracking tools, packet-crafting tools, and exploit frameworks should absolutely be considered (a discussion of which is beyond the scope of this appendix).

Port-Scanning Tools

Port-scanning tools function by attempting to connect to a host using a range of TCP and UDP ports. This information can then be used to determine which ports are listening, and thus which applications are probably running on the host. Port-scanning tools are one of the best ways to test your firewall ruleset, because the ruleset should allow traffic only on the ports that you have defined. If you port scan the firewall (or the IP addresses of the protected hosts the firewall is protecting) and find that it responds on ports other than the ones that you have defined, there is a good chance that the firewall ruleset is misconfigured and therefore may be exposing the protected host/network to external threats.

The most common and popular port scanner is Nmap. Nmap is an open source utility that runs on Windows, Linux, and UNIX hosts and can be downloaded from http://www.insecure.org. Nmap contains both a command-line utility and a graphical front end; however, the Windows graphical front end has not been maintained and updated for quite some time.

Running Nmap is a straightforward process. Running Nmap without any options brings up the usage screen, as shown in Example A-9.

Example A-9   *Nmap Usage Screen*

```
C:\Download\Hacking Tools\Nmap\nmap-3.93>nmap
Nmap 3.93 Usage: nmap [Scan Type(s)] [Options] <host or net list>
Some Common Scan Types ('*' options require root privileges)
* -sS TCP SYN stealth port scan (default if privileged (root))
  -sT TCP connect() port scan (default for unprivileged users)
* -sU UDP port scan
  -sP ping scan (Find any reachable machines)
* -sF,-sX,-sN Stealth FIN, Xmas, or Null scan (experts only)
  -sV Version scan probes open ports determining service & app names/versions
  -sR RPC scan (use with other scan types)
Some Common Options (none are required, most can be combined):
* -O Use TCP/IP fingerprinting to guess remote operating system
  -p <range> ports to scan.  Example range: 1-1024,1080,6666,31337
  -F Only scans ports listed in nmap-services
  -v Verbose. Its use is recommended.  Use twice for greater effect.
  -P0 Do not ping hosts (needed to scan www.microsoft.com and others)
* -Ddecoy_host1,decoy2[,...] Hide scan using many decoys
  -6 scans via IPv6 rather than IPv4
  -T <Paranoid|Sneaky|Polite|Normal|Aggressive|Insane> General timing policy
  -n/-R Never do DNS resolution/Always resolve [default: sometimes resolve]
  -oN/-oX/-oG <logfile> Output normal/XML/grepable scan logs to <logfile>
  -iL <inputfile> Get targets from file; Use '-' for stdin
* -S <your_IP>/-e <devicename> Specify source address or network interface
  --interactive Go into interactive mode (then press h for help)
Example: nmap -v -sS -O www.my.com 192.168.0.0/16 '192.88-90.*.*'
SEE THE MAN PAGE FOR MANY MORE OPTIONS, DESCRIPTIONS, AND EXAMPLES
```

Nmap supports both TCP and UDP port scanning, and for TCP port scanning it supports the following methods:

- **Connect scan**—This is a basic form of TCP scanning and uses the connect() system call provided by the operating system to attempt to connect to the remote host on the given port number and open a session. This is essentially the three-way handshake process, and although it provides a relatively certain method of identifying open ports, it is also easy to detect and is slower to perform a complete scan because of the additional overhead and wait time required for session establishment and teardown.

- **SYN scan**—This is the most common type of scan and is frequently referred to as "half-open" scanning because of how it works. For a SYN scan, Nmap attempts to initiate a SYN request to the target host on the given port number. If a RST response is received, the port is considered closed. If a SYN/ACK is received, the port is considered open. Nmap immediately sends an RST to tear down the session and proceeds to test the next port. This makes a SYN scan a fast scan to perform and complete, but it can produce incorrect results and requires root access on Linux and UNIX hosts to be run.

- **FIN stealth, Xmas tree, and Null scan**—These scanning techniques are all intended to be as quiet and difficult to detect as possible by sending packets that are out of context and have various TCP flags set (or unset in the case of a Null scan). The general concept behind these techniques is that a closed port is supposed to respond to a connection attempt with an RST, whereas open ports generally ignore these kinds of packets out of context. Nmap sends packets with the FIN flag (FIN stealth); FIN, URG, and PUSH flags (Xmas tree); and no flags (Null scan) in an attempt to "surprise" the host (that is, the host is receiving packets that it does not have a corresponding session with). The drawback to these kinds of scans is that although all hosts should support RFC 793, many do not and therefore respond inappropriately to FIN scans. This lack of support causes them to respond with an RST for all ports, when they should instead be dropping the packets on open ports. Therefore, these are rarely used.

In most cases, a SYN or Connect scan is more than adequate for testing your systems. Example A-10 shows the running of a SYN scan.

Example A-10   *Basic Nmap SYN Port Scan Against a Cisco Secure PIX Firewall*

```
[root@keoland nmap]# nmap -sS -P0 -O -vv 10.10.10.1

Starting nmap 3.93 ( http://www.insecure.org/nmap/ ) at 2005-10-04 14:10 CDT
Initiating ARP Ping Scan against 10.10.10.1 [1 port] at 14:10
The ARP Ping Scan took 0.01s to scan 1 total hosts.
Initiating SYN Stealth Scan against firewall.myco.com (10.10.10.1) [1668 ports]
  at 14:10
Discovered open port 443/tcp on 10.10.10.1
Discovered open port 25/tcp on 10.10.10.1
Discovered open port 21/tcp on 10.10.10.1
```

continues

Example A-10 *Basic Nmap SYN Port Scan Against a Cisco Secure PIX Firewall (Continued)*

```
Discovered open port 80/tcp on 10.10.10.1
SYN Stealth Scan Timing: About 32.99% done; ETC: 14:11 (0:01:00 remaining)
Discovered open port 110/tcp on 10.10.10.1
The SYN Stealth Scan took 65.80s to scan 1668 total ports.
Warning:  OS detection will be MUCH less reliable because we did not find at
     least 1 open and 1 closed TCP port
For OSScan assuming port 21 is open, 33480 is closed, and neither are firewalled
Host firewall.myco.com (10.10.10.1) appears to be up ... good.
Interesting ports on firewall.myco.com (10.10.10.1):
(The 1663 ports scanned but not shown below are in state: filtered)
PORT    STATE SERVICE
21/tcp  open  ftp
25/tcp  open  smtp
80/tcp  open  http
110/tcp open  pop3
443/tcp open  https
MAC Address: 00:0C:CE:E5:16:23 (Cisco Systems)
Device type: general purpose
Running: Microsoft Windows 2003/.NET|NT/2K/XP
OS details: Microsoft Windows 2003 Server or XP SP2, Microsoft Windows 2000 SP3
OS Fingerprint:
TSeq(Class=TR%IPID=I%TS=0)
T1(Resp=Y%DF=Y%W=402E%ACK=S++%Flags=AS%Ops=MNWNNT)
T2(Resp=N)
T3(Resp=N)
T4(Resp=N)
T5(Resp=N)
T6(Resp=N)
T7(Resp=N)
PU(Resp=N)

TCP Sequence Prediction: Class=truly random
                         Difficulty=9999999 (Good luck!)
TCP ISN Seq. Numbers: E44FD2A5 AA5F5E6D 8CCB934 69128FD1 6AD48312 4CDF45B5
IPID Sequence Generation: Incremental

Nmap finished: 1 IP address (1 host up) scanned in 68.462 seconds
            Raw packets sent: 5029 (202KB) | Rcvd: 25 (1244B)
```

Vulnerability-Scanning Tools

Vulnerability scanning takes the concept of port scanning to the next level. Now that you know which ports are open, which vulnerabilities might exist on the host that is listening on those ports? You can use a number of commercial and freeware vulnerability scanners to test virtually any system on a network, including firewalls. One of the most popular is the open source vulnerability scanner named Nessus. You can obtain Nessus from http://www.nessus.org/; it is freeware and can be installed on Linux/UNIX hosts (for testing of your own systems only) or is a commercial product for installation on Windows hosts (named Tenable NeWT).

Nessus operates in a client/server fashion with the server performing all the testing and scanning and the client providing the front-end configuration and reporting. You can install the client and server on the same system, or you can install the client on a remote system that will connect to the server. If configured in that manner, you can use a freeware Windows client named NessusWX to allow the Windows client to connect to the Linux/UNIX server. Nessus maintains a list of plug-ins that have been written to detect vulnerabilities; at the time of this writing, it contains 9700 plug-ins.

To run Nessus, you need to perform two steps. First, start the Nessus server. Second, start the Nessus client. You can do this by running the commands in Example A-11.

Example A-11   *Running Nessus on a Linux host*

```
[root@keoland nessus]# nessusd -D
All plugins loaded
[root@keoland nessus]# nessus &
```

Using the switch **&** specifies to run the command and return to the command line after the application has launched. When Nessus launches, you are prompted to log in to the server, as shown in Figure A-4.

Figure A-4   *Nessus Login Screen*

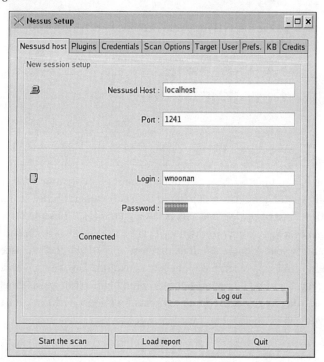

At this point, performing a scan is just a matter of navigating the tabbed screens and specifying the appropriate plug-ins to load, options for the scan, and target hosts. As shown in Figure A-5, if I want to scan Cisco hosts for vulnerabilities, I just ensure that I select the appropriate Cisco plug-ins and start the scan. Something to keep in mind is that not all plug-ins are considered "safe" to run. What that means is that some plug-ins are risky in nature and could result in the targeted host crashing or otherwise having a negative result. These "risky" plug-ins are identified by a red triangle with an exclamation point in the middle. Use caution when you decide to run these plug-ins.

Figure A-5   *Nessus Plug-In Screen*

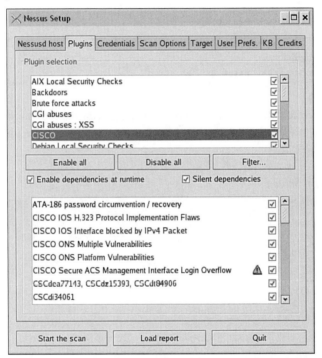

When the scan has completed, Nessus launches the report containing the status of what was detected, as shown in Figure A-6. Keep in mind that all vulnerabilities scanners make a best guess at what they believe is occurring, but this is not a guarantee. Consequently, you may find false positives, false negatives, or downright incorrect results. You always need to investigate the results of the vulnerability scan in more detail using more specialized tools to ascertain whether the targeted system is indeed vulnerable to the stated exploit. This last sentence is important to understand because a lot of companies think running Nmap or Nessus constitutes an audit. They do not! Anyone you pay to audit your environment who just performs those steps is ripping you off, because you can do that yourself for free.

Figure A-6 *Nessus Results*

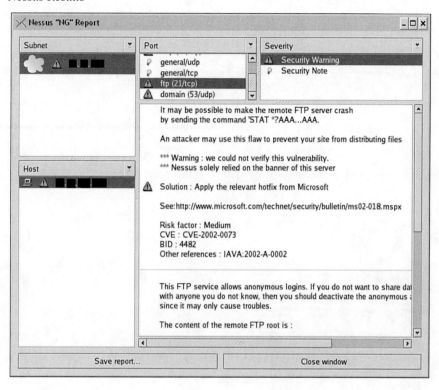

Firewall and Security Resources

This appendix contains web and book resources that reference the technologies and products discussed in this book. They provide excellent additional material for those who want to learn more about firewalls and security.

Firewall-Specific Information

NIST Guidelines on Firewalls and Firewall Policy, http://csrc.nist.gov/publications/nistpubs/800-41/sp800-41.pdf

Firewall Software and Internet Security FAQ, http://www.firewall-software.com/firewall_white_paper.html

General Firewall Configuration Guide, http://www.bolthole.com/solaris/firewall.html

Personal Firewalls for Remote Access Users, http://www.windowsecurity.com/articles/Personal-Firewalls-Remote-Access.html

Windows Firewall Features, http://www.microsoft.com/technet/prodtechnol/windowsserver2003/library/ServerHelp/f89a9126-078d-4be5-8696-61a238fb9114.mspx

Windows ICF, http://www.securityfocus.com/infocus/1620

Linksys Firewalls, http://www.linksys.com

Cisco PIX Firewalls, http://www.cisco.com/go/pix

Cisco ASA, http://www.cisco.com/go/asa

Yahoo! Groups PIX Firewall, http://groups.yahoo.com/group/PIX_Firewall/

Linux NetFilter, http://www.netfilter.org/

Linux IPChains, http://www.tldp.org/HOWTO/IPCHAINS-HOWTO.html

Firestarter, http://www.fs-security.com/

Firewall Builder, http://www.fwbuilder.org

Webmin, http://www.webmin.com

Transparent, Bridging Firewall Devices, http://www.securityfocus.com/infocus/1737

Transparent Firewalling, http://www2.linuxjournal.com/article/3246

OpenBSD Transparent Firewall Installation Guide, http://www.netikus.net/documents/OpenBSDTransparentFirewall/

Building Your Firewall RuleBase, http://www.windowsecurity.com/whitepapers/Building_Your_Firewall_Rulebase_.html

Usenet Firewall Newsgroup, comp.security.firewalls

Firewalls Mailing List, http://www.isc.org/ops/lists/firewalls/

Firewall Wizards Mailing List, http://honor.trusecure.com/mailman/listinfo/firewall-wizards

PhoneBoy CheckPoint Information Portal, http://www.phoneboy.com/

Firewall and Security Portal, http://searchsecurity.techtarget.com/

Firewall White Paper, http://www.firewall-software.com/firewall_white_paper.html

How Do Firewalls Work?, http://www.practicallynetworked.com/sharing/firewall.htm

Network Address Translation FAQ, http://www.vicomsoft.com/knowledge/reference/nat.html

What Is a Firewall Proxy Server?, http://www.akadia.com/services/firewall_proxy_server.html

Virtual Firewalls White Paper, http://intoto.com/product_briefs/Virtual Firewalls White Paper.pdf

General Security Information

Microsoft's Security at Home, http://www.microsoft.com/athome/security/default.mspx

Intrusion Detection FAQ, http://www.sans.org/resources/idfaq/

Intrusion Detection Systems FAQ, http://www.windowsecurity.com/articles/Intrusion-Detection-Systems-FAQ.html

What You Need to Know About Intrusion Detection Systems, http://www.windowsecurity.com/articles/What_You_Need_to_Know_About_Intrusion_Detection_Systems.html

Intrusion Detection Systems (IDS) Part 1, http://www.windowsecurity.com/articles/Intrusion_Detection_Systems_IDS_Part_I__network_intrusions_attack_symptoms_IDS_tasks_and_IDS_architecture.html

Intrusion Detection Systems (IDS) Part 2, http://www.windowsecurity.com/articles/IDS-Part2-Classification-methods-techniques.html

Host-Based IDS vs. Network-Based IDS (Part 1), http://www.windowsecurity.com/articles/Hids_vs_Nids_Part1.html

Host-Based IDS vs. Network-Based IDS (Part 2), http://www.windowsecurity.com/articles/Hids_vs_Nids_Part2.html

Log Analysis, http://www.loganalysis.org/

SecurityFocus, http://www.securityfocus.com/

SANS InfoSec Reading Room, http://www.sans.org/rr/

Windows Security Portal, http://searchwindowssecurity.techtarget.com/

Slashdot Technical News and Information, http://slashdot.org/

NSA Security Configuration Guides, http://www.nsa.gov/snac/

Insecure.org Security Portal, http://www.insecure.org/

Team Cymru, http://www.cymru.com/

Center for Internet Security, http://www.cisecurity.org/

Networking Portal, http://searchnetworking.techtarget.com/

Microsoft Security Home Page, http://www.microsoft.com/security/default.mspx

United States Computer Emergency Response Team, http://www.us-cert.gov/

Windows Security Exploit Mailing List, http://www.ntbugtraq.com/

The Register News Portal, http://www.theregister.co.uk/

IP Authentication Header, http://www.faqs.org/rfcs/rfc2402.html

IP Encapsulating Security Payload, http://www.faqs.org/rfcs/rfc2406.html

Additional Reading

Behtash, Behzad. *CCSP Self-Study: Cisco Secure PIX Firewall Advanced (CSPFA), Second Edition* (Cisco Press)

Cheswick, William, Steven Bellovin, and Aviel Rubin. *Firewalls and Internet Security: Repelling the Wily Hacker, Second Edition* (Addison-Wesley Professional)

Comer, Douglas E. *Internetworking with TCP/IP Vol.1: Principles, Protocols, and Architecture, Fourth Edition* (Prentice Hall)

Deal, Richard. *Cisco Router Firewall Security* (Cisco Press)

McCarty, Bill. *Red Hat Linux Firewalls* (Red Hat Press)

Noonan, Wes. *Hardening Network Infrastructure* (McGraw-Hill Osborne Media)

Shinder, Thomas W. *Dr. Tom Shinder's Configuring ISA Server 2004* (Syngress)

Vladimirov, Andrew, Konstantin Gavrilenko, and Andrei Mikhailovsky. *Hacking Exposed Cisco Networks* (McGraw-Hill Osborne Media)

Index

CISCO SYSTEMS

Cisco Press

3 STEPS TO LEARNING

STEP 1

STEP 2

STEP 3

First-Step

Fundamentals

**Networking
Technology Guides**

STEP 1 **First-Step**—Benefit from easy-to-grasp explanations.
No experience required!

STEP 2 **Fundamentals**—Understand the purpose, application,
and management of technology.

STEP 3 **Networking Technology Guides**—Gain the knowledge
to master the challenge of the network.

NETWORK BUSINESS SERIES

The Network Business series helps professionals tackle the
business issues surrounding the network. Whether you are a
seasoned IT professional or a business manager with minimal
technical expertise, this series will help you understand the
business case for technologies.

Justify Your Network Investment.

Look for Cisco Press titles at your favorite bookseller today.

Visit **www.ciscopress.com/series** for details on each of these book series.

Cisco Press

FUNDAMENTALS SERIES
ESSENTIAL EXPLANATIONS AND SOLUTIONS

1-57870-168-6

Voice over IP Fundamentals

A systematic approach to understanding the basics of Voice over IP

Jonathan Davidson, CCIE No. 2560
James Peters

ciscopress.com

When you need an authoritative introduction to a key networking topic, **reach for a Cisco Press Fundamentals book**. Learn about network topologies, deployment concepts, protocols, and management techniques and **master essential networking concepts and solutions**.

Look for Fundamentals titles at your favorite bookseller

802.11 Wireless LAN Fundamentals
ISBN: 1-58705-077-3

**Cisco CallManager Fundamentals:
A Cisco AVVID Solution**
ISBN: 1-58705-008-0

Cisco LAN Switching Fundamentals
ISBN: 1-58705-089-7

Cisco Unity Fundamentals
ISBN: 1-58705-098-6

Data Center Fundamentals
ISBN: 1-58705-023-4

IP Addressing Fundamentals
ISBN: 1-58705-067-6

IP Routing Fundamentals
ISBN: 1-57870-071-X

Network Security Fundamentals
ISBN: 1-58705-167-2

Storage Networking Fundamentals
ISBN: 1-58705-162-1

Voice over IP Fundamentals
ISBN: 1-57870-168-6

Coming in Fall 2005
**Cisco CallManager Fundamentals:
A Cisco AVVID Solution**, Second Edition
ISBN: 1-58705-192-3

Visit **www.ciscopress.com/series** for details about the Fundamentals series and a complete list of titles.

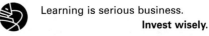

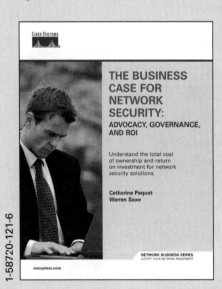

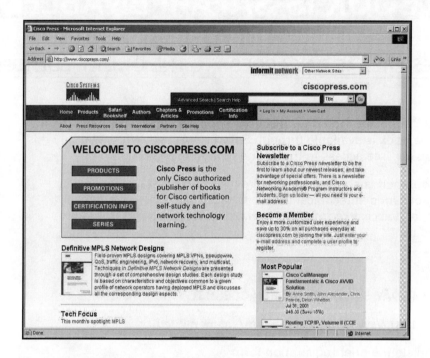
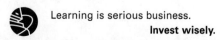

BOOKS ONLINE
ENABLED

THIS BOOK IS SAFARI ENABLED

INCLUDES FREE 45-DAY ACCESS TO THE ONLINE EDITION

The Safari® Enabled icon on the cover of your favorite technology book means the book is available through Safari Bookshelf. When you buy this book, you get free access to the online edition for 45 days.

Safari Bookshelf is an electronic reference library that lets you easily search thousands of technical books, find code samples, download chapters, and access technical information whenever and wherever you need it.

TO GAIN 45-DAY SAFARI ENABLED ACCESS TO THIS BOOK:

- Go to **http://www.ciscopress.com/safarienabled**

- Complete the brief registration form

- Enter the coupon code found in the front of this book before the "Contents at a Glance" page

If you have difficulty registering on Safari Bookshelf or accessing the online edition, please e-mail customer-service@safaribooksonline.com.